What readers and reviewers have said about
TALES OF ALASKA'S BUSH RAT GOVERNOR:

"Gov. Jay Hammond is a unique figure in U.S. politics. He was fiercely independent — to use baseball parlance, 'he called 'em as he saw 'em.' This book is a good read written by a good man."

President George Bush

"TALES OF ALASKA'S BUSH RAT GOVERNOR is entertaining, informative, and challenging — a rare combination for an autobiography . . . Jay Hammond's experiences in Alaska are described with inimitable style."

President Jimmy Carter

"BUSH RAT GOVERNOR is a joy and delight!"

Scott W. Reed, Coeur d'Alene, Idaho

"Your book made me laugh out loud — I enjoyed it exceedingly."

Robert Sheldon, Seattle, Washington

" . . . like a breath of fresh air at a time when we come to expect the worst of men in public life."   **David Hoffman**, Barrow, Alaska

"Readers will relish this book . . . "   ***Anchorage Daily News***

"Jay has led an amazing life, and his writing is full of self-deprecating, gentle good humor . . . "   ***Alaska Journal of Commerce***

"BUSH RAT GOVERNOR is readable, amusing, exciting, irreverent, and occasionally outrageous. The book is happily peopled by compelling real-life characters . . . "   ***General Aviation News & Flyer***

"The most exciting and stimulating reading of my 77 years."

Rev. R. L. Brandt, Billings, Montana

"I could not put it down — I don't think I have ever enjoyed an autobiography more!"   **Betty Miller**, Homer, Alaska

" . . . Among the best accounts of life in post-World War II Alaska."

Juneau Empire

TALES OF ALASKA'S

Bush Rat Governor

ERIK HILL / ANCHORAGE DAILY NEWS

The extraordinary autobiography of
JAY HAMMOND
wilderness guide and reluctant politician

Foreword by Kay Fanning

Epicenter Press
Fairbanks / Seattle

Epicenter Press

Fairbanks/Seattle

Epicenter Press Inc. is a regional press founded in Alaska whose interests include but are not limited to the arts, history, environment, and diverse cultures and lifestyles of the North Pacific and high latitudes. We seek both the traditional and innovative in publishing quality nonfiction tradebooks, contemporary art and photography giftbooks, and destination travel guides emphasizing Alaska, Washington, Oregon, and California.

Publisher: Kent Sturgis
Acquisitions Editor: Lael Morgan
Editors: Suzan Nightingale, Kent Sturgis
Research: Robert Clarke, Dermot Cole
Proofreading: Jean Andrews, Christine Ummel
Design and pre-press production: Laing Communications, Inc.
Cover: Elizabeth Watson
Printer: Transcontinental Printing
Text © 1994 Jay S. Hammond

To order single copies of TALES OF ALASKA'S BUSH RAT GOVERNOR, mail $17.95 (Washington residents add $1.47 sales tax) plus $6 for priority mail shipping to: Epicenter Press, Box 82368, Kenmore, WA 98028.

Booksellers: Retail discounts are available from our distributor, Graphic Arts Center Publishing ™, Box 10306, Portland, OR 97210. Phone 800-452-3032.

This title was originally published in March 1994, as a hardbound edition from Epicenter Press Inc.

PRINTED IN CANADA
First Printing April 1996

10 9 8 7 6 5 4

Library of Congress Cataloging-in-Publication Data

Hammond, Jay S.
Tales of Alaska's bush rat governor: the extraordinary autobiography of Jay Hammond, wilderness guide and reluctant politician / by Jay Hammond.
    p.   cm.
Includes index.
ISBN 0-945397-43-7 (SB): $17.95
1. Hammond, Jay S. 2. Governors—Alaska—Biography. 3. Alaska—Politics and Government—1959- I. Title.
F910.H36 1993
979.8'05'092—dc20
[B]
                                                      93-49357
                                                         CIP

To my grandchildren, and to theirs.

That my progeny will never know my parents is a treasure lost. With each passing generation, more coins of recollection are covered by the sands of time. This book attempts to mint from memory a few coins of my own and to strew them a bit more broadly than were those of my ancestors.

An autobiography grants a wonderful opportunity to relive one's life with suitable amendments or deletions. Hopefully I've but employed the latter. Like most politicians, who are unable to use lean when a fat phrase is available, I produced a manuscript that required massive rendering. Hence, many whose trails crossed (or collided) with my own have been deleted. To those who seek in vain to find themselves within these pages, your immense relief is gracefully acknowledged.

Table of Contents

Dedication   v

Acknowledgments   ix

Foreword   x

Part One: Laying the Kindling

1 • Molding the Clay   1

2 • Pelican in the Wilderness   15

3 • Befuddled Believer   23

4 • Serendipity Strikes   31

5 • Tour of Duty   41

6 • The Alaska Connection   53

7 • From Rainy Pass to Vulture Flats   61

8 • Twists in the Trail   73

9 • Macoola, Murder and Mayhem   79

10 • Partners in Crime and Comedy   89

11 • Ever Cry Wolf   101

12 • Alaska Master Guide No. 009   107

13 • Bush Piloting   115

14 • Statehood & Sciatica   121

Part Two: Striking the Match

15 • Reluctant Candidate: 1959   127

16 • Lies, Dam Lies and Politics   137

17 • Fish Tales of a "Grate" Communicator   147

18 • Bounced Back   155

19 • Green vs. Gold   167

20 • Prudhoe Bay and The Pipeline   173

21 • "Retired" and Retreaded   183

22 • The 1974 Primary Campaign   191

23 • Reluctant Candidate: 1974   199

24 • ". . . a lousy Governor"   207

25 • Hits and Misses: First Term   219

26 • Reluctant No More   225

27 • The Great Alaska Lands War   237

28 • Money, Money, Money!   247

29 • Four More Years   259

30 • Media Mania   269

31 • Life in the Governor's House   277

32 • Name Droppings   287

33 • Back to the Briar Patch   295

34 • Foes, Friends, Family and Faith   305

35 • Whither Alaska?   317

Epilogue   327

Appendix   331

Index   336

Acknowledgments

To ACKNOWLEDGE ALL WHO made contributions to this effort would leave but a page or two for text. While some might deem that a blessing, I'm not about to let my main abettors off unscathed.

For help in sifting rare, raw nuggets from massive mounds of clinkers; smelting these into some semblance of sense; then providing proper setting, I owe an immense debt of gratitude to Lynda Giguere, who deciphered my hieroglyphics; Bob Clarke, my agonized agent whose blistered hands wielded the largest shovel, longest; and Suzan Nightingale, who gave it all a final burnish.

Foreword

IT'S A RARE TREAT TO READ the memoirs of a canny politician who can write with humor and astonishing self-effacement. Jay Hammond was a politician who really did make a difference in the evolution of the 49th state during its most critical years.

Alaska might have veered wildly to the right or to the left during the heady decade of the Prudhoe Bay oil rush. It could have developed every acre from the mountains to the sea, or it could have locked away so much land that the Alaskan economy might have collapsed. That none of these extremes occurred was due to the steady hand of the Bush Rat pilot who steered the state through the turbulent air of the 1970s.

What makes this book so special is how that steady but innovative hand evolved out of the antics of an Adirondacks youth and out of the wild adventures of an Alaskan hunting guide, commercial fisherman, and bush pilot. From the tale of Hammond's fourteenth summer at Farmer Fred's, to his harrowing tumble over the falls as a teen-ager, to the tragic rafting accident after his term as governor, Hammond narrowly averts countless perils as both pilot and politician. He keeps the reader riveted to his humorous portrayal of eccentric, unforgettable characters. He interweaves his love for the wild world of nature with his more skeptical portrayal of the still wilder world of politics and with a dash of his homespun philosophy.

Tales of a Bush Rat Governor is an incendiary mix you won't want to put down.

Katherine Fanning
Former Editor, Anchorage Daily News
and Christian Science Monitor

Part One
Laying the Kindling

Scotia Parsonage, 1927. The first and last time they ever got me under a fedora. "Indiana Hammond" I was not.

1

Molding the Clay

IT SEEMED TO BE a stupid way to die — healthy, uninjured, driving a team of dogs just miles from home.

We'd turned onto the frozen Hayes River to get out of the deep snow, finding its rough cover of ice easy going in sub-zero weather. The dogs seemed to freshen up and catch a second wind.

Suddenly, with a rolling report like rifle fire, the shelf of ice underneath us pitched into the river. Dogs, sled and I pitched in behind it, dropping eight feet to the coursing water below.

To our good fortune, the fast-moving water was only two feet deep. However, the hole we'd fallen into was out of reach of the ice cover overhead and in the semi-darkness, the frantic dogs snarled and screamed as I fought to drag them and the sled away from the current to a small gravel bank. Soaking wet at 12 below zero, we had to get to a fire quickly.

Most of our gear had floated off when we hit the water. What remained lashed to the sled made it impossible to move, so I quickly cut loose the last of my load. Next, I freed the dogs and somehow worked the sled upstream beneath the gaping hole. Using the sled as a ladder, I got all seven dogs to scramble to the firm ice above.

In clothes by then frozen like armor plate, I struggled to climb the sled and to haul it up behind me. Shoving it across the ice to firm ground, as wet dogs squalled and shivered about me, I fumbled for the match case and a paraffin-soaked twist of hemp I carried in my parka.

With fingers brittle in the cold, at first I couldn't unscrew the cap. Using teeth and fists I got the cap off, but then I was unable to pluck out a match. I shook the case and dumped all but three matches in the snow. Holding one in my teeth, I scratched it on the serrated back of my belt knife, touched off my twist of hemp, and tucked it beneath some kindling. As the blaze grew, I toppled several small dead spruce and fed them to the fire. The dogs joined me as I stood gratefully near the leaping flames. We spent most of the day drying out, then hitched up and returned to camp.

I was new to Alaska then. It was not to be the last time I found myself on thin ice — or blistered between hot fires — but little did I guess the form these encounters would take in years to come.

Neither background, aspirations nor concept of moral turpitude suggested I'd go into politics. As a young boy growing up in an urban parsonage, I never dreamed my trail would wend its way from a remote cabin in Alaska to the governor's mansion. I may be the only politician who ever aspired to go back to a remote log cabin . . . and made it.

These days, what thin ice I may venture onto comes courtesy of Mother Nature and predators encountered again run on all fours.

This, then, is a story of serendipity's triumph over careful planning. That my life has been so enriched by those I've met along the way makes it as well a story of thanksgiving.

BORN IN THE GARMENT TOWN of Troy, New York, July 21, 1922 — some four years after my father returned from service in France — I have few recollections of life there as a Methodist minister's son. Only a fading montage of sepia memories remains:

Camping at Crooked Lake . . . Minnows gumming my toes while I screamed as though being consumed by piranhas . . . Cool nights buried in blankets while Mother or Dad read aloud *Tom Sawyer, Lorna Doone,* or *Robin Hood,* making them wondrous adventures never quite to be equaled . . . A fiery Christmas tree hurled through the parlor window of the parsonage when a primitive motion picture projector ignited its film . . . Daily vacation Bible school . . . Thanksgiving clan gatherings, Mother and Grandma Suzie preparing such Pennsylvania Dutch fare as crumb pies and other baked ambrosia no others could duplicate.

Memories take on sharper focus for the years after Troy: My father's massive yellow brick Methodist Episcopal Church in Scotia, New York, looming like some Crusader's castle to a six-year old boy . . . Kindergarten where little girls revolted at holding my warty hands to play "Farmer in the Dell." Great-grandmother Brown's cure of rubbing warts with an onion, burying it under a rain spout. Come the full moon, when the onion rotted, the warts would be gone. Sure enough . . . Heading for ski slopes in our old 1929 Buick and watching Dad career the hills in World War I hightops, long coat and never, ever, without a necktie . . .

One of my fondest memories is of three-year-older brother Billy brandishing a cavalry saber while hotly pursuing neighborhood bully Homer Barsillo. My glee in Homer's shrieks of panic was later enhanced by Billy's squalls as Dad applied a hairbrush to his undisciplined hindquarters.

Less fondly, I recall Billy demanding his small grubby sibling be observed washing before allowed to dine at the same table. Microbe-phobic "Bacillus Bill" considered me sort of an ambulatory, unlatched, Pandora's Box from which seeped all sorts of contagion.

Having inherited Mother's wit, intellect and nervous energy, it's amazing how he perverted attributes appealing in her to something appalling. Doubly amazing is how well he turned out. Chalk up yet another miracle to the Almighty who must have worked time and a half on that unmalleable clay. Certainly Billy's elevation from brat to beloved brother took several pratfalls en route . . . many at my expense — like the time I skipped up to the parsonage dinner table singing a lilting ditty Billy had carefully taught me. Imagine my surprise when the folks displayed something less than doting parental enchantment. Only because they believed it unlikely one so young could understand the forbidden four-letter lyrics was I spared that dreaded hairbrush.

Billy derived enormous pleasure in shocking an audience — his satisfaction directly proportional to depth of outrage incurred. A memorable example occurred at a gathering of the clan at Aunt Edith and Uncle Archie's.

Dr. Archibald Carter Worth was a diminutive eccentric never absent spats, a cigar of Churchillian proportion and intense opinions on any subject. These he embellished with a Brooklyn accent dipped in southern drawl and delivered as through a bull-horn. Archie was intensely proud to be related to "The Virginia Carters." On this occasion, several of his Carter kin had, for the first time, condescended to visit us "damn Yankees." In consideration for their sensibilities the picture of Grampa Hammond in his Civil War uniform was placed out of sight and us kids instructed to be on our best behavior. All for nought! Upon learning that some of the Carters came from Atlanta, Billy could not resist letting our choleric guests know he "had read lots about Georgia in diaries kept by grandfather during his 'March to the Sea' with General Sherman." We never saw them again.

I remember stealing apples from Mrs. Williams' MacIntosh tree, only to find my scurrilous act recorded in my brother Bill's secret dossiers, along with the fingerprints and "crimes" of other neighborhood miscreants. Later, I was not surprised when Bill got a degree in police administration and went on to a career in military counter-intelligence — only that he was exceptionally good at it and had metamorphosed from an insufferable pest into a fine man.

I first heard the word "marijuana" in the 1930s when would-be crime buster Bill found a few stalks growing in the local post office yard. Hardly a household word then, probably no one in town other than Bill would have recognized wild hemp. His study of arcane lore for "undercover" work equipped him with knowledge of matters completely unfamiliar to us common folk.

Fortunately for society, Bill went straight. In his library were books on safe cracking; cheating at cards; slot machine tampering; con-artistry; lethal substances and virtually all facets of illicit activity. Nothing delighted Bill more than the opportunity to flaunt his skills with practical application. I recall him basking before awe-struck church elders as he cracked open an enormous old safe to which they had lost the combination.

THE HAMMONDS RODE OUT the Depression Years in the small town of Scotia, New York. At Sunday morning services, Mother kept her two little monsters' heads bowed in devotions, to all appearances. Actually, we were preoccupied trying to untie wet, knotted rawhide pucker-strings on small chamois bags filled with candy. I remember seeing Dad's salary check of $45 a month, and playing slug-a-bed Saturday mornings hearing the 6 a.m. hand-cranking of Dad's old two-gallon freezer, concocting the best ice cream I've ever tasted. Sometimes we wore "hand-me-down" clothes from a couple of rich kids known by our generous and enterprising Aunt Edith.

Despite our limited income we seemed to have everything we required. I know now we certainly had much more than the average youth of today. If deprived, I never knew it. Unlike many contemporary parents who wish to give their kids "all the things we never had," I would deem myself most successful if I could give my children half of what we received: love in full measure, respect, security, sense of purpose and worth. Most importantly, my parents planted the seeds that ultimately gave root to a solid, sustaining spiritual awareness and acceptance of the teachings of Christ as the base upon which anyone can build a better life.

Those seeds first fell on rocky soil. For years, prayerful contemplation and things of the spirit were confusing impediments over which I nimbly skipped. The wild side of the street had brighter lights and far more fascination. That I ever crossed over, I attribute to my strong, loving parents who opened doors which, had they remained shut, would have prevented me ever knowing what truly abundant living is all about. That my father and mother were remarkable people occurred to me almost too late in life to tell them so.

Dad was Morris A. Hammond, the youngest of three sons who grew up in Saratoga Springs, doing chores in the lumberyard of his father, William Jefferson Hammond. Dad tended the neighborhood cows and nightly lit the town's gas street lamps. Dad's father and Uncle Delos, whom the former had packed out wounded from the fiery hell of the Battle of the Wilderness, constructed several buildings yet standing. My father pointed these out on frequent trips to Saratoga to visit his mother, Arabella Esther Ward Hammond, who survived her husband by some thirty years.

Fiercely independent, Gramma Hammond was justifiably proud of the job she'd done almost alone raising five children. All had been well educated, married accomplished spouses or gone on to achieve at least modest renown in their fields. Though she died when I was but twelve, I remember her vividly. Blessed with an off-beat sense of humor that I found delightful, it was her stupendous snoring and other idiosyncrasies that impressed me most. Late in her eighties, she was almost stone deaf. This, coupled with some afflictions not uncommon to aging digestive tracts, often caused me anguished embarrassment when I'd accompany Gramma in public.

I most clearly recall passage through the receiving line at the wedding of a friend of my cousin Blanche, at her parents' mansion in Saratoga, a baroque structure later featured as the setting for the film *Ghost Story*.

Arriving late in Aunt Edith's sedate 1927 Buick Phaeton, I helped Gramma out of the car and toward the smiling throng. Arm-in-hand we exchanged pleasantries with the guests. Lamentably, my ardent prayer for Gramma Arabella's bowels to behave during this rite of passage went unheeded by the Almighty. To my agonized dismay, while bantering with a local dignitary, a horrendous, rock-shivering blast billowed the bombazine at her backside. Had I been able to self-destruct, or transport to Samarkand, I'd have done so without hesitation. Gramma, meanwhile, unaware of her indiscretion, continued to work the crowd, accompanying her good humored joshing with a veritable barrage of gastric gunfire.

If ever a medal was warranted for service above and beyond the call, I earned it that day by remaining on the front lines squiring Gramma. Years later, my first exposure to enemy fire caused me far less distress.

WHILE I'VE NEVER ALLOWED blood lines to obscure family foibles, I can say without qualification my father was by far the finest man I have ever known. Blessed with a kind and gentle humor that served to obliterate the over-pious, self-righteous aura surrounding too many clerics, Dad came closest to successfully practicing the teachings of Christ than anyone I've ever known. It was a blessing to have but known him; to have been his son was reward beyond measure.

Much the same can be said of my mother, Edna Sterner Hammond. Her father, Jacob Sterner, a Stroudsberg, Pennsylvania attorney, died in his late thirties leaving his wife Sue Brown to raise their three girls single-handedly. Descended from a long line of Dutch Quakers, Mother's speech patterns had been pretty well stripped of colloquialisms in acquiring an English degree at Swarthmore College. Fortunately, her lexicon of traditional recipes remained unabridged.

Her real love, however, was literature. Words were ingredients of fare in which Mother found far more sustenance than she did in food, and these she dished up in enormous helpings. Yet so delightful was her self-deprecating sense of humor, one willingly went back for second helpings.

After years as a high school English teacher in Stroudsberg, Edna Sterner in her marriage to Morris Hammond brought a determination that her children

My dad with my older brother, Bill, 4, and me, 1.

would at least be exposed to "culture." She spent hours reading to us from the works of Shakespeare, Kipling, Dickens, Balzac and other classics. Similarly, an old hand-cranked Victrola inculcated both appreciation for and some knowledge of fine music. Opera was Mother's forte, and though in accompaniment her voice took on all the lilting resonance of a score of fingernails swept across a blackboard, we nonetheless, or perhaps because of, came to appreciate a well-executed obligato. I suspect I was the only kid in fifth grade at Mohawk School who knew Donazetti was not an infielder with the Brooklyn Dodgers.

MY BOYHOOD HERO was a wild-haired hellion three years older and seldom more than one jump ahead of the law. Jimmy Scott's crimes, however, weren't vicious, just high-spirited horseplay: pilfering fruit from neighborhood yards; trespassing on the forbidden grounds of the Minor estate; popping out street lights; hanging privies from telephone poles; or hopping fast freight trains as they slowed to pass through town.

Jimmy had a brilliant mind and exceptional athletic ability. Frequently, local policemen found each used to confound them. Many's the night I, hot on Jimmy's heels, fled the scene of some minor offense with our poor old pot-bellied village constable in hot pursuit until frustrated by an unscalable fence or precarious high voltage catwalk. Jimmy scampered across unafraid, while I followed in fearful ecstasy, discovering how life lived close to the edge held undue attraction.

One innovative challenge Jimmy devised served to sharpen both our photographic abilities and physical reflexes. Standing on the railroad tracks just in front of an onrushing train, we would snap pictures at the last possible moment. Then we'd compare contact prints. The one with the largest train image was declared winner! Very exhilarating and not messy at all; if one did not diddle unduly with focus or suffer low boiling point bowels.

Another boyhood friend who humbled me often was Bob Haigh. Totally fearless, even in his late sixties he remains a superb downhill skier and handsome as a matinee idol. At our fiftieth high school reunion in 1990 — my first — I was pleased to find I had magnanimously forgiven him for the many times he'd outshone me both at ski-racing and skirt-chasing. Of course, to forgive that he, unlike me, had retained a glorious mane of gray hair, would have been asking too much.

PERHAPS MY MOST UNFORGETTABLE youthful experience occurred in the summer of 1936. At age 14, I "hired out" as a farmhand for a dollar a day plus room and board. My ever-solicitous Aunt Edith knew a fat, jolly Dutchman who delivered farm produce to Saratoga. She put in a good word for me. Since at 14 I could easily pass for 18, old Farmer Fred hired me on the spot. My aunt was delighted since she, an ardent Protestant, had watched with growing alarm my increasing interest in Eleanor Barth, a sloe-eyed Catholic girl back in Scotia. Removing me from the proximity of that intriguing distraction was Aunt Edith's true motive. However, she cloaked it in such comments as: "It'll do Jay good. Fresh air, sunshine, and exercise."

Poor Aunt Edith would have had seizures had she known the truth. Fred's farm was far closer to "Tobacco Road" than "Walton's Mountain."

Hitchhiking to it one sunny June day, I vividly recall lugging my cardboard suitcase up the dusty lane to the house. Large, brightly painted barns and outbuildings contrasted remarkably with the decrepit condition of the old farm house itself. Peeling paint scrolled down the columns of its front porch and boards covered one broken front window.

As I rounded the rear of the house, the screen door flew open and, with a couple of capering hops, there appeared before me an alarming apparition. No more than four and a half feet tall and almost as wide, a potato-shaped old woman gaped at me through rheumy eyes. Her dried-apple face was framed in that stagged-off bob of gray hair common to female mental patients. Clutched between jaws unencumbered by teeth was a fuming corncob pipe. Removing it with a brown, monkey's paw she thrust its stem into my face cackling: "Who be you, boy? I'm old Mary."

Explaining I was a new hired hand got me nowhere. "You can't come in till you give Mary candy," shrieked the old crone, agilely skipping to bar my way each time I tried to reach the back door. Finally, the door was thrown open from inside and out barreled all three hundred and fifty porcine pounds of Farmer Fred, the owner. Giggling , he playfully cuffed Mary off to one side.

"Don't mind her, she ain't too bright. Just bring your things and we'll get ya' squared away."

Through the screen door, I entered a world such as I'd seen neither before nor since, save perhaps in some *Twilight Zone* re-run. In the huge woodshed, metal milk containers sat cooling in tubs of water. Cats scurried in every direction, aided in flight by Fred's lashing gumboots as we waded through them. In the kitchen, my nostrils were assaulted by a gut-clenching stench which, even today, occasionally seeps into memory.

Quickly passing into the dingy parlor, I saw, propped up in a bed, what appeared to be a shrouded mummy. From its head bindings, one glacial-blue orb rotated in its parchment-bound socket and followed our progress. The other socket was empty. Not a word was spoken. I later learned this was Farmer Fred's mother, confined to that living room bed for some dozen years. Whether her bed linen had once been changed in that time, seemed doubtful. However, the original wall coverings had been altered. Scabrous old wallpaper had sloughed off. In its place were patches of old newspapers. More cats, disturbed from their slumbers, arched and spit as we passed the old woman's bed. Lumbering up the rickety stairs, Fred showed me my room and left.

I looked around, appalled. A thin, stained and reeking mattress lay on a sagging army cot around which was clustered a battalion of empty beer bottles. A dozen used cuds of chewing tobacco pocked the floor amidst less identifiable — but even more disquieting — deposits. Everywhere, cockroaches scurried in idiotic abandon. Fat blow flies buzzed through an open window to dine rapturously on the filth.

Next day, I moved to the barn, which, even with its occasional rat, was far more hospitable.

That morning, I was introduced to the other hands over breakfast: Frank, Leon, John, Fred's father Eli, and Honey Lee. Frank handled the horses. Whether he'd been kicked in the head sometime in his career, I never knew. But when Frank's left eye was fixed on twelve o'clock, his right would lock on at three-thirty. Nonetheless, I learned Frank had a way of communicating with horses that was uncanny, a talent less perplexing when I discovered he almost matched them in intellect. Poor Leon, Frank's twenty-year-old son, was even less well equipped. On parole from a mental institution, his problems were compounded by being mute. John, on the other hand, was most impressive. Articulate, obviously well-educated, and ruggedly handsome, his most remarkable talents to a fourteen-year-old boy were his ability to shred his rolled-up shirt sleeves by flexing his eighteen-inch biceps — as well as snap caps off beer bottles with his teeth.

Eli, Fred's father, was a spry, wizened cricket of about eighty winters who, upon introduction, demanded I give him a six-figure number. "Here, write down any number," he said, clawing a stub of pencil and a shred of brown paper bag from his overall bib. "Now give me another six-figure number to multiply it." I did and almost immediately he called out the answer.

"Check it out, lad," said John. "Old Eli's got a built-in abacus board — never saw him make a mistake."

Eli's correct answer took me three minutes to work out on paper. Later, I discovered Eli's mind, while incredibly agile in math and total recall of Scripture, was muscle-bound when it left those arenas. But once he understood his instructions, he attacked a project with incredible vigor; pipe-stem arms and legs pistoning in accompaniment to a stream of incomprehensible chatter and song.

Only one of us could outwork old Eli: Frank's son, Leon. Poor Leon. Not only had he inherited all his father's mental defects, he had acquired some of his own. Though grotesque in appearance (I believe he had acromegaly), he combined incredible strength with the cheery disposition and intellect of a three-year old.

Honey Lee proved to be most intriguing of all. An eighteen-year-old ebony-black con artist with the compact build of a light-weight boxer, Honey had a rhinestone set splendidly in one front piano-key tooth. Honey combined a larcenous mind and murderous temper with one of the most charismatic personalities I've ever encountered. In a different time he could well have made it as a rock star or entertainer had he been able to forego fascination for crime and violence. Spawned in the swamps near Florida's South Miami, Honey told incredible tales of alligator poaching, bizarre sexual encounters, and of watching one of his seven brothers lynched with a baling wire noose that decapitated him when he fell from the tree limb on which he'd been perched, propelled by three .22 slugs fired into his rump. The entire family had been made to watch, according to Honey. To Honey's five-year-old mind, this nightmarish experience started a journey that eroded all qualms of conscience and replaced them with a strange amalgam of mostly savage, and sometimes sublime, visceral responses. Which would predominate was unpredictable. Whether Honey's mood swings were ruled by diet, hormonal imbalance or moon phases, I have no idea.

Old Mary and a buxom red-headed woman of about thirty prepared meals for this strange crew. I learned the earthy redhead, Lena, was a gypsy Fred had taken in to share his bounty and bed. Since in the 1930s cohabitation without matrimonial sanction was socially frowned on, I wondered what Father Eli, the Biblical scholar, thought of all this. To my awakening pubescent hormones it was, of course, most provocative. Many's the night I tossed restlessly, dreaming of booting Fred's ponderous bulk to the floor and scrambling into his bed. If Lena was ever aware of my nocturnal mental marauding, she gave no hint. We hardly exchanged a dozen words during my five weeks there.

My first breakfast was memorable, as were all meals at the farm. Mountains of eggs, hotcakes, biscuits, and pastries alongside a gallon crock of gravy in which floated unidentifiable chunks of meat. Soon enough, I found most meat was groundhog. Each day we'd take rifles into the field to replenish the larder.

Though somewhat greasy, groundhog was surprisingly good. Good, that is, until our cooks had their way. Their way was to cook entirely with butter. Eggs, groundhog, and hotcakes were all deep-fried in butter. Butter supplanted lard in the hotcakes, biscuits and pastries.

However, that butter was almost always rancid. While delivering fresh produce to Saratoga's restaurants, Fred collected foodstuffs consigned to their garbage. These included stale breads, pastries, sour milk and rancid butter, ostensibly to feed Fred's gargantuan hogs. Much, however, found its way to our table. Mealtimes were not a day's highlights. Fortunately, abundant fresh vegetables, raw potatoes and berries helped stave off starvation.

On that first day, after breakfast, another event hastened my move to the barn. I was hauling water from the big hand pump in the back yard when I heard strangled squalls, thumping, and high pitched giggling coming from the milk shed. Startled, I dropped my buckets and flung open the screen door on a shocking scene. There on the floor of the shed knelt Fat Fred astride Mary. One hand was clamped on her thrashing rump and the other on the back of her neck, holding her head under water in one of the milk-cooling tubs. With Old Mary's sneaker-clad feet drumming a tattoo on the shed floor, one nightmarish shriek after another drowned in gurgles as Fred periodically yanked her head above water and then plunged it back under.

"I told ya' I'd wash your mouth out again if ya said them dirty words," chortled Fred. "This oughta learn ya'."

Appalled by the sight, I'd like to say I hurled myself at Fred's hulk and forced him to stop. In truth, I did nothing but stand there, more sick than terrified, and hollered, "Come on Fred, cut it out. You'll kill her."

Clearly enjoying himself, Fred released his grasp reluctantly and took a menacing step toward me.

"Look here, kid, I run things around here. If you don't like it, pack up and run your way the hell out of here."

Badly shaken, I went back to work. The only reason I didn't accept his invitation was because someone who knew Fred's reputation had bet me I wouldn't last more than a week on my summer job.

From earlier exposure to works by Kraft Ebbing and Havelock Ellis, (sneaked by a classmate from the library of his doctor father), I had some small awareness of psychological aberrations. That Fred was a certifiable sadist I had no doubt; a conclusion reconfirmed when I saw him kill a cow by beating it with a shovel, giggling maniacally. The imprudent cow had stepped on Fred's foot. Since his concern for livestock seemed to outweigh that for humans I had little doubt if I'd tried to stop him, I too would have been joyously bashed. Terror gave way to nausea and I fled the scene to throw up outside.

Since the farmhands all detested Fred, I wondered why any stayed. In time, I understood. In almost each case, he had acquired total control over their destinies. Old Mary, Frank and Leon had been released from mental institutions with the understanding Fred would "look after them." Relieved of the financial burden, the government was pleased to farm out such unfortunates. Perhaps, like blessed Aunt Edith, it felt the fresh air and good food of farm life would be rehabilitative.

John was another "hand" Fred had by the neck. John once showed me old, yellowed press clippings which explained his plight. He was an escaped convict and Fred knew it. He had been a highly regarded school principal until a wealthy woman had set her sights on him. Flattered by her attention and impressed by her affluence, John was, at first, a willing target. However, after a year or so, her demands became more obsessive and his interest cooled. While seeming to accept this, the woman was inwardly bitter, according to John. She let him drive one of her cars out-of-state for a much needed vacation. Upon arriving at his destination, John was arrested by local police and charged with having stolen the vehicle and some jewelry which she'd hidden behind the back seat. He was sentenced to ten years in Dannemora Prison. However, en route he'd overpowered a guard and escaped. For twelve years he'd been on the run. How Fred had known of this I never learned. Given John's abiding and abundant thirst for beer, I suspect, after downing a dozen or so, he'd confided in Fred, just as he'd confided in me.

It was John who introduced Honey and me to the macho practice of snapping off bottle caps with our teeth. We took moronic pride in so doing. Honey Lee far out-machoed me, however, by learning to orally uncap while standing on his head and one hand.

If Honey Lee felt himself to be a repressed minority, he never showed it. He was clearly, as he liked to say, "the winkin' bull hog's eye" of the outfit. All hands seemed to look to Honey for leadership, whether in the fields addressing some burdensome chore or at the local tavern, where Honey matched or exceeded any feat of strength or agility.

During that summer I came to appreciate Honey Lee's mercurial temperament when he "saved my life" simply by ceasing to strangle me during a brawl in the barn. The fight was over a girl and it started largely as horseplay.

A week earlier we'd learned Frank was bringing his daughter Betty, to work at the farm. Reflecting on poor Frank and his son Leon's mental and physical shortcomings, we expected Betty would prove less a "dish" than a dented pot.

"She'll be the gal for you, Jigger," he snickered. "Trouble is, you'll need a muzzle and leash to take her home to your folks." I knew a little something about the price paid for jumbling defective genes. Strange traits were likely to surface.

So it was at breakfast one morning we learned Betty would arrive shortly.

"Control yourself. Don't let on you love her at first," chuckled Honey. "Matter of fact, a gal's much more interested if she thinks you're not available. Tell you what; I'll help. I'll say you're queer. That'll make you irresistible."

A few minutes later as we sat at the kitchen table, Frank's old Model T truck rattled up to a stop in the driveway. The door opened, almost as wide as Honey's mouth. Even at fifty yards it was evident Betty was a real beauty. Honey's rhinestone tooth flashed like that proverbial "bull hog's eye" and for once he had no earthy comment. Long legs briefed in cut-off bluejeans flashed like sabers as Betty strode to the kitchen door; oblivious or careless of the eight male eyeballs ratcheting at every step.

Sixteen-year old Betty proved to be well-endowed physically and at least adequate mentally; though in those pubescent years I fear the latter was of small concern. Somewhere between that Model T Ford and Fred's back stoop I fell in love. That affair was short-lived, however.

At noon Betty, Honey and I often took our lunches to the barn's hayloft and ate with a group of young berry pickers, trucked in from Saratoga. One sweltering day we were horsing around after lunch when Honey made some salty comment to Betty, the gist of which I've long forgotten. Half in jest, I told him to knock it off or I'd knock him over. When he continued to tease her, I tackled him to the hay and we thrashed around in what I thought was good natured fun. Not Honey. Perhaps too many years of old-time Deep South conditioning by what happened to blacks merely accused of making passes at white girls triggered a violent reaction. Grabbing me by the throat with iron fists he clamped down. A dark curtain, cross-hatched by a spray of shooting stars, began to descend over the sudden terror now shrouding my mind. As consciousness faded, I thrashed about ever more feebly in his furious grip, experiencing for the first time in my life the gut-grinding awareness this was probably the end of the line.

Suddenly, the shooting stars broadened into the glow of a comet as the curtain slowly ascended. Through it I saw Betty frantically jabbing Honey's ebony ribs with the butt end of a pitch fork. At least I think she was jabbing at Honey; I was the recipient of more than one prodding blow. At any rate, it worked. With an explosive grunt, Honey released his grip, leaped up and snatched the pitch fork. Scrambling to my feet, I debated whether to run or stand my ground in noble defense of the girl. Since Honey's walleyes and the tines of the fork were fixed only on me, it was a short debate. I soared off the side of the loft into the hay wagon below and bounced to the ground running.

Honey came through the air right behind me, pitchfork in hand. With a fifty foot lead, I wasn't too concerned until I raced around the corner and into the stable area, normally open to the barnyard. To my horror, the stable door was closed. Slamming against it, I frantically struggled to slide it back on its tracks just as Honey rounded the corner. Seeing my predicament, his rhinestone tooth flashed in hideous glee as he raised his weapon. Surprisingly, rather than charge like some errant black knight bent on skewering a craven opponent, Honey stopped and hurled the fork at me like a spear. Fortunately, pitch forks tumble in flight, rather than fly like javelins. Striking the wall sideways along-side my left ear, the fork dropped harmlessly to the floor — just as I shot through a gap in the door into the manure pile outside.

Later that day, you'd never have known Honey'd been hyped-up to murder. He was his usual, bubbly self. Seemingly, all was forgotten. The incident left one scar, however. Next day, Betty departed.

A TYPICAL DAY on Fred's farm started at five in the morning. Since I've never required an alarm clock, I had no trouble rising on time. Milking the cows before breakfast proved more challenging with Fred's pronouncement I'd be docked a dollar each time I didn't meet his schedule. Though I was initially promised a dollar a day plus room and board, Fred had several cute ways to spur work and cut expenses. Not only would he dock a dollar for missing a time schedule, he'd also do so if one failed to meet assigned quotas. For example, if I did not completely fill each box in a crate of berries in the time allotted, off came another dollar. Likewise, more than two trips a day to the outhouse or the water pump cost at least fifty cents.

After back-breaking days in the fields, we had supper at six o'clock. Most evenings at seven we'd leave with two teams to haul gravel until about midnight. Never have I worked harder for less.

On Friday evenings we'd drive to Luther's "Emporium" at Saratoga Lake for the club fights. Fred told Honey and me that for three fast rounds we could earn five dollars, which he'd hold for us until final payday. Though I was only 14, Fred told them I was the required 18 years of age. He also entered me under another name: Jigger Hampton. My boxing career was short-lived, however. I retired with two wins, a draw and a shameful weakness for tearing up when bashed on my nose.

My small pugilistic skills had been honed by one Dilworth Bower, an amateur boxer several years older than I who spent much time with our Boy Scout troop teaching this "manly art." The son of an elderly couple much beloved by our church congregation, Dilworth had seemed a splendid young fellow destined to make a name for himself. He certainly did. Several years later I read an article about America's most infamous mass murderers. To my astonishment, Boy Scout boxing coach Dilworth Brower had made the list by blowing away his parents, his in-laws, his wife, all their children and then himself!

Honey was a superb fighter who could have gone far. I doubt if he did, however. Learning from me that my father had an old World War I handgun, Honey begged me to steal and sell it to him. He quite unabashedly stated his prime ambition was to get into armed robbery.

Despite such appalling lack of redeeming social graces, Honey could be a delightful companion. I often wonder how he met his end. Odds are he never made it to thirty. My last recollection of Honey is seeing him leap from his cot, grab a shotgun and blow his pillow apart to "teach them damn bedbugs a lesson!"

Returning home to Scotia that summer, I'd earned a total of eighteen dollars for five weeks of the hardest work I've ever done. I chose not to dismay poor Aunt Edith. She never knew the "character-building experience" she'd promoted had been more corrosive than constructive. Happily oblivious, she sighed in relief on learning beauteous Eleanor Barth had, during my summer on Fred's farm, dumped me for somebody else.

*In 1940, I graduated from high school, then went into the
Canadian backcountry on a less than carefree canoe trip
before enrolling at Penn State.*

2

Pelican in the
Wilderness

THE LURE OF WILDERNESS ADVENTURE that eventually drew me to
Alaska beckoned long before. In high school, a cherubic lad named Robert
Nichols became one of my best friends — despite my corrupting his name to
"Rubber Nipples" — when we discovered a mutual aversion to the school social
scene. We preferred to trek through remote country or sample a new stretch of
trout stream.

Nip and I had many adventures together. Of course, show me an adventure and most times I'll show you a stupid mistake. That I've often subjected
myself to hardship and peril has been more the result of poor planning and
ignorance than bad luck or dauntless courage. I seemed cursed with a perverse
need to stand with toes over the ledge of some mental precipice, barely restraining
the urge to jump. Not that I liked being afraid. I abhorred it. Yet somehow, life
took on more vivid color and sharper dimensions when back-washed by fear.

In our last year of high school Nip and I came across an outdoor magazine
article recalling a canoe trip taken years before by the author. His description of
roiling rapids and other challenges had us romanticizing all winter long about
prospects of retracing his route.

Shortly after graduation in June, 1940, Dad drove us and our gear over the
border into Ontario. There, we caught a freight train north to Biscotasing, a
small mining town just in front of the Canadian backcountry.

For the first few days our adventure went well. The turbulent Missisagui
River was high and so were our spirits. As we ran rapid after rapid confidence
grew. Each dawn we'd launch the canoe, glide — or tumble — downstream
for several hours, then pitch camp and catch a few fish for supper. When the

15

campfire winked out, we'd unzip our sleeping bags and, bone weary, crawl into oblivion. It was Paradise.

The old map we'd gotten from a railroad official showed us landmarks on our route and stretches of river that required portaging. Carefully checking the map, we cautiously carried our canoe around the rougher water. We were at first properly respectful of this wildly wonderful place but became less so as the days and miles flowed by.

One crisp late August morning, we crawled from our tent to find ice on the water bucket. We noted the next portage was several miles downstream. Portages were usually marked on shore by a "lob tree" — a tall spruce from which the branches were stripped. Our map showed the portage required leaving the water a quarter mile above the rapids, near a side stream at which was located a prospector's cabin.

Coursing downstream on a river sparkling like molten silver, feeling the sun and spray fleck our bare backs with fire and ice, watching wedge after wedge of geese wing south, compelled us to conclude all was right with the world — and to ignore the fact something was very much wrong with our navigation.

Distances on our old map were represented, not in miles, but in time. Though we'd passed a small side stream, there was no sign of a lob tree or prospector's cabin. We had a good half hour, we thought, before coming to the next portage. Though a distant rumble suggested rapids ahead, we were little concerned as we sluiced around a wide turn in the river onto a boiling crest of fast water.

Suddenly, our daydreaming turned to terror. Up ahead, instead of a tumbling rapid was the edge of the earth! The panorama of river and forest continued unbroken for perhaps a quarter mile; then both disappeared beneath fuming mist.

By now the river's roar drowned out voice communication. Frantically thrusting his paddle as a bow rudder, Nip tried to pull us around to the left, towards less boisterous water. Matching his effort, I dug as hard with my longer stern paddle, and snapped it in half on a rock. Completely out of control, we shot through a funnel, slammed into a boulder, then broached and swamped. I pitched over the side and was swept downstream in the torrent. Unable to fight my way out of the vicious current, I careened off rocks, tumbled end over end and flooded all bilges. My trip through the quarter mile of chute leading up to the falls happened so fast I had no time to panic. Panic set in when I found myself slammed into a rock face at the top of the falls, where I managed to secure a handhold. From that precipice I was able to peer over the edge at spicules of rock far below, upon which thundering waters fell to be pulverized into vapor.

Unable to break the clutch of the current, I couldn't haul myself up the rock ledge. Instead, I clung, legs fluttering over the edge and, in horrified fascination, contemplated dropping into the mortar below to be pureed by a gigantic pummeling pestle of water.

The strain of fighting cold and current took both toll and time. Instead of ripping me loose in quick, merciful order, it left me to ponder my fate for what seemed an eternity. Realizing I could not avoid going over the falls, I nonetheless hung on for dear life. To this day, I can still see my fingers peeling, one by one, from that rock crevice to which I clawed in desperation. As the last one came loose, I shot over the edge. My last thought was to curl up like a ball.

Only later did I learn what happened from Nip, who was provided a ring-side view. When the canoe overturned, he clung to it as it swept down the chute toward the falls. Finally, the swamped craft momentarily lodged in some rocks and Nip scrambled to solid footing. The problem, however, was that Nip's island perch was near the lip of the falls. The river raging on both sides made it impossible for him to get to shore.

According to Nip, it seemed half an hour before he spotted my carcass, half hauled out on a sandbar downstream from the rock cauldron beneath the falls. For several minutes I did not move. Then I slowly gathered my scattered senses, sat up and took stock. Bleeding profusely from a battered head and kneecap, I had nothing to staunch the flow of blood. Bare to the waist before plunging overboard, the river had stripped me of my drawers, socks, and the lumberman's rubbers I had worn, unlaced, on my feet.

The icy water no doubt helped slow the bleeding, as did the leaves I tried to plaster over my wounds. Though the river's roar drowned out any possible verbal communication, it wasn't long before I saw to my great joy and amazement the tiny figure gesticulating wildly atop the falls. Then the horrid thought struck me: "He's in mid-stream with no way of getting ashore. Since he can't look directly over the edge, he doesn't see the granite boulders. He may feel since I made it, he can too." I had to get up there and try to haul him out.

Frantically, I beat my way around the base of the falls and up the steep cliff. But at the top the terrain was such I couldn't even see Nip from my side of the river. There was nothing to do but get upstream, above the chute, and try to swim across. Floundering through buck-brush and alders, I raced barefoot, mother-naked and bleeding, a quarter of a mile or so upstream. Here, though still fairly wild, the water narrowed and I thought I could cross it quite easily.

How wrong I was! Plunging in, I was once again swept downstream, emerging on the other bank just before the start of the final chute through which I had been sucked before. Reconnoitering, I found to my astonishment our canoe had swamped in some backwater at the top of the falls. Since we had lashed-in most of our duffel there was some rope to attempt a rescue. Would there be enough?

Nip's rock was about 60 feet or so out, and downstream. Because of the constant roar, we could communicate only by hand signals. My intent was try to raft a stick tied to the rope's end down to Nip in hopes he could grab it. I then planned to anchor myself behind a rock and haul him ashore.

Despite the hot sun of mid-day, the water was frigid. After several futile attempts to get the rope out to Nip, I just about iced myself over and was growing desperate. Finally, Nip, who was most precariously perched, hooked the line with his feet and reeled in. Clinching my end around my waist, I waded out to the anchor rock I had chosen and awaited his signal. Carefully knotting the rope into a sling at his end, Nip attempted to slip it under his hind quarters — and dropped it! I couldn't believe it! In disgust I hauled in the rope, untied his wet knots with fingers like brittle twigs, and started the routine all over again. Fortunately, Nip was able to capture the rope on our next try. Again, he fashioned a rope sling, and to my great relief, managed to lodge himself solidly within its confines.

With that, Nip leaped over the side — and panic leaped into my lap. Immediately, I was slammed up against my anchor rock. Water cascaded over me. I was unable to gain an inch on the line and barely able to breath. There we were, linked together in what could well be terminal tug of war neither could win. Half drowned and desperately clawing at the rope around my waist, I must confess: could I have done so, I would have cravenly shucked Nip to save myself.

Suddenly, to my dismay, the rope went slack and I knew I'd lost him. Plowing my way through the churning water back to the bank, I anguished over what I was going to tell Nip's folks. Then I saw him lying limp, face down in the slack water near shore at the crest of the falls, clutching some willows. Hauling his unconscious carcass out of the water, I did my best to revive him. At first spewing water, then an unsolicited display of what he'd had for breakfast, he sat up and looked at me in bewilderment, just before we both collapsed in hysterical laughter.

Nip was the first to recover. In my case, along with relief, shock set in and I became almost helpless. Nip, ever resourceful, took over completely. Hauling the canoe up the bank, he salvaged our gear and soon had a fire going. After drying some of the gear, he bound up my wounds and got some damp clothing on me. This included a pair of his much-too-short pants. Mine had gone overboard. His spare pair of shoes, however, were much too small for my bloody, bruised feet.

Toting canoe, our gear, and then myself down the steep bluff to the river below was a Herculean task Nip handled with remarkable ease for a lad of his stature. Though I was shivering in shock, and certain I could never again hear even a faucet run without drowning in terror, Nip persuaded me to climb back into the canoe and head downstream. It was the best therapy. Had I not done so, I suspect I'd have been forever hag-ridden by fear of fast water.

For the next two or three days we beat downstream without further incident, emerging at the little Ontario town of Hooverville. When the townsfolk heard our story they were amazed. A news reporter told me several people had perished over the years on that stretch of water, and to the best of his knowledge I was the only one to go over the falls and survive. Legend had it, according to him, that in the old days, local Indians disposed of captives and feeble elderly by sending them over what was locally known as "Squaw Chute."

Whether fact or fiction, I have no idea. Though over the years I've grown a little less confident, the former always wins over the latter when it comes to news coverage, I choose to believe it. Apparently, so did the people attending the little ceremony in Hooverville at which I was presented a small bronze medallion and a citation.

It was not my only citation on that trip. Having lost, along with clothing and shoes, my wallet containing identification and money, I was in sorry shape. Nip was only a bit better off, for I'd borrowed from his sorely limited wardrobe. We sold our canoe for twelve dollars and ignominiously hopped a freight out of Hooverville. It was now late summer and Canadian nights got pretty chilly. When we found the boxcar doors sealed, we tried huddling up on the tender immediately behind the coal burning steam engine. There, fuming hot cinders soon drove us several cars back, where by using our belts to lash our wrists to the catwalk atop a freight car, we could grab snatches of sleep between jouncings without rolling off. Occasionally on this long, illegal journey toward home, we'd find a box car door open and spend the night luxuriating out of the wind and rain. As we came into freight yards, however, we'd leap off when the train slowed down. Railroad officials back then did not take kindly to unsolicited, non-revenue customers. At each stop, yard cops searched the trains for freeloaders and unceremoniously encouraged their rapid departure — usually a fraction of an inch ahead of an orbiting nightstick. While we saw more than one head cracked, ours escaped unscathed.

During several days' cross-country travel by rail, foot, and thumb, we visited small restaurants or bakeries, and did manual chores for day-old bread and stale food. At last arriving in the border town of Petawawa, Ontario, we considered trying to cross the Roosevelt Bridge into northern New York. Having lost our documentation, we couldn't go through Customs. So we went around. Waiting for night to do a bit of prolonged, somewhat perilous swimming, we skirted the Customs station and crossed the St. Lawrence River into New York. Penniless and dripping wet, we were still many miles from home.

That evening after several futile attempts to hitch rides, Nip glared at me in the glow of oncoming headlights and shook his head. "No one's going to pick up an apparition like you. You've got three month's growth of hair and a beard that looks like it's been combed with an egg-beater. Your pants come to your knees and your feet are bare. You've got so much soot and grime ground into your hide you'd ruin a car's upholstery. Why don't you stand back, out of sight, and see if I can thumb someone down by myself."

He had a point. By contrast, Nip appeared almost couth. Beardless and far more normally clothed, his boyish good looks were less likely to prompt motorists to gun by, as they did when they spotted me.

Sure enough, on his very first try, a car slowed to a stop a hundred feet down the dark road. Elated, I popped out of the brush and sprinted alongside Nip towards our Good Samaritan. Nip and I flung open the door, about to offer our thanks. Instead, we gaped down the barrel of a huge handgun grinning at us from the fist of a burly gentleman garbed in the silks of the U.S. Border Patrol.

Once more, "adventure" translated into stupid mistake: In our attempt to outsmart the law, we had imprudently chosen to emerge from the St. Lawrence River, soaking wet, just across the border from Petawawa, where, in 1940, Canada had located a German Prisoner of War camp. Though we almost convinced our host we were neither Wehrmacht or Luftwaffers, he nevertheless hauled us to the jail in Rouse's Point, New York.

During intensive interrogation, an enormous state trooper entered the room. The border patrolman asked him if he could verify our feeble story. "Mack, this kid says he lives in Ausable Forks. That's part of your beat, isn't it? You ever seen him around there?"

Mack shook his head. "Can't say I have," he responded laconically.

"Well, that's not surprising," I explained hastily. "You see, while my Dad moved up there months ago, I've been completing my high school senior year in Scotia, New York."

"Hmm," said the trooper, "let's give your father a call. What's his number?"

Calling the number I gave him, the trooper waited for several rings before hanging up. "No answer. Who else do you know there?"

Actually I'd spent little time in Ausable; I knew almost no one. I'd made the casual acquaintance, however, of a very attractive ticket taker at the town's lone movie house. "Mary DeBlazio's a good friend. She takes tickets at the theater in Au Sable."

"Oh, you know Mary?" I was relieved to see I'd obviously caught his attention and was making my case. Eagerly, I proceeded to exploit my good fortune.

"Hey! You bet; I know Mary well. She's a great little gal. I see her every time I get to town."

I babbled on idiotically and before I was through you'd have thought Mary and I, who had spoken but three or four times, were about to elope. As I warmed to the subject of the lovely Mary, I began to sense the warmth of my bubbling enthusiasm was having a chilling effect on one very large trooper.

Later, the border patrolman explained why "Mack" had seemed less than enchanted to hear of my "affair" with the matchless Mary. "Mack's been going with Mary over a year now. They plan to get married next spring. If he had his way, you'd probably stay here until after the wedding. She'll have some explaining to do. Tell you what, we'll make some phone calls in the morning. I believe you fellas are telling the truth, but I've got to keep you penned up 'til I'm sure."

Nip and I spent the night locked up in a double-deck cage inside Rouse's Point jailhouse, luxurious accommodations compared to the catwalk of a freight car.

The next day after a few phone calls verified our status to our hosts' satisfaction, a deputy drove us to the edge of town, where we were deposited. Again deciding Nip stood a better chance of catching a ride unencumbered by this "apparition," we split up. Within a half hour Nip waved at me from a car which, on sighting me, seemed to accelerate. No matter, Nip was heading back by a different route to his hometown of Scotia, while I wended my way to Au Sable Forks.

On the back country road I traveled, traffic was very light. What little there was sped obliviously by my extended thumb which, I must admit, was occasionally shamefully propelled to my nose by their slipstream. As a consequence, I walked the full 18 miles in bare feet. Briefly my spirits soared when I came upon an orchard of MacIntosh apples beckoning succulently from behind a wire fence. Already savoring the tang of apple juice unclogging the dust from my palate, I prepared to slither under. Instead I squalled in anguish as high voltage coursed up my arm. That did it! People were no damn good! I would take to the hills and become a hermit. Civilization was not only a pain in the butt, but in most of the rest of my anatomy, as well.

Arriving in Au Sable Forks, my humiliation continued. No one was home and the parsonage door was locked. I had to climb a tree to the porch roof and enter through a second floor window. This was duly reported by alarmed neighbors. Fortunately, my father had returned home by the time the law arrived.

It was some time before I told Dad of my other brush with the law at the border. It was even longer before I got courage enough to go to the movie house where my "lost love" Mary took tickets.

Mother and Dad at home in Rupert, Vermont in 1951.

3

Befuddled Believer

IN MY EARLY TEENS, tragedy hit the Hammond family. While I'd been somewhat conditioned to death by loss of a beloved grandmother and a favorite uncle, I was unprepared for the agonies associated with mental illness. One day Dad called Bill and me into his study.

"Your mother's going through change of life, boys, and that can cause a woman some problems. Don't be surprised if Edna acts a little different. She'll be moody one moment and her usual, cheerful self the next. Just be patient, she'll get over it. Meanwhile," he added ominously, "as a precaution, don't leave any guns about."

I had already noted Mother had not been herself, but attributed it to the flu or medication. As weeks went by she became steadily worse. Gone were the bubbly sense of humor and constant chatter. No longer did she regale or recite to us. Instead, I'd find her sitting alone in her room, staring out the window. One would have to call her name repeatedly before she'd finally turn tear-filled eyes upon you. Then she'd just shake her head sadly and mutter, "Poor boys. My poor, poor boys. Why did I ever bring you into this world?"

After a suicide attempt it became necessary to institutionalize Mother at the mental hospital at Middletown, New York. For the next several years, Dad drove the long round trip almost weekly to visit her. Occasionally we'd accompany him, but reluctantly. I hated trips to Middletown. Preferring to remember my Mother as she once was, each journey further shattered memories of happier times.

My maternal grandmother, Suzie, took over domestic chores at the parsonage. Suzie was a beautiful, white-haired wisp of a woman who, though widowed in her early thirties, had reared three girls and sent them through college on money she earned as a seamstress. Suffering irregularly from severe migraine headaches, Suzie nonetheless assumed the responsibilities of raising a second family without complaint.

In the late 1930s Dad had been moved to a small, rural church in Au Sable Forks because the Methodist hierarchy, while most sympathetic to Mother's condition, felt the ministry of a relatively large congregation like the one in Scotia, required a pastoral helpmate. With Mother they'd gotten one of unflagging energy, good cheer and devotion. She taught Sunday School, led Ladies Aid and the Epreth League, played the piano and organ at prayer meetings, and mother-henned food preparation at church suppers. Moreover, she did it for free. Of course, it was unheard of in those days to supplant a minister's wife with an assistant pastor.

Mother remained hospitalized, undergoing shock treatments and who knows what else, during all my high school and college years. At times she'd be fairly lucid and we'd take her for a drive — once, briefly home for a visit. That almost ended in tragedy with another attempted suicide. Wakened by shouts from my Dad and uncle, I was badly shaken and walked the night through on the back roads of the sleeping village, wondering what had happened to the ordered world I'd once known.

Finally, the day came when Mother recovered. New medication plus shock treatments had apparently resoldered whatever wiring had been chemically short-circuited. In August 1942, I learned of this through a joyous letter Dad sent to me at Navy pre-flight school. His prayers had finally been answered. Perhaps the old boy had something there, I thought to myself. At any rate, he was taking Mother to his new assignment as pastor in Rupert, Vermont, where he was to be a "circuit riding" preacher to small churches in Rupert, West Arlington and Sandgate. I was granted leave to visit them. It was one of the best times of my life. Mother was her old self and could even joke of her life among the minions of Middletown.

ARTIST ROCKWELL KENT had been a neighbor when we lived in Au Sable Forks. Later we came to know Norman Rockwell, who resided next to my father's church in West Arlington, Vermont. Our church was featured in one of Rockwell's famous *Saturday Evening Post* covers, as were a number of Dad's parishioners.

Another friend of the family was an elderly lady who lived in the village of Eagle Bridge, New York. My folks frequently visited her en route to Rupert. When they introduced me to Grandma Moses, she had just turned 80, and had not yet achieved the worldwide acclaim that came later.

Life in the tiny, rural hamlet of Rupert was a dream come true for my parents. They were never happier. Dad raised a small garden of his beloved sweet corn and watermelons, declaring a preference for the "blossom end" of the latter as it was the sweetest. During the days I had with them, I too, had never been more content, for their joy rubbed off on all who knew them. I've never known a couple of seniors so deeply in love. This was shown more in the immense respect and consideration each held for the other, rather than couched in words. I'm not sure I ever heard them exchange much in the way of "sweet nothings," but there was much good-natured joshing, mostly on Mother's part.

Dad wasn't just a preacher, but a true practitioner of Christian charity. I realize now he was the most beloved and respected person I've ever met. He had not one phony nor mean cell in mind or spirit. By example, he served his Master far better than anyone I ever knew. My parents were sustained by a joyous, rather than somber faith. Instead of begrimed by fire and brimstone, one felt uplifted and cleansed in their company.

The only friction I recall between my parents was Mother's passion for, and Dad's against, antique shopping. The hills and dales of Vermont are pocked by almost as many antique shops as cows. While driving through that verdant countryside, when Dad spotted an "Antiques" sign ahead, his foot would automatically depress the gas pedal. Unless Mother shrieked, "Stop!" well before they rocketed past, Dad would win. If she succeeded in sounding off before passage however, he was subjected to a two-hour delay during which he would read the book he had brought along, just in case.

My father never spoke unkindly of anyone, not that he didn't recognize and regret their more obvious shortcomings. He simply abided by his basic credo to assess every prospective statement on the basis of three criteria: "Is it true? Is it kind? Is it necessary?" As a consequence — in contrast to Mother, who found those boundaries less binding when it came to gossip — my father was a man of few, but soft-spoken, words. Many's the time Mother would stray a little too close to one of those three parameters and Dad would quietly admonish: "Oh now Eddy, I wouldn't say that."

Since this expression was the trademark of a milque-toasty character on the popular Fibber Magee & Molly radio program, Mother started calling Dad, "Mr. Peevy."

"Mr. Peevy would take off and go straight up to heaven if I wasn't hanging onto his coattails," she'd sigh resignedly. "It's only my feet of clay that weigh him down."

Unfortunately, that ballast did not long enough serve as sufficient. The years of idyllic reunion in their beloved Vermont proved entirely too short. Dad found himself suddenly losing coordination and strength. No longer could he perform the daily exercise routine that had kept his powerful frame in excellent shape. A brief stint in his garden compelled him to collapse in exhaustion in his old Morris chair. His rich, resonant voice became hoarse. Speaking became difficult. A medical exam brought the dread verdict that, at age 70, my father had acquired *amyotrophic lateral sclerosis* — "Lou Gehrig's disease" — for which there was no cure.

My Father's decline was apparent and rapid. In seemingly no time he went from slow gait, to cane, to wheelchair. Speech became nearly impossible. His voice was almost an indiscernible whisper. That is, except in the pulpit. Incredibly, come Sunday morning he'd somehow recapture his vocal powers almost completely, delivering his sermons with humor and force. "The Holy Spirit simply seems to take over," was his explanation.

Many times over the years, I've been forced to conclude I've been a "victim" of serendipity; good things would happen to me in spite of myself. I now realize I was first "victimized" in the selection of parents. Morris and Edna Hammond were the best. After years of attempts to overcome their positive influence, I've no doubt it was their love and prayerful intercession that frustrated my efforts.

I FIRST BECAME AWARE of peculiar personal traits that confounded the fates during high school. They say courage and class are products of grace under pressure. Not so with me; pressure too often produced *dis*-grace, in athletics as well as in most other endeavors.

As in virtually everything I have undertaken in life, athletic performances were totally unpredictable, save in one regard: almost invariably I would start out like a world-beater and, through diligence, practice and determination, work my way slowly downward. The harder I'd try, seemingly the faster I'd fall. I'd do fine until I learned what I'd done was, for a tyro, impressive. Then, bathed in even lukewarm spectator appreciation, all the cogs, gears and levers would rust.

Take football as one example. In high school, on defense I played right end; on offense I played fullback because, in spite of my speed I was a fumble-fingered pass receiver. Though I relished the greater acclaim accorded offensive ball carriers, my abilities and attitude were much more in tune with defense. Rarely did anyone sweep our right end. At least that was my reputation until our coach announced he'd invited scouts from Southern California and Loyola to watch Saturday's game.

Before the game, I overheard him promoting me to the scouts. Unaware I'd been within earshot, the coach learned I'd overheard his praise. "No matter," he replied, "Jay'd be the first and only guy on the team to dispute what I said, and the last to let it go to his head."

I went on to prove such humility was fully justified. On a kick-off return, I fumbled. Later, breaking loose on a rare long yardage pass play, I surprised myself by catching the ball — then stumbled spectacularly over my feet. On defense, runners swept cleanly around my end as if by invitation, as I waved futilely at them from the ground where I'd been deposited. The harder I tried, the worse I performed. At the end of the game, I winced into the locker room while the two talent scouts winged back to the West Coast, never to be heard from again. It was a nightmare.

Scotia, New York, 1940. Number 19 had an impressive 18-point average — per season, not per game.

It was also a portent of my later life in politics.

Off the athletic field the humiliation continued. Classmates elected me senior class president with one ulterior motive: revenge for my having labeled many of them with ludicrous but adhesive nicknames. They, in turn knew all too well how sincerely I hated and shirked responsibility, formal attire and — Heaven forbid — public speaking. From this knowledge, they extracted full retribution.

One of the class president's duties was to introduce guest speakers at weekly assemblies. My first such dreaded assignment was to introduce celebrated track star, miler Glenn Cunningham. Standing off stage, I nervously went over my exceedingly brief introduction, waiting for the curtain to open. Suddenly, the awful moment arrived and a hand propelled me on stage just as an alarmed voice whispered, "Jay! For Heaven's sake, check your fly!"

Of course, stumbling onto the bare stage, I could not do so in full view of the faculty and student body. I looked in vain for a podium to hide behind, certain every eyeball in the auditorium was riveted on my gaping trousers. Unable to explore my condition covertly with a visual "down-check" or tentative thumb, I stood on center stage, transfixed and speechless.

"Please, God," I prayed, "if the end of the world is ever to come, Let It Be Now!"

When my prayer went unheeded, I opened my mouth to say something and was greeted with thunderous applause. Each time I tried to speak, vengeful applause drowned me out, prolonging for an eternity my embarrassed, presumed indecent exposure. To this day, the trauma sustained in that auditorium persists; I'm only comfortable speaking when seated, or half hidden behind a protective podium.

Other more inexplicable phenomena have played significant roles in changing my life. While these mostly took the form of oddball occurrences some might deem psychic, they helped crack open the door of my mind to the possibility, and finally assurance, that there are dimensions to life far beyond the mental and physical.

In those early years I had my first experience in what was, back then, deemed "the unknown," and today explained as telepathy. When sixteen, while walking through New York State's Lake George woods with friend Linn Adams, we came across a huge, fire-charred blowdown. Linn halted and opened his mouth to speak. Instantly, I saw in my mind, etched in bright green light, the words I knew he was about to utter.

"Hold it! You were going to say 'Thus die all denizens of the deep,' weren't you?"

Astonished, Lynn looked at me and gasped, "Yeah, I was. But how did you know?"

I was at a loss to explain.

The next year, during my first canoe trip with Bob Nichols, more experiences were triggered.

"Hey," Bob once started to say. Again words flashed in the green light of my mind.

"You're going to say, 'Let's visit Sabattus'." Since Sabattus was an old Indian after whom a small village hundreds of miles away was named, this made no sense at all. Nonetheless, Bob acknowledged that for some reason this was exactly what he meant to say.

A few hours later, looking at a row of Lombardy poplars, Bob opened his mouth to speak.

"Wait." I said. "You're going to say, 'Wouldn't that make a great wall around Dannemora Prison?'"

Bob nodded in astonishment.

I have never pretended to understand this phenomena. But there were to be many such experiences — each mysterious and some morbidly accurate.

I was commissioned as a 2nd Lieutenant in the U.S. Marine Corps in February 1943.

4

Serendipity Strikes

Starting in my last year of high school and continuing for almost three years, I was often incapacitated by excruciating headaches. My father took me to some fourteen specialists, including some from the Harvard Migraine Clinic. They X-rayed teeth and sinuses, examined my eyes, gave me hemoglobin shots, stuck pins in my feet, asked about my love life, manipulated vertebrae — and concluded my headaches were psychosomatic.

In the fall of 1940, when I enrolled in Pennsylvania State College's School of Mineral Industries to study petroleum engineering, I also went out for wrestling and football. Though a bit light at six feet and one hundred, eighty-five pounds, I played defensive right end and offensive fullback. With no such thing as platoon football in those days, one often played a full sixty minutes. Soon the headaches compelled me to turn down an athletic scholarship and quit football and wrestling. Not a day went by without a headache. Despite consuming fistfuls of aspirin, two or three "bone crackers" a week put me to bed by eight at night. I barely made passing grades. The only exercise I could tolerate, which at times seemed to ease the pain, was working out with weights.

I'd begun this activity when I was twelve, after hearing a doctor tell Mother, "You'd best give him piano lessons; he's much too frail for athletics." Consequently, an early issue of *Strength & Health* magazine prompted me to forsake the piano and hoist iron, even though everyone "knew" lifting weights "enlarged the heart" and "bound" the muscles. In those days, weight training was opposed by almost all coaches and medical doctors. Only a few "oddballs" engaged in it; most were mentally or physically lame, sick or halt. Among us were polio victims, runts, narcissists, and some having difficulty with gender

31

orientation. Small wonder at Penn State we worked out in a tiny anteroom in back of the bleachers.

Learning to fly was a diversion. Because I found it intolerable to watch a football game in which I couldn't play, I welcomed any excuse to let me be elsewhere on Saturdays. Flight lessons at a nearby airport accommodated my quirk.

In 1939, an aborted lesson in a neighbor's old Monocoupe had not entranced me. The engine failed before we got airborne. When I learned of the new Civilian Pilot Training program, however, I was ready to try again. For twenty-five dollars the government would train a student to fly, provided the trainee agreed to enlist in either the Army, Navy or Marine air arm "in the event of a national emergency."

WEEKS LATER, on a bleak Sunday, President Roosevelt dropped his "Day of Infamy" bombshell. A national emergency had arrived.

Enlisting in the Navy as a Seaman 2nd Class, I was soon on my way to Chapel Hill, North Carolina to join the 1st Battalion of pre-flight school in an experimental program designed to produce the "roughest, toughest, fighting men in any branch of service," according to press releases. This first effort was almost disastrous.

Physical fitness instructors, known irreverently as "jock strap admirals," each tried to maximize the time allotted for his particular sport. I recall one painful day when we were rousted out for a fifteen-mile, half-run and half-walking march at five a.m. On returning, instead of "falling out," many of us simply fell down exhausted. Next were bi-monthly "achievement tests." These required one to do all the push-ups, chin-ups, and sit-ups possible, perform jump tests and run an obstacle course. Afterward, I joined those losing breakfast. Then came sixty minutes of some of the roughest football I've ever played. Our team was coached by Jim Crowley of Notre Dame "Four Horsemen" fame. Most of us, including three All-Americans, had played college ball. In the blistering 95-degree temperature, it was the longest game I ever played. When it was over, up came lunch.

Next, our platoon moved on to the boxing instructors for a few fast rounds between which dry heaves took over. From there we went to our "regular activities." For me this was track and field. At both the beginning and end of each track session, it was once again around the obstacle course. My third and final circuit that day I suspect set records for time consumed; something I could not do with dinner. Then it was time to hit the books.

"Lights Out" came at ten and signaled an agonizing seven hours of high decibel, adenoidal serenading by one of my six roommates, a bulbous bugler known by his bunk-mates as "The Toad." He'd mastered the "hesitation snore": a long, whistling tremor on inhale, then — as you braced for the rock-shivering blast expected to follow — nothing. Nothing, that is, until you began to relax, only to snatch the covers to keep them from being stripped off your cot in the ensuing hurricane. That he was a nice guy while awake went for naught. I grew to hate The Toad after hours, and alarmed myself with all the bloody methods of dispatch that frolicked insanely through the back alleys of my midnight mind. Many nights I sought sanctuary in the "head," falling in and out of sleep astride a toilet bowl rather than succumb to the temptation to perform a tracheotomy on poor old Toad.

What effect did all this have on my aching head? After two weeks in pre-flight school, it became obvious I simply couldn't take anymore. Reluctantly, I slunk off to sick bay to seek a medical discharge. That day, no doctor was on duty; just a teenaged corpsman. Presuming he could hardly help me, I explained my symptoms anyhow.

"Oh," he said, "you need salt tablets."

He gave me a bottle of plain salt pills to take "after exercise, while hot and perspiring." This I did. Next thing I knew, my salivary glands began to clench and my stomach contents ejected.

A friend who'd had the same experience suggested I pick up some sugar-coated salt tablets and take them first thing in the morning. I did. Three days later, when I got up I gave my head the usual tentative shake to gauge where the day's ache would register on the Richter scale. To my astonishment, for the first time in three years I felt not even a tremor. From that day on, I've had no further trouble with severe headaches. Salt tablets continued as daily fare during my years in the service. I discontinued them only after I came to Alaska.

To this day, the annals of U.S. Navy medicine refer to the 1st Battalion of Chapel Hill Pre-Flight as the "guinea pig class." From us, the Navy learned a lot about what not to do to maximize physical conditioning. True, those few who had been grossly overweight and yet survived the program, were remarkably honed down. However, those of us who entered in good shape suffered the burn-out of over-training. In my case, records at the start and finish of pre-flight school tell a dramatic story.

At the 1st Battalion's graduation, a phalanx of Navy brass came to see the end-product of their experiment. They interviewed us individually as we handed them the results of our final physical achievement tests. I recall well the U.S. Naval Academy's football coach, Admiral Tom Hamilton, glancing at my final scores and proclaiming heartily, "Son, this program certainly has shaped you up. Let's see how much you've improved." Rifling through my file he happily announced, "Ahh, I see you trimmed off a lot of lard. You now weigh 181, but weighed 205 when you first came in. Excellent!"

His satisfaction changed to perplexity as he dug further into my file.

"Wait a minute. Your last achievement test shows you did eighteen chins and eighty-five push-ups. That's pretty good. But the first time you took the test you did twenty-seven chins and one hundred and fifty-seven push-ups? And you added more than a minute to your time on the obstacle course? Something seems all backward here."

Poor Tom. I ruined his day. Worse, it took me almost six months to get back in shape.

———————————

GOING THROUGH NAVY FLIGHT TRAINING in Dallas, serendipity again slapped me alongside the head. An unexpected visit by high brass from Washington prompted the base commandant to call an immediate parade and inspection. Cadets scurried frantically to meet muster in proper uniform. You might know, I couldn't find the right uniform cap. Realizing an even more capital crime would be to show up wearing none at all, I grabbed the only cap I could find and raced to "fall in." When the commandant spied me out of uniform, he was apoplectic.

Hammond!" he bawled, "At least we'll have the ranks in uniform. Get the hell up front and take charge of the drill!"

Thus it was when the two hundred-strong Cadet Corps marched in review before the visiting brass that day, one hundred and ninety-nine khaki caps were led by one of bilious green.

Furious for having again propelled myself to stage center when I would much prefer goofing off in the wings, I took out my anger on the troops, barking commands and putting them through a difficult, intricate drill. When we were dismissed, I slunk back to the barracks to await chastisement. That evening, I was ordered to report immediately to the commandant's office.

Expecting a verbal thumping, imagine my surprise when, after a mild rebuke, the commandant said, "I rather liked the way you drilled the troops today, Hammond, so I'm appointing you Cadet Battalion Adjutant. You'll have special duties but you'll also have special privileges. You'll receive written orders tomorrow as to your duties. That's all. Dismissed!"

Next day I received my orders, along with a commission as Battalion Adjutant and a copy of the glowing letter inserted in my personnel file attesting to my "exceptional leadership abilities"! While the orders described in detail my privileges as Battalion Adjutant, nowhere was there mention of additional duties. To this day, I do not know what they were. Talk about serendipity! By failing to make muster in proper uniform, I'd been awarded the best job in the Cadet Corps! I had almost private quarters; I could sleep until nine — rather than rise at five for calisthenics with the other cadets — have a leisurely breakfast of whatever I chose at special dining facilities, and the privilege of overnight liberty, off-base, every weekend, instead of suffering the curfew imposed on all others. Small wonder such experiences warp one's values. Burning desire and overt ambition never have paid off for me. The more ardently I aspired to something, the less likely I would achieve it. Take my prime boyhood ambition to build twenty-inch arms, and a later desire to keep all my hair. I achieved neither.

MOST CADETS WERE HAG-RIDDEN by fear of "washing out." To wash out was not a fate for dolts and dunderheads only. Some of the brightest cadets fell by the wayside.

Though I held a private pilot's license before enlisting, the Navy had its own way of flying and most instructors preferred to take students "from scratch," rather than attempt to reshape one already corrupted by learning to fly other than "the Navy way."

My close call with "washing out" came in the latter stages of primary flight training at Dallas' Love Field. We were flying Spartan Jeeps, Stearmans and N3N biplanes known as "Yellow Perils." I'd done quite well in the first phases of training. However, on one crucial check flight we were required to slip without power and hit a large circle chalked on the runway. I had hit one less than required.

My instructor was conciliatory. "I hate to do it, Hammond, but I have to give you a "down check." You missed a circle. You'll have no trouble connecting, next time around. Today you were just a little off." I did not share his confidence. For the next few days I had no trouble hitting the required number of circles, but at night I tossed in apprehension over my final check ride scheduled at the end of the week.

When the day arrived I slung on my parachute and waddled to the flight board to see what instructor I'd drawn. I prayed it would not be old "Down Check" Robins. Known for his vitriolic temper and seemingly sadistic delight in failing student pilots, Lt. Robins was the nemesis of the entire Cadet Corps.

A glance at the flight board confirmed my worst nightmares. I had drawn old "Down Check" himself. "That's it," I panicked, "I've had it."

Dejected, I climbed into the rear cockpit of the Stearman and awaited arrival of my check pilot. Without so much as a grunt of acknowledgment, the irascible, beetle-browed Robins hopped into the front cockpit, adjusted his Gosport and roared into it: "What the hell are you waiting for? Let's get going!"

Already near panic, I took another step toward its brink. With extreme deliberation, I carefully went through the Navy's standard eight-point check-off list: "Good Pilots Must Find Home To Land Safely." Gas, Prop, Mixture, Flaps, Hook, Tail wheel, Landing gear, Straps. Starting the engine and allowing more than sufficient warm-up, I began to taxi. Being extra cautious, I crept down the ramp, weaving back and forth in the manner prescribed to avoid obstacles.

Suddenly the controls jerked from my hands and a bellow blasted through my concentration. "For God's sakes, Hammond, what the hell are you doing? Let's GO! I haven't got all day and tomorrow!"

For the next hour I was subjected to a constant blast of invective and ridicule as I fumbled through maneuver after maneuver. Several times I had the controls jerked away as a withering stream of curses accompanied his demonstration of what I *should* have done. Long before the hour was up, I was

mentally packing my bags and wondering how I could weather the humiliation of washing out.

Finally, I could take no more. In the wake of another blast, I wagged the
controls, caught "Down Check's" eye in the rear view mirror and signaled he
now had the controls. I was through.

He returned immediately to base, landed, and without a word stalked from
the aircraft to the check board.

When I caught up with him, Robins was eyeing the board, chalk in hand.
Turning to me he growled, "Hell, there's nothing wrong with your flying."

To my astonishment, drawn on the board by my name was an arrow pointed
up. Without another word, Lt. Robins slouched off while I soared some ten feet
above ground to my barracks.

Few subsequent flights caused me more fear and apprehension, unless they
were night carrier landings. Certainly, my first combat mission was a piece of
cake by contrast. For this I must thank and salute my old nemesis, "Down Check."

ONLY AFTER BEING BURNED several times did I learn never to ask for the
assignments you want in the Navy. When I enlisted I asked to be sent to the
pre-flight school in Philadelphia. I was sent to Chapel Hill, North Carolina.
Then I applied for Basic Flight Training in Boston, and was sent to Dallas. For
Intermediate Flight and Instrument Training, I asked for Corpus Christi's
Cuddahy Field, nicknamed "Easy Acres." Instead I was sent to adjacent Cabinus
Field, which certainly deserved the contrasting title, "Eager Acres." For Ad-
vanced Training I asked for fighters and, you might know, I was put in Squadron
Seventeen, to fly battleship-catapulted "Kingfisher" observation aircraft. When
I ultimately was assigned fighter training, I received orders to Jacksonville, Florida,
rather than Cherry Point, North Carolina which I'd requested.

Even a request granted usually backfired. For example, during the last stages
of flight training, Naval cadets were allowed to apply for transfer to the Marine
Corps. Of course, we who were selected made much of the fact only the top
percentage of those who applied were selected. Navy flyers, of course, were quick
to assert that only the dregs ever applied. I recall one Marine selectee trying to
persuade his distraught girlfriend by phone that assignment to the Marines was
a singular honor.

"Why," he intoned proudly, "you should know they take only the top
percentage of applicants."

"Yeah," chortled an irreverent bystander, "the top ninety-five percent."

Though not quite the truth, it was close. In 1942, they were frantically seeking
replacements for Marine squadrons depleted in early South Pacific campaigns.

My motives for requesting Marine assignment were mixed. The one I pronounced publicly was a desire to get into A-20 As, light, twin-engine bombers.
Reportedly, these were incredible performers. A few new Marine squadrons of

these aircraft were allegedly about to be formed. My unspoken motives, I fear, were less noble. I did not at all find enchanting the idea of flying off aircraft carriers. Again, I might have known. Not only did I never get to see an A-20-A in combat, one of my first assignments was to a carrier. Since we were to fly old "birdcage" Corsairs — so named because of the confined view through the metal strapped canopy — and would lose or damage some eighteen planes through training accidents during my first two weeks at sea aboard one of the smallest "vest pocket" carriers in the Navy, my suspicions that carrier flying held undue hazards would prove well founded.

Curiously, before attempting our first carrier landings, we were subjected to conditioning seemingly designed to convince us we'd fail. First came simulated carrier landings ashore. After shooting a few dozen of these "spot" landings — during most of which we failed to catch the arresting cable with the aircraft's tail hook — confidence ebbed. What little remained drained completely when we were shown our last training film.

In it, planes slammed into the carrier's fan tail or its super structure; cartwheeled over the side; "spun in" on approach; dribbled over the bow from weak catapults; or rocketed into the barrier after shucking a tail hook. Moreover, the footage was spliced together in such a way as to make these hazards not seem the exception. Had I had the nerve, I'd have quit then and there. Instead, I meekly climbed into the cockpit and headed to sea.

When we rendezvoused with our carrier, a qualified carrier pilot established a landing pattern. I was fifth in line. As we circled the tiny postage stamp bucketing about in a heavy sea, I couldn't believe my eyes. "No way can I possibly land on that!"

Yet, one after the other, the four pilots preceding me did so. As I entered the traffic pattern, my feet skittered about on the pedals in a nervous tap dance accompanied by the baton of my control stick, which kept imperfect time. Somehow ignoring the mortal terror riding my shoulders like some insane jockey, I concentrated on the landing signal officer, and to him and the good Lord, commended my spirit. I recall well my last perception just before landing: "If those idiots can do it, so can this one!" This sustaining thought has since taken me through many trials and tribulations, for which I must pay homage to all other idiots in this world who have preceded me.

Years later, after thousands of hours flying Alaska's bush, landing on mountain tops, glaciers, river gravel bars, beaches and mud-flats, enduring fourteen engine failures, broken aircraft and bones, blinding snow storms, gale force winds and even the challenge of an aircraft whose rudder controls had been hooked up backward, I still have found nothing to hold a candle to the dark dread of that first night carrier landing. If night carrier landings were not as impossible as they first seemed, the best comparison I can make is to that of walking a railroad track. It's not tough at all, on the ground; but raise the track two hundred feet in the air and feel your pucker-string cinch!

While it may be true that there are old pilots and bold pilots, but none both old *and* bold, chances are even the former have been bruised. Such safety features as earplugs, earphones, or shoulder straps were not required back then. Consequently, most of us who flew open cockpits have long since lost the top range of our hearing. Similarly, many World War II vintage fighter pilots suffered whiplash. Among carrier pilots, one altogether too common distinguishing feature was the so-called "Mark VIII gun-sight nose." This crude relandscaping of one's features occurred often before the use of restraining shoulder straps at the abrupt stop of a carrier landing. Convenient optical alignment required the gunsight to be mounted but a few inches in front of one's nose.

MY FIRST BRUISING occurred on a night flight over Corpus Christi in 1942. While on this training mission a squadron of OS2C Kingfisher floatplanes were caught aloft when a dense fog rolled in from the gulf. In an effort to find our way to the completely obscured Laguna Madre seaplane landing area, virtual panic took over. The airwaves were cluttered with frantic pleas for assistance from fledgling pilots. A number of mid-air collisions occurred. Several aircraft and pilots were lost in what was deemed the worst training disaster in Naval aviation history. I came close to being among the statistics.

Just before becoming engulfed in fog, I noted a hazy red glow a few hundred feet under me. Assuming it was the boundary lights of our landing area, I started an instrument let-down. To my dismay, I broke through overcast to find myself careening down the main street of Corpus Christi! Hovering over me on each side were tall buildings — a fact attested to in the local paper next day by a hotel guest who, hearing a roar, peered out on a float plane "barreling along *beneath* my window."

Pulling up frantically, but now oriented, I headed back through the fog to our landing area, a few times en route slapped by the slip stream of another invisible aircraft.

When, by "dead reckoning," I'd felt I was over water, I set up my float-equipped aircraft for instrument landing. Few things so capture a pilot's attention as the question of where he's landing — especially when he's in "the blind." So it was that only emotional relief flooded the cockpit when my aircraft touched down on water in a smooth landing. It was relief short-lived, however. With a shocking jolt, my floats hit a sand bar and we careened to a sudden stop, high and dry. For the next hour I had a painful ringside seat at a slaughter. Panicked radio transmissions garbled airwaves as frantic pilots sought to land. Even though immensely relieved to be down, I realized I was still not home free when an aircraft spun out of the night and crashed no more than a hundred yards from me.

Paddling to the wreckage in my parachute-pack life raft, I was able to extract pilot Harry Moore and return with him to my stranded aircraft. His injuries were so much more severe than my own, I barely noticed my aching back.

Fortunately, as the tide came in, my aircraft floated off the sand bar and I was able to taxi to the seaplane station.

Next day, I could hardly get out of bed. However, since I desperately wanted to graduate with my class, I foolishly failed to report to sick bay. Only years later did X-rays reveal the old fractures of my lumbar and cervical vertebrae.

It's debatable whether these spinal injuries occurred then, or later, when I was forced to crash land a plane whose vertical stabilizer had been partly knocked off in combat. More significant is the fact, in the later instance, that lack of nerve helped save my life. When my aircraft was hit and I, in shock, noted the absence of tail feathers, my inclination was to bail out. I unbuckled my seatbelt and threw open the canopy. However, at six hundred feet, the water below seemed entirely too close and I chickened out. Since the aircraft was not doing anything drastic, I flew back to a beach where I landed wheels-up. Once again, my backbone executed a whiplash.

Later, I learned my failure to find nerve to jump was my good fortune. The waters were some of the most shark-infested in the Pacific.

Meanwhile, I had already taken a leap into the uncharted waters — of matrimony.

This had been prompted by a chance meeting with Henrietta Juve, sister of the Penn State friend with whom I'd enlisted. Dick arranged a date with "Hank" when she and her mother visited our training base at Corpus Christi.

Hank was a talented, tall, Nordic blonde beauty, unpretentiously honest and intellectual. She modeled for *Charm* magazine, played classical piano of concert quality and moved with unpostured poise through a world of sophisticates totally foreign to me. I, of course, took her away from all that, much to her mother's eternal resentment.

Hank and I were married shortly after I was sent to Jacksonville for advanced fighter training. At the time, I hoped my troubling doubts were normal pre-nuptial jitters. A series of tragic deaths in Hank's family had dissuaded me from further hurting her by insisting we hold off on marriage until I returned from overseas.

What raw cruelties come first camouflaged as kindness! Instead, I smiled and accepted congratulations — and felt sick deep inside, just as I would thirty years later on Election Night, 1974.

The first disruption of our union came soon after with orders sending me to the South Pacific.

Somewhere in the South Pacific, World War II.

5
Tour of Duty

To SOME WHO LATER HOPED to romanticize the Hammond image, my overseas tour was conspicuous for my having been assigned to Pappy Boyington's infamous Black Sheep squadron, VMF214. This is, one might say, true — but not accurate.

Originally known as "Boyington's Black Bastards," the Marine Corps high command demanded the squadron's name be de-salted to "Black Sheep." I was not a member of VMF214, except on paper, for more than a week while awaiting permanent assignment to another squadron. Not only had I never flown with Boyington, the only time I'd seen him fly was when he came flying out of an Officer's Club bar in a drunken brawl.

After reading autobiographies by General Chuck Yeager and Joe Foss, my "sea stories" seem so pallid as to not warrant repeating. About the only thing I had in common with these gentlemen was 20/10 vision. Certainly my combat experiences pale by comparison. Those that come to mind are either appalling, peculiar, or ridiculous. Bouts with jungle-rot, amoebic dysentery and other exotic forms of crud also are best forgotten. More spectacular by far than my engagements were those of others with whom I was privileged to serve. For this I was, and remain, most appreciative.

One of these was my good friend, Reiny Leu, with whom I had the distinction of serving for but one day as, respectively, Squadron Commander and Executive Officer of VMF211. Reiny also distinguished himself, reluctantly, in another regard. Returning from a mission one day, Reiny and his wing man encountered a mass of lumbering Japanese dive bombers. These slow flying aircraft cruised at a little over 100 knots and were virtually defenseless. More curiously, they had no fighter cover, so Reiny and partner set up for a turkey shoot. Charging their weapons, they made their first run. To Reiny's dismay his guns fired one shot, like a rifle, and jammed. Again charging his fifty calibers, Reiny swept in for another pass. Again his guns jammed. Furious and frantic, he made run after run, getting off but one round each time. Meanwhile, his wing man was raining planes out of the sky to become an instant "Ace" plus. It was a week before Reiny could see any humor in his situation; to the rest of his squadron it was clearly discernible, much to his disgust,

Whitey Kessler was another squadron mate whose experiences I didn't envy. Shot down, he spent three days in his life raft before being picked up by a U.S. torpedo boat. Blond and light complexioned, Whitey was almost fricasseed after three days in the scorching South Pacific sun. Still, he was several shades lighter red than he became in an experience we later shared.

We had just returned from a long flight from Zamboanga in the Philippines after raiding Japanese-held oil fields at Balacapapon in Borneo. The several-hour round trip challenged a Corsair's fuel capacity, to say nothing of one's kidneys. Such flights were known as "bladder-busters." Sure, our planes were equipped with so-called "relief tubes." Unfortunately, these were designed either by supermen or sadists. Seated on a parachute pack, only the most remarkably endowed could make the connection. With a funnel at the pilot end of the tube about the size of an eyecup, windage and elevation challenged one's marksmanship. To compound indignities, relief tubes clogged frequently. More than once I unclipped one from under my seat and extended it to the limit only to be showered by some perverse Venturi effect. Bad enough to be bathed in one's own body fluids; vicarious baptisms by previous pilots added insult. After a few such indignities, most chose instead to limit our pre-flight liquid intake and wait for relief after landing.

So it was at the end of our mission this day, Whitey and I leaped out on a wing and commenced tapping our kidneys. When taxiing, we'd seen some helmeted troops disembark from a Marine transport plane just in front of us. Now they dutifully formed ranks and stood at attention not too far beyond our trajectory. Suddenly, as if on order, all removed their helmets. Blond, black, brown and red tresses cascaded down their shoulders as the troop of nurses burst into catcalls, whistles and wild applause! Thunderstruck, Whitey and I momentarily froze on our perches, mouths and trousers agape. Then, as one, we leaped off and beat a hasty retreat, having just enough presence of mind to yank down our goggles for anonymity.

That night, it took us a while to crank up the courage to attend a dance the squadron put on for these itinerant Navy nurses, the first women from home most of us had seen in a mighty long time. Fortunately, none of them indicated we'd "met" before, so I relaxed. On the other hand, several seemed to grin a bit much when introduced to Whitey.

The evening provided further embarrassment. The old coconut plantation our squadron occupied was shared with giant lizards the size of Iguanas. While

Philippines, 1945. VMF211. At odds with the crowd, as usual, I'm looking off-camera in the lower-right.

these reptiles made fine stew, they lacked certain redeeming social graces; one being their vocabulary. Some swore these lizards, like parrots, could mimic speech and had been corrupted from too close association with the U.S. Marine Corps. Thus inspired, they would frequently shriek at high decibels an uncanny rendition of a most crude imperative directing one to perform on himself impossible sexual congress. These shocking screams were, more often than not, followed by the creature's maniacal cackle. While we'd grown quite used to this, not so the poor nurses. More than one amorous Marine had his moonlit pitch to a nurse plow into the dirt that evening. It's mighty hard to persuade a young lady you're sincere, amid obscenities screamed from above.

Another memorable squadron mate was "Murderous Manny" Siegel. Manny had made a name for himself before joining VMF211. With almost a score of Japanese planes to his credit, he was one of several Marine fighter pilots nudging Eddy Richenbacher's World War I record. Before his arrival, someone circulated a stateside comic book illustrating Siegel's exploits. Murderous Manny was depicted as a glowering, hawk-faced, blue-eyed swashbuckler with bulging biceps and shoulders hardly cockpit containable. Expecting some superman larger than life, we were appalled when Siegel arrived at mess and all five-feet, seven inches of this intrepid warrior slunk into view in the wake of an impressive nib, more suggestive of pelican than peregrine. Nervously swiveling his custard colored eyeballs, Manny timorously made his way to an empty spot at our table and asked if he might join us.

Manny's physical attributes may have been less than expected, but he soon won esteem, respect and affection from all. For one thing, he was a most improbable fighter pilot. A Jewish boy from New York's garment district, he'd never thought much about flying airplanes and only a friend's encouragement got him into flight training. Though his friend washed out, Manny, to his alleged surprise, completed the training — just barely. For one thing, his sight was not the best. For another, he was poorly coordinated; at least according to Manny. Both assertions were suspect when we learned he was also a talented artist. His most popular specialty was painting well-endowed female forms rivaling anything drawn by Vargas or Petty for *Esquire* magazine — the prime purveyor of 1940s print pulchritude. Manny's voluptuous vamps decorated "O" Clubs from one end of the South Pacific to the other.

Most fighter pilots are a bit wild-haired, cocky and convinced they're a cut or two above mere mortals. Not Siegel. Manny shrugged off any suggestion he was a top gun, attributing most of his kills to dumb luck. True, being in the right place at the right time is a large part of the game. Certainly, Manny did not seem to be the world's greatest pilot. Most of us could outdo him at dog fighting which he'd do only with reluctance, insisting his eyesight was too poor to chance a collision.

For a while I flew wing on Manny and at his request occasionally "talked" him down to the runway on landing.

"Jay, will you keep an eye on me to make certain I don't level out high?" Kidding? I'm not so sure.

Manny swore many times in combat he just closed his eyes and fired. He let his gun cameras and fellow pilots later confirm his kills. The most remarkable thing about his self-effacement was that both he and we apparently believed it. I'm sure this was why he was so well-liked. He made us all feel quite superior professionally.

"By George, if Manny can do it, so can I."

The rest of us had become so tired of trying to out-macho each other, someone who would readily acknowledge *you* were the better pilot was refreshing. Manny was a master at feeding egos. Apparently he'd learned early on we don't like or dislike others so much for what they are, as for what they make us think of ourselves, a ploy used by many successful politicians.

ONE DAY, SHORTLY AFTER the Battle of Leyte Gulf, our squadron was briefed by a most unusual source of intelligence — a captured Japanese infantry major. This episode first showed me a facet of the Oriental mind we find so inscrutable. Once conquered, Japanese troops I encountered became obsequiously subservient. While most would fight fiercely, often preferring suicide to capture, something in their code apparently compelled them to conclude if bested, they owed complete obeisance to their captors.

Not only did the captured major brief us on Japanese entrenchments dug in the hills not far from our perimeter; he asked to come along on a mission designed to dislodge them! We flew fighter cover for the light B-25 bombers that made the strike and were told by the astonished crew of the one on which the major flew, he had even asked permission to strafe his erstwhile comrades!

Later in China, I saw this attitude reflected in other Japanese POWs. Charged with conducting a transfer of fuel between the Marine Corps and the Chinese Nationalists, I had at my disposal a few dozen POW laborers. At first somewhat queasy about moving the prisoners from their compound with only two Marine guards, I was assured there was nothing to worry about. Of hundreds of our captive Japanese, to my knowledge none ever sought escape or was insubordinate.

The first time I used their captive labor I was astonished. Taking two truck loads of POWs to what seemed several acres of fifty-five gallon fuel drums, I instructed them through an interpreter to make room for additional storage by stacking one drum upon another. I assumed the task would take several days. To my surprise, when I returned that evening the job had been completed.

This began to change my attitude toward the Japanese. Like many Americans in World War II, I believed the Japanese fighting man was a sawed off, sub-human, sadistic brute incapable of improvisation. Deprive them of their leaders, we were taught, and their undirected "herd instinct" will be their undoing. We'd been conditioned in training to both hate and denigrate the enemy by leaders who'd have us believe we were far superior. I well remember my first sight of Japanese combat troops that called these presumptions into question. A score of captured Japanese Royal Marines was being transferred from one troop transport to another.

"Wait a minute. Where are all the bandy legged, bespectacled buck-toothed little monkeys they told us about?" I wondered.

These guys were all six feet or over and could have matched any drill team in spit and polish. This and subsequent encounters with the Japanese shook my earlier assurance of superiority.

In these days of Nikons, Sonys, Toyotas and TVs by Mitsubishi, it may be hard for some to understand how, prior to World War II, "Made in Japan" was synonymous with shoddy. Captured tanks, arms and aircraft seemed almost primitive by contrast to hardware available to U.S. troops. Upon their inspection, my first thought was: "Why in the world would the Japanese wage war with such second rate materiel?" After watching the fanatical energy and determination with which they waged it, my second thought was: "Why didn't they win?"

To fighter pilots like myself late to combat, the fanaticism of the Kamikaze campaign that emerged in the war's final phase was especially disconcerting. The essence of an aerial dogfight, for example, is basically a simple game of "chicken." Realization your opponent simply won't "chicken out," can trigger one's sweat glands.

Late in the war, on Okinawa, our Marine mechanics patched up a Japanese "Oscar;" a modified version of the Zero. Incredibly maneuverable, it could turn inside our F-4Us and also out-climb them. Yet sitting in the "Oscar," I felt naked and exposed. While our planes cupped us in armor plate, theirs had no such protection. To have flown an Oscar in combat must have been as disconcerting as playing in the NFL without pads, face mask or jock strap. Not that mine was an unusual concern for protection of manhood. A latent fear of most who played that monstrous game of chicken in aerial combat was the idea they might emerge caponized. I've long felt this unheralded fixation might be used to foreclose future wars. Somehow, if the Geneva Convention had only compelled armies to shuck their drawers in combat, I suspect aggressive ferocity might turn flaccid.

WHEN VMF211 MOVED from Saipan for the Philippines invasion campaign, General Douglas MacArthur directed that henceforth all reference to aerial activity be attributed to "MacArthur's aircraft," rather than distinguishing them as Army, Navy or Marine. Up to then, several Marine aces — Joe Foss, "Butcher" Hanson, Greg Boyington and Siegel, whom I had met personally — were bumping the World War I kill record of Eddie Rickenbacher. This distressed MacArthur, who wanted the Army Air Corps to retain the record. Consequently, Marine fighters were shunted away from choice areas of aerial combat and assigned air/ground support, or raids on shipping. Moreover, while virtually every Army pilot had a fruit salad of ribbons hanging in festoons to the navel, Marine pilots such as Butcher, one of the top Marine aces, were not even awarded an Air Medal until they downed almost a score of planes.

Hanson's accomplishments and those of other Marine pilots were finally recognized through the efforts of news commentator Walter Winchell. Winchell began a crusade against the inequitable treatment of Marine pilots by MacArthur, known irreverently as "Dugout Doug." Compelled by public pressure to recognize outstanding performance, even by Marines, MacArthur henceforth established a uniform process of awarding medals. This came a little late for many, including Butcher Hanson, who received his Congressional Medal of Honor posthumously.

MacArthur's "uniform process" of awarding medals also came a bit late for Marine pilots who looked forward to impressing Australian girls when they went to Sydney for R&R. Previously, any beribboned 22-year-old Army Air Corps colonel out-bedazzled the comparatively undecorated Marines of far lesser rank, in the eyes of the Australian ladies.

"My gawd! Everybody's a bloody 'ero!" one New Zealander rudely commented the first time he observed Air Corps pilots out for a night on the town.

By the time medals were being dispersed like Cracker Jack prizes, few Marine fighter pilots ever got a chance to make points with the ladies of Sydney by flaunting their ribbons. Suddenly, MacArthur's High Command deemed duty in Sydney too hazardous. Henceforth, Marine pilots were sent to Hollandia, New Guinea, for rest and recuperation. There was, admittedly, some method to what seemed at the time "cruel and unusual" madness. After a few days in Sydney, that most fabulous of all liberty towns, so freely flowed both alcohol and adoration, it took the average pilot a week or two to recuperate back at the front. By contrast, after two days in Hollandia, most pilots were eager to return to their island combat bases.

THE FIRST HINT I HAD the war's end was near came in a letter from home that mentioned "The Bomb." Neither I nor my squadron mates had heard anything of the first nuclear weapons dropped on Japan, yet apparently it had been widely broadcast in the states.

One night, shortly after receiving that letter, I was rudely awakened by what sounded like the arrival of Armageddon. All ordinance seemed to be going off, sirens shrieked and people rushed madly about, ducking for cover. Since we'd been told our area was secure and most Japanese troops, planes and armor had been recalled to their home islands to defend against the pending invasion, the mayhem took us by surprise. Diving out of my cot and grabbing a weapon, I dove into the nearest slit-trench — hoping it had not been converted into a latrine. Cowering there gratefully undefiled, I soon noted that, for all the bells and whistles going off, a number of men were running about clad in naught but

*My brother, Capt. William J. Hammond, and I were reunited
briefly in San Antonio, Texas in 1943.*

their skivvies and silly grins. Many were discharging weapons, but they were firing vertically, into the air, rather than horizontally at attacking invaders.

"What the hell's going on!?" my fellow slit-trench occupant commanded
of a particularly exuberant marine running within ankle grasp.

"Haven't you heard? The war's over!" he howled. Then downing dregs
from a bottle held in his left hand, he hurled it high in the air, fired three
wayward shots, and staggered off, giggling.

With war's end, servicemen awaited eagerly to return home. My wait was
far longer than anticipated. My back problems by now so severe it was difficult to fly for more than an hour or so, I went to the squadron doctor to start
turning wheels for a medical discharge. He counseled me not to go that route
if I hoped to get home in a hurry. The brass had established a point system to

determine in what order the troops would go home: so many points for years in the service, months overseas, combat duty, etc.

"Look," said the doctor, "you have enough points to be sent home in a couple of weeks. But if you try for a medical discharge you're liable to be here for a month or more while they unfurl the red tape."

I took his counsel and spent half a year regretting it.

Two days later, word went around that the brass was looking for volunteers to ferry a few Corsairs to Peiping for the Chinese Nationalists.

"What the heck?" I thought. "That'll eat up a week; when I get back my orders will surely be cut to go home. Besides, I'll probably never get to see China otherwise."

Our inauspicious departure should have forewarned me. We got caught in the backwash of the worst typhoon to hit Okinawa. Some good pilots were lost, including my wing man.

In light of the hazards encountered, on arrival in China we were informed Chiang Kai-shek himself would award us one of his country's highest decorations. I believe it was called the "Order of the Purple Chrysanthemum." Now *that* was a medal worth acquiring: a spectacular sunburst of gold plate, outdazzling in glint, if not glory, anything the U.S. of A. could award. Alas, it was not to be ours. Though Chiang and Madame came to greet us, we pilots were awarded only an embossed white silk scarf and an invitation to accompany them to the opera that evening. The only one to receive the Purple Chrysanthemum was a Marine colonel who, rather than having flown to China as a volunteer, came up by ship.

Shortly after our arrival, a huge communist offensive cut off all road and rail transportation out of Peiping. Our return would be momentarily delayed, we were told. "Momentarily" stretched into almost six months.

By now, the communist takeover was in full sway. If it was less hazardous duty than the island hopping we had recently been engaged in, as "guests" of the Nationalists, we were to suffer whatever "inconveniences" Chairman Mao and friends hurled at our hosts. Among these were the bombing of our headquarters building and the loss of virtually all our records.

During our prolonged China stay, we were given tempting offers to join the Chinese Nationalist Air Force and fly combat against the encroaching communists. Though the proposed pay seemed outlandish, few signed up. It was obviously just a matter of time before the communists would take over. The distinction between "haves" and the "have nots" under the old regime was simply too great. Since most Chinese seemed downtrodden, it came as no surprise to learn most of them felt any change in the system was bound to be better. We can argue the merits of a capitalism versus communistic society, but political subtleties are lost on a peasant whose head's just been broken because he failed to genuflect quickly enough before his lord and master.

I was appalled by the treatment of the average Chinese coolie. A number came each day to do menial tasks at the base where we were billeted. Each evening, as they filed past the Chinese guard post on their way out of the electrified barbed fence, each was searched. If contraband was found on them, they were severely beaten. I recall one unfortunate coolie who had hidden a ball of tin foil no larger than a walnut inside his quilted jacket. When his "crime" was discovered, he was compelled to hold out his hands, which were then broken by a club-wielding guard. Of course, as the Communist Red Guards themselves later demonstrated, the Nationalists had not cornered the market on cruelty. But the desire for "change" that propelled the Red Guards into power blinded many to the possible downside attending such change.

In 1946, I could have no idea that, thirty-four years later, one of the men fighting against our Nationalist hosts, Deng Xiaoping, would invite me to his country as the first U.S. governor to visit the People's Republic after diplomatic relations were restored in 1979.

As guests of the Chinese Nationalists we were housed and fed very well. The housing was primitive by U.S. standards, but the food was marvelous compared to the fare we'd received on the islands. As a bastard stepson of the Navy, and even less esteemed by MacArthur's Army, Marines were the last capillary in the South Pacific's long circulatory system. As a result, we became masters of midnight requisition and experimentation. For example, my diet in the islands included occasional water buffalo, monkeys and lizards. These were surprisingly tasty. None, however, could compare with camel, prepared in a variety of ways by innovative Chinese cooks. We ate splendidly. And though no dish is more "American" than apple pie, the finest one I've ever tasted (except my wife's, of course) was in China.

Vegetables, however, presented problems. Lush and tempting, these qualities were attributable to the rich night soil in which they were fertilized. To acquire this valuable resource, farmers erected roadside outhouses on which signs solicited passers-by to contribute.

For the same reason, our Marine "head" was considered a veritable treasure trove by these rustics. They would periodically descend upon it with long scoops and a couple of buckets suspended from a shoulder yoke known colloquially as a "yo-yo stick." Nodding and grinning, they would keep up a line of incomprehensible Mandarin chatter while happily mining an adjoining toilet seat shaft. All this proved disconcerting to those meditating nearby. As a consequence, our head was henceforth posted "off limits" to Chinese civilians. Relative peace and tranquillity returned. But only temporarily. One morning, to the dismay of Marines in occupancy, the whole building suddenly shuddered and collapsed into an enormous glory-hole which the innovative Chinese farmers had under-mined by excavating into the side of the slope on which the head had been built.

In the early spring of 1946, I was hospitalized in Peiping with amoebic dysentery when I received orders to return to the U.S., where I proceeded to Boston for discharge. My first evening in "Beantown" was marred by two Navy Shore Patrolmen who came to my hotel demanding to see my credentials, explaining I appeared much too young to be a Marine Captain. Curiously, while able to pass for eighteen when four years younger than that, at twenty-four I still could.

THE WAR YEARS MANIFESTED psychic phenomena even stranger than those I'd experienced previously. The first occurred in the Philippines.

One night I dreamed I was sitting on the porch of an old country store back at Round Lake, New York, owned by the uncle of my boyhood friend, Jack Hemstreet. Suddenly, around the corner of the store, stumping on crutches, shrouded in bandages and giving off that now familiar green glow, came Jack. Shaking his head in disparagement, Jack admonished, "Why aren't you fighting for your country, instead of just sitting here?"

Resentful, I responded, "What do you mean? I'm in the service, doing just as much as you, Jack!"

"No you're not," Jack intoned bleakly, "I've just been killed."

I shot bolt upright in a cold sweat. I hadn't even thought of Jack for at least five years. Why had I dreamed of him? Unless . . .

It was more than a year before I learned Jack had indeed been killed the same month I had my dream. Though I hadn't recorded the exact time and date to know his death was simultaneous with my dream, I have little doubt.

The second incident was more immediately appalling. At a morning briefing for the day's combat mission, a pilot in my four-plane division came to me at breakfast and hesitatingly told me the following: "You know, this sounds ridiculous, but I've got to tell you, Jay. Last night I had a very disturbing dream. In it while we were climbing to join you in formation, your engine suddenly quit. You 'bought the farm' when you tried to land, wheels-up, on the water. The only reason I'm telling you this is because I've learned to pay attention to such dreams. Please scratch your flight and let someone else fly the mission."

I told him his concerns were ridiculous. Still, his warning scurried around in my mind up to the time of take-off. How could I cancel a flight on such grounds? To do so would forever condemn me to being hag-ridden by superstitions. Squelching my niggling fears, I took off.

Climbing to altitude, I waited for my wingmen to group up in formation. The first two did so. As we circled, our fourth, the troubled dreamer, banked steeply, cutting inside the circle toward his position. Suddenly his aircraft pitched down sharply, prop windmilling. While we watched in agony and pled by radio for him to eject, he dove within a few feet of the water, leveled off briefly, and hit. Water sheeted in front as the plane came to a wrenching stop, nosed up momentarily, then disappeared beneath the brown flood. We circled for several minutes but nothing save an oil slick surfaced.

Clairvoyance? Self-hypnosis? Coincidence? All I know is that he was my stand-in for a role in some cosmic drama, the script for which he'd badly misread.

Our 1929 Loening Amphibian, "Old Patches," is now located at the Alaska Aviation Heritage Museum in Anchorage, where they plan to restore it to mint condition. So far no one's offered to do the same for me.

6

The Alaska Connection

MOST OF MY MILITARY SERVICE was spent in hot, humid climes for which I had little tolerance. Long before leaving the States, I'd sworn should I return, I was going north. Subsequent service in the South Pacific led me to amend my vow: "the farther north, the better." The opportunity to keep that promise came in 1943, shortly after completing flight training at Corpus Christi.

One blistering day while walking to my quarters, I approached a Navy lieutenant who appeared to be wearing a mask. On closer inspection, it proved to be a calamine-lotioned nose affixed to an epic sunburn. Astride the chalky nose, two ice clear blue eyes registered as much distress as I felt in the parboiling temperature.

"Where you from?" asked I.

"Alaska," said he.

My only exposure to Alaskans till then had been vicarious. In Au Sable Forks, we lived near the famed artist, Rockwell Kent. Having fallen into disfavor as a Nazi sympathizer in the late 1930s, Kent had gone into seclusion in upstate New York. Working for him was a former World War I German U-boat commander whose nubile daughter, Lydia, told me about their living with Kent in Alaska. In her photo album, towns like Seward and Anchorage seemed little different from the small towns in northern New York and Vermont. No igloos. No skin tents. Nothing exotic. Far more interesting than Alaska was the beauteous Lydia herself. In 1939, absent her presence, Alaska had little attraction for me.

But Alaskan bush pilot and hunting guide Lt. j.g. Bud Branham opened doors on a world I thought had long ago vanished. Under Bud's verbal brush strokes — and slides from home — Alaska loomed larger and far more vibrantly colored than I'd imagined: Dog teams. Traplines. Exotic peoples. Big game and tackle-torturing trout. Remote log cabins and hair-raising adventures.

After I'd extracted from Bud every possible dreg of Alaskana, we went our separate ways. Bud returned to Alaska in the Navy's wartime air/sea rescue service; I shipped out to the South Pacific. During the remaining war years we corresponded. From Bud, I learned of his trapping partner and fellow guide, Griff Quinton, then flying B-17s in Europe. In one of his letters, Bud said he'd written Griff about my possibly joining them after the war at Rainy Pass, a hundred miles northwest of Anchorage. Would I be interested?

Each hot, humid day reaffirmed my resolve to go north. Now Bud offered the chance, and even the fates seemed to take a hand. Not long after his invitation, I picked up an old copy of *Look* magazine from the mud outside my hut. Inside, an article featured "famed Alaskan bush pilot and big game guide, Bud Branham."

I rendezvoused with Bud and my wife, Hank, in Chicago. Bud was ferrying a plane to Alaska. Since we'd shortly be heading there to work with him, it seemed an appropriate opportunity for Hank to meet him. No time could have been less appropriate, of course. Looking forward to some time together after more than a year apart, Hank was less than enchanted to share that time with a third party. While she handled their meeting with indulgence and grace, it did little to establish a close friendship. Moreover, Hank much more readily than I, sensed certain traits in Bud which, when rubbed on mine, would prove abrasive.

Not long after, we journeyed to Syracuse, where I'd located a 1929 Loening amphibian bi-plane with a 400 HP Jacobs engine mounted on top. Cost: $4,000. The owner, Lee Nemeti, sold me the aircraft to pay for an operation on his four-year-old "blue baby" son, Lee, Jr.

Since the Loening lacked dual controls, I simply watched while Lee showed me how the controls operated. Then, I took it up solo. Previously I'd flown only stick controlled aircraft. The Loening was equipped with a wheel that proved a challenge. The plane bucked and pitched on take-off as I fought the controls.

With some airborne maneuvers, my confidence grew. After shooting some wheel landings, I felt ready to try one on water. This required retracting the amphibian's wheels. Making certain the indicator on the hand-cranked retraction system read "wheels up," I prepared to land on Cayuga Lake. Aware of hundreds of weekend bathers watching below, I glided the old bi-plane majestically over their heads. No sweat at all, I thought smugly. "I'll give the folks a show and grease in so slickly I'll hardly break the surface tension." Suddenly, at contact, the Loening's nose pitched violently downward; water geysered up as plane and pilot cartwheeled over and came to rest upside down. Hanging inverted from my seat-belt, I unbuckled and dropped head first into the rising water. Crawling along the ceiling to the rear hatch, I found it not yet submerged and climbed through to the tail where I perched like a bedraggled pelican. Some show!

Some observers had a simple explanation. "The pilot neglected to retract the wheels."

"But," I protested, "I did not forget! I checked the gear hand crank just before landing."

Later, when we hauled the Loening out of the water, examination revealed that a worm-gear in the retraction mechanism had jumped its track, preventing the landing gear from fully retracting, despite what the indicator arrow showed.

For the next six weeks, Lee and Irene Nemeti put Hank and me up in their home. Lee, a mechanic, supervised the Loening's repairs as we patched the plane. From the Nemetis I learned much of the warmth, affection and gastronomic capacity of large, Italian families. Every Sunday we were included in a gathering at Lee's parents' home where we'd stupefy ourselves consuming immense portions of pasta, interspersed with an incredible array of other Italian dishes. In the six summer weeks we were privileged to enjoy their warm hospitality, we grew to consider Lee's family part of our own and were shocked and saddened when, in Lee's absence, his tiny son went into convulsions and died in my arms. Little Lee's corrective surgery, now commonplace and nearly always successful, was scheduled to be performed in a few days. Tragically, it had been postponed from the previous month because of limited hospital facilities. Hank and I shared the family's grief while admiring the resolute strength with which they met adversity.

Finally, in late August, the Loening was fully repaired and christened "Old Patches." After loading the aircraft and bidding the Nemetis an emotional goodbye, Hank and I took off, headed north to Alaska. We almost failed to make it.

The Loening's tanks only held two hours of fuel. Cruising at eighty miles per hour, its range was less than two hundred air miles. After several long days of very short hops, we crossed into Canada above Great Falls, Montana.

A few days later, en route to Smith River, B.C., we ran into thick fog. No problem. The weather report indicated Smith River still had a 2,000 foot ceiling with good visibility. Having flown many hours on instruments — even though I had only "turn and bank" and "airspeed" indicators to fly by — I wasn't worried. Climbing enough to clear any protruding real estate, I concentrated on following the radio beacon to Smith River. Back then, we had no sophisticated navigational aids; just a blended Morse code "A" [dit dah], "N" [dah dit], low frequency signal which, when you were on course, gave an unbroken tone. Only if one slid "off the beam" could the "dit dah" or "dah dit" be detected, advising the pilot to change course.

On schedule, we got to the radio beacon's so-called "high cone" that oriented the pilot for approach to the airfield. When the high cone signal came over the radio, I commenced a descent. The ground beneath Smith River's high cone was, according to the chart, some few thousand feet below. Since they were still reporting a 2,000 foot ceiling, I had no concern about letting down through the dense fog. If troubled at all, it was by the fuel gages; they were bouncing off "empty." Again, no problem, we'd be down in five minutes, I thought.

Suddenly, at about 5,000 feet, through a rent in the thick, gray curtain of mist, I saw a sharp, rocky crag directly in front. Banking sharply to miss it, I caught sight of another, and then a third! We were caught in a pocket of pinnacles soaring up on every side into the layered cloud cover. Ice water hit the nape of my neck and washed down my back. I was certain we'd had it.

Bucketing around and around in a steep bank, just within the parameters of the craggy cul-de-sac, I expected a spire of rock to reach out of the fog and claw us into splintered oblivion any second. Near panic hit me like a basketball slam-dunked into my ribcage.

Hank, by contrast, seemed remarkably cool. Either she was unaware of our peril or had far more confidence in my abilities than was warranted. Suddenly, I spotted a possible alternative to what seemed an almost certainly fatal crash. Just below, in the crotch of two mist-shrouded crags, I saw a small, frozen pond no larger than a basketball court. At least the ice was level, I thought, and certainly no harder than rock. A normal landing was out of the question, but maybe we could slip in on crumpling wings and survive. The odds weren't good, but there seemed no other choice.

Starting a spiral descent in a steep bank, I broke through another layer of fog and saw, up a chute to our right, a different light pattern through the funereal gray of the mist. Dare I head for it? Crashing the aircraft on the small mountain pond was a poor gamble. Heading up that gray gullet looked a little better. Again going on instruments, I pulled the nose up and immediately lost all visual reference in the clotted mist.

Now a third "passenger" in the cabin almost took over. I could not shake the mad jockey of fear from his seat in my lap, gleefully flailing me into half-blind panic. Certain we'd hit an unseen mountain at any instant, I was tempted to close my eyes and throw up my hands when a sudden gust hawked us out of the maw of the gullet and into the sunshine over Smith River Valley!

Just as the basketball under my ribcage began to deflate and that wild rider slip off my lap, a new alarm grabbed my attention. The fuel gauge needles were no longer bouncing. The Jacob's engine had been gulping for over two hours. We should have been out of gas ten minutes ago.

By now I'd abandoned all reliance on radio. When not transmitting a splintered signal, the beacon was interrupted by static or, of all things, the ebb and flow of Mexican music from a station in San Diego! It seemed the fates were now trying to unspool my sanity. Far off to the right below, I could see a wide river bottom. Off to my left, a cloud of blowing dust marked another possible airfield site. Which direction to take? The dust cloud being closer, we gambled for it — and won. Smith River runway lay just below.

Were I to exercise literary license, the Loening's engine would sputter and quit just as I came into range of the field, requiring me to land "dead stick," without power. Not so. The engine didn't quit until after we landed.

Taxiing in, it gasped its last, having run on naught but fumes for the past half hour.

When I relayed my story to the Canadian Air Force personnel at Smith River, they registered little surprise.

"Oh," said one, "you got onto that split radio beam that runs into what we call 'Million Dollar Valley' because of the number of planes crashed there. Something between here and St. John causes the signal to split, sending a false beam up into those high peaks. During the war, a lot of planes got swallowed up in that area."

That "Old Patches" did not join them, I'd like you to believe was the result of superb airmanship rather than dumb luck, which is just one more term for my old friend serendipity.

The rest of our trip to Alaska was relatively uneventful. For me, the unforgettable highlight was crossing the border and finding almost untrammeled wilderness all the way to Fairbanks. To the left, the sun stained the flanks of the majestic Wrangell Mountains; to the right, unbroken miles of forest. We cruised at five hundred feet above virgin timber, streams undammed by other than beaver, and occasional moose, bear or caribou. I felt I'd finally come home for the very first time.

The September 1946 evening we splashed down on the Chena River, it seemed half of Fairbanks gathered below the Cushman Street Bridge to see our antique aircraft.

Looking back on the curiosity Old Patches evoked because of her age, I find it strange. In 1946, a 1929 vintage aircraft was but seventeen years of age. Nowadays, no one thinks anything of using aircraft at least twice that old. The plane I have in 1993, for example, was built in 1955. By contrast, thirty-year old cars are considered rare classics and seldom driven, save in parades while aircraft built in the thirties, forties, and fifties are in everyday use in Alaska. Many have not been greatly improved upon.

Though even today the airplane remains the prime means of access to most of Alaska, in the mid-forties far fewer people had that means available. A territory of some 365 million virtually roadless acres, inhabited by 72,000 people — half of whom resided in Anchorage — Alaska's more than 200 remote towns and villages were linked only by air or water. Many had no airstrips, so small bush planes equipped with floats in the summer and skis in the winter hauled the bulk of the freight and passengers at great expense. Unless one owned a plane, remote lakes and streams were all but foreclosed to the average Alaskan. Consequently, those who had planes were especially privileged. For years, I encountered almost no one while hunting or fishing in Alaska's back country. It was as though one owned the entire wilderness, and when the occasional interloper was encountered, I confess to a shameful sense of violation and trespass.

Though I sometimes lament I'd not come North sooner, actually I could not have imposed my almost half-century presence on a more intriguing era.

Those coming to Alaska twenty years earlier had little chance to sample other than small sips of what the Greatland could offer. Those who came twenty years later, while perhaps allowed more ample portions, were denied savors lost when too many cooks are obliged to water broth down for too many patrons. Few more than a dozen "work horse" bush planes occupied "stalls" at Lake Hood near Anchorage in 1946. Today, summer traffic there can be almost as busy as Chicago's O'Hare Airport, one of the busiest in the world.

Old Patches was perhaps more mule than work horse. Certainly she was both hammerheaded, sway-backed and stubborn, yet a consistent old bawd. In my recollection she would climb, cruise, glide — and stall — at about eighty miles per hour. Though I've since owned far sleeker steeds, the old girl occupies that special niche to which only prodigal kids or lame dogs find ready access.

Perhaps Old Patches attracted so much notice because she had two wings and a skid instead of a tail wheel. Few folk who hadn't flown prior to 1940 have seen either. Since many airstrips in Alaska in the 1940s were grass, a tail skid caused many airport managers to scream when divots were plowed up by my unwelcome visits. They were not subjected to many such visits, however. A month or so after arriving, the Loening's engine blew up in the air and dumped me in the trees bordering Shirley Lake near Rainy Pass. There it sat for years until finally hauled out by helicopter. The abused carcass of Old Patches now reposes in the Alaska Aviation Heritage Museum in Anchorage.

Aniakchak Bay bear camp, 1947. Assisting guide Bud Branham while learning to haul my own water.

7

From Rainy Pass to Vulture Flats

BRANHAM MET HANK and me at the small town of Talkeetna on the Susitna River, sixty miles due north of Anchorage. From there he escorted us to Puntilla Lake, on which I made just my third water landing in Old Patches. Taxiing to the beach, I had my first look at our third trapping partner, Griff Quinton. Most notable on this, our first day of acquaintance, was the skeptical look the sight of the old flying boat and its cheechako pilot brought to the face of this lifelong, woods-wise Alaskan.

Griff clearly doubted Old Patches could "cut it." He proved right. While the old horse would perform fairly well at sea level, the high elevation of Puntilla Lake greatly reduced performance. Only with half-full tanks and small loads could I get "up on step" and finally lumber off the water into the air. A further major shortcoming was, of course, the amphibian could not be used on skis, a serious liability in winter. Clearly, Old Patches had to go. Therefore, I told famed Bush pilot Bob Reeve and another interested party I'd be ready to sell, after making a couple more freight hauls.

But on what was to be my last freight trip to Anchorage prior to selling the Loening, bad weather forced a landing on Shirley Lake, where I holed up in one of our trapping cabins. When the weather cleared, I taxied to the far end of the lake and took off. A sigh of relief at just clearing the shoreline trees was premature. Suddenly, an explosive shower of oil blackened the windshield; followed by deafening silence. Some fifty feet above the treetops, I dropped the nose toward a less dense section of woods. Steering between two sizable spruce trees, I crumpled both wings at their roots. The hull plowed on into a beaver pond, careened across it and through the dam, coming to rest like a beached beluga. I was unscathed, save for a severe blow to the wallet. Our every cent had gone to purchase and repair the Loening. Though partly insured, it was years before I received payment. Problems encountered in this settlement process started the plunge of my pain threshold of tolerance for attorneys. But that's another story. Without Old Patches, or dollars, Hank and I were about to spend our first winter in Alaska.

That we didn't spend most of it together was not surprising. While Hank accepted her lot without complaint, asking her to share a remote trapline log cabin lacking plumbing with three males exceeded even my callused insensitivity. A few weeks after we arrived, I took her into Anchorage where she got a job as an assistant librarian and started teaching piano.

More than a hundred air miles away, Rainy Pass Lodge perched on the bleak shores of Puntilla Lake almost 2,000 feet above sea level in a broad valley framed by the Alaska Range. At a few hundred feet below timberline, only the rare, runty spruce tree made it past puberty. Since we depended totally on firewood for heat, we had to haul it from some distance away.

Though the lodge consisted of but one twenty-four by forty log cabin in which we lived, the care and feeding of its two insatiable wood stoves consumed an inordinate amount of our time — especially when only one of us was in camp.

Our only assured income were government contracts to carry mail to three remote villages, and to report the weather by radio, every hour from 6:30 a.m. to 6:30 p.m. The latter required one of us to remain in camp at all times. Since little wood had been gathered to meet winter's demands, it was necessary to cut and haul almost every day. When alone, this proved rigorous.

I've never required an alarm clock to waken on time, so arousal at 5:30 a.m. proved no problem. *Arising* was something else. Emerging from the cocoon of a warm sleeping bag into a crypt of sub-zero cold harks more of cheap death than to herald the life of a new day. Only by jump-starting with caffeine orally injected within the radiance of the well-stoked kitchen stove, could I thaw to function. The first chore was to race out in the frigid pre-dawn to check temperature, humidity and wind gauges; warm, then start the generator and flick on the transmitter, all so that at 6:30 a.m., bush pilots obliged to thread through Rainy Pass a few miles to the north would have the first clue whether they should fly or forget it.

Once these chores were done, if one was alone it was time to ready the big freight sled, lay out the harness, hitch up the dogs, toss ax and Swede saw aboard, then haul water fifty yards from the lake to the lodge. With luck, you'd remembered the day before to cover the ice hole with board and canvas to minimize depth of overnight freezing. If not, hacking a hole in the ice took some time. After the dishes were washed and morning ablutions performed — often done simultaneously — the next half-hourly weather report was due.

Before the short-wave radio cooled, it was dash again for the sled, cluck at the dogs and sail off to that small, far away patch of scraggly timber where you'd spotted an old standing dead spruce. Few trees exceeded twelve inches in girth at that altitude and these could be dropped fairly quickly with the hand-powered Swede saw — no such fripperies as chain saws back then. But by the time you trimmed branches, sawed sled-sized, eight-foot lengths and loaded up, it was touch and go to get back to the cabin in time to make the next half hour's weather broadcast. Back at the lodge, the load was dumped and the mad race to the radio won or lost. Our pay was docked for each one lost, so there was inducement beyond merely the zest of the challenge.

More than forty years later, memories of wood gathering at Rainy Pass Lodge incline me to keep at least a year's supply seasoning in one of three sheds at our Lake Clark homestead. I still have a Swede saw, but it's backed up by four gas powered chain saws. Why four? Simply because that's their comparative ratio of reliability to the faithful old Swede saw. Maybe that same ratio applies to reliability of my recollections. But in my mind's fading eye, I envision ever more clearly the hundreds of cords heroically cut by myself, while my two scurvy partners did naught but sometimes haul ashes.

The Swede saw was not the only toothed torture device at the lodge. Its indignities inflicted on flesh were nothing compared to those experienced when obliged to shake hands with the whip saw. Sawn lumber for floors and roofs was at a premium. The nearest lumber yard was more than a hundred air miles away. Either lumber was flown out, strapped to your plane's floats, or fashioned locally from raw spruce logs. To accomplish the latter required use of an 8-foot, two-man whip saw. One victim stood below in a deep pit amidst a blinding shower of shavings; the other perched precariously on a trestle along which he advanced as the saw blade slowly sliced another plank from the core log.

Talk about aerobics! A few sessions in the saw pit could render out copious quantities of cholesterol, lard and mineral salts, leaving little left of the operators save whang leather and quivering protoplasm. To this day I'm a bit troubled by all the non-productive sweat and energy so many expend solely for their own well-being on equipment that provides only resistance. If induced to ride one end of a whip saw instead, they'd not only fry off flab, the fitness fad would double the world's plank production.

When not tending the trapline, guiding sportsmen or keeping tabs on the weather, one of us would go into Anchorage to pick up mail and fly it out to the small villages of Skwentna, Tyonek and Alexander Creek. Our postal contract required these rural mail flights once a week in the old Stinson. There being no place to land with wheels near Puntilla Lake, we used skis in the winter, floats in the summer. My first float landing off the oceanside beach fronting Tyonek was almost as sensational as my first water landing in the old Loening. While I'd done considerable seaplane flying in Naval flight training, it had all been in rugged, single-float Stearmans, PBY flying boats or OS2U Kingfishers; the latter, designed to be catapulted off battleships, could land in huge swells and rough water.

That balmy day at Tyonek the ocean seemed placid compared to waters

I'd landed on in the service. A long, smooth ground swell was running before a light off-shore wind. I set up for landing, acutely aware of the host of villagers gathered to get their incoming mail. Gracefully settling into a trough between swells, I smiled smugly in anticipation of accolades my stellar performance would likely elicit. My smile almost smeared the instrument panel when, suddenly, I shot into the air, slammed into the next swell, almost flipped over and then, like a skipped stone, porpoised several times before being beached high, if not dry, by a breaker. Mercifully, nobody was so rude as to ask my name.

At Rainy Pass Lodge in the mid-1940s, there were no such distractions as TV, nor neighbors within fifty miles. Solitary evenings were spent mending gear, stretching furs, stoking stoves, and in endless reading. When more than one of us were in camp, the other often was called on to replenish our larder. Moose, caribou and ptarmigan were found in abundance nearby, so this was no great challenge. Not just any moose would do, however. Bud believed a bull, after the rut, was fit only for dog food. I remember my first moose hunt well. Now that the statute of limitations has long expired, I can confess it.

"We're low on fresh meat, Jay. Why don't you get us a moose?" Bud suggested one crisp winter morning. "But don't shoot anything other than a barren cow or a small 'mulligan' bull."

"A barren cow?" I said in surprise. "I thought it was illegal to kill cows. The regulations say that's not allowed."

"Oh, didn't you know?" Bud responded indulgently, "Those regulations don't apply to us who live in the bush. They're for city folk. We're exempted."

Gee, how considerate, I thought, shucking shells into the magazine of my old .303 Enfield.

Three hours later I spotted a young cow deep in a swale of willows, a hundred yards off. Only then did I question my ability to determine whether or not she was barren. Just a month or two after breeding, it hardly seemed likely she'd show signs of having conceived. Not to be dissuaded from taking my first crack at a moose, I assured myself she was a virgin and dropped her. Setting my old Kodak Retina on self-timer, I posed proudly alongside my "trophy."

My pride curdled in utter self-contempt when butchering revealed the moose I'd presumed was a maiden was to be a mother. I hastily hid the pathetic fist-sized embryo in the snow; but couldn't purge it from my mind's eye. While I never confessed my transgression, for years I stood condemned by self-judgment for what I felt was a despicable act. That forlorn fetus — amorphous glob of unidentifiable flesh — grew in my imagination to magnificent stature as the aborted, potential progenitor of the multitude which could have forever sustained moose herds all over Alaska.

It was only years later, as a wildlife biologist, that I came to question whether killing moose cows is always undesirable. The old adage holds that in killing a cow, you're killing two moose instead of one, the basis for our "bull only" hunting seasons. Yet when cows greatly outnumber bulls, more harm may be done to herd populations when bulls are removed. Since each bull can service no more than about twenty cows, should there be, say, a hundred cows per four bulls, potential calf production will be far less for a bull killed than for even a pregnant cow.

This is but one of many false presumptions some folks have regarding wildlife. So far as moose are concerned, it was years before I questioned another old wives' tale most hunters believe. Many assert a bull in the rut is inedible. Certainly, unless meat is carefully handled it can be easily tainted. However, if very carefully handled, I've found bull moose taken deep in the rut to be completely palatable.

The same is not true for rutting caribou bulls. I have several times taken great care to salvage and prepare their meat. No matter how it is handled, it tastes as though marinated in Purex. Completely disgusting!

IN MY FRESHMAN YEAR at Rainy Pass, the trapline proved my most demanding instructor. Failure to heed its lessons not only earned one poor grades, it could prove terminal.

Life on the trapline was, to say the least, rigorous. We ran more than a hundred miles of trapline, much of which now is traversed by the famed Iditarod Sled Dog Race Trail. Back then, dogs were our only mode of ground transportation. Snow machines were not yet available.

Though I'd experienced backbreaking farm work and stayed in excellent shape, breaking trail for a dog team through the deep snows of Rainy Pass to check traps at thirty below was a far greater challenge. Each day brought a new test for survival, and more than one night I slept out between a couple of fires or bedded down sandwiched between the dogs.

Sleeping bags were almost useless under such circumstances and I seldom used one — especially when it was very cold. It is far easier to rouse oneself and hustle wood to feed fires at forty below when one doesn't first have to shuck himself out of a sleeping bag. Two fires, or even three, is the secret. One fire takes care of only half your carcass. The other half freezes. Arising from a spruce bough bed to straddle a low fire in a long skirted parka was nothing short of Nirvana. Not fully appreciating the need for a coat of such long length might have foreclosed my state of bliss permanently, had I not learned a most painful lesson.

I'd taken the dogs up a wide valley traversed by our trapline. Bucking strong headwinds at twenty below, we were assaulted by a chill factor of about minus forty. Eager to reach the shelter of a line cabin quickly, I chose not to halt to tap my kidneys. Instead, I reversed position on the moving sled's runners and relieved myself off the stern.

Not much later, as the team pulled into the wind's icy blast, I detected a draft, along with an alarming sensation, centered just south of my short parka skirt. Checking, I found my fly was wide open. Distracting me from this development had been my freezing feet. In snow pacs too small, they were getting no circulation. On making camp I attended all my frost-bitten appendages. Not until I saw Doc O'Malley in Anchorage, however, did I learn to my great relief, minor surgery to trim off proud flesh was required only on my right heel! New foot gear and an *ankle length* parka returned with me to Rainy Pass.

DURING MY FIRST TWO YEARS in Alaska, trapping was my chief source of income. Griff and Bud were good teachers. Both were superb woodsmen, pilots and guides. In subsequent years I've come to appreciate their capabilities more fully, especially their training of dogs.

While more folks have become acquainted with dog-sledding with the increasing popularity of sled dog racing for sport, few have witnessed such superbly trained teams as those we had at Rainy Pass. These were big brutes, by contrast to racing dogs seen today — sixty-five to hundred pound malamutes, and red, so-called "MacKenzie River" huskies. To work with them was a joy — most of the time. Forgotten are the long hours of care and feeding. Only someone who's coursed dogs through snow-laden woods in the moonlight can fully appreciate the exhilaration of running a good team.

Each dog team takes on its collective personality. If you use them in the back country, they also take on the chore of occasionally saving your life. Many's the time in blizzard conditions I was certain the dogs were lost. Rather than argue, I gave them their heads and, sure enough, they got us to camp every time. The reading of totally obscured trails and the condition of overflowed river ice, I found, was much better left to the dogs. They were far more literate than I in that regard.

I didn't fully appreciate just how well trained Bud's dogs were until I saw others in action. Most teams require handlers to unsnap the dogs' chains, haul them — one at a time — to their harness positions and then hook them up to the sled, which must be solidly anchored to prevent them from racing off before the driver's ready. This procedure is commonly accompanied by wild bucking, plunging and barking. Not so with our dogs. Unhooked, they'd trot to their harness positions and lie down until hooked into their traces. There was little noise or plunging. Our sleds never required anchoring.

Once hooked up, the dogs would lie down to await command. We could leave them for an hour to go tend traps and they'd remain quietly in place where we'd left them. If you were dumped from the sled on a rough trail, there was no worry of being stranded. After running a few yards, the lead dog would detect your absent weight and stop in his tracks till you caught up. Upon return to camp the dogs were unhooked, and one by one, trotted to their individual stakes to await chaining. The only times our dogs broke training was when game was about. Should they encounter a moose or caribou, the urge to sound off was irresistible, a welcome warning to the driver. Aside from then, they ran in silence.

On the trapline, one's anticipation of even such rude fare as a peanut butter sandwich or can of frozen fruit at the next line camp prompted single-minded dedication akin to the quest for the Holy Grail. It's curious how life takes on more vivid dimension and color in the shadows of hazard than while basking in the sunshine of ease. So it is, during wartime or the earlier years of a marriage, we have greater appreciation of those who ride with us on that roller-coaster careening between terror and the elation of merely surviving. Dissatisfaction seems to set in when we finally "have it made" and sail into safe harbor. More careers and relationships seem to run aground on the golden sands of success than splinter on the rocks and shoals of a shared struggle. Perhaps our real enemy is ennui. Life lived on the brink in wartime or on a high country trapline, allows little time to entertain boredom.

———————

TRAPPING IN THE 1940s was a good source of income until Asian fur flooded the market. A cherry red fox pelt, worth a hundred dollars in 1946, brought no more than five dollars a year or two later. By 1947, while awaiting my share of our yet unsold winter furs, I hit financial rock bottom. "Tell you what," said Bud, "you make one more run pulling traps, then take all our fur to town, sell it and get paid off."

On that final trapline trip, I found heavy wet snow and very hard going. Breaking trail for the dogs, my snowshoes clogged up with pounds of slush. In a few hours this took its toll. Excruciating pain erupted down my right leg from a crater of agony in the small of my back. Unable to snowshoe further, I had to crawl to unhitch the dogs and make camp. When I failed to return in a day or two, I knew, someone would come looking. Bud found us. Loading me in the sled, he broke trail back to Puntilla Lake.

When I was able to walk in a few days, I flew our furs into town. Since they didn't sell immediately, I arranged to have my share sent to Fairbanks where I hoped not only to seek treatment for my back, but to shore up my marriage.

I reached Fairbanks with 25 cents in my pocket and not much more in our bank account. Unlike several who came to Alaska destitute and became rich, I arrived with a pretty good stake and seemed headed for destitution. After a chiropractor pounded me back into functional shape, I looked for work while Hank began teaching a new crop of piano students.

To get a job, I had to join a labor union. It was not a happy experience. I went to work as a laborer at Ladd Field, an Air Force base outside of Fairbanks. Having worked on jobs where one was rewarded according to effort, I had trouble getting used to one that paid precisely the same whether one worked like a dog or simply dogged it. To me there is no more difficult work than that which requires you to appear busy when you're not. Rather proud of my tolerance for hard physical work, I hauled and fetched a bit more enthusiastically than some fellow laborers felt appropriate.

"Hey! Leave half of those two-by-fours and slow down. You're making it tough on the other guys," our shop steward advised. "This contract is cost-plus; there's no hurry."

It took a few weeks, but I finally learned the knack of looking busy while doing nothing at all. When there was no task at the moment to do, I'd walk around and around the job site carrying a few sticks of lumber, or make several trips to the head. As my shop steward's approval grew, my self-respect dwindled. Rather than maximize productivity, the main goal seemed to prolong it. I sorely resented being party to this sorry process, let alone paying dues for the privilege. Subsequently, of course, I've come to appreciate abuses by management which led to the counter-actions by labor. I can't say I think much of either.

My return to "civilization" only made me miss the bush that much more. But our marriage was straining from separation, so I remained in Fairbanks on a job that held little attraction, despite the fact serendipity once again "victimized" me. Though much preferring physical work to the responsibilities of supervising, I was made labor foreman. This, of course, required me to do no real labor whatsoever. To my shop steward's distress, I ignored this constraint. It was not the union however, but fate, which made me pay for this indiscretion.

One day, heaving a large case of tar up to my shoulder, I felt something give. Pain rocketed down my right leg. The tar hit the floor with me right behind it. X-rays were taken and I was sent home. I was limping the five miles to where we lived when an ambulance, siren shrieking, lurched to a stop alongside. Two attendants jumped out.

"You Hammond?" one asked. With acknowledgment, they grabbed me. "For heaven's sake get in. You've got a broken back!"

Rushed to the hospital, I was carried to the emergency ward where I was swaddled in a full-body cast and popped in bed. Next morning I came to appreciate more fully one labor union benefit when its agent came to help me apply for workmen's compensation. For the next few weeks, it was my sole income; then it too, dried up. One morning the union man returned. Shaking his head sadly, he said, "I don't know just how to tell you this, so I'll just let you read this letter."

Physicians who had reviewed my case had written: "In examining Mr. Hammond's X-rays we conclude the fracture of his fifth lumbar was occasioned by a pre-existing condition which so eroded the vertebral structure as to permit collapse under excessive pressure. In our view the pre-existing condition suggests either cancer of the spine or tuberculosis. Accordingly, Mr. Hammond's claim is disallowed."

"Sorry," said the union rep, "there's nothing more we can do. Since you're a veteran, we'll have the VA man come see you."

A day later, a Veterans Administration representative came to my hospital room. Reviewing my case, he took all pertinent data to a local orthopedic surgeon, Paul Haggland. In my first consultation with Dr. Haggland, a ray of hope penetrated my dark depression.

"You know," said the doctor, "I don't think you've got a cancer or TB at all. It looks more like some sort of an infectious process. Though now healed, it so eroded the bone it finally collapsed. Your military records show you were hospitalized for amoebic dysentery in China. I'll bet we're looking at an old amoebiasis infection. I'm going to recommend you be accepted as a VA patient with a service connected disability."

He did. The VA agreed with his diagnosis. Over the next several weeks I received treatment courtesy of the VA at the base hospital. On discharge, I was told I'd have to wear a full-body cast for another few weeks and perhaps a back brace thereafter. My options somewhat restricted, I decided to return to college. Having had two years of petroleum engineering at Penn State, I enrolled in a kindred course at the University of Alaska, Fairbanks.

ONE DAY WHILE HITCH-HIKING before classes commenced, I was picked up by a distinguished looking, middle-aged gentleman who, noting my body cast, was most solicitous. When he revealed he was an attorney, I should have been forewarned it was not compassion that prompted him to probe further.

In the course of explaining, I mentioned the loss of my Loening and the difficulty I'd had securing the insurance settlement. I heard his cluck of sympathy but failed to note the drool on the steering wheel as he salivated in anticipation of plucking and broiling his passenger "pigeon."

A few days later he telephoned. "I've contacted the company that insured your aircraft. As a qualified claims adjuster who has worked with them frequently, I've been authorized to process the settlement. If you'll come down to the office and sign some papers, we'll get this thing settled."

Profoundly grateful, I agreed to do so that afternoon, blissfully unaware he was simply pre-heating the oven.

The papers he'd drawn up were described as "routine." I read them carefully and, after inquiry, was assured his fee of one third my settlement was "standard practice." Too dumb to get a second opinion, I signed and profusely thanked him for his help, unaware all he'd helped was himself — to his pigeon's last nest egg.

Though partially plucked, it was three weeks before I felt the oven's heat and smelled smoke. The agent from whom I'd purchased my aircraft insurance called, at long last, to advise my settlement would be shortly forthcoming. In grateful response, I voiced appreciation for my attorney's effective intercession on my behalf.

To my dismay, the agent called back to advise me the insurance company had not only never heard of this parasite, it never authorized fees to be subtracted from claim settlements to pay adjusters.

"You've just kissed a third of your settlement bye-bye, I fear," he commiserated. "Too bad you didn't call me before signing those papers."

I hung up in a cold sweat. Or was it simply a final basting? Whatever, I'd at least let the would-be "cook" know I was on to his swindle.

His secretary answered the phone.

"No, I'm sorry, he's out of town for a few days. May I help you?"

Suddenly I had an inspiration. "Look, I'd like to check my file to see if I turned over all the papers he asked for. May I come by to the office?"

"Certainly," she replied graciously.

An hour later, after obtaining my file and perusing its papers in her presence for an appropriate period, I began gathering them to return to her. To my feigned chagrin, they slipped from my hand, cascading in every direction. As she knelt to help me pick them up, with her back to me I retrieved the signed copy of our "agreement" from the file cover where I'd clipped it, and slipped it inside my shirt. Ultimately my insurance was paid in full, and my shyster friend, rather than dining on pigeon, was left with only the file's droppings.

I agree, it is grossly unfair to base my assessment of the integrity and character of lawyers on that initial encounter. Accordingly, I have since mellowed somewhat. However, while Christian charity demands I open my heart to attorneys, it disinclines me to do the same with my wallet. Lamentably, far too often circumstances have compelled me to do so. I now accept lawyers reluctantly, as an evil necessity. Nevertheless, be forewarned: to pay their fees is to do naught but encourage them.

WITH THE INSURANCE SETTLEMENT, Hank and I purchased an acre of land from then-university president Charles Bunnell. Irreverent student property owners, resentful of the "exorbitant" $400 we were charged per acre, had named these lowlands below the president's house, "Vulture Flats." Several years later, when the community held an election to formalize the name for its new post office, Vulture Flats was among the proposals. Much to my disgust they elected instead the uninspiring name, "College," by which it is known today. I far more appreciated living in Vulture Flats.

In 1948, we built a small house on our Vulture Flats property. Shortly after moving in, our daughter, Wendy, was born. To augment my GI Bill assistance, after I recovered sufficiently from my back problem, I did a little trapping around Fairbanks, worked as museum assistant curator and maintenance carpenter at the university. When my back improved, I joined two other students in an acrobatic dance and hand balancing act which we performed at various service clubs or night spots for a few dollars and meals.

Meanwhile, my college curriculum took one change and then another. I switched from Petroleum Geology to Anthropology, to Pre-Med, and finally graduated in 1949 with a degree in Biological Science. An experience in our Optical Mineralogy class prompted my first transfer.

Usually my grades ranked me the second best student in the course. The sole other student, Ed Heiser, was first. On one surprise quiz, however, I got 100 percent, while he muffed the question: "Define specific refractivity."

"What's the proper definition?" Ed asked our instructor.

Whereupon the professor repeated verbatim language I'd used on my paper. At the time of the quiz, however, I had not known the answer and simply dreamed up something in pedantic language to disguise my ignorance. Surprised to hear this shot in the dark ricochet off my instructor, I checked the book. The true definition was entirely different. It seemed our elderly instructor had a photographic memory. However, while this faculty imprinted easily when exposed to trivia, unfortunately it had never been exposed to the academic formalities required to certify a Geology professor. When it was discovered our professor had no proper degree, he was assigned to other university duties.

In fairness, our inept instructor taught me one thing: So long as you state something in bold, obscure, confident terms, chances are most folk will believe you. The more confidence and obscurity the better. Folks are reluctant to admit they have no idea at all what you're talking about. In teaching, preaching or politics, this is doubly effective if one has an authoritative voice with which to make such pronouncements.

This incident first made me aware of how important to a politician's success are assertive speech and voice timbre. The most intelligent, handsome political aspirant, if endowed with a weak, hesitant voice, will most likely fall on his or her face. Conversely, some of the most physically and mentally bereft candidates captivate voters by asserting inanities in stentorian tones.

In the case of our old professor, his acoustical fidelity might have been on target but his academic accuracy missed by a country mile. When this became clear, both Ed Heiser and I concluded our interests lay more with living creatures than fossils, be they found in rocks or classrooms. We switched from Geology to Biological Sciences.

After graduating in 1949, I took a job with the U.S. Fish and Wildlife Service as a pilot and government hunter. That decision put the final strain on an already tenuous marriage.

Daughter Wendy, husband Per and grandson Nick, Phnom Penh, November 1991. Wendy's unselfish service to the world's less fortunate tells me The Rev. Morris Hammond's spirit is alive and well.

8

Twists in the Trail

INITIALLY HEADQUARTERED in Anchorage, my work as a government hunter required frequent prolonged absence from home. One year I was in the field 278 days. Then, in 1950, I was transferred to the southwest Alaska fishing village of Dillingham, on Bristol Bay, assigned to fly federal game warden Bob Mahaffey on his patrols, in addition to conducting my predator/prey studies on the Alaska Peninsula's caribou herd.

Hank had been teaching piano to augment my $6,800 annual salary. Loss of her income, coupled with Dillingham's high cost of living compounded our problems. Though Hank did far more than her share to adjust, our marriage broke up. She and our daughter Wendy, then two, returned to the Juve family home in Ohio.

Unfortunately, the marriage had been too loosely knit from the beginning. We were one of those couples who married young because of the war, not in spite of it. Hank had done her best to keep the union intact and I realize now how few women would have tolerated conditions I imposed on her, such as living in a small wilderness cabin with two other men besides her husband. Our problem centered on my inability to reconcile having married more with my head than my heart. My head told me I had a wonderful woman for a wife — brilliant, talented, beautiful and understanding. What else could one want? My heart told me fate had unfairly entrapped me before I was ready.

Our inevitable divorce was all the more guilt-ridden by the loss of Wendy, from whom I've received a series of wonderfully literate and sensitive letters from exotic locations around the world. I count among my greatest losses the fact I had never really gotten to know her. In more recent years, the fates have been kinder. The daughter of whom I am so proud and whose acquaintance I now enjoy, Wendy's unselfish service to the world's less fortunate tells me the Reverend Morris Hammond's spirit is alive and well in another generation. After a stint in the Peace Corps, Wendy went to work for *Redd Barna*, a European version of *Save The Children* after serving several years in Thailand and Cambodia. At this writing, she's on assignment in the Sudan.

Back then, however, I was devastated. Many years passed before I shed an enormous burden of guilt and accepted the fact our union was doomed from the start. Even if Alaska had not become an alluring mistress with which Hank could not compete, our backgrounds and interests were simply too different. Selfishly, I would not forego the far greater fulfillment I found exploring the Greatland's wild attractions than existed amid "civilization." And the painful fact is, the niggling doubt I guiltily hid on our wedding day never lifted.

It was not the last time I would reap the bittersweet harvest of being swept along by someone else's expectations.

––––––––––––––––––

I RETREATED TO THE COMFORTING isolation of work. As with any job, there were downs as well as ups. The highs so exceeded the lows, however, that I knew I had the best job in the world. Virtually my own boss, I could not only call my own shots, but select my own targets. Provided almost unlimited use of a government aircraft, I explored almost every lake, stream, valley and mountain range from the Aleutians north to the Kuskokwim River. Other assignments took me almost everywhere else in Alaska, a vast, mostly uncharted territory. If others had been there before me, almost nowhere did I encounter their "sign."

It was as though I was the first to unlock a vast trove of fabulous, untrammeled treasures. Long before anyone read about scores of bear congregating to feed on salmon clogging McNeil River, I came on some sixty-four brown bear there while flying stream surveys to determine salmon spawning dispersal. Once I was compelled by weather to land in a very shallow, weed-filled lake near a small stream where torpedoing shapes I'd assumed from the air to be silver salmon were actually tackle-torturing, ten-pound-plus rainbow *trout*. Totally unsophisticated, the brutes rose to almost every fly, indicating they'd never been fished!

The adventures were endless. Recovering thirty-six tusks one day while beach combing the Walrus Islands near the village of Togiak; gunning for waterfowl in Izembek Bay as a half million Black Brant geese eclipsed the sun; landing for the first time inside the eerie, moonscaped crater of Aniakchak volcano; cruising the entire shore-line of remote, forty-five-mile-long Lake Clark, in search of a prime spot to homestead. And finding it!

While most of these treasures remain today, to those privileged to be among the first to discover them, they've lost some luster; one can no longer view McNeil's bears without first securing a permit. The Ungaluthluk River that produced those gorgeous rainbows was "discovered" and wiped out years ago. It's now closed to fishing. Beachcombing for walrus tusks is forbidden to all but Alaska Natives, and the Walrus Islands comprise a sanctuary with tightly controlled access. Seasons on some waterfowl species are closed; bag limits severely curtailed for others. Of course, the sun over Izembek Bay remains blotted out most of the time. But inclement weather alone accounts for this now, with little help from whistling goose wings. Along with other waterfowl, Black Brant have greatly declined. Homesteading? It's no longer permitted.

HOWEVER SORE MY LAMENT for those yesterdays, it's more than offset by appreciation of a treasure that even today proves my best Alaska discovery: Bella Gardiner.

Fellow Fish and Wildlife agent, Bob Mahaffey, inadvertently provided the "map" to this treasure when we were confined to Dillingham by poor flying conditions one wintry afternoon.

"Hey, it's 'tight-shoe' night at the Willow Tree Inn. Betty and I are going to the dance. Why don't you come along?"

At first I declined. Since the breakup of my marriage I'd become even more reclusive. Socializing held no attraction.

"Aw, come on. It'll do you good. If nothing else, you'll get a bang out of watching me make an ass of myself trying to do those sexy new dances. Know what I mean? Without the music everyone'd be arrested."

Eventually, I agreed to go. My reluctance was due more to fumbling feet than a dislike for dancing. Yet that night, a very pretty part-Eskimo girl proved so remarkably adroit at evading my clumsy clod-hopping, I was deluded into thinking myself exceptionally feather footed.

Seventeen-year-old Bella Gardiner was not only most attractive, she had a gift too rarely found. She was an excellent listener. When one spoke to Bella you had her undivided attention. In turn, her responses were remarkably intelligent, honest and incisive for one so young. I was intrigued.

A few days later I was lunching at the Green Front Cafe, then Dillingham's only restaurant, when I encountered Bella and her father. Tom Gardiner, a craggy old Scotsman in his early seventies, had come to Alaska in 1898 to follow the gold trails. Some fifty winters in the north had done little to thaw the burr encrusting his rich Highland brogue.

When gold fever abated, Tom settled in Dillingham, where he fished commercially, trapped, ran mail by dog sled and acted as jailer. At age 46, he married a 16-year-old orphaned Eskimo girl and fathered three sons and three daughters. Locally, Tom was legendary, not just for putting up splendid smoked salmon, but for siring the best-looking clan of kids most folks had ever seen. Though I'd met only Bella, I became an instant believer in this local legend.

Suddenly, I began to have lunch almost daily at the Green Front. But I refrained from drinking its water, which the cafe's owner had drawn from a well

Bella and "Daniel Jones," last of my sled dogs, in 1953.

located at the base of the local cemetery. Consequently, orange juice was the only Green Front potable I would consume.

Bella shattered my assurance I was avoiding contamination when she advised me the orange juice was reconstituted with water drawn from the fearsome font below the cemetery. It struck her as enormously funny at the time, and perhaps prompted her father to take pity and invite me to dine at his home the next evening. I accepted with enthusiasm. There I was able to verify Tom's reputation. The smoked fish was superb. The girls were beautiful and the boys all handsome. Their mother, Lydia Gardiner, a quiet, eagle-eyed observer, spoke volumes without uttering a sound.

I enjoyed Tom's adventurous tales of the gold rush days, but it was Bella who intrigued me most. Added to her list of talents was that of exceptional cook. I was entranced.

Later that summer, I visited Bella and her mother at their salmon setnet site. There I came perilously close to destroying what progress I'd made in her pursuit. Offering to lend a hand with the harvest, I waded out, picked the few sockeye salmon enmeshed in their net — then lost them all in the surf! Bella was incredulous. I was mortified.

The next day was her parents' wedding anniversary, a good excuse to stay and try to redeem myself. With no means of baking a cake at their tent camp, Bella had arranged for the local cannery chef to do so. We walked in from camp to pick up a huge, two-tiered creation, lavishly festooned with candied flowers, gobbets of icing and inscribed, "To Tom and Lydia on Their 25th Anniversary."

The route back from the cannery required our crossing wet, mossy planks laid across an expanse of swamp. Hoping to make amends for yesterday's bumbling, I insisted Bella let me carry the boxed confection. Always the gentleman, I let her precede me across the first plank. She did so with grace and assurance, then turned to witness my progress — just as my feet shot out from under me. In my ungainly swan dive, I hurled the cake high in the air where, to Bella's horrified eyes, it ejected from its cardboard carton and, in dreadful slow motion, executed a twisting half-gainer to splash upside down into the swamp!

With a shriek, Bella dove in to retrieve it. This time *I* did the listening. Mercifully, some imprecations hurled at me were in Yupik, and before I could translate, Bella ran out of breath. Gaining her second wind, the misery of the drenched object of her disaffection overwhelmed her. To my vast relief, she collapsed in hysterical laughter. I was in love.

My mother, upon learning that the girl I intended to marry was part Eskimo, expressed unfeigned delight. "Oh Jay! I'm so glad to have our stale old Anglo-Saxon genes get a shot of new, vibrant blood. I can't wait to meet her!"

Valedictorian of her high school class, Bella received a scholarship to the University of Alaska where she enrolled that fall. The following September 1952, we were married and moved to King Salmon, where I continued to work as a government biologist, pilot and hunter.

Of the good fortune showered on me over my life, by far the most surprising and treasured is Bella. I've been blessed with a partner who is not only a wonderful wife, mother and baker of the finest comestibles I've yet wrapped a lip over; she is the most honest person I know. Most amazingly, she remains an excellent listener . . . to tales, I fear, often more than twice told. Could it be she's deaf? If so, it's her only defect, and one I gladly ignore.

Our first house was a wooden, sixteen-by-sixteen World War II hut I salvaged from nearby King Salmon Air Force Base. With no plumbing, we packed water and used an outhouse. We lived very frugally. But Bella brought to this lifestyle just as much uncomplaining grace as she brought to the Governor's House some twenty years later.

Frequently, she'd accompany me in the field in pursuit or observation of both predators and their prey. Our chief quarry were — whisper the word — *wolves.*

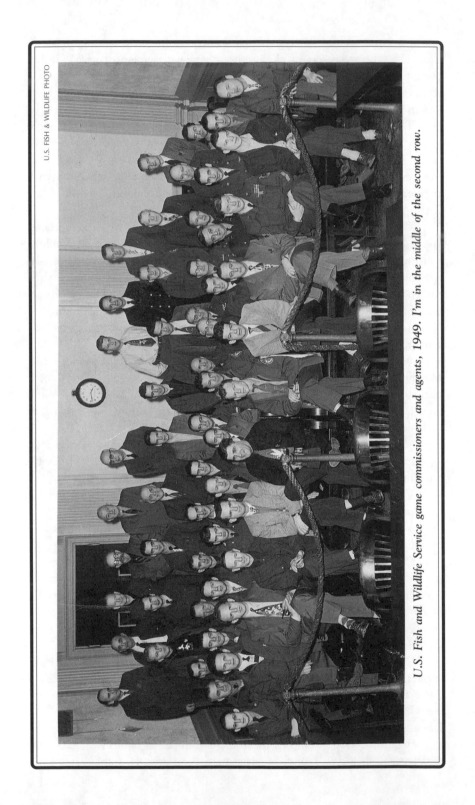

U.S. Fish and Wildlife Service game commissioners and agents, 1949. I'm in the middle of the second row.

9

Macoola, Murder and Mayhem

ALASKA IS A LAND OF SUPERLATIVES — some of lesser renown than others. We've seldom bragged, for example, of having the nation's highest per capita rate of alcoholism, unemployment, divorce, venereal disease, child abuse, rape, suicide and murder. Yet in my first ten years in Alaska, I once tallied sixteen homicides in which I knew both victim and culprit. An imaginative variety of methods were employed; perhaps the most unusual means of dispatch was visited upon one Naknek barfly who was terminally swatted with a Mix Master.

But each killing had a common denominator: alcohol. For many years, alcohol-induced "confusion" was every bit as effective a legal defense in Alaska as temporary insanity. "Oh well, the poor devil didn't know what he was doing. He was drunk."

Whether alcoholism is a disease or not, I can't say. Certainly, we treat it like no other. When we determine the causative factors of most diseases, we either immunize people, reduce their exposure, or prohibit products deemed harmful. One case of botulism, for example, results in the immediate recall of a food product. Gonococci, herpes, streptococci, typhus, and multitudinous causative organisms, including the AIDS virus, are militantly warred upon by society. No one would dream of permitting their sale for profit, much less provide government licensing. Yet, we all know the causative factor of alcoholism is alcohol. No one ever "caught" the disease without first ingesting it, save those innocents born with fetal alcohol syndrome. Still, we permit its ready availability to almost anyone despite the high incidence of infection, an inconsistency I find troubling.

MY FIRST CONTACT with an alcohol-induced homicide came during my first winter in Dillingham while flying game warden Bob Mahaffey on patrol.

As we cruised up the Kejulik River, which flows into Becharof Lake, we flew over the cabin of a white man known as Murphy and considered stopping for coffee as we had a few times before. Circling, we saw no chimney smoke, only two old dog team trails leading from the cabin door, and fresh wolf tracks going directly into the windbreak. Deciding to land to check things out, we skied in and made our way through crusty March snow to the cabin. Inside the windbreak hung the remnants of an illegally poached moose. Wolves had left the carcass in tatters.

Bob was ecstatic. "I finally caught the old boy red-handed! I knew he'd been busting moose on a regular basis; now I can prove it." That he could happily accept the comfort and coffee of one's household and then throw the book at the occupant might seem peculiar to some. But they did not know Bob Mahaffey. Bob was a remarkably personable fellow of enormous energy and dedication to doing things by the book. He believed by constantly ranging the country, thus instilling fear of discovery in the hearts of would-be fish and game violators, he could significantly curb their transgressions.

But for one game warden to cover such an immense area was, of course, impossible. Besides, the "bush telegraph" always radioed word well ahead regarding Bob's whereabouts and likely time of arrival. Listeners responded. Salmon gill nets used to snare ptarmigan were hastily taken down; traps removed from beaver houses; caches emptied of illegal carcasses; spring geese consumed and all evidence buried or burned. Arriving at these remote trapping campsites, Bob would be greeted effusively by owners exuding total innocence. To most it was sort of a game. Usually, when someone was guilty and they knew Bob knew, they would openly challenge him to make a case. The problem was finding proof. Occasionally, Mahaffey would — like the time a leg ladled from a "ptarmigan stew" we were served grew the webbed foot of an out-of-season duck.

When he had sufficient proof, Bob issued citations with such good humor even the culprits found it hard to hate him. Besides, apprehension often simply meant a free flight to town where the wrongdoer could get in some shopping or dental work. Fines levied back then seldom equaled transportation costs.

On this day, opening the back door of Murphy's cabin, we entered, looked around briefly, and finding no evidence anyone had been there for several days, departed. Because Murphy was a "three time loser" — a thrice convicted felon; his unavailability for immediate arrest or chastisement was an enormous disappointment to Bob.

Again airborne, we decided to follow the sled trail leading south from the cabin. After about fifteen miles, we found it led to an old sod hut — known as a "barabara" — used by one Jake Gregory as a trapline camp. His dogs were picketed in the willows nearby. Jake himself emerged from the semi-subterranean hut as we flew in for landing.

Jake told us the following story: He had sledded over to Murphy's for a visit about two weeks before. Murphy, his wife and their small boy were there. They invited Jake to stay the night. That evening, they broke out a crock of "macoola" and began to party. Macoola, or "bewhack" as it is sometimes known, is a brew of fermented beans, raisins or anything else which, when placed under the stove, increases in potency. Consuming the two or three gallons Murphy had been brewing for several days, all became drunk. According to Jake, husband and wife got into a squabble. Finally, in exasperation, Murphy had shouted at his Aleut spouse, "Well, if you don't like me, why don't you shoot me?"

Musing on this intriguing suggestion but briefly, Mrs. Murphy pulled an '06 off the gun rack and obliged Mr. Murphy with a .220 grain slug through the sternum. Then, somewhat chagrined, if not sober, she and Jake had gathered up Murphy's mortal remains, dressed him in his best clothes and laid him out in the back bedroom with the family cat "to keep shrews off of him." The next morning, properly remorseful, Mrs. Murphy vowed she and her small boy would return with their dog team to her home village of Egegik, where she would turn herself in to the marshal. Jake had then driven his dogs back to his trapping camp.

Most disappointed he now would never apprehend Murphy, Bob suggested the least we could do was stop at Egegik to make sure Murphy's wife had indeed turned herself in.

Checking with Egegik Marshal "Speed" Huff, we found she had neglected to do so. After we'd remedied her oversight, Speed said he would go directly up to the Kejulik, and haul in Murphy's body.

Three aircraft landed next day at the scene of the crime. Entering the cabin, Speed went directly to the back bedroom which we had previously not investigated. Flinging open the door, he was almost bowled over by a squalling white cat. A very *fat* squalling white cat. Stretched out on the bed were the grisly remains of Murphy. The cat, of course, during its two weeks confinement, had nothing to feed on save shrews and Murphy's carcass. Obviously, he had much preferred the latter.

Lurching out of the cabin retching, Speed pulled his revolver and sent the cat in vivisections to join its much-loved master. Since the body had been subjected to alternate freezing and thawing in the early spring weather, it took careful handling to haul it to the aircraft. Unfortunately, there was simply no way Paul Nekeferoff's PA 11 could accommodate its passenger save by stuffing Murphy, head first, into the plane's baggage compartment. In such undignified posture, Murphy made his last flight to Egegik.

Not so Murphy's widow. If she did any time at all, I never knew it. To my knowledge, the most anyone ever got out of the whole affair was aversion to large white cats. My gorge still rises when I see one.

As a postscript, I'm sorry to say, not too many years later Bob Mahaffey was shot dead by *his* wife.

PERHAPS THE BEST EVIDENCE of then prevailing judicial attitudes regarding "bush justice" occurred in the multiple homicide trials of Billy Nekeferoff, brother of Paul.

Billy was a remarkable little fellow with an extraordinarily long rap sheet. The list of charges against him almost exceeded his height — a few inches over five feet. But what there was of him was tough as a wolverine. And like the wolverine, what Billy could not consume, he'd rip apart or defile.

With dimpled cheeks red as apples, crystal clear glacial blue eyes, and a shock of straw colored hair, Billy looked for all the world like a cherubic choir boy. Yet this benign facade disguised as lethal a creature as I'd ever encountered. By the time I'd come to Bristol Bay in the late 40s, Billy was already a legend. In the ensuing thirty years or so I knew him, incredibly, he seemed to age not at all. Years ago when he told me it was his sixty-fourth birthday, he looked to be in his late thirties. While the ravages of a life badly misspent seemed to mark Billy's features no more than Dorian Gray's, they sure added much to his legend. Billy's reputation for violence was such that mothers used him as the local boogie man to keep contentious children in line.

One fishing partner and two trapping partners of Billy's had disappeared while in his company. Only the body of the ex-fishing partner, Bob Pesterfield, was ever found. An old rodeo rider with a steel plate in his head, Bob had simply fallen off their fishing boat one night, according to Billy. Yet I'm told when Bob's body was recovered several weeks later, the steel plate in his head had been badly dented.

One gruesome tale circulated by Billyphobes was, I'm almost certain, untrue. Allegedly, someone had stumbled by chance into his trapping camp at Alinchak Bay and found skinned human hindquarters hanging beneath his driftwood cache. True or not, there was plenty of other evidence Billy was a psychotic killer. Like the murder of Henry Miller. A derelict alcoholic, Henry was what was known as a "dehorn" in the Bay's fishing villages.

One night when Billy was staying with Henry in his Naknek shack, they argued. Billy disliked arguing. It made him nervous. To avoid such unpleasantness, while Henry lay on his cot smoking a cigarette, Billy shot him.

When his body was discovered, Billy confessed to the crime and was flown to Anchorage for trial. The incredible particulars of this trial were reported to me, as follows, by an attorney assigned to the case. When asked how he pleaded, guilty or not guilty, Billy at first pled guilty.

Either because of Billy's angelic appearance or his apparent hearing loss, the judge would not accept this plea as final. First assuring Billy's hearing aid was turned up full volume, the judge offered him some defense counseling. "The record shows Henry Miller escaped years ago from jail in Coffeeville, Kansas, where he'd been incarcerated for murder. Obviously, he was a man of violent and unstable temperament. Could it be that you'd gotten into an argument and you killed him in self-defense?"

"Uhhh . . . Yeah!" was Billy's enlightened response.

"In that case," continued His Honor, "you might wish to change your plea to 'Not Guilty.' " Billy complied happily.

Throughout the course of the trial, the curdled milk of human kindness dribbled down from the bench. On it, Justice skittered and skated about. Its final pratfall occurred when Billy was asked why, after he'd shot Henry once as he lay in his bunk — virtually incapacitating him — had he again shot him as he crawled across the floor seeking escape?

Billy's reasonable answer, "Why, to put him out of his misery, Your Honor."

Such compassion won Billy only a couple of years "vacation" on Washington's McNeil Island prison. It seemed no time at all before he was back in Naknek, terrorizing the neighborhood. What with several bar room assaults, a stabbing with a round tipped butter knife and two or three cases of suspected arson, Billy was occasionally removed from the local scene. But every summer, come fishing season, there he was, making his rounds through the alders.

Before I concluded Billy was dangerously psychotic, I had no qualms dealing with him. He'd always been very friendly to me. Frequently he'd charter me to fly him in and out of some remote area where he intended to trap. Curiously, on three of these occasions, he had me fly back later to retrieve his backpack, hearing aid and rifle. In each instance, oddly, these three crucial items had been left behind.

After the murder of Henry Miller, Billy became less friendly to me. He threatened to kill the local magistrate, Iris Jensen, who had first arraigned him. Since Iris and I were good friends, I suppose Billy's paranoia included me as one "out to get him." I first became aware of this while shopping in Naknek's grocery store. Spotting me, Billy hissed, "Hello enemy, I hear you're looking for me."

Surprised, I hastily assured him I was neither an enemy nor looking for him. But he'd have none of it.

"I know you're out to get me," Billy said. "Don't be surprised if I get you first."

Not long afterward, I encountered more evidence of Billy's increasingly malevolent maraudings. One day I flew into the Becharof Lake bear camp of Kodiak guide, Park Munsey. Park wasn't there, but his wife invited me up for coffee. She and a couple hunting clients told me the day before Park had landed his float plane and taxied up the slough a hundred yards or so from the cabin where he'd tied down. While securing the aircraft, Park was accosted by a wildly gesticulating Billy who burst out of the brush to confront him. As his wife and clients watched from the window in growing dismay, Billy suddenly launched a round house right and knocked Park kicking. Leaping on top, Billy then grabbed Park by the throat and started banging his head on the ground. Galvanized into action by this display, Park's wife and the hunters raced to Park's rescue. I was told they virtually had to beat Billy off with rifle butts. Finally persuaded to let go, Billy leaped off and fled into the brush, swearing revenge.

"What in the world was that all about?" inquired Park's dismayed rescuers.

Rubbing his bruised throat, Park croaked, "Something about his mining claims. He said I'd been shooting holes in his claim notices from my plane. When I kinda' laughed and told him a bear had probably chewed them, he came completely unspooled. I couldn't believe it. The last thing I ever suspected was that he'd coldcock me." Park, though of modest size, was himself tough as nails. Had Billy not caught him unaware, I suspect a battle royal would have taken place.

From his cabin, Park radioed the state troopers in Kodiak. The latter's response was a groaned, "Why didn't you shoot him? Oh well, we've got another body over here we think we can connect him to. We'll come over and pick him up."

If they did, Billy wasn't in custody long. That winter, Park's bear camp was burned to the ground. The next year his neighbor guide, Jackie Myers, had his camp and boat torched.

That Billy did both arson jobs nobody doubted. Yet despite the fact his round-trip snow trail was found to lead from his camp to Jackie Myer's location, Billy was never convicted.

Years later, while governor, I received an impassioned plea from Billy asking for a pardon. Believing the *possibility* of my granting it might dissuade him from trying to carry out his previous threat, I stalled, telling him I'd have to review his record. I found not a rap sheet but a *ream* cataloging an appalling list of transgressions. Fortunately, I never had to increase Billy's disfavor by telling him I could not swab clean such an immense slate. Shortly after, game warden Dick Dykema told me Billy apparently had "gone to the Great Trapline in the Sky," for he has not been seen since.

MAYHEM IN THE BUSH led to occasional requests from local marshals to help them enforce the law. I found few of these ventures much to my liking. However, they elicited my profound respect for the nerve, if not the common sense, exhibited by some of these doughty men who wore the badge in Alaska's bush.

Take the case of the "Wild Killer of Ugashik." I'd received a radio request from Marshal Sam Rick to fly him and his deputy into the small village of Pilot Point on the Alaska Peninsula. Here we were given details of a murder committed a few days before. At the height of a wild party, one Valentine Sapsuk had shot a reveler and, taking a local woman hostage, fled upriver.

We searched for many hours by plane and later by foot and boat without finding a trace of Valentine. Several winter months went by. Occasionally, I'd get a call from Sam and we'd fly off to investigate another clue. One such call was prompted by the kidnapped woman's return to Ugashik. She'd found a skiff and escaped, she said, while Valentine was distracted butchering a moose. She told us locations of several of Valentine's hideouts. We checked each but found nothing.

The following March, Valentine's brother James, notified us he had found a note in his cabin on the Dog Salmon River asking for supplies to be delivered there. I flew to King Salmon where I met Sam and two companions, one a deputy marshal. To my dismay, I learned the other was an Anchorage newspaper editor. My concerns were allayed somewhat when the journalist revealed he shared my distress over flamboyant and inaccurate reporting. I cited several stories where activities in which I'd been involved were grossly distorted. He assured me sensationalism affronted him in the extreme; only hard facts would be reported. Thus deluded, we flew off for Ugashik, where we met brother James. James advised that Valentine, who had tuberculosis, would like to give himself up, but feared he'd be shot if he did so. We assured James we had every intention of taking his brother alive and would provide him protection.

On the way upriver to the Dog Salmon cabin, we landed to "de-coffee" and refuel. While pouring gas from the two five-gallon cans we'd carried along, we spotted a couple of wolves emerge from the brush far downriver and cross to the opposite bank. Though several hundreds yards distant, the deputy marshal fired a few futile rifle shots. Meanwhile, the newspaper man busied himself taking pictures.

Later, at the Dog Salmon cabin we circled above to see if we could pick up a trail. Though several days old, we found Valentine's tracks. Followed by air, they led a few miles onto a ridge between the Dog Salmon and Ugashik rivers. There they were lost in a maze of moose tracks.

Circling for several minutes and about to discontinue the seemingly impossible search, I noticed what appeared to be an unnatural pile of brush. I pointed it out to Sam. After several more circles we saw Valentine scramble out of the brush pile and appear to aim his rifle at our aircraft. We quickly departed and landed a half mile away on a small tundra pond. Making our way toward Valentine's "camp," Sam plotted strategy.

"You two cover us. Jay and I'll go directly to Valentine's camp." Somehow I didn't find this approach too appealing and must admit I permitted Sam to lead off well in advance while I cravenly scurried from one bit of cover to the next.

Soon, we came to an open area of frozen swamp. At the far edge we saw Valentine, rifle at port, peering in our direction. I hunkered down behind a small ridge expecting Sam to do the same. Instead, Sam stood up in full view and started directly toward Valentine. I did not share his fortitude. Instead, I fixed the front sights of my Springfield on the small distant figure and cowered behind my embankment. To my great relief, Valentine laid down his rifle and came forward to meet Sam halfway. I shortly joined them.

Valentine, up close, looked pathetic. Little more than five feet tall, his hundred or so consumptive pounds were wrapped inadequately in the remnants of the clothes he'd escaped in. He seemed truly glad to see us, relieved that his attempts to evade the law were finally over. Understandable. He'd been on the run for several cruel winter months. Later we learned we'd come close to his camps many times. Had he wished, he could have picked us off like clay pigeons.

Before we flew our prisoner back to town, we went to look at Valentine's hideout. It was incredibly primitive; nothing more than a hollowed out pile of brush with just enough room to accommodate his small body. Yet he'd holed up in that brush pile more than a month in sub-freezing weather.

Making our way back to the aircraft, the Deputy Marshal and editor rejoined us. The latter got his exclusive interview.

When the newspaper story emerged a few days later, I was appalled. Headlines read: "Wild Killer of Ugashik Captured." Beneath was a picture of the valiant manhunters and quarry. Trouble was, without a score card, it would be very hard to tell just who were the good guys. Sandwiched between Sam and me was the diminutive Valentine. He was the only one holding a rifle.

The article itself was worthy of the most lurid tabloid. It said we'd been "forced" to fire at a pack of wolves menacing us when we'd landed to refuel. Only the most incredible tracking prowess had led us to Valentine's "fortified" lair. Only the most astute and courageous strategy permitted us to take him without bloodshed. My respect for the media ratcheted down yet one more notch.

An epilogue: To my knowledge, only one of the eight people in attendance at the lethal party that started the whole affair has survived. The rest were all in turn killed by either knife, gun or other means of mayhem. In each instance alcohol played a key role. The lone survivor? Who else but old Valentine Sapsuk, "The Wild Killer of Ugashik." He regained his health while spending a short time in prison, and then returned home to Pilot Point.

*"Firepotting" was required to start an aircraft
engine in cold weather.*

10
Partners in Crime and Comedy

I SUPPOSE I SHOULD have expected sensationalized coverage of the "wild killer" story. Almost no newspaper account of events in which I'd played a role seemed totally accurate. This conclusion is not exclusive to public figures and politicians. I find virtually everyone who's been reported on finds it true.

Another time I was interviewed by a newspaper reporter shortly after I'd returned from the village of Mary's Igloo, where we'd shot several wolves decimating a reindeer herd. My wildest imagination could not have dreamed up the quote attributed to me: "According to Hammond, once more his efforts have saved the Eskimos from starvation." Good grief!

As if that weren't outlandish enough, in his book, *Of Wolves and Men*, writer Barry Lopez blindly repeated that specious bit of nonsense as gospel more than 30 years later!

An even more ludicrous story, about one of the very few charging bear I'd been forced to shoot, increased my distress with reporters. As a Fish and Wildlife agent, I was required to keep a daily diary from which monthly reports were sent to our Anchorage headquarters. There, reporters often found in them grist from which to turn out half-baked Alaskana. On this occasion I'd been tending traps near a dry creek bed by Big River. Suddenly, from out of the willows burst a cow moose. Behind it bounded a large, chocolate brown bear. Unable to catch the moose, the old fraud soon gave up the chase to snuffle around for ground squirrels, looking as though this was what he'd had in mind all along.

At first, he was a good hundred and fifty feet from me, working his side of the creek bed as I did mine. As we progressed, however, the bed narrowed and I found myself paying more attention to the bear and less to my business. When he came within fifty feet, to spook him I threw a rock. To my surprise, it hit him in the rump. To my alarm, rather than spook, he came at me, all stops out. Normally, I'd have fired a shot over his head to dissuade him but neither time nor space permitted. The flood-swollen Big River at my back provided a most uninviting escape. With the bear almost upon me, I reluctantly put my sights on his chest and knocked him down. He came immediately to his feet and scrambled for cover. Before I could get off a second shot, he skidded and collapsed, stone dead.

At the time, I was contemptuous of most "charging bear" stories and wondered how to explain this one. Examining the carcass, I found one of the brute's tusks had been shattered and the shard of an old bullet remained in his jaw. A suppurating mass on his shoulder testified to a probable recent fight with another boar over some fickle female. Under his hide, I found three different sizes of birdshot. This old boy had every right to have a mad-on for mankind.

Along with the hide, I submitted my report to the front office where a naive reporter found it and structured a wild story. In fairness to her, I must acknowledge certain details were happily fleshed out by my fellow agent, Bob Burkholder.

After writing a reasonably accurate account, the reporter took off on a flight of fancy fueled by Burkholder. It went like this: "Hammond, a rather large fellow, commonly wears one of those hairy Canadian sweaters. A wolf trapper by trade, not surprisingly he often smells like something other than human. Given how brown bear have very poor eyesight and this was the mating season, you get the picture. To put it delicately, to save himself from a 'fate worse than death,'" according to Burkholder, "Hammond had no choice but to shoot the amorous animal whose only crime was to fall in love"!

BURKHOLDER AND I often teamed up on fiascoes that made the papers. One February in the early 1950s we were stationed with game warden Bob Baker in Kotzebue. Back then, Kotzebue had no winter airstrip. Aircraft were staked out on the sea ice, where we used axes to cut ice bridges for tie-downs. One day a severe winter storm hurtled out of the southwest. With high winds blowing snow, it was a good time to catch up on reading, sleeping, or playing chess.

That evening, while engaged in the latter, a frantic pounding on the front door stopped the game. Fellow U.S.F.W. agent Bob Baker hollered at the pounder to enter. Stumbling in out of the dark came Gene Joiner, colorful bush pilot and publisher of a widely read pot-boiling paper, the *Mukluk Telegraph*.

"Hey," Joiner begged, "can you guys give me a hand securing my plane? The wind's blowing so hard I can't get her tied down by myself."

Donning parkas, we went hand over hand by guide rope down to the sea ice. Visibility was nil and shrieking wind made walking difficult. The chill factor was almost a hundred below. Somehow we got to Joiner's plane. Unlike other planes, his was facing out of the wind. We moved and securely tied it.

Groping back to the cabin, Burk and I resumed our chess game when we heard the wind suddenly scream from a different direction. It was now gusting over ninety miles per hour, blowing squarely on the tails of our aircraft. Such tail winds can crumple wings like tissue paper. There was nothing to do but try to turn our planes more nearly into the wind. Again we made our way out into the howling gale. Without powerful flashlights and guide ropes we'd have been quickly disoriented. But turning the aircraft was absolutely impossible. Drifted snow was solidly packed half-way up the fuselage. Able to do nothing, we stumbled back to Baker's cabin fearing the worst.

When the storm finally lifted, our fears were realized. Several aircraft, including ours, had at least one crumpled wing. A Waco belonging to famed bush pilot Archie Ferguson had been almost denuded of fabric. An Aeronca owned by Archie's son, Bill Levy, had both wing tips touching the ground. Baker's Gullwing Stinson had lost its ailerons. The only unscathed aircraft was, you guessed it, Gene Joiner's.

A few weeks later, someone came up to Burk and me chortling, "Have you guys seen the latest issue of Joiner's *Mukluk Telegraph*? His headline reads: 'The $6,000 Poker Game.' It says, 'While drinking beer and playing poker, Fish and Wildlife agents Bob Burkholder and Jay Hammond let the wind damage their government aircraft to the tune of $6,000.'"

Burk was no more livid than I. "That ungrateful louse! After we helped him save *his*, he'd do a thing like that! Tell you what, dammit; let's take a vow. The first one who sees him clobbers him." We shook hands on it.

I fear I broke that vow. When I saw the actual news story, I cooled somewhat. Rather than a "$6,000 poker game while drinking beer," it read a "$4,000 chess game while drinking coffee." Bad enough, but not quite so reprehensible in the eyes of our supervisors. Another reason for not fulfilling that vow was that almost twenty years went by before I saw Joiner again. Not only had he aged even faster than I, he'd also lost several fingers and toes to frostbite. Punching out the lights of a crippled old man no longer seemed worthy. Besides, I'd developed a perverse admiration for the irascible fellow.

Years later, I learned Joiner made a small fortune selling jade mineral claims, then moved to Great Britain where he purchased a peerage. In his wake he left some rough-cut journalistic gems. Perhaps most lustrous was one mined from the *Mukluk Telegraph* about Archie Ferguson.

Diminutive Archie was thoroughly Scotch, save in verbal expenditures. As bush pilots competing for business, Archie and Joiner hated each other. Hence this piece for his paper's "society page":

"Local buffoon and windbag, Archibald F. Ferguson, recently departed for the states in company with his combination business-partner and mistress. We hope they have a pleasant trip."

ANOTHER EXPLOIT briefly put Burk and me in jail — an item I carefully neglected to include in subsequent resumes. U.S. Fish and Wildlife Service biologist Ed Chatelaine called us into his Anchorage office one blustery winter day and assigned us the mission of culling an old injured buffalo bull from the Delta herd.

"But make sure nobody sees you. Delta folks don't take kindly to those they might think are poachers."

Forewarned, Burk and I headed up the Glenn Highway. Passing very few people, we bucked drifting snow all the way to Paxson's Lodge, where we stopped for coffee and spent a convivial half-hour chatting with the owner and other locals. Setting out again, we wondered how long it would take to locate the injured bull.

Luck was with us. A few hours later, cruising down an unplowed side road, we spotted the animal, and waited as it lumbered into range.

When the bull reached a flat below a steep bluff, we dropped it within a hundred yards. While skinning it out, a pickup pulled alongside our Jeep. The driver crested the hill and looked down on two "poachers." Deciding we'd best explain, we showed him our badges and authorization papers.

"Please don't tell folks hereabouts one of their bison's been shot. It'll only confuse and upset them," pled Burk.

"I understand. Not a word," the truck driver assured us and left.

Loading hide, head, and meat into our Jeep and under a canvas, we started back for Anchorage. Stopping again at Paxson's we were surprised by the sudden chill. The previously-friendly owner nodded sullenly; customers shunned us. Obviously, the truck driver had not kept his mouth shut.

Back on the road after dark, our gas gage reading "empty," we decided to refuel from two five-gallon Jerry cans. Pulling off the road, we saw a car directly behind us do the same, presumably to see if we were okay. Burk and I held the rifles that had been propped between us as we piled out of the Jeep. Striding purposefully back to the car, Burk approached the driver's side, intending to thank the occupant for his unnecessary offer of assistance. At the driver's window Burk saw the car belonged to the Territorial Highway Patrol. Earlier he had told me a new patrolman, Phil Ames, had been assigned to the area. Burk was anxious to meet him.

"Hi. What's your name?" Burk inquired.

"Phil Ames," responded the driver.

"I've been looking for you," said Burk, shifting his rifle to his left hand to put his right through the half-open window.

Mistaking a handshake for something more ominous, the trooper frantically rolled up the window and raised his service revolver. Burk, startled by this rebuff to his friendly overture, jumped back as though already shot. "Hey, wait a minute. What's going on?"

"I don't like what you fellas have in your truck."

At that moment, from the other direction another Highway Patrol car, siren blaring, cut in front of our Jeep, and screeched to a stop. Two eight-foot, four hundred-pound patrolmen emerged with guns drawn. Not only had the loose-lipped truck driver passed the word all down the highway, the Paxson Lodge proprietor had called our Fairbanks office to check our story. Totally unaware of our assignment, agent Ray Wolford swore his office would have been the first to know of such a venture, since Delta was in his district. Accordingly, he'd notified the Highway Patrol to arrest the two poachers.

By now, our Anchorage office had closed. With no one to confirm our explanation, Burk and I spent the night in jail at Gakona. Verifying our story to the patrolmen next day, Ed Chatelaine apologized profusely for failing to notify Wolford of our nefarious mission. At least I think he apologized. Most of his words were choked off by laughter.

BOBBY LEE BURKHOLDER was one of many colorful coworkers in my years with the U.S. Fish and Wildlife Service. But none were daubed from a more vivid palette than Aleutian Wildlife Refuge Manager, Bob "Sea Otter" Jones.

Insufferably erudite and opinionated, Bob rubbed hair wrong on some folks. Having heard of his legendary exploits, I was surprised at our first meeting. I'd expected someone larger than life. Shoot! This skinny fellow would be hard-pressed to cast a shadow, I'd thought. Jones soon earned my respect, however. When it came to tough going, his shadow was always well out in front of mine. Once I got to know him, I developed enormous admiration and affection for Bob and discovered many redeeming virtues.

My most memorable venture with Sea Otter occurred in the early spring of 1955. I am reminded of it every step, every day, ever since.

I'd been sent to Cold Bay to pick up Bob and fly him around his remote Aleutian district.

Climbing into the Supercub, Jones asked me to fly him to King Cove, a small fishing village a few miles away. It was a rare day for the lower peninsula — calm, sunny and just above freezing. Having no airstrip, the only place I could land at King Cove was a small frozen pond from which the local cannery pumped water. Since the pond was bordered by an elevated six-inch pipeline, margin for error was minimal. Still, "a piece of cake" for an old carrier pilot, I thought.

One problem. Kids were skating on the pond. A low pass cleared them off to one side before I squared away for landing. Since there was no wind and the ice was especially slick in the sunny, 40-degree weather, I decided to land on wheels rather than pump down my skis. On glare ice, metal skis seem to speed a plane's momentum on touch-down. I had little enough runway as it was.

Nose high with a power-on approach just above stalling, I neatly put down at the edge of the pond. Rather than slow down once power was cut, my tires skittered over the water-slick ice with almost no frictional drag. The far end of the pond was coming up fast. No problem. A controlled half ground-loop on glare ice will reverse one's direction, if you catch it with throttle just right. Before I could execute this maneuver, however, the children skated back onto the ice beside and behind the plane, and I suddenly had a very serious problem. Unable to reverse direction without imperiling the skaters, I had to ride it out, straight ahead.

Our speed reducing less rapidly than the diminishing distance to the pipeline, I had one option. Unbuckling my seat-belt and flinging open the door, I bailed out and grabbed the wing strut, bracing both feet before me for additional drag to stop us before we hit the beach. It worked all too well. Frozen in the ice was a wooden crate, one sharp edge above the surface.

My feet hit full force. The aircraft swerved and came to a shuddering halt, well short of the pipeline.

But something was drastically wrong. Letting loose of the wing strut, I collapsed. Seeing I was unable to stand, burly Mike Utech, a renowned bear guide, easily hoisted my two-hundred pounds and packed me to the village school house.

There, a teacher professed knowledge of First Aid. Foolishly, I took his advice and plunged my feet into hot water. It was the worst thing I could have done. My ankles swelled like turgid sausages. Since there were no other aircraft or pilots at either King Cove or Cold Bay back then, radio calls went out to the Coast Guard in Kodiak and Fish and Wildlife in Anchorage. Both said they'd dispatch aircraft to pick me up as soon as weather permitted.

For the next three days, a typical Aleutian storm centered over the area. With two broken ankles, the wait seemed interminable. The first night was the worst. When the initial shock wore off, my ankles blazed in constant pain. A fist-full of aspirin knocked the edge off only a bit. To keep my mind from my problems, Mike and friends decided I needed company. Propping me up in the cannery dining hall on a folding bed, they proceeded to party most enthusiastically all night.

The "party" lasted almost three days. Daily, the weather as well as my ankles got worse. Swollen enormously, subcutaneous hemorrhages radiated a sun-burst of colors from the broken bones and blood vessels. Unless treated soon, I would have real problems. On the fourth day, we decided I could no longer wait if I was to save my feet. During a brief weather break over King Cove, I told Bob that, together, we ought to be able to fly into Cold Bay where a larger plane could more easily pick me up. "You climb in the back seat and put your feet on the pedals," I said. "I'll work the hand controls." Ever venturesome, Sea Otter agreed.

That day we learned something new about an old adage: Two heads may often be better than one, but the theory unravels when both try to control the same set of feet.

Lining up for a take-off I shouted to Bob, "When I yell 'left or right' you press on the proper pedal." Adding throttle, we bucketed over the ice.

"Left!" I shouted as engine torque pulled us to the right. Abruptly we lurched to the left. "Right! Right!" I hollered as we lumbered over the ice. And so it went. Screeching "Right! Left! Right!" over the engine's roar, we lifted off. Like a bird be-sotted on over-ripe berries attempting to pluck insects out of the air, the plane clawed erratically for altitude.

Airborne, I wondered how to get us down safely. Neither had to be told our system didn't work well. If worse came to worst, I'd thought I could force myself to press on the rudder pedals. Soon, it was apparent I couldn't, even if my life depended on it.

The trip back to Cold Bay took an agonizingly long fifteen minutes. A crosswind gusting to forty knots made our landing approach an epoch in error. Unable to use any rudder to "crab" or hold the wing down, I couldn't counter the crosswind and we sailed sideways down toward the runway. Somehow the aircraft survived the rough impact and subsequent ground loop. Shuddering to a stop, I cut the engine as Sea Otter clapped me on the back in relieved exaltation.

I was carried to Jones' small quarters to wait for a weather change. It did. The next three days it screamed and stormed as it can only on the threshold of the Aleutians. Not even birds could fly.

Bob did his best to pull my mind up from my ankles. His most successful effort was unplanned. He'd just gotten a new .257 Roberts-Winchester rifle of which he was intensely proud. An excellent shot, Bob would exhibit his prowess at the least provocation.

While Jones sat at his typewriter one morning pecking out paperwork, the irreverent Mike Utech, who'd come over by boat from King Cove, decided to pluck at Bob's plumage to see if he could get him to fly off his perch. This was a favorite parlor game of those who'd been bruised by Jones' scathing derision. "Bob," said Mike, "if that new .257 is so hot, you ought to be able to bounce that raven off that pole over there."

Peering out the window, Bob spotted the bird perched thirty feet off the ground some hundred yards away beyond the next row of old World War II huts. "Nothing to it," scoffed Bob. "Of course, there's no shooting allowed on base. Besides, ravens are protected, as you very well know."

"You're just making excuses," Mike's needle probed deeper. "You know damn well you couldn't hit that bird if you burned a whole box of shells."

That did it. Jones flew off his desk chair and squawked, "You wanna bet? Five bucks says I drop him first shot!"

"You're on," chortled the plumage plucker.

Unlimbering the .257, Bob set his scope at its highest power, braced the barrel on the door frame and fired. Like a plumed-out clay pigeon, the raven exploded in a cloud of black feathers. Only as they floated downward did Bob spot what Mike had seen all along. Almost directly beneath the raven's pole, but sporadically hidden behind the next row of huts, was the menacing figure of one Maggie McNease, the local magistrate. In those days she and Sea Otter constituted all the law to be found on the lower Alaska Peninsula. In prosecuting fish and game violators, old "Law and Order" Jones frequently admonished McNease for not being tough enough. Jones seemed satisfied with no less than public flogging, as a prelude to hanging; whereas, Maggie, considered by Bob a sniveling sentimentalist, was perfectly willing to forego the flogging — and go straight to the rope. As the ruptured remnants of the raven fluttered down on her, Maggie let loose a shriek that struck terror into Sea Otter's heart.

"Oh my God!" he bellowed, frantically looking about for sanctuary. Finding none, he dove to his desk chair and started pounding his typewriter as though he'd been doing nothing else for the past hour.

Meanwhile, Maggie gathered her skirts about her considerable person and, like a tornado, swirled toward the sound of the shot. She didn't have to ponder its source for very long. As Jones pecked frantically on his typewriter attempting to exude innocence, someone surreptitiously opened the door. Mike's retriever, Rowdy, who'd been tremulously whining at the window in total frustration, rapturously burst forth to join "the hunt." Nose to the ground, he almost cut the legs out from under poor Maggie as he scurried to retrieve the blasted bird. Securing it in velvet jaws, Rowdy raced back toward Bob's quarters for petting and praise.

All this, of course, went unobserved by Sea Otter, buried behind his typewriter, pummeling away at any semblance of having sinned. None of this, however, was lost on Her Worship, the magistrate. Hurricane Maggie bore down like a billowing thunderhead, just paces behind Rowdy, who, bounding in through the door, proudly trotted over to Sea Otter to place the shredded bird at his feet. Tail thumping happily, the dog awaited his anticipated accolade, not realizing he had suddenly metamorphosed into a 'smoking gun.'

"Aha! You!" thundered Maggie who proceeded to verbally draw and quarter Bob before a most appreciative audience.

DESPITE SUCH DIVERSIONS, by now I desperately needed medical attention. Nearly a week had gone by. Aflame with pain, I got almost no sleep. My swollen ankles began to resemble those elephant foot wastebaskets so esteemed by "great white hunters," gross conversation pieces totally devoid of aesthetics.

The only solution was to fly myself back to King Salmon through the storm. However, since the flight required refueling, someone had to accompany me. A brave lad who'd had a couple hours of flight training some years before volunteered.

This time we tried a different approach. Double splints were rigged for both ankles. These extended below my feet and above the knees. I found I could exert pressure on the foot pedals through the lower ends of the splints. But these wouldn't allow me to flex my legs sufficiently to sit in the front seat of the Cub. I could fit, however, in the roomier rear seat, and use its dual control pedals.

Two more problems. Both the "stick" and throttle controls had been removed from the back seat. We solved this by inserting a long screwdriver through the floor boards to engage the stick controls, and connected a rod to the front throttle so I could operate it from the back. We hoped.

Taking off into barely flyable weather, we managed safe landing at Port Moller where my passenger re-fueled the aircraft from the two five-gallon cans on board. Aloft again, bucking snow squalls and strong head winds, it was after dark when the lights of King Salmon finally appeared. Squaring away for a landing, I felt my passenger's nervous hand on the control.

"I've got it," I shouted, giving my "stick" a shake to so indicate. In the process I pulled the screwdriver out just as we were about to touch down. The plane's nose shot upward in a left bank approaching a stall. Frantically reinserting my screw driver, I shouted again, "I got it!" Dumping the nose, we made a less than picture-book landing.

An ambulance standing by took me to the Air Force dispensary where I spent the night happily sedated. Next morning I was flown to Anchorage by military transport and lodged in a World War II "elephant hut" that comprised part of the old 5001st Army Hospital at Fort Richardson.

Examining my injuries, doctors deemed it necessary to reduce the swelling before surgery. For this, they elevated my feet in a traction harness and confined me to bed. The third night so trussed, I awoke to screams as smoke and flame billowed down the hospital hall into our ward. Panicked patients on crutches and in wheelchairs frantically lurched by my bed to escape the fire, every man for himself. Attendants and nurses, two of whom were to die in the fire, were occupied elsewhere and unavailable. Unhooking myself from traction, I slithered over the side of the bed to the floor and, on hindquarters, slid my way out the door into the snow. There I was soon gathered up and bustled by ambulance to the new Alaska Native Health Service Hospital.

Indignities heaped on my person were not ended, however. In the course of my stay at the ANS Hospital, a front page news story appeared with an accompanying photograph: "Native women from Alaskan villages await the birth of their children at the new ANS Hospital." In the picture, perched on a hospital gurney amid a number of demonstrably pregnant females, was myself, looking for all the world like some surfeited sultan in the midst of his harem.

The severity of my injuries required an ankle fusion and several months' recuperation. During this period, Bella and I bought a small restaurant in Naknek. The name "Model Cafe" proved a misnomer. After months of stumping around on crutches as a short order cook, I was happy to turn this non-profit enterprise over to someone else.

BEFORE GOING BACK TO WORK, I had a chance to test my ankles prospecting for uranium with Lake Clark old-timer Brown Carlson and his son-in-law, Tommy Myers.

Born almost 80 years before in Norway, Brown had been a circus acrobat and a sailor aboard tall ships. Jumping ship in 1906, after having seen the world, Brown found his way to Lake Clark and decided that was where he would stay.

When I met him in the late 1940s, Brown had lived almost alone in the bush for forty years. This isolated life had done little to obscure his eccentricities. Brown carried on lengthy two-way conversations with himself and with other wild creatures, and delighted in the amazement that his remarkable physical prowess elicited from onlookers.

I once took an orthopedic surgeon and physical therapist up the lake by boat to visit Brown. Approaching from a hundred yards away, we saw him emerge from his cabin, race to the beach and execute a handspring. From a distance, his age was not apparent and my companions simply chuckled at what appeared to be a youngster showing off. As we came closer their jaws dropped. That youngster had aged some sixty years. Cackling in delight at their astonishment, Brown led us to his cabin for coffee as stout as the expectorate from the Black Bull tobacco plug he munched. We also fed off his famed strawberry patch.

Years before, Brown had told me of a trip he'd made in 1925 on which they'd located what his geologist companion called pitchblende — a brown and black lustrous mineral containing uranium. The mineral having small value then, Brown thought little of it. Considering Brown a bit more than simply "bushy," I too thought little of it.

Later, when uranium fever hit, I showed Brown uncaptioned pictures of uranium ore. Without hesitation, he plucked from the pile a photo of high-quality uraninite ore from the Belgian Congo.

"That be it. Looks like black glass with yellow flowers in it" was his description.

My interest leaped. Perhaps Brown was not as bushy as I thought. That afternoon, we flew to Lachabuna Lake and hiked into the higher country.

Though my ankles protested, I was determined to see if the doctors had been correct in predicting that my days of climbing were over. I found I did fairly well but only by walking backwards while climbing. During the first few miles Brown kept up a running chatter — "Hi, Mr. Ptarmigan, Old Brown's back. What think ye of that? Hee, hee, hee!"

I began questioning my sanity for not more deeply doubting his. Were the wear and tear on my ankles worth a wild goose chase led by a senile old man?

Then Brown hollered: "Under that big spruce is where I cached some diamond drills."

Sure enough, we found a set wrapped in moldy canvas. Later, Brown pointed to an outcropping, "You'll find a cinnabar vein over there." Finding it, I thought, "Maybe the old boy's not lost all his small change after all."

My spirits by then transcended the pain in my ankles as we made camp. For Brown, this simply meant curling up under a piece of canvas. Tenderfeet Tom and I cut ourselves spruce boughs and beded down in mummy bags beneath a tarp.

At dawn, I could not stand on my blazing ankles. "What now?" I wondered. "Tom and Brown will have to arrange for a helicopter to come get me."

Swallowing a fistful of aspirin, I waited fifteen minutes, then hauled myself hand over hand up a small tree and took a step. AGONY! Then another. Agony. I took a few more steps — intense but tolerable. In a hundred yards either I had grown numb or activity lubricated what joints I had.

Halfway up a steep slope, Brown hesitated. "Let's see. I think it's over this way."

After an hour's search, he headed in the opposite direction. Since snow still adhered in spots, Brown concluded that his black glass with yellow flowers must yet be covered. Dejected, we made our way back to the aircraft and to Lake Clark.

Brown died years ago at 96, his search uncompleted. To this day when I fly over the area I sense somewhere below he's still looking for those elusive yellow flowers.

A few months after our futile prospect, while cooking on a job I'd gotten for him, Tommy was knifed by two drunken soldiers at King Salmon. He left behind three small children, a fine wife and a sick feeling I somehow was responsible.

THROUGH MY FISH AND WILDLIFE YEARS in Alaska's bush, those strange prophetic dreams kept occurring. In February 1955, Bob Jones, Bob Meyers and I had been sent to desolate, abandoned Amchitka Island in the Aleutians to live-trap sea otters for transplant. The only three humans on the island, our sole communication with the outside was a radio transmitter we installed.

Amchitka had been vacated ten years before, at the end of World War II, and its crumbling military structures were infested with rats. In our hut during meals we sat at a broken table, shooting rats with revolvers as they emerged from rotted floors and walls, drawn by cooking odors. At night, I experimented with placing the legs of my metal cot in pails of water to frustrate their insistence on invading my bed. It didn't work. Sleepless hours were passed by kicking the scurrying creatures off my blankets and puckering even more tightly the hood of my sleeping bag to keep them from filtering in.

Such conditions, of course, can induce disturbing dreams, and this night a particularly distressing one crawled up from my subconscious. This time I dreamed vividly my father had died. The next day a radio message verified the fact. Since Dad had been dying from Lou Gehrig's disease for many months, his passing was not surprising. That I somehow knew the exact time and date seemed something more than coincidence. Telepathy? Probably, but certainly at mighty long range. Morris Hammond died in New Jersey. His son dreamed it near the International Dateline, beyond the curvature of the earth, several thousand miles to the northwest.

*Government hunter for the U.S. Fish and Wildlife Service,
1950. This got me into trouble with conservationists in
1974 — and still does today.*

11

Ever Cry Wolf

LET ME CONFESS I am not a wolf expert. Of course, like almost everyone else, I *used* to be. But that was before I'd trapped for a living, earned a degree in biology, spent seven years as a government hunter and more than half a lifetime in the bush with opportunity to track and observe hundreds of these remarkable predators.

When I arrived in Alaska in the mid-forties, few defended the wolf. Territorial politicians made points with constituents declaring that if elected, they'd increase the wolf bounty. Bounties were paid not only on wolves, but coyotes, wolverine, seals, Dolly Varden trout and even our national emblem, the bald eagle. The prevailing attitude was "kill all the varmints!"

Perhaps aversion to politicians inclined me to take a contrary stance — a pattern that was to plague me during my own political career when I always seemed out of cycle with the politically correct view of the moment.

So it was during my senior year at the University of Alaska in Fairbanks that I wrote an article decrying the newly expanded U.S. Fish and Wildlife Service Alaskan predator control program. This generated far more criticism than commendation. Among my critics were Maury Kelly, head of the Service's Predator Control Division in Alaska and legendary wolf trapper Frank Glaser. Both came to visit me at the university museum where I worked as assistant curator. With good humor and patience, they made a rather good case that I didn't know what I was talking about. Despite our differing views, I liked both men. Kelly was a small, affable fellow, seemingly as unencumbered with guile as hair. Glaser was a lean, leathery old mountain man who'd probably spent more time than anyone chasing wolves.

One by one, they disputed my arguments. No, they didn't fly around "broadcasting" poison baits from the air. No, they weren't intent on extermination. No, neither strychnine nor cyanide incurred significant secondary poisoning of other creatures feeding on poisoned carcasses. No, wolves did not kill only the lame, sick or halt; nor did they take only what they required. To illustrate one misperception, they showed me a letter from an outraged amateur trapper:

Gentlemen:

You bastards! You've poisoned my trapline! I found these poison pellets scattered around my traps. Now there's no fur left in the entire area!

The letter was wrapped around a pint-sized ice cream container filled with ptarmigan droppings!

Still skeptical, I stuck to my guns. Finally, Kelly made an offer: "Why don't you take a temporary job with us and see for yourself?"

With some reluctance, I agreed. I was to remain on that job for the next seven years.

During that time, many of my preconceptions were called into question. Some were demolished. As experience grew, assurance dwindled: Perhaps I'd not had all the answers. While the wolf hardly seemed the vicious killer many contended, neither was it the selective culler of the weak asserted by those who'd enshrine it as nature's most noble embodiment of untrammeled wilderness.

Unfortunately, even those few who get to see wolves usually see but one dimension. Exceedingly rare are those privileged to observe the entire kaleidoscopic character of this elusive animal. Even they disagree.

One prime dispute is the impact wolf predation has on prey. That control of wolves could so dramatically affect prey populations came as my first surprise.

In 1948, the Alaska Peninsula caribou herd numbered less than two thousand, down from an estimated sixty thousand. Prior to introduction of reindeer, old-timers tell me no wolves were seen in that region. From twice yearly counts we found calf survival increased dramatically after two hundred and fifty wolves were eliminated by trapping and aerial hunting. The herd soon expanded tenfold. At the same time, wolves also increased far beyond previous levels, indicating selective control of predators can ultimately increase *their* numbers as well.

But don't wolves take only what's needed? I once found twenty-seven reindeer killed in one night by six wolves. Little other than tongues and livers had been scissored out.

But don't wolves selectively cull only the weak? In studying condition of bone marrow, body fat and disease presence in many wolf kills, to our surprise, we found if any selection occurred, it seemed for prey in prime condition. And why not? Having watched wolves pursue caribou on many occasions, I'm convinced they can easily bring down any herd member.

But isn't aerial hunting despicably unsportsmanlike? Perhaps. But it is far more challenging than the average hunt for big game, especially when one does it solo, flying and shooting simultaneously, as I often did. Check the box score.

I suspect the percentage of aerial wolf hunters clobbered far exceeds attrition in any other "sport" hunting activity.

Ironically, major critics of the federal control program were the same Alaskan Territorial Department of Fish and Game biologists who — after discovering for themselves how dramatically predator reduction increased prey populations — advocated the state's own wolf control program years later.

They proposed to achieve this selective control "surgically" — and in the process cut their own throats. The scalpel involved shooting from helicopters only target area pack members to which a radio collared "offender" had led them. The howl this proposal elicited literally reverberated around the world. Even those favoring wolf control bridled at such an "outrageous" proposal. "Why can't wolves be controlled by hunters and trappers instead?" they demanded.

The problem, of course, is that public hunters, rather than pursuing "culprit" wolves in target areas where prey may be in short supply, are attracted to areas of high prey and predator populations — where no wolf control is justified.

Unfortunately, most people's thoughts on wolves appear to spring from their hormones rather than their heads. Moreover, depth of passion seems inversely proportionate to degree of knowledge. Though perhaps I've observed more wolves than most "experts," I feel myself far less an authority than do many who might be hard-pressed to state with assurance from which end of the wolf emerges the howl.

Certainly, the pendulum of public opinion now stands at the opposite end of the arc from where it stood when I first came north. Rather than expendable "vermin," wolves are ascribed unrealistic nobility. If that pendulum must lodge in either extreme, I prefer support of the wolf.

Having concluded the truth lies somewhere between, I've been thumped on both sides by that pendulum's swing. Though I've long ago hung up my guns and traps, some environmentalists still unearth old pictures of me holding a dozen wolf hides and label me a wolf hater. Conversely, those who yet believe the wolf a despicable killing machine assert I'm responsible for their increase because I helped curb the use of poison and eliminate bounties.

And increase the wolf has. Forty years ago, many more wolves were trapped than today. Aerial hunting was open everywhere and poison was commonly used. A fifty dollar bounty was paid. What's more, the wolf's prime prey species, caribou, were far less abundant in much of Alaska than now. Yet the wolf easily survived this onslaught. By contrast, the state's recent modest and selective wolf control programs pose far less threat to wolf survival.

Nonetheless, it has engendered far more controversy. Animal rights groups have organized "howl-ins" and urged tourists to boycott Alaska until we mend our ways.

Author Farley Mowatt's *Never Cry Wolf* did much to swing the pendulum of public opinion to where it is now. Yet I'm told the book is a distillate of alleged adventures he experienced the few days he'd worked for eminent biologist, Dr. Frank Banfield, who was investigating the decline of Canadian caribou.

Studying wolf scats in a small area only, Mowatt asserted caribou provided but a negligible percentage of the wolf's diet. Small wonder! In his report, Dr. Banfield notes that during Mowatt's study, there were no caribou within two hundred miles of his study area!

Literary license has done much to shape, some say warp, public attitudes. Certainly *Red Riding Hood, Never Cry Wolf* and Barry Lopez' *Of Wolves and Men* have done far more than the most exhaustive scientific studies to sway public opinion. That such opinion is fuzzy is not surprising.

During the 1993 Alaska wolf controversy, at least three times, the media repeated ridiculous information about me provided by Lopez. In *Of Wolves and Men*, he asserts that I worked as a government hunter "killing three hundred wolves a MONTH" (emphasis mine), and repeats the asinine comment attributed to me: "Once again, I've saved the Eskimos from starvation."

Lopez never interviewed me. Three hundred wolves a month? That's twenty-five thousand wolves during my seven years as a government hunter! Three hundred wolves a *year* would be exaggeration enough. Still, that's less than a third of today's average yearly take by hunters and trappers, which, by contrast to the "old days" is far less than Alaska's annual wolf pup production.

Today's Alaskan wolves are hardly endangered. Nor will they likely be. Enlightened public attitudes will prevent any but — perhaps *even* — the most restrictive wolf control efforts.

I RECALL WELL my last wolf hunt. It was in March 1956. Bella often came along on these aerial exercises. She was there for the finale. Sometimes she'd act as gunner, but usually she'd simply load the shotgun and hold it until I'd lined up the plane, ready to shoot. The day was clear and sunny as we flew some 200 miles down the Alaska Peninsula. Even though tracking conditions were good, we encountered almost no sign of wolf.

Finally, we picked up the trail of a lone wolf near Sandy River. With practice, tracks are fairly easy to read from the air, especially in winter. It's not hard to distinguish one species' trail from another. Moreover, as a small mound of snow is kicked up ahead of each track, in good light one can determine which way the trail leads. This one wound through willows, over ridges and creek bottoms, then through alders up into the high country. We coursed it almost twenty miles. Finally, we spotted a lone wolf ghosting through the buck-brush toward an open saddle, devoid of cover.

The early spring sun was long and low on the horizon as I timed our approach across the saddle to coincide with the wolf's charge into the open. Raising the upper door panel, we were buffeted by a sixty-mile-an-hour blast of frigid air. Bella handed me the shotgun.

Dropping half flaps, we came in low and slow to the left rear of the wolf's tail. Bucketing desperately through deep snow, the big gray was an easier target than most. I fired. Banking around to check, we saw him, crumpled and still, in the spume of snow kicked up by his final plunge. Pumping down the plane's hydraulic skis, we landed and came to a stop a few yards from the carcass. The wolf was a bone gray, almost white, male. In the rictus of death he'd bitten through his tongue. Save for blood from that wound he appeared unblemished.

In the failing sunset, Bella and I silently looked on what minutes before had been a magnificent symbol of wild, raw freedom. The elation of successful chase was totally absent. It was at that instant I decided it was time to hang up my guns. Bella agreed.

My reasons were both physical and philosophical. Physically, the Alaska Peninsula caribou herd had recovered. From less than 2,000 animals it had risen to well over five times that number. While local residents attributed this to our help in removing more than 250 wolves from the range, I make no such assertion. Perhaps it was in spite of, rather than because of, our efforts.

Philosophically, I had no zest for continuing efforts that no longer seemed necessary. Not long after that disturbing last hunt, I submitted my resignation.

By 1958, I was beginning to lose my stomach for guiding, finding that the hunted were often more noble than the hunter.

12

Alaska Master Guide
Number 009

LEAVING GOVERNMENT SERVICE left me and my family without a pay-check for the first time in seven years.

Steady jobs are not plentiful in rural Alaska. To make ends meet I was obliged to wear many hats.

In the summer, Bella and I fished commercially. I did some charter fly-ing and gave flying lessons. In the spring and fall, I guided hunters and fishermen.

I'd been an assistant guide to Bud Branham during my college years. At that time, one had to reside in Alaska five years, get recommendations from guides and clients for whom you'd worked, and pass both written and practical tests to get a Registered Guide license. Consequently, prior to statehood in 1959, guiding was a proud profession. You received a badge from the Territorial Game Commission and were, in essence, a warden sworn to uphold fish and game laws. Not that there weren't some "bandits" who abused the profession, but most Alaskan territorial guides were excellent woodsmen who held reverence for both the wildlife and the land — a far different breed than many of the renegades who came later.

Unfortunately, that changed with statehood. Out went residency and ex-perience requirements; in flooded hundreds of newcomers, a lot of whom were con artists with no regard for anything but the fast buck.

Suddenly, any drugstore cowboy with a Supercub on big tires could be-come a guide and compete with the most experienced outdoorsman, particularly if he had no conscience. Too many were well qualified in this regard. By fly-ing a few hours in game country, almost anyone could locate a bear, moose or caribou and then land, dive out and shoot. Herding game by air to hunters on the ground became commonplace, along with client horror stories of being bamboozled by some bandit "guide."

Later, Alaska was to flush out most of these bandits and reinstate a five year "experience" requirement not based on an unconstitutional length of residence. A new category of "Master Guide" was established, awarded only to those with fifteen years of guiding experience without a game violation, and with affidavits from other guides and clients attesting to their superior capability and ethics. I began guiding with some sense of pride years ago. Despite these pruning processes and other improvements, the practices of some "guides" are such I'm sometimes ashamed to admit I still hold Master Guide license number 009.

This disenchantment has been compounded by my growing recognition that far too often, the hunted out-noble the hunter. Some hunters lack any reverence at all for wildlife. They distress me with their dedication simply to hang a head on their wall as evidence of some perverse need to prove their manhood. If their quarry fails "to make the book," — Boone and Crockett Club records — they feel their time and money are wasted.

There were, of course, notable exceptions. One was Dr. Richard A.C. Gilbert, my first bowhunting client.

As a Fish and Wildlife agent, I'd advocated legalizing bowhunting in Alaska, though I'd never done any myself. When Dick Gilbert wrote that he'd like to bowhunt brown bear, moose and caribou in a two-week period, I was intrigued but a little skeptical.

The day after Dick and hunting companion Dr. Joe Goldzier arrived we all flew to Chignik Lake. There we unloaded and spent the day readying camp. Though late in the afternoon, Dick wanted to hunt.

"We'll just have to humor him," I told fellow guide Griff Quinton. "I know it's a waste of time. But it's obvious he's going to feel cheated if we don't take him out hunting this evening. Let's walk his butt off and simmer him down."

Starting a brisk pace up the beach, we virtually double-timed to the point of exhaustion. Three hours later, two "rugged" Alaskan guides dragged dejectedly back to camp, well in the wake of our supposedly Cheechako client. The Eastern city-slicker had made us hard-bitten bush rats look like Girl Scouts.

In the morning, a skiff of October snow was falling and ice crusted the water buckets. Undaunted, Dick trekked naked to the lake and plunged in while Griff and I cowered shivering by the stove. After breakfast, Griff and I took Dick to Clark River. Passing through Chignik Village, we stopped for coffee with matriarch Dora Andre and her husband John. The elderly couple were good friends and fine people.

When we left, Dora said if we'd bring her some bear meat, she'd make a roast and have us to dinner.

Dick and Joe were delighted by the invitation. Griff and I were dismayed. We'd tried brown bear and didn't like it. Not only tough and fishy, a skinned brown bear looks much too human. Eating one seems almost cannibalistic.

An hour or so later, hunting along Clark River, we spotted a respectable brown bear feeding on salmon. Picking a vantage point behind a high river bank, we began a stalk to bring us closer to the bear.

When about eighty yards away from our quarry, I was astonished to see Dick send an arrow five feet over the bear. He then ran a few steps forward. At fifty yards, out sailed another shaft that caught the bear in the rump. Squalling, the poor beast dove for the brush. Rather than risk the wounded bear's escape we were forced to shoot it.

"What happened?" I asked peevishly. "I thought we were going to wait until we got within twenty yards before shooting."

Dick was embarrassed. "I don't know what got into me. I guess I thought it was the only shot I'd get. Besides, those guys are so big it looked a lot closer."

We skinned the bear, packed the hide with a ham, and started back to camp. It was a fine trophy bear, but not a bow kill. Still, it exhausted Dick's bear tag.

That evening, Dora's delicious pot roast gave the lie to assertions brown bear fed on salmon are inedible. We all went back for seconds.

I guided Dick Gilbert again a few years later and he took a fine trophy brown bear with a single arrow. The intrepid doctor went on to international fame as one of the few who have actually taken — by arrow only — brown bear, elephant, lion and water buffalo.

ANOTHER HUNTER I GUIDED matched Gilbert's enthusiasm and tenacity. Author Lucy McConnaughy, with her husband Mack, had booked an ambitious two-week hunt. I told them we'd try first for sheep, then bear, then — time permitting — moose and caribou.

We lost the first three days, locked in at my lodge by high winds and foul weather. Finally flying to the sheep hills, we ran into severe turbulence in the mountain passes. Mack announced he was airsick. Solicitously, Lucy handed him her rain parka.

"Take this. Use the hood. We'll wash it later."

Mack grabbed the makeshift barf bag and barely had it in position before jettisoning his breakfast. But rather than the hood, he discharged into the parka's sleeve, the cuff of which led to his lap. For the next twenty minutes, despite open windows and buffeting slip-stream, Lucy and I fought the urge to either join Mack in disgrace or pitch him over the side. After landing, we made camp while poor Mack meekly swabbed out the aircraft.

Early next morning, we climbed to where we spotted a group of six rams. Addressing Mack to one fine trophy and Lucy to another, I advised that they shoot simultaneously. Mack dropped his ram, but Lucy's mortally wounded ram was about to dash over a ridge when I dropped it.

"I sure wish you didn't have to shoot my ram," she said. "I wanted to take it all by myself." Lucy didn't fault me; she was dissatisfied with her performance. "No, I can't claim that as my ram because I didn't actually kill it."

A guide often must finish off wounded animals for clients who conveniently forget this when re-living their hunt. Until Lucy, none of mine had resented it, since I always told them in advance if a wounded animal seems likely to get away, I'd try to finish it.

Mollified not in the least, Lucy told me not to kill her bear for her, "no matter what. I want to do it entirely on my own." I made up my mind to let her.

Unfortunately, it was a commitment I couldn't keep.

Instead, a few days later, after first emptying her rifle, Lucy exhorted me to dispatch a charging wounded bear. I needed no prompting. We leaped aside as the poor beast crashed to the ground between us, shot through the left eye.

Two days later, I was guiding Mack when a bear caught our scent and went for cover. Mack shot once. The bear rolled, then got to its feet and disappeared into the alders. An hour went by with no movement in the brush. Knowing the bear was wounded, I'd hoped by now he'd either expired or at least stiffened up to the point that going into the brush after him would be somewhat less exhilarating.

Suddenly, a patch of grass I'd been watching flickered. I tried to point it out to Mack, but there was no further movement. "If you think you've located him, shoot," Mack suggested. "Maybe you'll shag him out to where I can get a crack at him."

I fired in the general area where the grass had moved. The brush erupted as the bear lunged to its feet, spun around, tore at the alders then dropped, all four legs in the air.

When we examined the carcass, Mack whistled. "Holy cow! Look at this. You shot out the left eye!"

While of such sharpshooting legends may well be born, in my case they simply helped abort whatever blood lust for hunting I may have had. Increasingly, I preferred seeing game on the hoof, not as a horn or hide on the wall. On the other hand, some of the most ardent hunters I know exhibit far more appreciation and reverence for big game — and a willingness to pay for its well-being — than do most of those who oppose hunting.

FISH, OF COURSE, are not considered "big game" by some. But don't try to tell that to the sportsman who travels from Europe, Japan or Chicago to lay a fly on an Alaska wilderness stream to tempt an angry salmon or rainbow from icy water.

Long before I read Norman MacLean's fine book, A River Runs Through It, I too, was "haunted by waters." But for the most part, these are friendly shades which, in my sunset years, conjure up warm reflections. Like that time world-class flycaster Chuck Walton taught me the art of raising huge rainbow by working a black bass bug in fast water.

That late September day must have been programmed by Walt Disney. I'd flown Chuck and his sons into Katmai's Brooks River long after it had been deserted by summer vacationers. Though racing, gin-clear water crackled ice crystals against our waders, a confused autumn sun baked deep heat into our backs as though it were mid-July.

We shared the wild river with only sixteen other fishermen, all Alaska brown bears. By noon, using Chuck's bass bug technique, all of us had hung onto a score or more superb fish; having pinched off the bugs' barbs, these gorgeous fighters were easily released to fight another day.

During the morning, first a cow moose and calf had trotted past us within rod's length. Not long after, we looked up to where on the bank a lynx lay, blasting us with weird laser-green eyes. Rounding the next bend of the river, we spooked a bull moose wearing a rack as big as a king-size recliner.

Stopping for lunch on a sand bar, I noticed some Canada Jay camp-robbers perched in a spruce tree, eyeing us hungrily. They must have been starved, (I could almost detect beaks dripping saliva), for when I held up a bit of sandwich, two flew down posthaste. One perched on my wrist, pecking the bread. The other lighted atop my head awaiting his turn, then took it.

After some minutes of toying with these airborne burglars, we vacated our sand bar to accommodate a huge brown bear shouldering aboard to investigate. Not wishing he should perch on anyone's head, we discretely made our way down river with everything but a fancy, leather-bound coffee thermos, which our sand bar's new owner happily proceeded to shred. As we slunk out of sight around a curve in the river, we caught sight of a family of otter disporting like clowns in a backwater pool. They continued their unstructured games until a wolverine waddled out of the brush to the pond's edge, upon which the otter snorkeled off downstream to less crowded waters.

Silent until now, Chuck shook his head in disbelief. "My God! How long did it take you to rehearse this act? A guy could spend years in the woods without seeing the wildlife we've seen here today."

Though my nonchalance implied such displays were old hat, truth to tell, I'd never seen anything quite like it either. If the good Lord has days like that in store for those who keep the faith, the "saved" should have no complaint.

SOME OF MY MOST MEMORABLE expeditions were undertaken for clients who, armed only with camera and film, wanted merely to see and record Alaska's wildlife. No subject was more prized than brown bear, magnificent brutes in their natural setting. But wading through brush in bear country, whatever the purpose, one should still stay on one's toes. When the brush is too dense, it can lead to unwelcome intimacy.

Todd Sheldon, his boys, Mike and Bill, and I went to photograph bear at Cleo Creek on Becharof Lake. Todd, my close friend and owner of the famed Mepps spin-fishing lures, is an indefatigable outdoorsman. Despite some eleven major operations to replace, modify or reconstruct various arthritic appendages,

Todd made annual pilgrimages to Alaska for many years. Having long ago collected one of each of Alaska's big game trophies, rod-wrenching rainbows and salmon, Todd hunts mostly with camera now. On this rare, warm September morning we were working our way to the upper reaches of Cleo Creek, where bear congregate to feed on red salmon spawning in the shallow water.

"Todd, we've got two choices," I advised. "We can wade directly up the stream bed, or stay out here in the open and take the higher country where we can look down on the stream from above the brush line. But if we stay up high, we're liable to stink up the country and drive the bear off the creek."

"Let's stay up high and out of the brush, regardless," he answered, no more eager than I to endure the clutching fingers of buck brush, thorns and alders.

Our way up the ridge led us a few hundred yards upwind of the stream. Sure enough, our scent soon spooked two bear from the creek's lower reaches. Stopping to mop his brow, Todd reconsidered.

"Guess we should have stuck with the stream bed after all. Let's go back and give it a try."

Eyeing the hundred yards of thick, witch-head alders we'd have to go through to get back, I was not enthralled. Yet I had to agree.

Coming off the hillside we were engulfed immediately in heavy cover. Laboring toward the stream through ever thicker brush, we were forced to crawl. Pushing a .12 gauge shotgun loaded with double-O shot ahead, I wriggled slowly through the tangled undergrowth. Todd followed with his movie camera. Mike brought up the rear. I'd purposely placed two rattling canisters of film inside my shirt to help herald our presence; with the wind at our backs, I wasn't too worried about surprising a bear. I was more concerned they'd all be gone by the time we got to the stream.

On my knees, I reached out with my left hand to raise an alder branch high enough to slide under. Simultaneously, to check a different route, I looked to my right. As I did, I put my left knee on another branch to bend it down.

Suddenly, everything exploded. Alder branches and shotgun bucked up in my face and threw me backward on Todd, who in turn flattened Mike and Bill. Towering high above us was the loudly complaining brown bear I'd kneeled on. Highly indignant at being so rudely wakened from his lunch-time nap, the brute lunged at us once, then lumbered, bawling and scolding, off into the brush.

Had I been more alert and agile, I'd probably have shot when it lunged. Instead, I was entangled with my clients for long moments later. Chalk up another for my old friend serendipity. Had I but wounded the surprised behemoth, hot indignation would have boiled into fury. As it was, he'd been remarkably tolerant of our kicking him out of his bed.

OF THOSE WHO'VE LIVED among brown bear, no one did so with such intimacy as Howie Bass. Howie had a consuming passion to learn everything about these giant omnivores. Forsaking the corporate comforts of his family's shoe-building empire for an old trapping cabin on Becharof Lake, he indulged that passion for several years. With the finest movie-camera equipment, Howie filmed an incredible array of brown bear activities. I have no doubt his film library included more fine bear footage than exists anywhere.

At six-foot-four and two hundred forty pounds, Howie was an imposing figure. Far from being intimidating, he was a gentle giant. With shoulder-length hair and spaced-out smile he was a classic flower child of the 1960s, alienated from society, who'd taken to the wilds to commune with nature.

I got to know Howie pretty well, though often he soared mentally at an altitude for which I'd not been granted clearance. He felt far greater kinship to wild creatures than to humankind.

When I suggested that he forego fondling bear cubs in their mother's presence, he expressed surprise.

"If I should be killed by a bear," Howie explained with an indulgent smile, "I'd not mind at all. I can think of no more noble way to go in total harmony with both Mother Nature and my Karma."

No doubt he meant it. Howie certainly ignored precautions. Firearms repulsed him. In amazement and no small alarm, I once saw him advance with microphone in hand between two battling boars, adroitly ducking flailing claws, to record their primal combat.

Some years later I received a letter from a private investigator requesting information on Howie's disappearance, noting, "As he was last seen near your Becharof Lake camp, perhaps you can provide some information."

I could not. I suspect Howie was dispatched to his reward "in harmony with his Karma" by some accommodating bear.

What happened to Howie's thousands of feet of splendid bear footage? I'm told that the year before he vanished, in a fit of deep depression, he hurled it into the Fairbanks dump.

My souped-up Cessna 170 near "Lake Clark International."
Landings on the narrow, rocky beach can grab one's attention,
especially in a 30-knot crosswind.

13

Bush Piloting

ONE AFTERNOON ON A GRAY October day, we were flying far down the Alaska Peninsula, which thrusts like the chin whiskers of a belligerent Uncle Sam westward toward Asia. Ragged banks of fog and snow squalls clogged the valley leading to the mountain pass I hoped to thread. Thirty-knot gusts from the southeast bucked over the ridges and clawed at my Cessna 185 floatplane. The turbulence bounced us like a mouse batted by a cat. My concentration oscillated from a rock-strewn stream bed fifty feet below, to canyon walls just off my wing tips, to the gray curtain ahead.

Suddenly, from just behind me came a drunken moan followed by frantic thrashing. My fingers sought the comfort of a .44 Magnum revolver stashed under my seat. I glanced at my huge passenger. Mouth frothing, he floundered on the cabin floor. Fixed on me were his evil, red-rimmed eyes — discomforting as twin barrels of a shotgun.

"Please, Lord," I breathed in silent supplication, "please let those ropes hold."

I winged the Cessna around and headed back downstream. The last thing I wanted was to try placing a bullet between those pig-like eyes if my passenger freed himself and attacked. The cabin of a Cessna 185 seems mighty small when a crazed passenger goes berserk. How could I get my aircraft safely out of that troubled sky — and myself unscathed with it? I had agreed to haul my passenger, not kill the both of us.

After he had terrorized a number of people, the authorities had chartered my plane. Although he was sedated, it took several men to truss him in a strait jacket and load him aboard the aircraft.

"You have at least two hours before he recovers," the arresting officers declared. Since my destination was less than two hundred miles away and the floatplane cruised at 125 miles per hour, it appeared I had ample time. But I was unaware of bad weather sneaking into my flight path. After an uneventful hour and a half, fog, snow squalls, and scud had enveloped us, forcing a change in course. And now, my passenger had aroused from his stupor.

While his bonds were strong enough so long as he was tranquilized, I doubted they would hold once he fully recovered, and I did not care to find out. Locating a suitable lake, I landed and taxied toward the beach. Once aground, revolver in hand, I leaped out and slogged around to the passenger door. Though his protests were increasing, I was able to cut some of his lashings. I grabbed his legs and hauled his bulk through the aircraft door. He flopped onto the floats like a sack of potatoes, then rolled into the water.

Reluctantly rejecting an inclination to let him slip beneath the surface, I grabbed a handful of hair, held his head above the water, and cut the remaining bindings of his canvas strait jacket. When he recovered enough to keep his head above water, I backed off and waited while he hauled his 600-pound carcass to shore. With tooth-popping coughs, my passenger — an Alaskan brown bear — wobbled up the beach and out of sight into the alders.

During the more than forty years I've flown in Alaska, my passenger list has included momentarily expectant mothers (fly low; high altitude brings on labor), freshly apprehended murderers, live beluga whales, seals, wolves, wolverine, coyotes, caribou calves, moose, swans, and bears. I have also flown people who have been injured or frostbitten, or those whose bodies had been frozen solid, as well as other unfortunates who had died from heart attacks, drownings, or other terminal events. An assortment of unhappy endings seems to lie in wait for the ill-prepared, unfit, or imprudent who venture into Alaska's remote bush.

Of all my various passengers, few have conducted themselves better than the several tranquilized brown bears I have hauled. One exception involved the redecoration of my aircraft's interior by a young bear suffering from a gastrointestinal disturbance. It seemed he had recently consumed a cathartic concoction of vegetation used by brown bears to purge their systems after hibernation.

Although I've flown over virtually all of Alaska's bush country since 1946, I am reluctant to call myself a true bush pilot. That term belongs to those helmeted, white-scarfed stalwarts who, prior to World War II, had pioneered air service into those remote areas where no pilots previously ventured. Flying strictly by the seat of their pants, they braved frightening experiences unknown to many who flew in their wake.

Their Bellancas, Travelaires, Sikorskis, Wacos, Stinsons and Fokkers were patched together in ways that violated all of the known rules of aerodynamics. Yet, like a bumble bee ignorant of the laws of physics that say it cannot fly, they flew. In threading their way across the vastness of Alaska, they cross-stitched together remote villages and brought them in contact with the twentieth century.

Navigation aids such as radio beacons were absent. Instruments were sometimes as primitive — and useless — as a string stretched between two windshield braces, serving as an "artificial horizon" to one old-timer. But he said it made his passengers feel better when he told them its purpose while flying in white-outs. "I.F.R." in those days stood not for "Instrument Flight Rules," as it does today, but for "I Follow Rivers," a system that anyone who flies much in Alaska must learn, despite today's array of navigation aids.

The classic description of manned flight as "hours and hours of boredom interrupted by moments of stark terror" evolved long after the first true bush pilots ventured into the North. Before then, by all accounts, "stark terror" clearly predominated. Engine and structural failures were common. Most flights were far from routine with no airway charts, no radio beacons, no runway lights. For that matter, there were few runways. Most villages, mining camps, or traplines required pilots to set down on gravel bars, mud flats, ridge tops or beaches. A ballpark served as an airstrip for the bustling city of three thousand called Anchorage. In the winter, ski-equipped aircraft offered comparative safety and wide use — frozen waterways for landings were found almost everywhere. Floats, of course, granted similar advantages in the open-water season.

Though off-field landings were common, not *all* were planned. Thirteen of mine were due to engine failures. Mercifully, most of these were little more than humorous or humbling.

Perhaps the most humbling occurred on a flight with fellow government hunter Joe Miner. We were flying an old pre-World War II Piper J5C known as the Gray Ghost to Nome from Kotzebue.

It was a glorious spring day when we started. We'd shucked our skis for wheels since most snow was gone. Joe had been at the control for some time when he suggested we land on a sand bar to "de-coffee."

"Why don't you take it the rest of the way into Nome?" Joe suggested.

Switching places, we lumbered off the sand and continued toward Nome — failing to notice I'd left my old friend serendipity on the ground.

Within minutes the ceiling lowered and the engine began to act up. A stiff wind bounced scud through the foothills, cutting visibility to a few miles. Meanwhile, the steady washing-machine whir of the Ghost's power plant changed to a tortured howl, interrupted by frequent hiccups.

Suddenly the engine quit. Heading into the growing gale, I searched in vain for a landing site, frantically goosing the fuel primer to restart the engine. Not more than 20 feet from the ground, the Ghost belched a few times and once more began to growl. Climbing a few hundred feet, we'd begun to relax when the process repeated itself.

And so it went. Full carburetor heat did not help. Only by pumping the primer could we bring the Ghost back to momentary life. By now we were over the lip of Imorak Basin, yo-yo-ing up and down on our way toward Teller, a small village north of Nome.

"If only she'll hang in another five minutes," I thought, "we can make it."

The thought no sooner entered my mind than it was purged by one final retching gasp of the engine.

With only two hundred feet between us and the seething mass of broken ice cakes below, leisurely selection of landing sites was foreclosed. Off to the left, amid the white rubble, a small "island" of gray protruded. Less than a hundred feet long, the gravel ridge was strewn with boulders. Kiting down in the thirty-knot wind, the Ghost settled on the rock heap like a helicopter. It rolled a few feet, and, as Joe and I sighed in relief, gently went up on her nose, slightly bending the prop.

We threw a line around the tail wheel, pulled her down to a more dignified posture, and, heaping rocks on our snowshoes, secured the aircraft to these make-shift tie-downs. After walking five miles across the rough ice into Teller, we radioed for a small plane to fly us to Nome. From there, we caught a commercial flight to Anchorage.

Two weeks later I went back with a mechanic and a new prop. I hadn't bragged about the spectacular job I'd done bringing the Ghost down on a postage stamp, but with some shameless pride I anticipated the mechanic's awe when he discovered my remarkable feat.

He expressed awe, all right. The ice had melted and there sat the Ghost perched on a hundred foot heap of rocky rubble. Alongside lay five miles of beautiful, ice-free, hard-packed sand beach. What had seemed at the time a superb accomplishment — admittedly made possible only by near gale force wind — now looked like a stupid mistake. My explanation did little to boost my stock with the mechanic, especially when he had to replace not just a prop, but the entire engine, whose crankshaft had bent when the Ghost had "genuflected."

Most of my mishaps bruised my pride more than myself or my aircraft. Too many of these "adventures" involved pilot error — though I much prefer the more dignified term, "calculated risk."

MOST ALASKANS ACCEPT FLYING in small planes as a way of life. Unfortunately, it too often proves a way of death, as well. Few Alaskans haven't known someone killed in a plane crash. Most fatalities result from pilots trying to buck weather. The problem with bucking weather, of course, is that bad weather bucks back. Such accidents seem to increase during hunting season, when persons who fly rarely the rest of the year try to play weekend bush pilot.

Like the rest of Alaska, the skies are more crowded than they used to be. Alaska now boasts the busiest float plane lake and the highest number of private pilots per capita in the country. Still, flying through a snow-dappled mountain pass escorted by a full moon or spotting a herd of caribou thundering below is as magical as ever. I think of the flying pioneers I was privileged to know — Sig and Noel Wien, Bob Reeve, Mudhole Smith, Archie Ferguson, Sam White and Ray Peterson — and I count myself lucky to follow in their flight paths.

Bella and the girls at our first cabin at Lake Clark. This picture was taken in 1959, the year Alaska became a state.

14

Statehood & Sciatica

BY THE LATE 1950s, the cumulative effects of plane crashes, trail mishaps and other forms of abuse had me spending almost as much time on my back as in the bush. In the last half of the decade, I was hospitalized five times — almost totally incapacitated for periods averaging nine weeks.

These began after I'd broken both ankles in the King Cove accident. The fusion of one ankle joint caused a slight starboard list which, in turn, aggravated old back problems. Though I always had several days' warning, when the first spasm hit, I was unable to stand and almost helpless. A dull cleaver clubbed at the small of my back while hot rockets of agony screamed down the sciatic nerve of my right leg. Had my life depended on rising, I could not have done so.

For five years these episodes followed a pattern. I'd be fine for a few weeks. Then it would start all over again: First, sciatica, then a sledgehammer of pain would drop me in my tracks and I'd be back in the hospital for several weeks.

This presented real problems. Since my activities as a guide, pilot and commercial fisherman took me to remote areas, it seemed clear I could no longer safely function alone. Once, while visiting my cousin Blanche at her Schuylerville, New York, home, pain dropped me to her living room floor. In an attempt to move me to a bedroom, something sawed through a nerve ending and partially paralyzed my right leg. After they simply shoved an air mattress beneath me, I spent the next ten days in a sleeping bag, sandwiched between a divan and a grand piano, contemplating my fate if this had occurred in the bush.

Theories on back treatment had changed dramatically over the years. This had done little to bolster my confidence in the medical profession's omniscience. Initially, treatment consisted of total bed rest, traction, and heat application.

Because traction always seemed to aggravate my condition, spinal fusion was suggested, then rejected in favor of outfitting me with a full back brace. This contrivance was not only bulky, it seemed to have no beneficial effect. Worse, the metal brace wore out the seats of my pants. Doctors concluded I should have the fusion after all, and one morning I was rolled onto a gurney, given a shot of dope, and wheeled to surgery.

There, however, two orthopedic surgeons debated over my carcass. One ready to cut and fuse; the other felt my back problems resulted from old injuries that triggered muscle spasms. These, in turn, he felt, put pressure on spinal nerves causing pain and paralysis. Once injured, the nerves took several weeks to recuperate.

"Back operations don't always do the job," he told me. "Maybe we can put you on an exercise program to tone the muscles and prevent spasms. If it doesn't work, we can do a spinal fusion."

Happy for reprieve from the knife, I was rolled back to my ward to begin this new exercise program.

The next morning, shortly after breakfast, a strange, unkempt little man bounced into our "back ward," gleefully announcing he was the new physiotherapist who'd soon have us malingerers leaping from our hospital beds, if only to escape his tender ministrations. His bloated cigar-butt body stuffed into straining, stained hospital whites did little to identify him as a therapist. Watery, pale blue eyes, one of which was cocked forty-five degrees from the other, did even less to convey professional competence. My suspicion that he was simply a bull cook who'd wandered in from the mess hall during coffee break soon gave way to the certainty that he'd escaped from the psycho ward two flights above.

Coming to my bed, he grasped my right ankle in one hand and placed the other on my kneecap.

"Surely he's not about to do what I fear he might do," I thought in panic.

To those who've experienced *sciatica extremus*, the mere suggestion of lifting the afflicted leg an inch off the bed brings on paroxysms of agony. Yet, leering gleefully into my eyes, he chortled, "Okay, Sonny, smile!" and jerked my leg upward.

I did my best to transform the resultant girlish scream into something a bit more masculine. I failed. Repeatedly, the "Sorcerer's Apprentice," as he soon became known, pumped my rigid leg upward, simultaneously pumping from me a glissando of shrieking protests. After twelve repetitions, during which I frantically struggled to reach a bedpan with which to bash my tormentor, he suddenly stopped.

Tenderly replacing my abused limb under the covers, he grinned, "Come on, 'fess up, Sonny. You feel lots better now, don't you?" Incredibly, I did.

There followed a daily exercise regimen totally at odds with any previous treatment I'd heard of before. No more traction. Alcohol rubs instead of heat. Muscle relaxant pills. Stretching and strengthening exercises five times a day. From the outset I registered daily improvement. Each morning I could raise my right leg an additional inch or so. When able to point it straight to the ceiling, all pain had gone.

Whether more Marquis de Sade than Mother Teresa, I owe an enormous debt to the Sorcerer's Apprentice for his exercise program. He spared me the knife, returned me to my normal activities, and rid me of that ponderous back brace and the potential disgrace of inadvertently "mooning" through the shredded seats of my trousers. I was soon able to resume guiding as well as fishing commercially for salmon on a wooden Bryant thirty-two-foot drift gillnetter I owned with a remarkable little fellow named Jimmy Drew.

Jimmy was not just a top flight mentor and partner, he was a good friend. Having fished for several years on the old double-ender sailboats to which Bristol Bay drift fishermen were confined before 1952, Jimmy knew the treacherous sands, tides, flats, and shallows of Bristol Bay as well as he knew the fine table set by his wife, Bertha. Jimmy was as generous imparting his knowledge to a Cheechako fisherman as Bertha was in setting another place for this frequently unannounced guest. The Drew household was ever joyous and bustling; their hospitality without reservation. I've been privileged to invade the former and abuse the latter for almost forty years, and still they make me feel welcome.

Jimmy and Bertha were born on the shores of Iliamna, Alaska's largest lake. Their mothers were Native women; their fathers respectively, Scotch-Irish and Scandinavian. Of Jimmy's seventeen brothers and sisters, only nine lived to adulthood. Several were claimed by the stormy waters of 95-mile long Iliamna or other coastal dangers of Bristol Bay. Survival meant learning those waters well.

Jimmy and I were among the last Naknek residents to take advantage of the federal government's Homesite Program. Prior to statehood, five acres of land could be claimed and secured for a small filing fee and survey cost, if one built a habitable dwelling. The Hammonds and the Drews did so next door to each other.

Naknek had no public utilities of any kind back then, so Jimmy and I bought an old five-kilowatt Witte electrical generator. An artifact when we got it, we nursed it for several more years to provide power to our own and three other households. It was far from adequate; we made frequent frantic rushes to the generator shed, racing to pull the switch before everyone's circuits blew. Despite this, the old Witte served us pretty well, graciously delaying its final death throes until Naknek's first power plant came on line — almost. One evening about the time Alaska became the forty-ninth state, the Witte disemboweled itself in total exhaustion and sent a piston cannonading through the side of the shed.

WHEN ASKED TO DESCRIBE NAKNEK, I used to tell folk it was a small, treeless, wind-swept Bering Sea fishing community of about 300 souls: a great place to live, but I wouldn't want to visit there. Redeeming social virtues were far less abundant than the tens of millions of red salmon returning annually to spawn in its watershed. This, the world's largest sockeye run, attracted multitudes of fishermen to cash in on the harvest and take their pay elsewhere. Despite extractions of billions in resource wealth from adjacent waters, most villagers lived in small shacks with no plumbing. Garbage was hauled over the river banks in hopes it would flush out, come spring.

In short, Naknek was a prime example of the same "rip-off-and-run" affliction debilitating most Alaskan coastal communities — great resource wealth but little means to manage it for local benefit. As a consequence, "outsiders" were not enthusiastically welcomed. "Statehood" was seen by many as the answer to many problems.

One of the most persuasive arguments for statehood was that we could gain control over our fish and game resources. Alaskan fishermen had long felt abused and dominated by federal fishery management and its excessive accommodations to absentee processors and fishermen. Certainly, as an employee of the federal Fish and Wildlife Service, I'd witnessed management decisions that led to these conclusions. Fishing period openings and closures were often dictated by canneries' processing capabilities, rather than for sound biological considerations. More than once, valid decisions made by local Fish and Wildlife personnel to close river systems because of inadequate escapement to spawning grounds were overturned from Washington under pressure from the "Salmon Industry."

Of course, fisheries and wildlife were not the only natural resources Alaskans wished to control. Extensive mineral deposits, timber and oil were all seen as potential means of supporting a state government.

Yet too often, self-serving arguments used by some statehood proponents seemed contrary to fact. Justifying means to their ends were the trade for many running for office. This did little to attract me to politics.

Prior to 1959, however, it was unthinkable for a political aspirant not to advocate statehood. Having no such ambitions, I had no qualms voicing my opposition. Not that I opposed statehood idealistically. After all, taxation without representation was as valid a complaint in 1959 as it had been in 1776. What troubled me was there seemed too many slurred-over questions and unexplored alternatives to statehood, and those most ardently advocating the idea often seemed would-be political plum-pickers aspiring to elective office.

Some of us believed commonwealth status, such as Puerto Rico's, might avoid imposition of federal income taxes and yet achieve a greater degree of self-government. But little reasoned debate was allowed. Anyone daring even to question statehood was branded either a "pinko," a paranoid or, to some Alaskans the most scathing of all charges, an "environmental preservationist."

Excuse me, but when most politicians line up on the same side of an issue and militantly rail against those expressing alternatives, I grow suspicious. The role of devil's advocate becomes irresistible. It compels me to pry up rocks and to open closed minds to examine the pallid creatures that scurry from light. So it was with statehood. With our tiny population, minimal tax base and heavy dependence on federal spending, I questioned Alaska's ability to finance and administer statehood.

"Why, with our small population, virtually any idiot who aspires to public office is likely to get elected," I asserted imprudently.

There are those who insist I subsequently proved this point, on several occasions.

Part Two
Striking the Match

Clem Tillion explains my decision to grow a beard as an effort to hide a hideous birth defect — my face. This was taken during my early years in the legislature.

15

Reluctant Candidate: 1959

I LAUGHED IN UTTER DISBELIEF when Naknek school teachers Mark and Harry Davidson suggested I run for the first Alaska State Legislature.

"Hey," they argued, "Denny Moore's the only one who's filed. He doesn't have a ghost of a chance. He's controversial to begin with, and he's declaring as a Republican. Someone's going to file as a Democrat and win hands down. You ought to do it."

"Humpf!" I snorted. "I don't want anything whatsoever to do with the rascals in politics, and I can't imagine anything worse than spending the winter forced to listen to a bunch of politicians pontificate. Besides, I voted against statehood. Forget it."

Mark and Harry were back a few days later. "Jay, you've got to reconsider. Some carpetbagger went into Anchorage, got the Democratic party's blessing and filed for our House seat. He's new here, with no idea what our problems are except what he hears in the bars. Please reconsider."

I said I not only had no desire to run, but coming from Vermont and a long line of Republicans, I'd dare not defile the family escutcheon by defecting to the Democrats.

Mark and Harry wouldn't give up. "Well, it's a cinch a Republican can't win in Bristol Bay. File as an Independent. All you have to do is get a petition signed by a certain percentage of voters."

I restated past protests and dredged up new ones. Still, they hammered away. "You'll never forgive yourself if some idiot goes to Juneau by your default. Besides, here's a chance to do something about all those things you complain about. At least consider running as an Independent."

To get them off my back, I said I'd *consider*, but only if they wanted to go to the trouble of passing around a petition. *I* certainly wasn't going to do it. Enthusiasm apparently dampened, they left. Pleased with having wormed out from under the guilt they'd tried to lay on me, I felt the matter closed.

Two days later Harry and Mark were back waving a lengthy list of signatures in my face.

"Okay, we've done our part; let's go sign you up. You promised."

"Hey, I only said I'd *consider* it; not that I'd actually *run!*"

But the Davidsons were not dissuaded. Obviously, they'd translated "consider" into "commit." Having gotten more than enough signatures — no doubt telling each signer I'd promised to run — they acted as though I'd broken my word. Maybe they also knew I was a sucker for such posturing. More than once I've gritted my teeth and gone spinelessly along when someone convinced me they believed I'd made a commitment, even when I knew I hadn't. Being a very slow learner, it was several years before I learned to avoid such traps.

"Okay, okay, okay. I'll file even though I never said I would. But don't expect me to campaign. That's where I draw the line. Running around flashing the incisors and pestering people to convince them what a fine fellow you are, is not my idea of acceptable public conduct. It ought to be outlawed."

Bella was dismayed, too. I assured her we had nothing to worry about. Not only would I not campaign, but by then, a respectable Native candidate from the far larger village of Dillingham had filed to run as a Democrat. The likelihood of a non-party white man from tiny Naknek defeating a lifelong Dillingham Democrat, seemed to pose little hazard. I went blithely about my business. On Election Day, bad weather prevented my flying home to vote.

Though I deem the right to vote sacred, demanding one do so in ignorance strikes me as profane. We should be at least somewhat informed on candidates and issues. For those who are not, far better counsel would be to stay home. Voters are too often confronted by candidates as indistinguishable as blackbirds on a fence, though some may change plumage during campaigns. Hopefully, at least one will metamorphose into a sparrow hawk if not a soaring eagle. Should that not occur, however, voters should be given the means to shoot down the biggest turkey. Why not permit us to cast negative votes to subtract from that candidate's total?

———————————

TO MY DISBELIEF, the people of Bristol Bay apparently were more disgruntled with my opponents than me. They elected me to Alaska's first state legislature. Typical of communications back then, I didn't even know it until weeks after the early November election. Results weren't in until after Thanksgiving.

In January 1960, neither Bella nor I was enthusiastic about pulling up stakes, taking the girls from school and leaving for Juneau. Once involved in the legislative process, however, I found it intriguing. Being the first year of statehood, Alaska's entire government mechanism had to be pieced together and given a trial run.

To my surprise, most legislators didn't fit my previous perceptions of politicians. Perhaps inspired by the historic significance of molding a brand new state, most seemed unusually dedicated, idealistic and disconcertingly honest — if somewhat naive. As Eugene McCarthy once observed of successful politicians, "Most have to be smart enough to get elected and dumb enough to believe they can make a difference." No doubt, the greatest opportunity to make that difference was granted those of us privileged to serve in that first legislature.

Since our pay was only $2,500 a year, plus $40 a day for expenses, most of us couldn't afford to sit long in session. We had to get home to make a living. In those early years, we hit the ground running when our planes landed in the nation's only state capital not connected by road to any other city in the state. We worked weekends, holidays and evenings. Having no secretarial help nor staff, we did all our own research and wrote all our own bills and correspondence. Some of us sent newsletters to constituents, paying postage from our very small salaries.

Years later I reflected that the only legislative session of the twelve I attended that truly warranted more than ninety days was the first, when we set up the entire state government. And we did that in but eighty-seven days. As revenues and salaries increased, Parkinson's Law prevailed and work expanded geometrically. During the first thirty days of subsequent legislatures, there seemed no sense of urgency. Life in Juneau collecting tax free *per diem* beat hauling wood and water back in the village, or trying to make it through the winter on last summer's pay day.

In Alaska, nothing so boils the bile of the news media, and subsequently the public, as the perception of lawmakers frittering away time in extended session. At each election, challengers scourge incumbents with "do nothing" charges, vowing, if elected, to change all that. Many tried, including myself. Since critics presumed we remained overtime just to multiply our *per diem* checks, I once successfully proposed we limit *per diem* payments to but ninety days. My measure passed.

On the ninety-first day we repealed it.

I pondered other approaches, my purpose not solely selfless. I was impacted financially when ever-longer legislative sessions eroded my spring guiding business. Another time, I introduced a bill that would eliminate *per diem* entirely, but add the equivalent of ninety days *per diem* to legislators' salaries. If we exceeded ninety days, additional costs would come out of our pockets; if we adjourned in less than ninety days, legislators would pocket a minor windfall. This wasn't merely a healthy incentive to expedite business; how refreshing it would be to have the media castigate us instead for spending too little time in session! I couldn't even get that bill out of committee.

I soon learned that within this committee system lay the major problem. Almost every year, extra weeks of time and millions of dollars are expended because of arbitrary powers granted committee chairmen. It goes like this: a crucial piece of legislation falls into a committee chairman's clutches to become trading stock, moldering in his locker until whatever legislation the chairman covets is enacted. This happens time and time again. I recall one instance where six weeks and several million dollars were squandered before an obstinate committee chairman, an attorney, by holding a critical bill hostage, forced the passage of one piece of special interest legislation designed to bail out one of his clients.

In theory, a simple majority can vote bills out of a chairman's grasp, but it's almost never done. Fear of retribution prevents it. Those who dare defy the "sanctity of the committee system" — as it is piously termed by those most expert in abusing it — find themselves stripped of powers and their own pet legislation buried.

In the U.S. Congress and in state legislatures across the land, awesome powers of committee chairmen often lead to abuse and confusion. A favorite ploy of minority members, for example, is to "move" to bring a bill out of committee, knowing majority members will vote "no." The minority's intent, of course, is simply to embarrass majority members by forcing them to vote against the *motion*, so they can later use the "Nay" vote to tell voters majority members voted against the *bill*. Come election time, they'll trot out a list of measures their adversaries voted not to extract from committee to demonstrate they, unlike their opponents, have no such callous disregard for widows, orphans, students, veterans, minorities and the down-trodden.

Not only totally phony, the process confuses the public about where those who voted against extraction really stand on the issue.

To frustrate this public disservice, I once naively proposed a "secret ballot" be allowed on motions to extract bills. This intrigued freshman legislators, but horrified old hands who held committee chairs.

Without a process to allow or compel all members to vote their conscience, public presumption that "one man, one vote" provides equal representation is ludicrous. Unless your legislator holds a committee chair, you're being short-changed. In the Alaska Legislature I've frequently seen a lone, obstreperous chairman frustrate the will of every other lawmaker, as well as the governor.

Wherever this system is in place, including Congress, a more equitable division of power among legislators is long overdue. I still believe the best way to achieve this would be to allow a secret vote on motions to bring bills to the floor. Nothing more effective could be done to cut excessive session length, ballooning blood-money budgets designed to buy off arbitrary chairmen, and the public deception that now prevails. Don't hold your breath for this to happen, however. If there's anything we politicians find distressing, it's to have our inconsistencies consistently flaunted. I must admit I happily took advantage of the system myself, on occasion. Of course, I first had to be re-elected.

TWO THINGS HAPPENED in my first term that perhaps influenced my political career more than any others. The first was assignment to the House Natural

1st Alaska State Legislature
1959
House Of Representatives
Warren A. Taylor, Speaker

Robert R. Blodgett (D) Teller
Frank E. Cashel (D) Sitka
Francis X. Chapados (D) Fairbanks
John E. Curtis (R) Kotzebue
Peter M. Deveau (D) Kodiak
William M. Erwin (D) Seward
Charles E. Fagerstrom (D) Nome
Helen A. Fischer (D) Anchorage
James E. Fisher (D) Anchorage
Charles J. Franz (D) Port Moller

Oral E. Freeman (D) Ketchikan
Robert Glersdorf (D) Fairbanks
Douglas Gray (D) Douglas
Richard J. Greuel (D) Fairbanks
Henry L. Haag (D) Kodiak
Jay S. Hammond (U) Naknek
Harold Z. Hansen (U) Cordova
Donald Harris (R) McGrath
John S. Hellenthal (D) Anchorage
Earl D. Hillstrand (D) Anchorage

James Hoffman (R) Bethel
Andrew Hope (D) Sitka
James J. Hurley (D) Palmer
Axel C. Johnson (D) Kwigok
Charles M. Jones (D) Craig
Peter J. Kalamarides (D) Anchorage
Bruce Kendall (R) Valdez
John E. Longworth (R) Petersburg
R. S. McCombe (D) Chicken
Russ E. Meekins (D) Anchorage

James E. Norene (D) Anchorage
John Nusunginya (D) Barrow
Grant H. Pearson (D) McKinley Pa
Allan L. Petersen (D) Kenai
John L. Rader (D) Anchorage
Morgan W. Reed (D) Skagway
J. Ray Roady (D) Ketchikan
Robert E. Sheldon (D) Fairbanks
Dora M. Sweeney (D) Juneau
Warren A. Taylor (D) Fairbanks

Esther Reed—Chief Clerk

Mary Nordale—Assistant Clerk

Peggy Benesch—Assistant Clerk

The 1st Alaska State Legislature, House of Representatives, 1959. I'm third from the left in the third row (wearing a tie!)

Resources Committee. This was not merely where I felt most qualified, the committee was chaired by Democrat Andrew Hope of Sitka, an elderly Tlingit Indian who, in some respects, seemed a vest pocket version of my father.

Andy, who had been in the territorial legislature, assigned to me increasing powers and duties normally reserved for the chairman. This was heady stuff, since it enabled a great deal more "moving and shaking" than normally accorded a freshman lawmaker. Of course, as an Independent, I could never hope to assume a chairmanship. This was reserved for members of the dominant party.

This, plus the fact the state election code was amended in 1961 to make it extremely difficult to run as an Independent, reluctantly compelled me to abandon my Independent status. As one of only two Independents in the House, I received a certain amount of wooing from both sides of the aisle. Democrats made the better case.

"Look, you seem to be reasonably bright fellow. You have almost no chance winning as a Republican in your rural district. Why not file as a Democrat?"

I was tempted. Frankly, legislative service had blurred my perception of partisan distinctions. Without a score card you wouldn't know who was what. A magic "D" affixed to my name on the ballot would surely enhance my chances. Yet, at one time I'd been conditioned to believe most Democrats were wastrels, n'er-do-wells or crooks. My years in Bristol Bay had done little to change my mind. After all, virtually every wastrel, n'er-do-well and crook I'd encountered there was a Democrat. It took much more time than it should have to realize this only seemed to be the case because, back then, there were almost no Republicans there.

But because my accursed blue-nosed New England conscience would not let me enlist as a Democrat merely to facilitate re-election, I filed as a Republican. To my surprise, I was re-elected. Since I did virtually no campaigning and sent no flyers announcing my Republican enrollment, perhaps my mostly Democratic constituents were not aware of my apostasy.

After more than twenty years in politics, I'd say most office holders, regardless of party, are less despicable opportunists than they are idealists who foolishly believe they can make a difference. That so few do is as much a fault of the system as it is self-delusion.

One who did make a difference in Alaska was Clem Tillion. Given the flowering self-importance seeded in too many politicians, I was intrigued on returning to the House in 1962, to find a brash iconoclast had clod-hopped into our midst, trampling verdant egos en route. When I heard of Clem, a commercial fisherman like myself, I looked forward to meeting him. To my surprise, I found I already had, during the 1940s in Fairbanks, where we, like many families, had our drinking water delivered by truck.

Lo and behold, the new legislator from Homer turned out to have been our water truck "Gunga Din." Some fifteen years and fifty pounds had been added, but there was no mistaking him.

Though Clem says recollection of my first glimpse of him on the House floor is fancifully over-blown, it remains firmly fixed and I'll not let facts erase it. His shock of red, Woody Woodpecker hair, barely contained by an old derby hat, had the luster and texture of Brillo. In a 1930s belted, Glen-plaid suit of his father's burnished to an almost metallic patina, he looked like something from "Guys and Dolls" sired by "The Great Gatsby." Other witnesses present that morning perhaps remember best his prehensile-toed feet perched atop his desk, flexing in happy, unfettered abandon. Clem later explained that only when unshod could he think freely.

This once caused caustic Rep. Wendell Kay, an Anchorage attorney, to castigate Clem for lack of shoes and failure to stand when addressing the Chair. Kay suggested the location of Clem's brain prevented it from functioning properly when constrained by standing in shoe leather. Tillion's laconic reply, delivered through the unmuted bronze bullhorn that passed for his voice, accepted Kay's theory.

"Brain location is indeed a primary consideration; to function fully one's gray matter must not be subjected to undue pressure. This, of course," Clem guffawed, "is why barristers *must stand* when they speak."

Clem worked at cultivating the image of a simple rustic. With ample arable ground to work with, he played the role of country bumpkin to perfection, up to a point. That point arrived when some city slicker, smugly assuming he'd outmaneuvered a yokel, had Clem, with a chortling bray, hand the slicker his severed head.

"RepTillion" became one of Alaska's most accomplished leaders. In the process, he provided the comic relief necessary for some of us to endure what he termed "The Puzzle Palace."

Of course, other early House members helped provide that comic relief, sometimes inadvertently. Bob Blodgett from Teller often played a leading role. Known as "the Heller from Teller," Blodgett was given to lengthy, malapropic debate on any subject. He'd have his say, then sit down, cock his feet on his desk, and bury his head in a newspaper to convey total disdain for any rebuttal. To counter Blodgett's rude arrogance, I rose one day to berate one of his pet projects. As I sat down, Blodgett predictably jumped to his feet, spluttering in protest. At that moment, by pre-arrangement, all other thirty-nine members, including the Speaker and even demure little old Dora Sweeney, threw their feet on their desks, unfurled newspapers and began to read. Blodgett wound down like a hand-cranked Victrola. But not for long.

Blustering again a few days later, Blodgett threatened to fast until a pet bill was passed. Tillion, with a toothy grin radiating all the winsome benevolence of a rutting barracuda, simply asked, "Promise?"

Challenged, Blodgett was true to his word, up to a point. He began his fast but curiously seemed to lose little weight. "Before" and "After" news photos showing him standing on scales clad in naught but his drawers, were revealing. In the former, an aggressive paunch is most evident. In the latter, however, the strain of sucking his gut in has caused his fingers to flex. From an unfortunate camera angle, what is no doubt the thumb of his off hand, appears to emerge from his Fruit of the Looms. The effect is alarmingly unstatesmanlike, especially in a family newspaper!

With entirely too many legislators perfectly willing to watch him waste away, Blodgett did the predictable. One day he collapsed on the House floor and was rushed to the hospital. There, doctors found nothing wrong, and over his violent protests, discharged him. On his unwilling return to chambers, he immediately demanded the floor to berate his tormentors.

Whereupon he received the following "Owed to Bob Blodgett."

> *"What in the world was that rude noise I just heard?*
> *Was it Blodgett muttering 'foul'?"*
> *I fear his impassioned words were drowned out*
> *By a heart-rending stomach growl."*

EARLY IN MY LEGISLATIVE YEARS I discovered that most politicians are inclined to take ourselves much too seriously, a posturing that prompted me to prick pomposities, mine included, when things got too tense. The sharpest bodkin, I found, was rude verse. It could jab without incurring excessive pain or outrage. I found I could say things in rhyme that would not be tolerated if said straight out. Usually the "subject" would join in the laughter, and only later detect the bloodstain on his ego.

As it was, Tillion inspired more of my rude verse than anyone. Some of this threatened our friendship, which got off to a shaky start his first month in the House. All votes back then were verbal roll calls recorded by the clerk. I've long forgotten the matter before us, but the vote is very clear in my mind:

"Devaugh?" — "Aye"
"Hammond?" — "Aye"
"Kendall?" — "Aye"
"Rader?" — "Aye"
"Sweeney?" — "Aye"
"Tillion?"... Silence. Again, louder:
"TILLION?" No response.
"MISTER TILLION!"
"Uhh? Here!"

"No, Mr. Tillion," the Speaker scathed, "we're voting on House Bill Fifty-six, not recording who's present. You've already established your *absence*. Now let's have your *vote*."

After the roll call, I asked for the floor to make an observation in my first "Owed to Clem Tillion."

"Mr. Tillion, please answer when your name is called.
Could it be that you're sleeping? Or simply enthralled
With the summer attire of those bits of fluff
Who stroll by the window while you sit on your duff
Making laws often dealing with public decorum.
Despite knowing full well you intend to ignore 'em?"

At recess, Clem groaned, "Did you have to do that the very first time I had a hometown constituent in the gallery?"

Despite such abuse, somehow, we managed to strengthen our friendship over the years, each remaining the other's firm supporter in the frequent occasions such was required. Like the time I was campaigning in Cordova. After a luncheon speech, I mingled with guests. Suddenly, my arm was grasped by a large, florid gentleman who spluttered: "You should do something about your friend Tillion. I'm the local mortician and some of the things that man says about my profession are libelous. Why, do you know," his indignation rising along with his color, "he even referred to us as *prostitutes*!

"Oh," I said to appease him, "I wouldn't get too upset over that. Now had Clem equated you with *attorneys*, for whom he has real contempt, you'd have a right to be affronted. By contrast, you have no idea in what high regard Clem may hold prostitutes."

Clem seems quite content to pretend such a general lack of social graces. In social situations, however, those graces are more than provided by his remarkably charming and understanding wife, Diana, a successful artist at both easel and cookstove. That our trail and the Tillions' so infrequently cross, is one of my greatest laments in leaving politics.

As usual, I'm the one without a tie. Over the feigned protests of "RepTillion" (far left) and me, the House Resource Committee gleefully voted my rewrite of a controversial bill out of committee — fulfilling my hope that they would not bother to read it.

16

Lies, Dam Lies and Politics

CAMPAIGNING AS A REPUBLICAN in the early days of statehood was especially challenging in rural Alaska, where registered Democrats out-numbered Republicans about six to one. If elected, it was in spite of being Republican, never because of it.

Even so, the overwhelming majority of Democrats in the legislature were embarrassed when a few Democrat-dominated bush districts sent an occasional Republican to Juneau. To fix this, they created for the 1961 Election what we, the offended, termed "The Idiot Bull's-Eye Ballot Box."

This unholy device, cynically calculated to take advantage of the then-relatively unsophisticated political awareness of Native villagers, was simple in design, but most devious. At the top of each voter's ballot were two circles, one marked Democrat, one Republican. Checking either one automatically cast a vote for that party's entire slate of candidates. A name checked on the list below for a candidate from another party was nullified.

The hope, of course, was to confuse folks into thinking they simply were designating party preference and still free to cross-vote. In village after village, where votes cast for me were subsequently taken away, people said they'd been asked by local party workers if they planned to vote for Democrats Bob Bartlett, Ernest Gruening, or Bill Egan. Since all three were perennial Democratic favorites for most Alaskans, the question virtually assured an affirmative answer. "Well then, just mark the Democrat 'bull's eye' and all three will get your votes automatically."

The foul ball flung by the Democratic legislature ricocheted off the "Idiot Ballot Box" and beaned them. That year an offended electorate replaced many

137

Democrats with Republicans. The House was split twenty-twenty and required a coalition organization.

I declined an opportunity to become Speaker in order to retain my seat on the House Natural Resources Committee. Alaska's Constitution, unlike those of other states, gives its citizens collective ownership of all natural resources. This causes state government to lean more toward those who would develop those resources instead of conserve them. Consequently, I much preferred my Resources Committee's duties to those required to referee a House equally divided — a task that devolved on Anchorage businessman Bruce Kendall.

To the surprise of many, Kendall proved an excellent Speaker. Eager to warrant support from both sides of the aisle, impartiality became his prime rule and he demanded total decorum. This was especially remarkable, since his own most memorable past performances involved serious breaches of such. Like the time he'd taped a pistol cap to the Speaker's gavel and almost blew old Warren Taylor out of the chair and into cardiac arrest. Or the time he passed by the ceiling-high pile of paper festooning the desk of pack rat Benny Leonard, surreptitiously torching it with a cigarette lighter.

AS CHAIRMAN OF THE RESOURCES COMMITTEE, at long last I had an opportunity to enjoy the arbitrary and capricious powers I had criticized so often before. Though other chairmen abused those powers in behalf of special interests at the expense of the broad public interest, I, of course, self-righteously rationalized my abuse as clearly in the public's behalf.

Early in the session there fell into my clutches a Joint Resolution, already unanimously passed by the state Senate at the request of Alaska's U.S. Senator Ernest Gruening, expressing the state's ardent support of, and urging the U.S. Congress to appropriate money for, a huge hydroelectric dam to be built on the Yukon River at Rampart.

Perhaps nothing did more to exacerbate environmental awareness in and outside Alaska than the Rampart Dam debate. It was without doubt, a major turning point in the nation's belated concern with environmental abuse. Consequently, credit Senator Ernest Gruening with fathering Alaska's environmental movement, though this is a paternity charge he might dispute.

Since legislative rules dictate all measures concerning the state's wildlife, lands and waters be processed through the Resources Committee, there was no way to keep the joint resolution out of my grasp. Much to the dismay of dam proponents, I eagerly accepted the measure — and promptly buried it.

On the wrong side of the popular political issue of the moment as usual, I thought the immensely popular Rampart Dam proposal was a monumental boondoggle, not only because of its enormous financial costs. According to virtually every knowledgeable biologist, the dam's environmental consequences would be devastating. Moreover, there appeared to be far less expensive and more reasonable alternatives.

But in Washington, Senator Gruening was determined to get federal funds for Rampart as his legacy to the people of Alaska. So powerful and respected was he, it appeared possible he might pull it off. I was one of a very few legislators dumb enough to publicly question his motives and the viability of his proposal. In the wake of this indiscretion, not only was I opposed in the next election by one of Alaska's most popular political giants, all those who were entranced by prospects of profits from the huge construction project verbally burned me in effigy. Newspapers throughout the state provided the tinder.

While I'd like to have readers believe fearless courage of conviction bolstered my stand, little was required. Representing remote Bristol Bay fishing communities, I knew few of my constituents saw any benefit in Rampart's construction. Indeed, the history of salmon destruction caused by high-rise dams did little to spur enthusiasm among fisherfolk anywhere. Thus it was serendipity again that played a part in my re-election to the House. An election eve newspaper headline trumpeted: "Lone Naknek Legislator Opposed to Rampart Dam."

This won more votes in my district than it lost — the first of many efforts by opponents that backfired and returned me to public office.

As the Rampart resolution languished in my custody, the statewide media bombardment demanding its passage intensified. Aimed directly at the "obstructionist" Resources chairman, some shrapnel ricocheted off my Republican cohorts for not persuading me to discharge the resolution from my committee. Three newly elected Republicans from Fairbanks, Ed Baggen, Forbes Baker and Jim Binkley, were particularly peppered. The *Fairbanks Daily News-Miner* launched a prolonged salvo from which they sought cover.

"Look," pleaded Baggen, Baker and Binkley, "we know you don't like the Rampart resolution, but won't you please let it out for a vote? Vote against it if you must. But we're getting killed at home for not acting on it. Our constituents are overwhelmingly pro-Rampart and they simply don't understand why bills aren't voted out of committee over the chairman's objections."

"But," I started to protest, "the resolution contains inaccuracies."

They interrupted, "Okay! Then correct them. Just get it out soon. Please!"

Since the "three Bee's" were among my favorite legislators, I said I'd indulge them to this extent:

"I'll let the committee vote for or against the discharge of a properly worded version. If the majority favors it, I'll cough it up."

Their apprehension eased, the three grateful Bee's buzzed off. In line with my commitment, I rewrote the resolution without any help whatsoever from its originator, Senator Gruening.

Originally, the Resolution had read, in essence: "Whereas, this wondrous project would provide a super abundance of CHEAP POWER at virtually NO ENVIRONMENTAL COST; and whereas, the Development and Resources

Corporation, a PRESTIGIOUS AGENCY engaged by the U.S. Corps of Engineers, has DEMONSTRATED the MARKETABILITY of Rampart power; Now, therefore, be it resolved that the PROLONGED AND EXCESSIVE COST AND ENVIRONMENTAL STUDIES CEASE and the Congress APPROPRIATE SUFFICIENT FUNDS TO COMMENCE CONSTRUCTION. (Emphasis added.)

Of course, we politicians never use few words when hundreds will do. The original resolution took three type-written pages festooned with hearts and flowers to say little more than what is condensed above.

My amended version, while leaving undisturbed most of Gruening's flamboyant bloom, applied some corrective pruning to the root stalk. It now read essentially:

"WHEREAS THIS WONDROUS PROJECT WOULD PROVIDE A SUPER ABUNDANCE OF CHEAP POWER AT VIRTUALLY NO ENVIRONMENTAL COSTS only if proponents are correct and opponents deluded; AND WHEREAS THE DEVELOPMENT AND RESOURCES CORPORATION, a promotional agency hired by the corps of engineers to further their project, has SUGGESTED THE MARKETABILITY OF RAMPART POWER; NOW THEREFORE, BE IT RESOLVED THAT all authorized environmental and economic studies be fully funded and completed *before* construction may be commenced."

Since one of my very first legislative lessons had shown me the attention span of the average politician is about thirty seconds, I gambled on few of my committee members taking time to read my "corrections," especially if these were camouflaged appropriately within the foliage of the original version. It was a good gamble. They gleefully voted it out of the Resources Committee, over my fake protests.

Legislative rules, however, require *amended* joint resolutions be read aloud in entirety before the full body. Fearing exposure at this point, I confided in cohort Clem Tillion. As I pointed out my remedial amendments, Clem's toothy grin threatened to circumnavigate his head.

"Wonderful! But you'll never get away with it."

"Probably not," I agreed, "but it's worth a try. Just make sure you join me and vote against it. That may delude them into thinking it's okay."

As the clerk began to read the resolution to the momentarily attentive legislators, the first few paragraphs led them through the original garden of cloyingly flowery verbiage I'd left untouched. Then relaxing, most of them flew mentally off to other realms to roost. As the clerk droned on, I could almost see the nictating membranes drape down over bored eyeballs. Then John Rader, a long-time Gruening fan and ardent Rampart proponent, almost spooked the flock.

As the clerk monotoned through the new language I'd inserted, John, who'd been following none too intently, leaped to his feet, brow furrowed. "Wait a minute, Mr. Speaker. What goes on here?" he demanded.

But Representative Warren Taylor, perhaps the most strident example of what I'd irreverently termed the "Rampart Regardless" mentality, waved Rader impatiently back to his seat. "Sit down, John. It's alright. I've read it."

Not fully reassured, John nevertheless sat down to await the final vote. His apprehensions were set to rest only when both Tillion and I "stridently" voted "Nay!" The amended resolution passed overwhelmingly and was sent back to the Senate. There, after checking to see how "environmentalists" Tillion and Hammond had voted, the Senators concurred unanimously. The Alaska Legislature's Joint House and Senate Resolution on Rampart Dam was signed, sealed, endorsed by the governor and sent to the U.S. Congress and an increasingly impatient Senator Ernest Gruening.

Not long after, Gordon Watson of the U.S. Fish and Wildlife Service returned to Juneau from Washington. A long-time Gruening flagellatee for his temerity to challenge the Senator's facts at several public hearings, Watson quivered with ecstasy.

"When that resolution hit Congress you could hear Interior Secretary Stuart Udall shriek from two blocks away: 'You mean to tell me the Alaska State Legislature passed this resolution? I can't believe it. It's the first intelligent thing they've had to say about Rampart!'"

Senator Gruening, on the other hand, was apoplectic. The fact Tillion and I should have been absolved (after all, we voted against the resolution), did not mollify or confuse him. He knew full well who was responsible and never let me forget it. My efforts to atone by submitting a resolution to name the far less objectionable, Susitna-Devil Canyon Hydro Project as "The Ernest K. Gruening Memorial Dam Site," did not reduce his wrath. To the contrary, he felt it was my rude intent to imply his prime interest all along had been to have an enormous boondoggle named for him. That posterity might view far more kindly one responsible for a boondoggle of less outrageous proportion seemed to escape him.

While charity was admittedly not my prime motive, I've little doubt had Gruening backed off from Rampart and supported Devil Canyon instead, that project would now be in place. Not only were conservationists supporting Devil Canyon as an alternative to Rampart; Congress would have welcomed this far less expensive project and paid handsomely to get the tenacious Gruening off its back.

Though the economic and environmental costs of Rampart were in-calculable, its appeal to the "Rampart Regardless" fraternity was such it came surprisingly close to being authorized. Construction workers and contractors were understandably bedazzled. Politicians drooled at the thought of bringing home not just the bacon, but the biggest whole-hog of all. Super patriots favored it for being "larger than any dam the Russians have." Newspaper editors rhapsodized, calculating the multitude of new subscribers flooding to Alaska for the boom.

So monumental were even the *acknowledged* environmental costs in loss of habitat to fish and wildlife that when these concerns finally surfaced they proved a major obstacle to the dam. *Unacknowledged* environmental costs were far greater. At risk of losing their jobs, concerned Fish and Wildlife officials showed me privileged information that revealed field personnel had been directed to cut their assessments of waterfowl losses virtually *in half* to avoid the wrathful Gruening's threatened budget cuts.

So extreme were arguments put forth by some Rampart supporters, even those normally indifferent to all but the most extreme environmental abuse were aroused. For example, I recall an impassioned floor speech by attorney Warren Taylor in which he termed "ridiculous" concerns of those who worried that total inundation of an immense area of prime Yukon nesting ponds would damage waterfowl: "Why everyone knows ducks *love* water. The enormous lake Rampart Dam would create just gives them that much more water to love," he pontificated.

Ironically, more than twenty years later, Alaska environmentalists lined up almost unanimously in opposition to the smaller Devil Canyon project they once supported as an alternative to Rampart. Years and millions of dollars have been invested in economic and environmental evaluation of Devil Canyon. Still, questions remain. Costs have escalated enormously and potential alternative power sources, such as immense coal and gas reserves, have been discovered. No one, however, even mentions Rampart anymore, and those of us who had opposed it are indulged, if not forgiven.

ISSUES LIKE RAMPART only helped to lower my pain threshold for some attorneys yet further.

As legislators, trial lawyers are the most adept in attuning their arguments to expediencies of the moment. As "hired guns," many are little more than philosophical prostitutes more intent on winning jurors than justice. It's only natural they bring some of this unsavory talent to the legislative process. But the public interest is serviced, not served, when they do. In my first years in the legislature I was appalled by the efforts of some attorneys to bail out or accommodate their clients, ever trying to water down existing statutes and penalties. A favorite device was to insert in the law, the words, "*knowingly and willingly did commit*" or to gut another law's intent by changing "*shall*" to "*may*"

Many times I heard attorney-legislators argue persuasively one way in behalf of a measure, only to argue precisely the opposite on another which embodied the same principle, when their political or personal interests were served.

A classic case in point related to the 1964 earthquake. In that devastating event, many Alaskans lost their homes but were faced with continuing mortgage obligations. Thanks to a benevolent federal government and the ensuing rebuilding boom, the earthquake ultimately proved to be an economic boon to many Alaskans.

Among measures submitted by Governor Egan at the special session he called in the quake's aftermath was one that would have paid off major portions of mortgages for those who had lost their homes. As Egan's proposal made no distinction based on need and provided no assistance whatsoever for, say, the elderly couple who had painfully paid off the mortgage on the home they'd lost, it seemed designed primarily to bail out bankers, and actually rewarded those who had the largest outstanding mortgages, many of whom were millionaires. I recall one wealthy legislator-lawyer privately express embarrassment in having to vote for a bill which, in essence, handed him more than $50,000. He, of course, overcame his embarrassment and stalwartly cast a "yes" vote, nonetheless.

To the amazement of many, including the governor, the legislature at first turned down this measure. In speaking against it, I pointed out how, in addition to the inequities mentioned above, many attorneys in the group had reversed philosophical arguments they'd made on another issue.

That issue had been a bill to increase parental liability for incidents where a juvenile's act of vandalism incurred property damage costs for an injured party. Several attorneys had argued vehemently that this was inappropriate. They contended the injured party had the opportunity to secure adequate property insurance. By failing to do so, he, not the juvenile vandal's parents, should assume the cost of property loss or repair.

For earthquake victims, however, the attorney-legislators completely reversed this argument. While earthquake insurance could have been purchased by Alaskan homeowners — fully aware they were living in one of the world's primary quake zones — few, if any, had bought it. Despite this "oversight," the government was now being asked to bail them out. Confusing.

I concluded that the distinction between these two sets of seemingly similar circumstances was that the former offenders — parents of delinquent children — were potential fee paying clients; the latter offender was God, (as in an *Act of God*), from Whom no attorney has yet secured a retainer.

Some attorneys were the very best legislators I've known, but their presence was countered too often by the worst. Certainly there seems to be no greater conflict of interest than to write laws upon which one's livelihood directly depends.

Serving in the legislature with attorneys forced me to conclude that more than Murphy's and Parkinson's laws hold sway in government; so do Hammond's Laws Numbers One and Two.

Hammond's Law Number One is: *"The abundance of discourse is inversely proportionate to the significance to the subject."* Thus we find the legislature debating more than a week a resolution designating "Alaska Square Dance Day," while spending no more than five minutes to pass a multi-million dollar appropriation.

Hammond's Law Number Two holds that: *"The Number of sides to a given issue is double the sum of the square of the number of attorneys debating it."*

FRESHMEN LEGISLATORS SOON LEARN no issue resolves into simple black and white; nor for that matter, clearly graduated shades of gray. Once attorneys daub away at them, they span as well, all the colors of the rainbow.

That's not to say attorneys don't make a significant contribution. Few who were present can ever forget the high point in the legislative career of one Alaska lawyer-senator, George McNabb.

Through interminable hours of mind-numbing debate to amend a bill, George exploited the stunted attention span of his colleagues. After some thirty seconds, most politicians will bob their heads, smile, or grunt to show they're still with you when mentally they've long departed. Thus it was when Senator McNabb adroitly slipped an amendment into a long list of "clean-up" statute revisions, it passed unanimously. Only later did the lawmakers learn to their horror *they had abolished their pay* — a heinous act immediately remedied.

WHETHER THE CUMULATIVE EFFECTS of such legislative realities produced some sort of hypothalamic overload or accelerated brain cell death during my last session in the House, I had my final and most irrefutable experience with telepathy.

One morning at breakfast I told Bella my vivid dream of a visit from our long-time friends Dick and Iris Jensen. Both were in California for the winter and not due back for another two months. The most peculiar aspect of the dream I described was a comment Dick had made as he sat at our lunch table.

"Come out to the airport with me, Jay; I want to show you something."

In my dream we were immediately transported six miles to Juneau's airport along the Gastineau Channel in the shadow of Mendenhall Glacier.

"Look there!" Dick pointed. Crouched in the channel's low tide like a beached whale was, of all things, the gray hulk of a submarine. "I picked it up for a song," said Dick. "It's just what we need."

The dream had been so intense and so absurd, I described it later that morning to a fellow legislator, Charlie Franz, who also knew the Jensens.

Arriving home for lunch that day, who's sitting at the table but Dick and Iris Jensen. I started to tell them I'd dreamed about their visit. Before I could get around to the particulars, Dick interrupted.

"Hey, I've got the answer for providing electrical power to Naknek. I found some surplus submarines for sale in San Diego. We could sail one up, anchor it in the river and generate all the power the village needs."

Bella and I looked at each other and laughed. Maybe our laughter, not the legislature, affronted the cosmic communicator who'd apprised me since childhood of things to come. But not once since then has prophecy, outlined in eerie green fire, come through the channel. It's just as well. I sleep better for it.

Dana and Heidi and the encyclopedia set I bought from a fast-talking salesman so my kids would be exposed to "culture" in tiny Naknek.

17

Fish Tales of a "Grate" Communicator

THOUGH I FOUND MY SIX YEARS in the House challenging and enjoyable, in 1965 I debated running for a fourth term, for several reasons. All involved money.

With increased competition in a district expanded by reapportionment, I would have to campaign seriously for the first time. In my past three elections, I neither needed nor knowingly accepted campaign contributions. All offers of financial assistance were declined; checks were returned to senders with thanks, but no thanks. While most politicians feel we can't be bought, I feared accepting campaign money suggested just the opposite. In the one instance when contributions had been made to my campaign, it exacerbated this fear.

In my third run for the House I had been approached by fishing, timber and oil lobbyists, each offering to contribute $500. Grateful but firmly declining, I asked why they would be interested in re-electing me. "After all, I've thrown curve balls at all of you; as a suspect conservationist, I'm hardly the darling of your bosses. Why would you want to help me?"

Their response was they at least knew where I stood. Even when it was in the middle of their backs, they agreed I was at least fair enough to hear their complaints and inflict pain equally.

Imprudently, I mentioned this curious offer and its rejection, to my then "campaign manager," a volunteer who, I learned to my chagrin several weeks later, had gone to the three lobbyists and told them we would accept their donations after all! By the time I discovered this, however, their money had been spent. Though discomforted, I was persuaded by colleagues there was really nothing sinful in accepting donations, so long as they in no way influenced one's vote on legislation. Somewhat mollified, I thought little more of it and went on to win re-election, after which I was again assigned chairmanship of the House Resources Committee.

One of the first bills consigned to my tender mercies was one substantially raising taxes on Alaska's oil industry. Rather than even consider the bill's merits, my inclination was to immediately move it out of committee and promote its passage. "Here's my chance to demonstrate the $500 oil contribution in no way influences my decision," I thought. But of course, it almost did just that in reverse. Concern for my "pure" image almost prompted a knee-jerk reaction as unfair as would have been my opposition just to please "big oil."

I agonized over this issue unduly. Finally, after careful study, I voted for the tax increase. This eliminated any future agonizing; no more offers of campaign assistance were made by oil, timber or fish interests.

Reluctance to seek financial support ill-equips one to run for political office. When I once confessed to an audience, "I'd rather wrestle naked at high noon on the court house steps than ask for donations," someone in the back yelled, "Hammond, I wouldn't give a nickel to your campaign but I'll pay fifty bucks for a ringside seat at the court house!"

Most politicians profess to love campaigning. I find most of it repugnant. The sleight of hand, rancid red herrings, smoke screens and flashing mirrors too often employed, submerge substance in style. Issues are beclouded. Candidates are begrimed. In the process, I've seen too many decent, competent and hardworking candidates wiped out by some far less worthy opponent who is more adroit at such tactics.

My financial concerns increased with lengthening legislative sessions eating into seasons when my family earned our livelihood. At one time sessions lasted but 90 days. Now, they had not only eliminated my spring bear hunting season, they were invading our commercial salmon fishing summers.

Amid all this, one other money matter helped quench whatever embers remained of that "fire in the belly" that prompts most politicians to run. This was the tempting possibility of staying home in Naknek to help harvest the potential of a new form of local government I'd planted seeds for in the legislature.

THIS SEED-SOWING HAD BEEN PROMPTED by my resentment that, despite extraction of literally billions of dollars of fish from our back yards, most coastal communities were little more than rural slums. Absent formal municipal structure and an appropriate taxing authority, residents of villages like mine were forced to watch virtually all of their local wealth leave — in the pockets of others from elsewhere.

By 1965, however, the legislature had finally provided the tools for these communities to lever themselves from destitution. Most important of these was creation of a new form of local government.

When Alaska approached statehood in the late 1950s, cities and counties across the nation were wrestling with inefficiencies and duplications that complicated traditional city-within-county governments. To avoid these problems, Alaska's Constitution established a unique concept. Known as boroughs, these were intended to be the fundamental structure for local government.

Two types of boroughs were contemplated: organized and unorganized.

To form an organized borough required a majority vote of those residing within its proposed borders; approval by the State Boundary Commission; election of a mayor and borough assembly; and assumption of the usual powers accorded local governments, such as power to tax and ability to provide public health, safety and education services previously provided for by the state.

All those areas in Alaska not choosing to become organized boroughs would comprise the state's Unorganized Borough. The legislature would serve as its assembly and impose whatever taxes required to provide basic services.

Attractive enough on paper, in practice, the organized borough concept had little appeal to most communities. After all, why should they tax themselves to pay for services received from the state, gratis? Understandably, during the early years of statehood, there were no organized boroughs in Alaska.

At the same time, the legislature was loathe to act as an assembly for the Unorganized Borough, and thereby become both imposer of local taxes and provider of inadequate services. Consequently, legislators had little enthusiasm for subjecting themselves to heat generated by local school boards, public utility districts and other entrenched local bureaucracies. Not surprisingly, lawmakers chose to move proposed borough legislation to the ever-popular back burner. There it simmered and stewed until increasing publicity over failure to meet our constitutional mandate compelled us to at least take off the lid and once more sniff the issue.

Still not entranced with the odor, we followed another enshrined governmental tradition: we clapped the lid back on and assigned the whole mess to a "Study Committee."

To head the committee, the Speaker appointed an irascible representative from Cordova named Harold Hansen, known to both friend and foe as "Horrible." A man of caustic wit and an unquenchable thirst for high voltage spirits, "Horrible" loved to flail tormentors on the House floor at the slightest provocation. While seldom actually drunk, "Horrible" was even less often cold sober, and many colleagues hoped the borough study assignment would somehow get lost in the alcoholic haze they presumed befogged "Horrible's" mind. The problem was, "Horrible" drunk was still sharper than most of us sober.

Resentful of being handed a hot potato in hopes he would drop it, Hansen fashioned his committee into a pressure cooker. Meeting daily on a grueling schedule, committee members whipped out a remarkably comprehensive piece of legislation in short order and tossed the blistering spud back into our laps. Chagrined, we had little choice but to pass it, earning "Horrible" Hansen the sobriquet, "Father of the Borough Bill," a paternity charge he contended was a blot on his family escutcheon.

Imperfectly formed as it may have been, borough government appeared to me to have the potential to address traditional problems confronting fishing communities such as ours in Bristol Bay. There, even the most basic amenities long taken for granted elsewhere were almost non-existent. No sewer or water systems. No municipal light or power. No telephones. No police. No fire-fighting equipment. No health care. Few local service roads — and those in sorry disrepair. No high school. Few airstrips. Not even designated garbage dumps; trash was often simply dumped over the river bank to be flushed out to sea come the spring flood.

Borough government was, theoretically, now empowered to address these problems. But to do so not only required local acceptance of the borough concept; it required more money than could be raised by traditional sales or property taxes on a few hundred residents.

In my third year in the House, I'd laid groundwork on which I felt a successful borough might be structured in Bristol Bay. First, I'd sponsored legislation doubling the percentage of the state's raw fish tax remanded annually to municipalities where the fish had been processed. Though this alone would have done much to help finance borough government, I increased this potential with legislation that would empower boroughs to impose a local "use tax" on fish, as well. Unlike the raw fish tax paid to the state by fish processors, the "use" tax would be paid to the borough by fishermen.

With both of these sources of funding in place, there remained the task of selling the borough concept to unwilling buyers.

Most fisherfolk are fiercely independent. Like small farmers who once dominated American agriculture, most choose to live free under the least government possible. It seemed almost impossible to convince them to impose a tax on themselves. However, there was one very strong interest that might induce them to do so.

In the mid 1960s, most rural Alaska villages had no high schools. Children were shipped off to church or government boarding schools, far from home and family, around and outside Alaska. Most parents wanted local high schools, but high costs made their funding virtually impossible for state government, much less small rural villages.

To help local school financing, I had sponsored legislation requiring the state provide 80 percent of construction money needed to build schools. In addition, I had sneaked into the final version of a new state revenue-sharing bill a subtle way to disperse millions more to communities than my urbane colleagues deemed appropriate.

In doing so, I once more demonstrated a shameful willingness to slip under the counter something I could not sell over the top. Only now that the statute of limitations has expired am I willing to acknowledge the malice of forethought and disgraceful connivance involved.

With these funding sources in place, I considered how to make the best sales pitch. Having learned my direct pitches too often fall short, I decided to hide the ball in my glove.

At my behest, a citizen's study committee was formed. I felt that, as a politician, any argument I made for borough status would be suspect. Instead, I pointed out that we could easily fund a borough through fish taxes, and that those who would pay the most by far lived outside the borough.

"Some have even suggested," I noted, "all taxes paid by locals could be refunded, and there'd still be enough money to construct our long-dreamed-of high school."

Piously, I added, "as representative of all the people of Bristol Bay, I, of course, felt obliged to *oppose* creation of a borough because, while most of my constituents would share costs, only residents of the borough (Naknek, South Naknek and King Salmon) would reap the benefits. This would be grossly unfair." To complete the ruse, I then voted, "No."

Not unexpectedly, my colleagues showed no such unselfish concern. Only one other joined in voting against creating a borough. One of those voting for it later told me he'd planned to vote "No" until he heard my reasons for doing so.

Happily accepting the committee's rejection of my "Minority Report," I drew up proposed borough boundaries, including waters open to commercial fishing. These were approved by the state, and in 1963 our three communities became Alaska's first organized borough. However, it was to be another two years before I was to explore the intriguing potentials of borough government to a far greater degree.

In both 1964 and 1965, Bristol Bay was declared a disaster area because of depleted salmon runs. When then Democrat Governor Bill Egan appointed Dillingham Democrat Joe McGill to distribute emergency food to the twenty-three villages in my district, I suspected Joe was being groomed to run against me. This proved true.

In 1965, facing this formidable competition in a district made larger by reapportionment, by the time I bestirred myself to campaign, it was too late. When I'd fly in to visit, villagers would ask: "Joe says just send him our grub orders and he'll take care of them. Can you do that?" When I admitted I could not, they'd look at each other, nod, and disappear behind inscrutable eyes. Long before the polls opened in November, I knew I'd lost.

An earthy ex-Marine wounded on Guadalcanal, Joe had come to Alaska in the 1940s, married a local woman and settled in Dillingham, Bristol Bay's largest community. Having enlisted underage, Joe's formal education had been cut short. But his robust vocabulary, resplendent with all the ruffles and flourishes common to bar and barracks, gave Joe a much better facility for communicating with constituents than I ever had. To the average fisherman, much of my convoluted effort to communicate was boring and incomprehensible. Many people told me they simply didn't understand what I was talking about — and concluded I didn't either. Always intrigued with lexicology, I have an unfortunate penchant for substituting a complex word for the simple. This, coupled with a facility to become enmeshed in my own verbiage, I was told, was why our fellow fisher folk felt more at home with Joe. He won handily.

At first, feeling somewhat affronted, I admit taking some solace from a Juneau attorney's comment: "Hammond, the problem is you just don't represent the people of Bristol Bay. And you ought to be damned proud of it!"

I was not. Failure to communicate with constituents is no cause for pride. It wasn't that I hadn't tried. I answered all correspondence and sent monthly newsletters. But these are no substitutes for spending a few days in each village, "coffeeing up" or buying the boys a beer in a local bar. Since I dislike coffee and beer and did not frequent bars, I was no match for Joe. It was not just his remarkable bladder capacity or greater tolerance for the inebriated; Joe dealt more effectively with everyday concerns.

I was ever trying to pass legislation dealing with such concepts as enhancing financial aid to local communities. Joe underlooked these broad themes for local capital projects like schools, roads and structures of tangible brick or concrete. The latter, of course, are bread and butter issues to most voters. To secure $10,000 for a highly visible construction project wins many more points in the villages than, say, funneling an unprogrammed $1 million into the coffers of local government.

Though I'd successfully sponsored legislation that ultimately inundated my community with millions in annual income, not half a dozen locals were aware of it. Instead, some people still asked, "What's Hammond ever done for us?" Had one-tenth of the millions I'd secured for Bristol Bay villages gone instead into so-called "pork barrel" projects, I'd have won far more points with the rank and file.

Despite my humbling defeat in 1965, I wasn't too resentful. Only a few weeks after the election, to augment my flying, fishing and guide businesses, I became the part-time manager of the Bristol Bay Borough. Now I faced the intriguing challenge of using the management tools I'd forged while still in the legislature.

These tools proved far more difficult to wield than imagined. Each attempt to sculpt a new means of sustaining local government from the vast resource wealth being extracted was met with blade-blunting resistance. While what emerged was but a caricature of what I'd intended, the frustrations, mashed thumbs and gashed fingers incurred were, years later, to spur efforts to accomplish at the state level what I'd failed to do at the local.

Shortly after taking that job, a cursory study showed almost ninety-seven percent of the payday from fish caught within our borough's boundaries left in the pockets of folks who lived elsewhere — most outside Alaska. Even though a modest three percent "use tax" on fish would glean $97 from non-residents for every $3 paid by locals, my first ordinance proposing the tax was voted down.

Convinced voters didn't understand what a good business deal I'd offered, I took to the stump, wrote newsletters and held public meetings. To heighten interest, I suggested we form "an investment corporation" from our annual bounty of fish tax dollars, and *"grant each local resident one share of stock for each year they resided in the Borough."*

Invested prudently, I pointed out, our annual stock dividends from what might be termed, "Bristol Bay, Inc.," would far exceed their fish tax payments. A second vote failed by an even greater margin. Obviously, I had again garbled my message.

Clearly, new tactics were called for. I abandoned the Bristol Bay Inc. concept for "an offer they couldn't refuse." As mayor, I sponsored two ordinances: Ordinance A imposed the three percent fish tax. Ordinance B abolished all residential property taxes, with one proviso: *Ordinance B became effective only upon passage of Ordinance A.*

A majority voted for it, realizing their current residential property tax was far larger than the likely amount of their fish tax.

In the first year, abolished property taxes cost borough coffers only a few thousand dollars. In their place came hundreds of thousands of new fish use tax dollars. The measure was soon tested by affronted non-residents but upheld in court, as the tidal wave of new revenues continued to flow into the borough treasury.

These dollars, added to those coming with the redoubling of remanded state raw fish taxes, the new revenue sharing bill, and the new bill providing eighty percent state funding of school construction, almost drowned the new borough in dollars! Our "rural slum" had become what a *Fortune* magazine study called *"the richest municipality in the nation,"* in terms of borough income per person.

Parkinson's Law asserts government will always expand to spend every available dollar. The Bristol Bay Borough proved no exception.

I had hoped to prevent this through the Bristol Bay, Inc. concept. With its defeat, I next hoped exemption from residential property taxes might do so. However, when the legislature made it illegal to grant this exemption, it, in essence, made a liar out of me, for I had "sold" the fish tax as a trade-off. Thus instead of each borough resident receiving either a dividend or tax reduction, all of the borough's new wealth went into more government.

In 1965, the borough budget totaled $35,000. My part-time salary was $8,000. My full-time secretary got $12,000. By contrast, in 1988 the budget was $4.7 million! The manager's salary was $80,000, there were 21 full-time employees and — you guessed it — property taxes have gone up!

It would be another ten years before the basic dividend concept would prove itself as the Alaska Permanent Fund Dividend program. That it took me nearly 15 years to sell the citizen-owned investment account — later, immensely popular — attests to my inability to communicate.

Dana and Heidi at ages three and six. Spending time with the girls was a blessing found in my respite from public office.

18

Bounced Back

SEXUAL PECCADILLOES OF POLITICIANS rate second only to those of TV evangelists in terms of public fascination.

Nothing more delights the masses than reaffirmation that the trousers of the pompous and pious come off one leg at a time, as do those of us common folk. But just as it is with us common folk, trousers are sometimes shucked in the wrong places.

While some public figures admonish us to ignore their private lives, few of us do. Perhaps, as most contend, bedroom behavior has little bearing on standards of statesmanship. But I'm not assured those who casually break vows of marriage find it all that more difficult to break oaths of office. Moreover, I find it curious when some who claim they'd not dream of picking the public's purse, have no qualm stealing another's spouse.

Certainly public figures are subjected to extraordinary pressures, temptations and scrutiny. The trick is to avoid the *appearance* of evil — for it can get you into just as much trouble as the practice. Suspect situations may have been encouraged, anticipated, or totally innocent. But once made public, they are accorded the worst possible interpretation.

Like the night in Juneau's Baranof Hotel when, clad only in a wet towel, I was almost caught trying to drag a naked, screaming young redhead into a room. As the statute of limitations has expired, along with further political ambition, I can now reveal the facts of this sorry affair.

I'd been out of the legislature almost two years and missed it little more than I would have a bleeding ulcer. But as mayor of Bristol Bay Borough, I had to travel to Juneau to testify on some local issue. I took a room at the historic

Baranof Hotel, three blocks from Alaska's Capitol Building. Around seven that evening, I was emerging from a hot shower when I heard a horrendous screaming outside my door.

"HELP! MURDER! RAPE! MY GOD! HE'S KILLING ME!"

Frantic and imploring, the woman's screams so curdled my blood it may not have flowed freely brainward, for I simply grabbed a towel, wrapped it sarong-like around my wet body and dashed into the hall, fully prepared to do battle. Of course a small school boy could have rendered me *hors de combat* simply by snatching my towel.

To my astonishment, instead of a burly rapist assaulting some terrified victim, there was only one person. On her knees, screeching at the top of her lungs, was a stark naked young redhead. Obviously spaced out on something, she continued to shriek: "MURDER! RAPE!"

Hoping to calm her down and help her to her room, I grabbed her wrists to pull her to her feet. In that position, I heard many feet pounding up the stairs. Mercifully, my mind flashed on the picture about to unfold for the would-be rescue party.

"Wait a minute," I thought, "with nothing but a towel between us, I'm caught trying to drag a naked, protesting woman into a hotel room? No way!"

Ungraciously dumping the still screaming woman like a sack of potatoes, I leaped back to my room a split second before a throng of security men, bell-hops and clerks arrived on the scene.

More than most folks, politicians are naturally, perhaps even appropriately, presumed guilty until proven innocent. To say I'm glad I never had to explain my presence in the Baranof hall that night, understates my relief.

ON THAT SAME TRIP, I met an old legislative colleague, Marc Jensen, who urged me to file for the Senate seat created by the newly-structured election district encompassing my home town of Naknek.

"Forget it," I said. "My guiding-fishing-flying business is going too well and I'm enjoying more time with Bella and the girls." Heidi was ten now; Dana seven. It was a relief not to have to pack up each year and move to Juneau for the session.

Marc insisted I at least come with him to the Office of Elections and fill out the papers. "You never know who'll run for that seat, Jay. At least cover your bets. I'll hang on to the papers unless you tell me you've changed your mind." Protesting I had no desire to get back into politics, I nevertheless went with him and made out the papers, extracting his assurance to not submit them unless he heard from me.

A few weeks later I was astonished to read in the paper I had filed for the state Senate. When Marc was able to slip a word in among the heated abuse I heaped on him over the phone, he explained how my old campaign manager

Dick Jensen, (no relation), and Senator Brad Phillips had both told him to file my papers.

"I thought they'd gotten the word from you to file," Marc said.

In fact, I had talked with Dick and Brad, imprudently mentioning my conversation with Marc and the fact he held my filing papers. They'd taken it from there. To this day I don't know who paid the filing fee. I didn't. The law says the applicant must pay the fee. Could it be all my subsequent actions in elective office might be null and void because I was improperly seated?

Bella was not overjoyed, but accepted the inevitable. Once again I hadn't the courage to "just say, 'No.'"

THE NEW SENATE DISTRICT was enormous. Almost seven hundred and fifty miles long and two hundred and fifty miles wide, it stretched from Port Heiden on the Alaska Peninsula to Wiseman on Alaska's Arctic Slope. Twice the size of my home state of Vermont, and almost totally roadless, it included all three Native language groups, Eskimos, Aleuts and Indians — plus urban white-collar workers employed at the communications site at Clear. To say concerns and interests of these constituencies were sometimes at odds, understates my challenge. That they elected me, I credit largely to John Sackett.

John had filed for the House seat representing the upper portion of my Senate district. An articulate, brilliant young Athapascan Indian of sometimes mercurial temperament, John was one of the first Alaska Natives to declare as a Republican. Without question, his support secured me the Native villagers' vote.

From his mother Lucy, John had inherited sharp intelligence plus a sweet and sour disposition. As a friend he was expansive and charming. As an opponent, he could be cold and formidably caustic. If there were still royalty among the Athapascan people, Johnny would qualify. Only in his early twenties, even village elders held him in high esteem. He had an almost frighteningly regal aura about him at times, similar to that which I suspect intimidated those early unfortunates who, in their last seconds, looked up into the obsidian eyes of a Mayan high priest surgeon about to perform the ultimate bypass. Not a few times I watched John verbally tear to ribbons some poor unsuspecting slob on the floor of the Legislature. At times John even let me play the sacrificial role of "tearee."

Traveling with John was enlightening. It was remarkable to watch this gifted speaker metamorphose from young executive to Yukon River villager. Left behind were the clothes from Saville Row or Bond Street. The grad student vocabulary was replaced by patois peculiar to Native communities. Phrases, for example, like "What time is it?" came out "What time it is?" or when citing the date, the specific month is followed by the word, "month," as in, "Russian Christmas comes in January month."

John not only helped me in all his district's villages, he learned some things from the people I would not have known otherwise. In one village, he was told people were not going to vote for me because, "as an Army Sergeant in World War II," I had "beaten a Native soldier to death in Shemya" in the Aleutians.

OF THOSE WHO HELPED ME campaign that year, the most refreshing if less productive contribution was made by one of my favorite curmudgeons, crusty old Don Harris.

Don, a hard-bitten and biting gold miner and construction contractor from tiny McGrath is himself of precious mettle. Serving with him in the legislature, I came to appreciate his uncommon sense and total integrity, even though I personally stood a bit to the left of where some say Don plants his ultra-conservative shoe pacs — a step or two left of slavery. Compared to Don Harris, Calvin Coolidge was a radical liberal.

Alice, Don's remarkably self-sufficient Athapascan wife, shared both his fiercely independent philosophy and suspicion of all things governmental. So I wasn't surprised to find campaigning with them somewhat different.

Don was running for re-election to another House seat within my new Senate district. "Why don't you campaign with me?" he offered. "We can fly around in my plane and I'll introduce you to your new constituents."

The wisdom of accepting his gracious gesture came into question at our first stop, the village of Nikolai. Upon landing, villagers descended on us, shouting complaints and demands.

"Don Harris! How come you didn't get more money for our community hall? Our sewer and water? Our schools? Welfare?" They chorused.

After a few minutes of this one-sided conference, Harris threw up his hands and bellowed, "If you guys would just get up off your asses and hustle, you wouldn't need all that damn welfare money!"

Wow, I thought as I mentally subtracted Nikolai from my prospective vote tally, that's a different approach!

On another campaign stop in Holicachuk, Don was greeted sourly by Village Chief Henry Deacon. "Don Harris! Did you get my letter?" asked Henry.

"Yes, Henry, I got your letter," Harris acknowledged.

"Don Harris, how come you didn't answer my letter?" Henry admonished.

"Because, Henry, the only appropriate answer would be a punch in the nose."

And so it went. Not surprisingly, Don's refreshing candor failed to win him re-election; nor, I suspect, did our close association do much to advance mine. Sensing this, when it came time for my next campaign, Harris told me:

"Jay, you know I support you one hundred percent; but I promise not to tell anybody."

I suppose I should have anticipated Don's campaign attitude when he explained to me why it is that elections are held during the fall rutting season of our bull moose: "It's the time of the year when the neck swells up, cutting off the flow of blood to the brain."

To offset Don's "contributions," I tried a new campaign ploy. In the past, the villages of South Naknek, Nondalton, and Manakutuk always voted solidly Democrat. Knowing Manakutuk was the only one of these villages where I had any support at all, with little to lose, I took a new approach.

"Look, for years you folks have complained about not getting basic projects. Maybe you've not gotten them because Democrats in Juneau know they don't have to give you a thing and you'll still vote Democrat. Why don't you shake them up, like Nulato did some years ago? They always voted Democrat and were completely ignored. Then one year they voted Republican. To bring them back to the fold, Governor Egan showered Nulato with capital projects. Who knows? It might work the same for you. Besides, it's not a sin to vote Republican once in a while."

To my surprise, for the first time, all three villages voted not just for me; in 1966, they helped elect Alaska's first Republican governor as well.

WALTER J. HICKEL was a successful Anchorage businessman and party fig-ure who ran on the slogan: *"There's a Better Way."* Apparently, most Alaskans agreed, because he unseated popular two-term Governor Bill Egan, who had never lost an election. Contributing to Bill's defeat was his perceived effort to bend Alaska's constitutional limit of two consecutive terms. Bill claimed he'd not served two *full* terms because illness had delayed his second inauguration by a few weeks.

A dynamic and successful entrepreneur with huge ambitions and energy to match, Hickel seemed to many just the type of go-getter to "get our state moving." But when a grateful Richard Nixon kept his promise and named major fund raiser Wally his Interior Secretary, Hickel resigned and left for Washing-ton, two years into his four-year gubernatorial term. Lt. Governor Keith Miller then filled the governor's chair.

Prior to leaving, however, Wally left a few footprints behind — some on the fabric of government, some on Alaska's landscape, and some on the hind-quarters of Clem Tillion and me.

Initially, I'd been favorably impressed with Wally's "take charge" approach. A no-nonsense sort, he'd attack problems head on. When you and he were on the same side, this was refreshing and sometimes rewarding. Once, some Senate action I'd taken helped further his wishes. I was immediately called to his office and offered the cabinet post of Fish & Game Commissioner.

"I know it doesn't pay much, but it's more than the legislature," said the Governor. "And we'll help you get a house. I think you'll find you can do quite well."

I was touched and appreciative. But not that touched. "Governor, thanks for the offer, but I have to decline. While we're in accord on some issues, I believe fish and game management should be removed to the greatest extent possible from politics. You appear to feel precisely the opposite. I suspect I'd not last six months as commissioner."

"Nonsense," said Wally. "I don't want a 'Yes' man in that job."

My instincts told me he'd have even less use for a "No" man. Like a self-fulfilling prophecy, from the moment I declined his offer, my rapport with Governor Hickel began to slide. My association with Clem Tillion greased the skids.

Before that descent, however, Wally named both Clem and me as advisors to the International North Pacific Fisheries Management Council. As the only Republicans with commercial fisheries experience back then, we were, I suppose, logical choices. Moreover we were both among the legislature's leadership; Clem as House Rules chairman and I as Senate Majority leader.

Once a week, Governor Hickel would hold Republican leadership meetings in his office. These were relatively informal affairs where one could let the hair down. To Tillion, that meant he could as well cock his unshod feet up on the governor's coffee table. While this irreverence no doubt affronted the imperial aura Wally seemed to prefer, he was tolerant of Clem's insouciant attitude. Until Rep. Tillion breached a more basic protocol.

Hickel had just finished an impassioned plea on some matter — and at impassioned speeches, Wally was gifted. During delivery, one was caught up in the Hickel enthusiasm. Such verbiage, however, like Chinese food, often seemed to satisfy for the moment, but later left one less than fulfilled. After this particular serving, Clem sat back with his Peck's Bad Boy grin aimed directly through the "V" gunsight of his stockinged feet at the governor, who, having concluded, awaited appreciative response. Instead, he got a full dose of pure Tillion.

"Well, Governor," drawled Clem, "that's a might pretty speech. But you ain't changed a thing. I can't go along with you."

With that, a startled aide hustled us from the office where, from beneath the closed door, blue smoke began to curl.

A few days later, in Washington D.C., Alaska's Democratic U.S. Senator Bob Bartlett gleefully announced to the press a letter had been received from Governor Hickel, demanding Tillion's removal from the North Pacific Fisheries Management Council. Hickel issued a heated denial. No such letter had been sent, he asserted. He had simply asked that room be made on the council for his Fish and Game Commissioner, Augie Reetz.

I had no quarrel with that, only with the possibility Clem might be dumped to create the vacancy. Accordingly, I wrote a Senate resolution pointing out how Clem's first-rate performance had earned him such high regard among his commission colleagues, they'd elected him chairman. My Resolution also mentioned Bartlett's allegation that the governor had requested Tillion's dismissal and Hickel's assurance that this was untrue. It went on to laud Tillion's outstanding service and urged his retention on the INPFC.

A fellow State Senator, Bob Palmer, agreed to co-sponsor the resolution. It was not the last time Bob would regret doing so.

On the day we introduced it, I feared we'd triggered an after shock of the 1964 Good Friday Earthquake. While no cracks appeared in the Senate chamber ceiling undergirding the governor's office, light fixtures shook and windows rattled. When our Tillion resolution landed on the governor's desk it caused the greatest eruption yet witnessed by the quivering, wall-eyed aide sent to summon Palmer and me to Hickel's office.

"Be forewarned," the aide admonished, "he's really hot and wants to see you both immediately."

Dutifully, Palmer and I marched upstairs and were hustled into Wally's presence by a nervous receptionist. Hickel wasted no time with amenities.

"#&**%&#?%&" he shrieked. "WHAT THE HELL DO YOU THINK YOU'RE DOING?!"

From then on he grew less convivial. For the next ten minutes, we were subjected to an increasing crescendo of outrage. At its apogee, I seem to recall, the governor was all but down on the floor, chewing the carpet and pounding his fists. Palmer contends my recall is faulty. Neither of us dispute the thrust of the governor's message: "HOW CAN YOU TWO COMMEND AN S.O.B. LIKE TILLION WHEN YOU SHOULD BE COMMENDING ME FOR THE JOB I'M DOING AS GOVERNOR?"

At first we thought he was joking. I'm afraid we may have smiled. But as he continued to berate Tillion in language as blue as a barracks ballad, we realized he was serious. Though four years in the Marine Corps had accustomed me to hot verbal reamings, finally, even I'd had enough.

"ALL RIGHT, GOVERNOR," I yelled over the din, "I'll withdraw the resolution and rewrite it. I'll commend YOU for demonstrating unusual wisdom in selecting a person of Tillion's caliber to serve on the INPFC."

If the first gush of abuse had been alarming, the second was an appalling flood tide. On its crest, Palmer and I tumbled out of the office.

This was not the end. A few days later, Senator Bartlett not only reasserted his charge the governor had requested Tillion's dismissal; he said a new request had been made to dump Hammond as well.

The piranhas of the press, of course, schooled happily on such tidbits, nibbling all parties involved. For weeks they'd reported Bartlett's allegations and Hickel's denials. Their final assault was headlined one evening in the *Fairbanks Daily News-Miner*: Bartlett Arrives; Tillion Letter In Hand.

Before this bomb could explode in papers everywhere, its fuse was snuffed out. Next day, the worst flood in its history devastated Fairbanks — a cataclysmic event mercifully sweeping "The Tillion Affair" to oblivion. Some lamented Tillion and I weren't swept along with it.

THE TILLION RESOLUTION was only the first blow to what had been an amicable relationship with Walter J. Hickel. The *coup de gras* came not over fish, but musk oxen.

Alaska's last indigenous musk oxen had been killed early in the 20th Century. Years later, a group of these shaggy beasts was transplanted from Greenland to Alaska's Nunivak Island. Protected there, they so flourished that by the mid 1960s, they threatened to over-populate their range. As Chairman of the Senate Natural Resources committee, I was approached by concerned Fish & Game biologists.

"There's just too many of them. We need to cull some old bulls to invigorate the herd. We could go ahead and kill them ourselves, or we could allow a limited hunt. The department could issue game tags for hunters, but we couldn't charge for them without legislative authority. If the legislature will establish a tag fee, the state could realize revenue from the project, rather than simply expense. Natives could act as guides and their villages would get all the meat."

As musk oxen had been protected for years, my committee had some apprehensions about proposals to hunt them. But the administration's biologists made a good case. Accordingly, we passed a bill that imposed, as I recall, a tag fee of a thousand dollars for non-residents and five hundred dollars for residents.

To our astonishment, Hickel vetoed the bill and rebuked the legislature for "authorizing a hunt on these defenseless creatures;" likening them to domestic cattle. "Why, you can walk right up to them," said Hickel, "stick your gun barrel in their ear and blow them away. That's no sport."

Since his administration had broached the proposal, the governor's words prompted an indiscreet response when I took the Senate floor to try to overturn his veto.

"Contrary to the governor's message," I began, "the legislature is not advocating a hunt, but merely assuring if such a hunt occurs, the state will realize some financial benefit from it. Whether a musk ox hunt occurs is up to the administration. Whether they can charge anything for it is up to the legislature. Therefore, the only distinction between our positions is, we believe musk ox tags worth five hundred dollars and a thousand dollars respectively; the governor, by his veto, has determined them to be worth nothing."

I did not have sense enough to leave the matter there, adding:

"So far as his charges regarding the domestic nature of musk oxen," I went on, "from my experience, the average moose or bear hunt is hardly more exhilarating. In fact, approaching musk oxen at close range in the wild can be downright zestful; as anyone would learn should we require them to be taken only as the governor suggests.

"This prompts an observation I'd like to read into the record. It's a prospective obituary which I'd not be surprised to see published, should the governor pursue his style of musk ox disposal. I then read the following "Owed to Wally Hickel":

> "Wally Hickel's long gone to meet his maker.
> It seems that while he was acting as Musk Ox caretaker
> He decided to prove a point he'd made
> That the Musk Ox, being so gentle and staid,
>
> Would simply just stand there and let you insert
> Your gun in its ear and not do you hurt.
>
> But the Musk Ox, of course, is a shaggy beast,
> And to those unfamiliar it is not in the least
>
> Simple to quickly and surely discern
> The Musk Oxen's bow from the Musk Oxen's stern.
>
> And Wally, poor Wally, somehow I fear,
> Approached the wrong end, his gun held like a spear.
>
> With a confidence borne we suspect from confusion
> Walter J. shocked the beast with a most rude intrusion.
>
> With a bellow of outrage and rock-shivering grunt,
> The Musk Ox exploded and with one mighty punt,
>
> Booted poor Wally clear up to Nome,
> In somewhat less time than he might have flown.
>
> And the last words uttered by Walter J.?
> 'Again I have proved 'there's a better way!'
>
> Now there's a moral to this sorry tale of woe.
> You better hear this, before Musk Ox hunting you go:
>
> Even domestic Musk Oxen turn suddenly feral
> If one doesn't take time to warm UP his gun barrel."

Wally was not enchanted; especially by my rude reference to his campaign slogan, "There's a Better Way." Years later — when we ran three times against each other for governor — his disenchantment seemed compounded by outrage. Accordingly, he came across to some as too uptight, humorless and excessively ambitious, while I appeared a disturbingly irreverent clown with insufficient ambition for the job.

To the latter charge, I plead guilty. When it came to politics, as in many other of life's activities, I preferred to be a loner. Political power or leadership positions simply did not entrance me — not because of selfless humility. I simply didn't want to bear the burdens of hard work and the responsibilities that come with such jobs. Some folks thrive on pressure; I wither.

Despite my best evasive efforts, events of the later 1960s succeeded in lobbing several heavy hot issues into my lap.

Some years, Lake Clark never freezes, and travel can be zestful. The closest road system is 150 miles away.

19

Green vs. Gold

NUMEROUS ISSUES HAVE PITTED Alaskan against Alaskan over the years, cacophonic conflicts that have compelled politicians to dance with alacrity between warring factions to seem in step with each. By contrast, being tone deaf and fumble footed, I seemed to step on the toes of both sides. Unlike the consummate politician who can convince both advocates and opponents he is with them, I convinced each we were at odds.

The pitched battle between "developers" and "conservationists" provided a showcase for my political shortcomings. Nowhere are such conflicts more easily triggered than in Alaska. This is understandable. After all, the two types of persons most inclined to come to the Greatland assure it.

One type are folks who, fed up with environmental degradation and people pressures found elsewhere, flee to Alaska believing it the last redoubt of pristine wilderness and broad horizons. Here they can indulge in lifestyles which, if not long since lost elsewhere, are at least suppressed in their native states. These people have read Robert Service and Thoreau. They arrive with romantic notions of life in a remote homestead cabin away from the urban rat race.

Along with these would-be rustics, however, comes another type of "pioneer" no less determined to find a different kind of "good life." Jobless or discouraged by conditions "back home," and hearing tales of common, unmonied folk striking it rich in Alaska, they flood north intent upon exploitation. It's inevitable that the shovels and picks of these treasure seekers often bruise environmentalists' toes.

Empathizing a bit with both factions, often I placed a foot in each camp, only to find I'd stepped into a campfire. Inability to see but one side of an issue

JAY HAMMOND COLLECTION

View from our front window at Lake Clark. One awestruck cameraman asked, "Why would you ever leave this for public office?" That question often resurfaced around three in the morning.

compounded political pain. How I envied those who saw issues in clear black or white rather than unfocused gray.

At first, I naively attributed this to greater sensitivity or intellect, and pondered both sides of a conflict in public. Only after much punishment did I learn more astute politicians ponder such questions in private. The most successful learn more quickly than I how voters want their leaders to take strong, unequivocal positions with absolute confidence in their omniscience. The electorate does not suffer lightly one who admits he may be as confused as they are.

Until I learned this lesson, opponents happily bombed me with charges of inconsistency. Although I might be in accord with them ninety percent of the time, that ten percent deviation enraged extremists on both sides. Some conservationists believed I should do all in my power to stifle growth and development; some developers were certain I aspired to "zero growth" and would return Alaska to a howling wilderness.

Since my heart, if not always my head and gut, was more green than gold, I took perverse but imprudent delight in outraging developmental extremists who were convinced my policies on Alaska's natural resources were a conspiracy to propel Alaska back to pre-Gold Rush conditions. I did not sit down to a standing ovation when I told the Anchorage Chamber of Commerce:

"Now I know there is some apprehension in the business community that

Hammond, with his perceived environmentalist views, will somehow stifle economic development, hurl Alaskans out of work, create a mass exodus and devastate the economy. Some have asserted if I have my way I'd make the entire state one huge, national park; fence it in and throw away the key. That's not only untrue, it's absolutely ridiculous. You have nothing to fear in that regard. It could not happen here. *Your city does not merit park status. It has already degenerated beneath acceptable environmental eligibility requirements.*"

I confess to more empathy with environmentalists than with rabid developers. Except for those most extreme, I often found them better prepared to back their positions with factual data and intelligent argument. By contrast, their opponents' arguments were too often more visceral than cerebral. This seemed especially true, of course, when an environmentalist position conformed to my own. Getting my head to modify the environmental bent of my heart, took a bit of doing. After all, I was a boy who lamented he'd not been born a hundred years earlier and able to pursue the life of the legendary mountain men.

To this day I can empathize with those two old mountain men in A.B. Guthrie's classic, *The Big Sky*. Riding through a vast western grassland, backdropped by the shining spires of the Rockies, one grizzled oldtimer reins up. Squinting into the setting sun beneath his horny palm, he sees, far away, a lone, covered wagon. Turning to his companion he sadly laments, "By God, she must have been pretty once!"

Likewise, I hold a deep respect for the colorful and out-spoken cowboy artist, Charlie Russell, whose finest hour perhaps came when a group of Montana boosters asked him to address them. Introduced as "one of Montana's true pioneers," old Charlie rose and glowered at his audience.

"I ain't no pioneer. In my book, a pioneer is a man who comes to a virgin country, traps off all the fur, kills off all the wild meat, cuts down all the trees, grazes off all the grass, plows the roots up and strings ten million miles of bob wire. A pioneer destroys things and calls it Civilization. I wish to God that this country was just like it was when I first saw it, and that none of you folks were here at all!"

Charlie probably got even less applause than I did from the Anchorage Chamber of Commerce.

CONFLICTS BETWEEN DEVELOPERS and environmentalists came into sharper intensity as the 1960s progressed. One that seemed especially ludicrous was the proposal to detonate an atomic device on the Aleutian island of Amchitka to test the efficacy of nuclear explosions as a construction technique. Though today this seems hardly imaginable, developmental extremists were ardent supporters, "visionaries" who felt the potential of nuclear power to reshape the earth by blowing out deep harbors — or vaporizing transportation routes through impeding glaciers — would facilitate Alaska resource development.

Environmentalists were aghast, concerned not only for marine mammals and other wildlife, but unwilling to add another dash of Strontium 90 to an already polluted biosphere.

When a reporter asked my views on what was called "The Cannikin Project," I said it was abominable even to consider an atomic blast on an island where remnant species of endangered sea otters are found. "If they must use an island location for their test, they should at least find one where the indigenous species aren't endangered."

"Do you have such an island in mind?" the reporter asked.

"Certainly. Why not Manhattan?"

Disparate views on the pending Cannikin blast split the State Senate almost in half. Proponents were stroked by the pro-development *Anchorage Times*, which supported the blast, while the environmentally-oriented *Anchorage Daily News* threatened to flog all those who did so. Not wishing to take any lumps on the issue, legislators did our usual dithering dance all around it while both papers fumed.

A small device was eventually detonated, fulfilling neither advocates' hopes nor opponents' fears.

IT WAS AROUND THIS TIME I composed an "Owed" that convinced Alaska pro-development forces we were at odds. It was occasioned by the discovery and development of oil reserves on the Kenai Peninsula and in Cook Inlet, both areas known for their rich fish and wildlife resources. Prudhoe Bay was yet to be discovered in the late 1960s, when I wrote:

"ALASKA 1984?"

Remember how lousy things used to be?
Before we had oil, fish cluttered the sea.
And Cook Inlet's waters were coffee hued,
Instead of the shimmering sheen of crude.

But it didn't take long to cover the mud
For it's a very short step from crude to crud.

Yes, that black gold sure out-glitters the old silver hoard
Since we reconstituted our Fish & Game Board
with oil stockholders who seldom think petty.
After all, for Commissioner, we got J. Paul Getty.

And remember all those stupid, dumb clucks
Who complained we might lose a few million ducks?

(A duck, you'll recall, had webbed feet and a bill.
The last one expired the year of the "Spill").

How lonely 'twas then to roam about, man;
Clean out of sight of a friendly beer can.
Now you can roam the most remote out-croppings
And find you're picking your way through the people droppings.

Water drunk years ago was new, and untried.
It's a wonder somehow so few people died.

True, now that we've grown a great deal more chummy
Our water does tend to be a bit gummy.

But you know doggone well when you slake your thirst
The guy survived who drank it first.

Back then, of course, we had garbage dumps,
Where refuse was piled in unsightly humps.

We've leveled these out now and you can discern
Nice level garbage wherever you turn . . .

And so on and on. Unfortunately, in the late 1960s, I had no idea how prophetic this "Owed" would prove to be in 1989 when the tanker *Exxon Valdez* disemboweled itself on Bligh Reef.

The trans-Alaska Pipeline. While there were many who'd send me down it, I managed to stay on top of the tube — but just barely. Unfortunately, the pipeline's route may have cost Alaska and the nation billions of dollars.

20

Prudhoe Bay and The Pipeline

IN THE ENERGY-HUNGRY WORLD of 1969, on the far northern coast of the Arctic Ocean, North America's largest oil field was discovered under the frozen tundra.

To the United States, with its insatiable appetites, Prudhoe Bay's billions of barrels of oil was heralded as but one more fat item on the energy menu. But to Alaskans, it was seen as the end of dark poverty and the dawn of prosperity. As Alaskans eagerly awaited the "boom" after so many decades of "bust," thousands from elsewhere began flooding the Greatland, detonating a population boom of their own.

As wells were drilled, the burning question was how to bring this far off North Slope oil to market. In that regard, my views differed from most Alaskans'.

For most of my twelve years in the Alaska Legislature, I'd been able to avoid significant leadership responsibilities. Being in the Minority helped. But after 1966, Republican seats increased. As third senior Republican, I moved up to Majority leader in 1969. In the Senate reorganization of 1970, to my consternation, a secret ballot dumped me unceremoniously into the Senate President's chair — furniture I soon found both hot and confining.

Without doubt the most discordant note I would strike while in it was the long primal scream reverberating from my bucking head-long into plans for the proposed trans-Alaska pipeline.

By 1970, most Alaskans favored construction of an "all Alaska" pipeline from Prudhoe Bay 800 miles to the Alaska seaport of Valdez. Congressmen from the Midwest, thirsting to receive Alaskan crude, preferred an alternative route through Canada.

The prospect of an immense construction project all within Alaska, estimated to cost at least $900 million, had state developers drooling. They argued against a Canada pipeline, asserting it would be far more expensive than one running 900 miles across Alaska to tidewater. The additional costs of tankering oil down the West Coast, then piping it 1,700 miles to the Midwest were ignored.

Winning their specious argument may have been one of the most costly mistakes of the 20th Century.

Ignoring not only comparative costs, "All Alaska Pipeline" advocates stirred public fears that piping Alaska oil across foreign soil would expose it to hazard. This jingoistic argument not only overlooked the many pipelines through which oil had for years freely been flowing between our two nations — if it came to a "battle of the spigots," Canadians stood to lose far more than Americans — it failed to foresee the eventual necessity of first tankering, then piping Alaska oil through Panama, thereby enriching the volatile dictatorship of Manuel Noriega, who did indeed come to pose a threat to our energy security.

Even more important, ignored were two other major items that would do much to impact Alaska and the nation, economically and environmentally.

First, virtually every economic study then available concluded Alaska, oil producers and the federal government, all would derive far more revenue if our oil were transported by a trans-Canada route than through a trans-Alaska line — unless Alaska crude could be sold to the Far East, in which case economic benefits were a "wash." Far cheaper costs of shipping oil in foreign tankers to Japan would provide the state with tax revenues comparable to those derived from transport across Canada. Likewise, shipping Alaska oil to Pacific markets would realize more revenue both to the Federal treasury and producers. The economics seemed irrefutable.

The second definitive issue was raised by conservationists. Most favored a trans-Canadian route since confining the pipeline to the corridor of the Alcan Highway would cause far less environmental disturbance than running it through virgin wilderness. Not only was this a time when immediate and long-term economic and ecological advantages seemed to coincide, the Canadian route also would preclude hazardous tankering of oil through pristine Alaska waters and down the Pacific Coast — a fact that prompted Prince William Sound's fishermen to vigorously oppose the all-Alaskan route.

As the debate raged on, none foresaw the coming 1973 Arab Oil Embargo, fueled in part by Alaskans insisting on the all-Alaska route, thereby delaying flow of Alaskan oil. Environmentalists vowed to sue to stop the pipeline unless alternatives to the all-Alaska route were studied, as required by the recently enacted National Environmental Policy Act. Their suit also charged trans-Alaska planners with ignoring Rights-of-Way statutes and land claims.

Having read these economic and legal studies and believing conservationists had a valid case that could stymie pipeline construction, I felt prudence dictated we examine their charges more closely. To encourage this, I wrote a resolution. Its essence was: "Whereas, several studies conclude Alaska would annually glean millions of dollars more by transporting oil through a trans-Canada pipeline than by an all Alaskan route, (unless our oil was destined for Pacific markets); and Whereas, environmentalists can halt pipeline construction through legal actions, unless laws requiring examination of alternative routes and rights of way are adhered to; Now, Therefore, be it resolved: *All economic studies be evaluated by the State to determine the comparative long term financial returns and, as required by Law, that alternative pipeline routes be assessed and pipeline Rights of Way be brought into compliance."*

In retrospect, the resolution seems innocuously appropriate. At the time, you would have thought I'd debauched Mother Theresa! Before the explosion, however, as I carried the resolution to the Senate chamber, I encountered my unfortunate friend Senator Palmer. Showing him the resolution, I asked if he'd like to join me as a co-sponsor. Bob read it; concluding it contained nothing more than plain common sense, he agreed. I suspect I could have persuaded others to do likewise. However, in a rush to get the measure in before deadline, I showed it to no one else. Poor Palmer. If he'd not learned from co-sponsoring my pro-Tillion resolution that had led then-Governor Hickel's molars to mow carpet pile, this imprudence soon taught Bob a far harsher lesson.

The resolution triggered an unbelievably violent response. Oil companies, of course, saw "unnecessary delay" in further studies; but particularly outraged was Robert Atwood, publisher and editor of the powerful *Anchorage Times*. In Atwood's first editorial blast, Palmer and I were accused of everything from insurrection to insanity. We were anti-Alaskan, anti-American, anti-development, anti-business and, that ultimate of all denunciations in the *Times'* lexicon, "environmental preservationists!"

While the din of Atwood's denunciations still echoed around the state, Alaska Teamster boss, Jesse Carr, already the most powerful political force in Alaska (even Anchorage police would be represented by the Teamsters in negotiations under Carr's reign), weighed in with earthier appellations.

Initially, most abuse was heaped on Palmer, who in my absence, took a phone call from the *Times*. Naively, Bob assumed a logical explanation would satisfy anyone of reasonable intelligence. Few appeared to be listening. Instead, an even more vitriolic editorial followed, most of the fallout landing unfairly on Palmer.

Meanwhile, conservationists, again demonstrating they do their homework more thoroughly, laid credit for the resolution at my feet. They, of course, felt it splendidly appropriate. These circumstances brought a toothy grin from Clem Tillion. "Hammond, you did it again. You introduced legislation for which you get all the credit and Palmer gets all the blame." That luxury did not last long.

Some editorial commentary attributed the most preposterous ulterior motives to Palmer and me. Some were so ludicrous Palmer and I wondered if someone was joking. Imprudently discussing this possibility within earshot of the press, I noted a *Times* reporter frantically scribbling notes.

That evening's *Times* story was fairly accurate. However, its editorialized headline — something like: "Hammond and Palmer Laugh Over Pipeline Flap" — inspired an outrageous flight of editorial fancy based, not on the content of the news story, but on their editorialized headline, a favorite *Times* "journalism" device.

Palmer and I were excoriated for "laughing" about Alaska's jobless, the state's depressed economy, small business bankruptcies, needy Natives and bedeviled taxpayers generally, to say nothing of Veterans, children, the lame, the sick and the halt.

Other legislators quickly got the message and placed as much distance as possible between themselves and pariahs Palmer and Hammond. One, Representative Maury Smith, a popular Fairbanks newscaster, frequently had expressed environmental concerns in the past. His reaction surprised me most. "Shocked and outraged" by our perfidies, he could not believe we were serious. Didn't we know Fairbanks was barely hanging on by its fingernails economically; and that the pipeline was the lifeline by which his community and most of Alaska, could be rappelled to fiscal security?

A year or so later, his words came to mind when I read in the *Fairbanks Daily News-Miner* that long-time local newscaster Maury Smith, after some 40 years in Alaska, had decided to leave. He cited as reasons the profound change and disruption of his cherished Alaskan lifestyle brought about by pipeline construction.

To give the legislature a chance to offset charges that Alaskans were environmentally insensitive, I introduced another resolution. This one simply said Alaskans would support the pipeline route which, through study of alternatives, proved to be first *environmentally*, and only second, most *economically* desirable from the state viewpoint. But so gun-shy had fellow legislators become, they would do nothing but plunge full speed ahead in blind, obedient support of the trans-Alaska route. Any suggestion we even look at alternatives triggered tirades from the *Times* and other media. The resolution failed. So did my next attempt — to reverse environmental and economic priorities and thus get the legislature's actual stance on record.

My revised resolution read: "The legislature supports the Alaska route *whether or not it is the most environmentally or economically preferable.*" This proved too candid. The body rejected it by gleefully clouting the Senate President (me) in open floor debate.

Still not content to leave bad enough alone, I scrubbed more salt into my wounds. To claims by "Outsiders" that Alaskans were greedy, blue-eyed Arabs more concerned with economics than environment, I responded such charges were simply not true. "Even though it appears in the long term we'd make far more money going through Canada, and in the process, avoid the environmental threats of tankering oil through our pristine waters, Alaskans are able to rise above such selfish monetary considerations. *We're willing to do it wrong even if it costs more!*"

That did it. Almost no one in Alaska, save of course, "preservationist extremists" dared suggest we even *look* at a Canadian route for fear of being branded a "crackpot conservationist like Hammond" by the state's most powerful newspaper and labor union.

Clearly, Alaska would experience far less environmental trauma with only six hundred overland miles of pipeline construction across its wilderness than nine hundred miles to Valdez — not to mention the pollution hazards of tankering via Prince William Sound and down the Pacific coast. The fact that the planned pipeline terminal at Valdez would be erected on a major earthquake fault was also not mentioned, as I recall.

In any event, transporting our oil through a single, 2,100 mile trans-Canada line to the Midwest would clearly be less costly than tankering *past* West Coast ports — which is precisely what happened when the southern pipeline fell through and inadequate West Coast refining capacity required North Slope crude to be shipped to the Panama Canal. There, supertankers had to be unloaded onto smaller vessels able to navigate the isthmus. These took the oil another 1,500 miles north to the Gulf of Mexico, to refineries in Houston. From there, of course, the product was piped north and east to the marketplace. Some Alaska oil didn't ship north to Houston, but went all the way to the East coast for refining and sale.

If there has ever been a greater waste of energy and economic potential than what Alaska and the nation paid for the All-Alaska pipeline route, I don't know what it might be. It has already cost uncounted billions of dollars and has been a major contributor to the nation's enormous trade deficit.

Most economists in 1970 agreed; only if Alaskan oil was shipped to neighboring Pacific Rim nations, did the longterm economic impacts on the state become a wash with piping it via a trans-Canada route. There's no doubt this was intended. Japanese interests admitted such negotiations were under way.

This revelation only further infuriated Midwestern congressmen who wanted Alaskan oil to flow to *their* refineries. When Congress threatened to halt pipeline construction until assured no Alaska oil would be sold to the Japanese, pipeline owners and proponents of the trans-Alaska route, scuttled negotiations and gave their word not to ship Alaska oil abroad. Instead, they'd just ship it twice that distance around the coasts of North and Central America — each additional mile of transportation costs deducted from the wellhead price of the oil. Since severance taxes on oil extraction are based on the price of oil at the wellhead, *less transportation costs*, obviously the lower the transport, the higher the tax revenues. Don't even mention the additional energy wasted in this most inefficient boondoggle.

To require compliance, Congress enacted the Federal Ban on Alaska Oil Export, a classic perversion of so-called "Free Trade" still standing in 1993, as we bash Japan's "unfair trade policies." The last time the United States embargoed oil to Japan, it led to war. With the international trade deficit this embargo has made possible between our two nations, perhaps Japan should have been more patient — or did we win World War II? I can't seem to recall.

The full costs paid to secure approval of the trans-Alaska route may never be known. Lost revenue and energy are just a part of it. Certainly, the one-third greater pipeline construction costs expended in Alaska *might* have provided more jobs and contracts for locals, as proponents promised. However, since most pipeline workers were imported, and many of the bigger contracts went to Outside firms, it's hard to quantify how much more Alaskans benefited in the short term — if at all — than had much of the pipeline gone through Canada.

True, the greater length of pipe in Alaska, and the number of capital projects located in the Port of Valdez, are values added. Yet countering these are the costs of state services required to offset population explosions in communities like Fairbanks and Valdez. Both pleaded for the trans-Alaska route, but were the first to come begging the state for multi-millions in "impact money" to offset spiraling demands for government services that came with the "boom."

Subsequently, of course, the massive 1989 *Exxon Valdez* spill in Prince William Sound has illuminated other costs of the route.

Economic studies financed by Alaska Legislators John Sackett, Al Adams and Jan Faiks, indicated by 1987 Alaska had lost an estimated *$15 billion* as part of the price paid for the all-Alaska Pipeline. Since Alaska crude sells at a lower price than imported oil, the higher price it would bring on the world market has cost the national treasury many billions as well.

But in 1970, none of this could be proven, especially to people who didn't want to hear it. And, as my controversial resolution forewarned, the pipeline was delayed when environmentalists won a court injunction based on the project's failure to comply with EPA regulations and rights-of-way stipulations. This delay played a large role in the economic upheavals caused by the Arab Oil Embargo by slowing America's industrial machine to a virtual standstill, marooning motorists on highways while others fought for places in long gas lines, and fueling one of the worst inflationary periods of this century.

During this catastrophe, rather than admit their undersight, pipeline promoters blamed all ills on environmentalists: "Preservationists Delay Pipeline" headlines screamed. As my good friend Kay Fanning, then-publisher and savior of the more even-tempered *Anchorage Daily News*, has pointed out, the Alaska Oil Pipeline galvanized the nation's environmental awareness. But up here, "environmentalism" became a dirty word. And the President of the Alaska State Senate was, if you believed what you read in the papers, the dirtiest preservationist of them all.

It's true. "Preservationists" did delay pipeline construction. But rather than blame "environmental preservationists," far greater blame should be laid at the feet of those "developmental preservationists" who would preserve every exploitive, "damn the torpedoes, full speed ahead" environmentally insensitive despoiling technique of the 19th Century. By ignoring laws of the land and the forewarnings of those who promised to force legal compliance, they, not the environmentalists, caused the costly delay.

Forgotten by many who still curse environmentalists for these woes is the fact that during the delay, construction techniques were upgraded and engineering problems resolved. Now, even some of the pipeline's most ardent promoters admit that, without these improvements, the line might well have proved a disaster. Today they point with pride to what environmental activists compelled them to do.

MY PIPELINE RESOLUTION began my fall from grace on the editorial pages of the *Anchorage Times*, a plunge that was to accelerate for the remainder of my political career. Frequently, I helped grease the skids by imprudently tilting with Bob Atwood on his own editorial page. For politicians, this is at best not too bright; at worst, terminal. Yet I succeeded, once, in getting the legislature to join in, unwittingly.

As Senate President, in the wake of an editorial I felt a particularly outrageous distortion, I wrote another resolution that said, in essence: "Whereas, the members of the Alaska Legislature are ardent champions of Freedom of the Press; and Whereas, however, we believe one of its prime Freedoms should be Freedom from Falsehood; and Whereas, it is important in these critical years for Alaskans to be fully apprised of the many controversial issues confronting them so they can form intelligent opinions; and Whereas, while most reporters do a reasonable job gathering and conveying facts, their reports unfortunately sometimes undergo distortion enroute to the editorial page and confuse the public; Now, Therefore, be it resolved such lamentable editorial practices cease."

When the resolution was read on the floor of the Senate, Lowell Thomas Jr. innocently rose and was recognized.

"Mr. President, I certainly agree with the resolution. We've all been offended on occasion by undue editorial license. However, this is unlike any resolution I've seen before. It's not addressed to Congress or anyone. To whom is it to be sent?"

Whereupon by pre-arrangement rose Juneau Senator Bill Ray, frequent victim of Atwood's continuing campaign to move the State Capital to within the *Anchorage Times'* circulation zone.

"The Chair recognizes the Senator from Juneau," I intoned with as much solemnity as I could muster.

"Mr. President," barked Ray, "I move and ask unanimous consent this resolution be sent only to Bob Atwood, publisher of the *Anchorage Daily Times*."

Hastily slamming my gavel before someone could protest, I pronounced, "Without Objection. So Ordered!"

I'm told when Atwood received the single copy of an official Senate reprimand, he was furious. Many Anchorage legislators were his personal friends and he was incensed at their failure to object to the resolution, or at least to its single referral. Of course, they'd had no chance. As word of this humiliation circulated, my standing in Alaska's largest newspaper was not enhanced.

Before the pipeline resolution, *Times* editorials had been very kind. More than once they had lauded my actions as Resource chairman, including efforts to reconcile conflicts between conservationists and miners on fisheries issues. Upon my election as Senate President their praise was lavish. No longer. I was continually blasted, sometimes even with cause. That often no cause was required at first confused me. Only later did someone purported to be "in the know," assert the basis for Atwood's violent reaction was his large property holdings which would appreciate should the trans-Alaska route be selected. Now *that*, I can understand, if true.

Today, while most Alaskans support oil export, they seem to forget they bargained away billions of dollars with the right to sell Alaskan oil to Japan as part of the price paid to secure the all-Alaska pipeline route. Midwestern congressmen have not. Every time the export ban expires, out comes the sale agreement and the economically damaging embargo is sustained. Oddly enough, in the Democratically controlled U.S. House, Alaska's only member, Republican Don Young, voted to extend the ban. That's a shame; for both Alaska and the nation would be much better off, financially and in energy conservation — not to mention Free Trade and the balance of payments — if the ban were removed. In addition to greater federal and state revenues to help tilt the balance of payments deficit more to our advantage, it might be a step toward a sane national energy policy now sorely lacking.

Instead, Alaska oil, on its way eastward through the Panama Canal to Gulf states and beyond, passes Mexican oil, on its way westward to Japan. This is ridiculous. What we should have done, of course, is simply swap, drum for drum, Alaskan oil for Mexican — and enrich the treasuries of both nations. This issue, I regret, once more demonstrates the ability of politicians to subordinate our nation's well-being to demands of local constituencies.

MY PIPELINE RESOLUTION won enmity from almost every quarter. Governor Bill Egan, an ardent advocate of the all-Alaska route, was no exception. Thanks to the governor's tender mercies, and the new re-apportionment plan he was obliged to draw up in its wake, I was again prompted to leave public office, a departure mourned neither by Egan, the multitude of special interests aligned against me, nor myself.

"What? Him governor? Naaaaw!!" Still, some folks claimed they'd vote for me BECAUSE of the beard.

21

"Retired" and Retreaded

POPULATION CHANGES brought by the tide of people flooding to Alaska for pipeline jobs allowed Bill Egan to again redraw the boundaries of my election district. This time, he thoughtfully expanded it to include the hometown of one of Alaska's most powerful Democratic senators, George Hohman of Bethel.

After six years in the Senate and six in the House, the fading attractions of public office did little to inspire the enormous effort to defeat Hohman — if indeed, he was beatable. A member of the Senate Finance Committee and an extremely shrewd "pork" processor unencumbered by concerns beyond securing many times his district's share of the state's annual budget, George took extremely good care of his friends. While this attribute later earned a criminal indictment, expulsion from the Senate and a term in prison, by 1972, it had only won him re-election by huge pluralities. I found it difficult to believe the governor was unaware of this when he planned his reapportionment, or if so, that he shed many tears when apprised.

The challenge of running against Hohman and the unpopularity of my views on pipeline routing made the option of spending more time with my family in the real Alaska all the more appealing. In 1972, I announced from the Senate President's chair my plan to retire from politics. The standing ovation from my colleagues, I chose to believe was due to my past performance, not my pending departure.

In the midst of these somewhat emotional proceedings, Beverly Keitahn, the lovely and extremely competent Senate Secretary who sat on my left, handed me a note. Since it was signed with the initial "B," I presumed she had written it. It read: "You horse's ass! Why did you have to go and do that?"

The demure Beverly always performed her duties with lady-like decorum, her blush threshold easily exceeded by the slightest off-color remark. Accordingly, I found her comment uncharacteristically terse and salty.

Scribbling my response, I returned the note. Flaring crimson, Beverly almost fell off her dais. Hastily she scratched another note, informing me *she* had not written the original; she'd simply relayed it from Senator Bill Ray!

With my retirement, Edgar Paul Boyko, a colorful criminal attorney, prognosticated in his weekly column, *The Roar of the Snow Tiger*, how Governor Egan, in reapportioning my district to make it virtually impossible for me to win re-election to the Senate, might prompt me to go after Egan's seat instead.

No one thought this prediction more silly than I, unless it was Bill Egan. We laughed together over what we believed was just another "dropping" in what some called "The Spoor of the Snow Tiger."

Boyko, a near-brilliant, articulate and flamboyant crusader for often outrageous causes and perceived as defender of the usually guilty, often requisitioned the courtroom as a laboratory to perform lobotomies on whatever body of law affronted him at the moment. To some, he came off more scoundrel than swashbuckler. Verbally capering about like a mad scientist constructing a monster from spare parts, Boyko would gleefully present his end product to judge and jury to await their accolades. That he ever succeeded in conning them into believing Jack the Ripper was really Jack Armstrong, was surprising. That he did so often suggests a degree of competence I am loathe to admit.

I have a shameful bias. There are certain criminal lawyers who, in my view, are retained mostly by the guilty. Their retention, I assume, is nothing less than admission of guilt. Certainly if *I* were guilty I'd hire them. My brief stint at law enforcement corrupted me into believing most brought to trial are, in fact, guilty. True or not, there are enough guilty people faced with court proceedings eager to purchase the services of a good criminal lawyer to keep that species fully employed. I admit my attitude is cynical, prejudiced and unfair. Unfortunately, it is also too often true.

A loquacious and interesting character, Boyko had the discomfiting habit of penetrating one's territory by standing nose-to-nose; frequently to deliver off-color observations or raunchy jokes. I later learned this proximity was due to poor eyesight. But few things more disturb me than to be brought unwillingly into obscene conversation. Only a breath length away.

I must say, Boyko's poor eyesight did nothing to hamper his selection of female companions. One in particular remains vividly etched in memory. During Boyko's short tenure as Governor Hickel's Attorney General, she appeared with Boyko when he gave testimony at an evening meeting of some Senate committee. I sat in the second row directly behind them. Mini-skirts had just made their debut in Alaska and some of us were still a bit shell-shocked by their revelations. Boyko's secretary wore one of bright pink which seemed to drape distractingly no more than six inches below her navel. I tried heroically to avoid more accurate visual measurement. Not all my senatorial colleagues were so successful.

Senator Jay Kerttula, from Palmer, is a man like myself, cursed with an affliction altogether too common in politicians: the inability to use few words when many will do. Given to subjecting captive audiences to lengthy pontifications whenever the spirit moves him, testifying this evening he was especially so moved. Kerttula has a wondrous facility for stringing words together in such a manner which, if you're not listening closely, seems to make sense. The more one tries to stay on track, however, the more confusing the trail becomes. One soon finds himself clawing through a tangled undergrowth of verdant verbiage, bearings awry. For this talent, Kerttula has become affectionately known as "The Great Knik Wind" — a blustery climatic disturbance that frequently blows off the Knik River in his Senate district.

On this evening, Kerttula outdid himself. Taking the stand, he verbally circled and probed, cavorted and crept through an Amazonian rain forest of issues, most of which bore not the slightest relationship to the subject at hand. It was a superb filibuster, designed simply to retain his vantage point in the witness chair — aimed directly at the mini-skirted target some ten feet away. Of course, Kerttula, ever the consummate fraud like most of us who succeed politically, attempted to cover his motives for holding the chair by clothing his testimony in especially heart-felt pathos and concern, all the while innocently swiveling his eyeballs over his entire audience rather than rudely locking onto his true objective. It was a masterful demonstration. Except for a touch of floridity and beads of sweat on his brow, he almost carried it off. From my location immediately behind Boyko's secretary, I was able to track the course of his probing eyeballs and note the point where his pupils periodically dilated.

At the close of Kerttula's testimony, which consumed the remaining time allotted, committee member Lowell Thomas Jr. came up to me totally perplexed. "You know, I had a martini for dinner this evening," said Lowell apologetically. "I'm not ever going to do that again before a committee meeting. I didn't think it would affect me so, but I couldn't begin to keep track of what Kerttula was saying."

"Don't worry, Lowell," said I. "You weren't supposed to."

Characters like Kertulla had added color and zest to my twelve years in the legislature. On my departure, I found I missed folk like him a lot more than the fray.

ALMOST A YEAR AND A HALF after my retirement from the legislature, happily engaged again in guiding, flying and fishing around our Lake Clark homestead and my summer fishing base in Naknek, the political years seemed far behind. Had it not been for bad weather, they might have stayed there.

On a stormy September afternoon in 1973, I was sitting in our Naknek kitchen drinking coffee with Jack Rawlings, a sport fishing client from California. A cold rain beating the windows from overcast skies had prevented our flying to one of Jack's favorite trout steams, and we were holed up. A phone call interrupted.

"Hello, Jay? This is Ron Somerville."

"Who?"

"Ron Somerville, of the Alaska Department of Fish and Game."

"Yeah, Ron; what's up?"

"Well, a few of us were sitting around talking and we think you ought to run for governor."

When I stopped laughing, I told him to forget it.

"I'm not interested in bleeding myself white financially for the privilege of saying I ran unsuccessfully for governor. Besides, I've been out of the swim for almost two years and I've no desire whatsoever to get back in the water."

"Well," he persisted, "would you consider running if we put together a campaign organization and came up with some funding?"

To end a ridiculous conversation, I told him, "Those would be the *only* conditions under which I'd even consider it. I've seen too many folk all but bankrupt themselves running for office. It's bad enough if someone wants the job more than anything in the world. To pay that price for something I *don't* want would be asinine. I wouldn't spend a dime on such a Mission Impossible."

Ron mumbled something and we hung up.

Jack, overhearing the conversation, was intrigued. "I think you ought to do it," he said.

"Forget it," said I.

"Well," he said, "if you change your mind, let me know. There'll be a campaign contribution in the next mail."

"That's one check you'll never have to write," I assured him. "The next to last thing in the world I want to do is run for governor. The *last* thing I'd want would be to win. I look at no politician with any degree of envy, especially the Governor of Alaska, particularly these days. I much prefer life outside the political arena, throwing rocks in, rather than trying to field them."

Anyway, I told Jack, I was much too selfish to give up a lifestyle I relished for one so programmed and restrictive. Just the social obligations of the office were enough to horrify me. I'd spent entirely too much time in the bush to be comfortable living full time in a city. I hadn't worn a necktie for almost two years and hoped never to see one again.

When we went fishing later that day, I felt the issue was laid to rest. But Ron called again about two weeks later.

"Well, we've put together a campaign organization and come up with some money. You said you'd run if we did."

"Hey, wait a minute. I only said I'd *consider* running if those conditions were met."

"Well," he asked, "will you at least meet with our group on your next trip to Anchorage?"

A short time later, I fired up my Cessna and flew in to meet Somerville and his "campaign organization" — all six of them. While I knew I'd made no commitment, despite my protest it was apparent they were convinced I had. Still lacking courage to stand up to those who would hold me to promises I'd never made, I caved in and reluctantly agreed to file. But I reaffirmed my opinion that their idea was ridiculous and my determination not to spend a penny of my own money.

"I'll run only to the extent funds are available."

As I recall, at the time I agreed to file there was about eight hundred dollars in the campaign war chest, with "commitments" for a few thousand more.

Well, I thought, nothing to worry about. I'll run till the money runs out and return to the hills where I belong. When I told Bella, she was apprehensive.

"What have you gotten yourself into now?"

"Nothing to worry about," I said. "I'll run for a week or two and when the money's gone, come on home."

WHY RUN AT ALL? Well, here was a chance to tour the whole state on someone else's money, sounding off on matters that had long irked me: Imprudent sale of oil leases in pristine Kachemak Bay; the decline and neglect of our fisheries; burgeoning unhealthy growth that couldn't pay its own way; failure to provide means by which some of our prospective oil wealth could be saved for future generations — not blown on instant gratification for those here now — and the inequitable distribution of benefits spinning off from that wealth.

With Alaska soon to be awash in "one-time" oil dollars, it seemed everyone knew how to spend it. The common source of these dreams was what someone once termed the "Edifice Complex," capital projects to build, build, build, with no thought about how to maintain all these structures when wells went dry and money stopped flowing. I had no desire to be the chief executive charged with trying to manage these problems. But I couldn't pass up a free ride to stress to whoever was elected governor that such critical issues could not be ignored.

MY MOST PROMINENT OPPONENTS in the 1974 Primary were former Republican Governors Hickel and Keith Miller. If by some miracle I made it by them, I'd have to face Alaska's most popular politician, Governor Bill Egan, running with his peripatetic lieutenant governor, Red Boucher, former mayor of Fairbanks, Alaska's second largest city. Both Hickel and Miller's political base was Anchorage, home to half the state's population. Weighing in from Naknek, population two hundred and fifty, with little money, even less name recognition and no hope of winning, I could be as outspoken as I liked. And I liked that a lot.

So did the media, which gleefully reported any rude comments I made. The first was my response to a reporter who asked if I was surprised Wally Hickel had come back from Washington to file for governor.

"Yes," I replied. "I thought he had his eye on the presidency . . . as a stepping stone to higher office."

Curiously, that spring I, a Republican, had been invited to emcee part of the annual Democratic Legislative Dinner in Juneau, probably for the same sport Romans had cheered in the Coliseum. Finding myself seated at the head table next to Governor Egan, who'd retired me many months earlier, I decided to cooperate with the Games and announced my candidacy for Governor.

Egan elicited great belly laughs — in which I joined heartily — when he expressed the "mortal terror" my candidacy struck in his heart.

"Why I understand Hammond has all of three percent name recognition among the electorate," chortled Bill. "It's going to be tough to beat such stupendous odds!"

Egan, whose ability to recall names was legendary, in contrast to my own inability to remember either names or faces, had reason to feel complacent. Not only did every Alaskan know Bill's name, he seemed to know their's as well. When I took the podium to respond, I acknowledged the governor's superior capacity for name recollection, but assured him, come Election Day, he'd recall mine even if I could not recall his.

All in the spirit of good fun, everyone seemed to enjoy the evening's "roast." For all the flippant comedy in the room that night, no one knew better than I, my candidacy was the biggest joke of all.

In Naknek before the race for governor with three of my favorite women, daughters Dana (left), Heidi and Bella. My oldest daughter, Wendy, was overseas in the Peace Corps.

22

The 1974 Primary Campaign

MY THREE GREATEST DISADVANTAGES in the Primary were my name recognition — except among pipeline boosters who viewed my candidacy unfavorably — lack of money, and consequently, an absence of credibility with Alaska's voters.

The three went hand in hand as I stumbled along, foot in mouth. Often the media helped me insert it by quoting me accurately, if not completely: When a reporter asked why I'd been reluctant to run, I'd responded: "Because of lack of funding and ability to put together an effective campaign organization." The ensuing news story: "Hammond says he is reluctant to run because of lack of funding and ability."

In spite of my floundering, I had one advantage over widely favored front-runners, former Governors Hickel and Miller. In 1974, a state campaign spending limit prohibited gubernatorial candidates spending more than forty cents times the population of Alaska. Not that we ever expected to raise the roughly $180,000 permitted. "Big spenders" were going to the competition. But candidates who could raise far more were severely handicapped from "buying" the election outright. The campaign spending cap served to even the playing field somewhat, even though we had but a few thousand dollars in our war chest. What we had in abundance was people asking not only "who" was this bearded bush rat running for governor, but "why?"

Soon after I announced, my name recognition was enormously enhanced when my good friend Lowell Thomas Jr. teamed up to run as my lieutenant governor. The idea of "teaming" was a first for Alaska — or so I thought. Up until 1974, candidates ran separate primary campaigns, the winners teaming up to run as a ticket only in the general Election. But Lowell informed me we were not the first to think up this ploy. According to Thomas, he'd declined just such a offer in 1965, when Wally Hickel asked him to team up in the 1966 primary. A major fund raiser for Nixon, Wally assured Lowell if Nixon won in 1968, he'd be rewarded with a Cabinet post and Lowell, as lieutenant governor, would become governor. Lowell's rejection of this offer was a measure both of his character and the luster his name added to our ticket.

Wally Hickel was undoubtedly my most visible and well-heeled primary opponent. But there were two other, even more potent opponents standing barely off stage, throwing garlands to Wally and garbage at me: *Anchorage Times* publisher Bob Atwood, and Teamsters Union boss Jesse Carr, the most powerful political force in Alaska.

Both men shared Wally's blind boosterism. Like him, neither had apparently met a development project they didn't love. As I, on occasion had asked rude questions regarding objects of their affection, all three took delight in searing me with the "Zero Growth Hammond" brand. Accordingly, barrages of egg shells, coffee grounds and political excreta were showered on me daily in the *Times*, weekly at Teamster meetings, and bi-monthly in the union's newsletters. Perhaps because of this, no candidate had so widely disparate a group of supporters as we did in 1974. So varied were their political views it's a wonder we could get them in the same room. A phone call to Avrum Gross, former head of Alaska's American Civil Liberties Union, makes the point.

"Mr. Gross, my name is Spike McVaugh. I'm chairman of the local John Birch Society and I'm supporting Hammond for Governor. To my dismay, I find you're supporting Hammond for Governor. What's going on here? I've never agreed with you on anything before. Maybe we'd better get together and talk."

They did. Incredibly, each came away with grudging respect for the other and, more surprisingly, with their support for me still intact.

I'M PROBABLY THE LEAST QUALIFIED to analyze the 1974 primary campaign. I didn't plan it, I never knew a lot of what was going on. I only knew I had no chance of winning. It's easy to ignore just what's going on when you have nothing to lose because you don't plan on winning.

Not only was I unknown from a small, remote village with no political base, I was opposed by almost every major interest group in the state: the Teamsters; the AFL/CIO, the state employees' unions, the National Education Association; the State Chamber of Commerce; the most powerful elements of Alaska's media, and — last but not least — the Alaska Republican party, whose golden boy was, of course, Wally Hickel.

All the above should have been sufficient to assure defeat with no effort on my part. Nonetheless, I fancifully calculated how I might "blow" any chance of election, just to be sure. In Alaska, that should be easy. Speaking kindly of either the

federal government or gun control ought to do it. Yet I was already on record opposing statehood — which suggested I was soft on the "Feds — and my gun control
pronouncements were so convoluted both sides on this issue had already condemned
me. When a reporter asked if I favored gun control, I'd answered: "Of course. And
I've been controlling my guns for years — with no help from bureaucrats, thank
you." There seemed little more I could do, short of self-immolation.

Compounding my dilemma was the increasing number of good people
deluded by my candidacy and willing to work hard and hand over money to
help our campaign. They were committed even if I was not. When I lost, I
didn't want anyone to be able to say "you might have won if you had just done
what we asked." Accordingly, I told my campaign people I'd let them wind me
up as they wished. I vowed to go where they said, when they said, and soon was
immersed in all the abusing indignities election campaigning requires.

Bob Palmer had signed on as my campaign manager. One of his early
tactical suggestions concerned my beard. To sanitize my image, Bob advised I
shave.

I didn't care for his suggestion, but promised to "take it under advisement."
Again serendipity stayed my hand and saved my face.

In an Anchorage store one morning, a clerk looked up. "Hey! I know you.
I saw you on TV. Man, you got my vote. Any guy with the guts to wear a beard
and run for governor's gotta be different. Those clean shaven guys try to im-
press us they're honest and we *know* they're crooks!"

I told this to Palmer and said if I didn't deserve to be governor with a
beard, I didn't deserve to be governor without one. "Abe Lincoln did all right,
you know."

"Yeah," sighed Palmer. "Look what happened to him."

OUR CAMPAIGN STRATEGY was simple. Various organizations and media
provided candidate "debates" which got us good exposure at no cost. Since we
had little cash, these events were important. Meanwhile, the key in my back
would be wound to show up for debates, and to campaign by that time-honored,
low-cost practice known as door-to-door voter solicitation. At first I did not
look forward to either. Later, I found them far less onerous than imagined.

Unfortunately, organized confrontations between candidates seldom con-
stitute true debate. Most are little more than "show and tell" posturings that do
little to enlighten the electorate. My first such confrontation was a function
where each candidate was asked to state why he should be elected. The three
previous governors — Egan, Hickel and Miller — spoke first, stressing their
experience. As "tail end Charlie" with nothing to lose, I left their flight path.

"I'd like to caution my opponents about the campaign bumper stickers
they've chosen," I began. "They suggest supplemental slogans to complete the
thoughts conveyed. Take Wally's campaign slogan for example:

"Wally Hickel — He Can Handle It

"Then why didn't he?" I asked, hoping to remind the audience Hickel had quit his governor's job in midterm.

"Or take Keith Miller's campaign slogan:

"Happiness is a new Governor

"Not one of these three old ones?" I asked, pointing to each of the three former governors on the dais.

"As for Governor Bill Egan, whose slogan warns Democrats not to defect in the Open Primary to elect a weak Republican candidate, here's a bumper sticker slogan he can have for nothing:

"No Fair Thinking — Vote Straight Democrat"

I SOON FOUND THESE so-called debates a lush gathering of over-ripe egos. Inevitably, a candidate would expose a tender pomposity ripe for pricking. At almost every debate, a panel member would ask the candidates why each felt most qualified to govern the state. The first time this question was put to me it came from a journalist exuding scorn. It seemed incomprehensible to him that a bearded bush rat from Naknek, with virtually no administrative experience, would have the audacity to run against Walter J. Hickel, whose remarkable energies, legend has it, parlayed 35 cents into millions; or the natty Keith Miller, who appeared always to have just emerged from a Band Box; or Bill Egan, three-time governor who made political points as "the friend of the Common Man."

"Well," I admitted, "I sure can't out-hustle an 'erg' like Wally; or 'out-couth' Keith Miller. But there's a lot of folks out there who'll tell you I'm *twice* as common as Bill Egan."

When next asked why, with my comparative inexperience, I felt entitled to vie with these three vastly more experienced administrators, I explained, "Actually, I have an unfair advantage over the other candidates. After all, the prime criterion for a top notch administrator is his ability to select persons more competent than himself to fill positions of authority under him — and I have a much broader field to choose from than these other fellows." It was true. Unlike the others, I was beholding to nobody.

This question came up again and again. On our final televised confrontation, I was again asked: "Why do you think you're the most qualified to become governor?"

"To the contrary," I replied. "I don't for a moment believe I am the most qualified to become governor. There are many Alaskans more qualified than I. Isn't it a shame none of them are running?"

Notwithstanding attempts to make light of my shortcomings, administrative inexperience and low name recognition continued to limit my credibility as a serious candidate. A chance to distinguish myself came when I addressed the Alaska Press Club. Afterward, I thought I'd extinguished myself instead.

My plan was to use the large assembly of reporters to make two points. The first was central to why I was going through the campaign; the second was to establish my right to campaign when everyone seemed to discount my candidacy almost as much as I did.

I began by launching a sermon I was to preach *ad nauseam* for the next eight years. At the time, it was an issue virtually no one in Alaska was addressing, gubernatorial candidates least of all.

"Alaskans should beware: some economic growth can be malignant. Unless development is environmentally sound, desired by a majority of Alaskans, and can pay its own way without burdening the state and the taxpayer, I'll oppose it.

"The state already is overpopulated economically. With the nation's highest unemployment rate, it's obvious there are too many people here for the jobs available. Unless new jobs go to Alaskans already here, some kinds of growth will simply compound our problems; because traditionally, for each new job created, three or four new job seekers flock up here to compete for them. When are we going to learn that malignant development is not only environmentally pollutive; it can be economically pollutive as well? Pump it into the mainstream of our economy and it can quickly turn black ink to red."

Up until then, all Alaska's media had heard from political candidates was knee-jerk support for any development that created new jobs. Asserting these jobs might cost the state taxpayers more than they were worth, was a heresy that seemed to capture my audience's interest. While I had that elusive commodity in hand, I felt compelled to state why I believed I was at least *entitled* to run for governor, despite my lack of recognition, funds, organization or administrative experience.

"It's true I've not had the 'office-bound' administrative experience of my opponents. But perhaps there's something else I can offer. I know a little something about the problems facing Alaskan homesteaders, because I've been one! I know something about the problems facing:

"Alaskan guides — because I've been one!

"Alaskan trappers — because I've been one!

"Alaskan bush pilots — because I've been one!

"Alaskan veterans — because I've been one!

"Alaskan students — because I've been one!

"Alaska's federal employees — because I've been one!

"Alaska's mayors — because I've been one!

"Alaska's small businessmen — because I've been one!

"Alaska's disabled and hospitalized — because I've been one!

"Alaska's unemployed — because I've been one!

"Even Alaska's incarcerated — because I've been one of those, too!

"But perhaps most important, I know a little something about problems facing Alaska's Native villagers, because I've been privileged to live among them for more than a quarter century. Yes, my opponents may have more impressive credentials, but none exceed my concern for this state and its future. Unlike so many who come up here simply to rip us off and run, I intend my bones to molder in Alaska forever."

By now I had become so emotionally wound, I choked up and had to sit down, certain I'd blown it. Once more, serendipity — in the form of a colorful curmudgeon and iconoclast host of the Press Club luncheon — came to my rescue. Anchorage radio personality Herb Shaindlin rose as I sat staring morosely at my uneaten dessert.

"Wow! INCARCERATED? This guy sure has grabbed my attention. If no one else gives him a chance to win, I'm betting before this campaign is over, his opponents will know they've been in one hell of a race!"

Within days of my Press Club outburst, Hammond/Thomas had come from a "no show" on the political Richter Scale to challenge Wally Hickel for the Republican Primary lead. People began coming out of the woodwork in multitudes — many not so much for me as against the network of interests opposing me. Accepting their small, hard earned cash in campaign contributions, I no longer felt comfortable merely getting an all expense paid trip simply to tell Alaskans what we should worry about for the future. These people were serious about me trying to win, even if I hadn't been.

Now, if I lost the election, I didn't want them to be able to blame only me. Accordingly, I bit the whole bandoleer of bullets and tackled even the most onerous campaign tasks.

Of all the campaign chores imposed on me, personally soliciting votes on door-to-door treks through city neighborhoods turned out to be the least repugnant. Surprisingly, this approach seemed to pay off more than any other. Issues, positions and past performance play minor roles in most elections, I fear. Certainly more people told me they voted for me because I took the time to visit them than for any other reason.

Door-to-door visitations were not without hazard. I was bitten three times (by dogs), cussed out by a cantankerous old-time Democrat, and kissed by a wavering Hickelite — a crickety, little old lady who vowed even though she intended to vote for Wally, I did seem "like a very nice man."

Once, I was nearly arrested. I'd borrowed a car to "work" an east Anchorage neighborhood. I parked and went down the street to the first house, dutifully carrying my sack of campaign propaganda. When no one answered my knock, I moved on, spending the next few hours rapping on doors and leaving flyers. Returning to the car, I stopped and knocked on the first door again. Still no answer, I then returned the car to its owners. The next day they told me they'd been called by the police.

Someone in the neighborhood had reported a suspicious, bearded prowler park his car and go up on the porch of vacationing neighbors. He'd been seen leaving the porch a few hours later, carrying a sack. The police accepted my explanation, but the experience did suggest some interesting campaign tactics. For a shameful moment I considered going around ripping off vacant houses and leaving calling cards with, "Thanks for the campaign contributions. Love, Wally."

This gave rise to the realization I'd far rather run my opponent's campaign than mine. Instead of enhancing my own name recognition, it might be more fun to expand my rival's by handing out non-functional campaign trinkets with his name and picture: cheap combs that shed teeth to the gumline the first time they're pulled through hair; packets of needles without eyes; ball-point pens minus ink; etcetera, etcetera. Coupled with community-wide distribution of non-removable bumper stickers pasted "face in" on windshields, I could do a lot to improve my opponent's name recognition.

Despite such flights of fancy and my original intention to run a losing race, in neighborhoods the polls showed public awareness and support for Hammond/Thomas growing rapidly. We had become more than merely viable; we suddenly found ourselves leading the pack, momentum building, with election day coming up fast.

Pundits explained this phenomenon many ways. It was the post-Watergate era; Richard Nixon had just become the first U.S. president to resign, and public disenchantment with traditional politics and politicians gave even a bearded bush rat some appeal. In itself alarming; more so were the multitudes contributing to our campaign. Finances had always been very tight, but as our war chest began to swell, for the first time I faced the unlikely prospect that, if we weren't careful, *we* could be the poor souls faced with resolving the insurmountable problems I'd been pointing out.

A number of unusual circumstances coalesced in 1974 Alaska. Growing environmental awareness certainly played a key role. While most Alaskans looked eagerly forward to the "boom" promised by pipeline construction, many others were apprehensive. Eskimos and Indians shared with them concerns for habitat destruction and decimation of fish and wildlife. Alaska's work force feared most jobs would go to non-residents now arriving in droves. Still others worried over increases in crime and other social impacts. I shared these concerns. Consistently harping on my "healthy vs. malignant growth" theme only increased the invectives thrown by Hickel, Atwood and Carr. But these, I believe, often worked to our benefit as the polls showed Hammond/Thomas going upward apace.

When the final tally was counted, we'd won the Republican primary by 7,874 votes. Aided no doubt by Democrats crossing over to give Bill Egan a lesser opponent in the November election, we had won even in Anchorage, "impregnable" stronghold of Hickel, Atwood and Carr. The latter two were now even more determined to keep me from the governor's chair.

I asked my campaign manager Bob Palmer if it was now time for me to shave off my beard.

"Don't you dare!" he admonished.

*Far more at home with real people than with politicians, I
immensely enjoyed trips to rural villages.*

23
Reluctant Candidate: 1974

HARDLY BELIEVING VOTERS had chosen me over two of Alaska's previous three governors in the primary, I now faced the third, incumbent Governor Bill Egan. Unquestionably the most popular politician since Statehood, Egan had, in his Lt. Governor, Red Boucher, another indefatigable campaigner. Yet oddly, the general campaign opened with us enjoying a substantial lead in the polls.

Political campaign experts believe if you peak too soon, the only direction you can go is down. In this "worry" lay my last hope of avoiding a mantle of responsibility that every day looked more like a hair shirt. I took comfort in knowing our large victory margin in the open primary was to no small degree aided by many Democrats "crossing over" to eliminate Hickel, whom they considered a far greater threat to Bill Egan in November.

When Egan and Boucher came out flailing away at Lowell and me, I took a different tack. Rather than plow into my opponents' shortcomings, I preferred to let them do so themselves. This sometimes reaped a rich harvest.

Bill Egan had tilled, planted and fertilized ground some weeks before by resurrecting my Senate vote against his first proposed Department of Environmental Conservation. Egan charged that despite attempts to color me "green," my vote showed I was actually a black-hearted despoiler, unconcerned with clean air and water. I countered this charge by calling his Conservation Department proposal a "paper tiger" he'd not only failed to equip with dentures, but wired its jaws to prevent even "gumming."

Expanding my rebuttal, I said, "to assume my vote against that toothless creation indicates my lack of environmental concern is as ridiculous as saying Governor Egan's recent veto of millions for the University of Alaska, demonstrates *his* lack of concern for education. There were other compelling reasons, I'm sure. There *must* have been."

Egan was furious. In a subsequent press release the extensive list of his actions on behalf of education was exceeded only by the number of ways he chose to chastise me. At the apogee of his apoplexy, we appeared before a gathering of educators in Fairbanks, headquarters of the university. Knowing Bill still seethed, believing I'd charged he was soft on education, I decided to decompress the palpable tension in the audience.

"Ladies and gentlemen" I began. "Many have the impression the governor and I are at odds over education issues. Nothing could be more removed from the truth." I went on to cite our mutual support for program after program of import to those present.

"Though at times we may differ on details, let me tell you of the enormous regard I have for Governor Egan. Certainly no Alaskan has for more years evidenced greater dedication to serving this state. I consider myself privileged to have worked with a man who has so exhaustively labored in behalf of all Alaskans. Moreover, I'm proud to call Bill Egan my friend. If I lose this election, there's no one I'd prefer to have best me."

After several more glowing accolades, I walked over to Bill, reached out to shake his hesitant hand, and pronounced loudly for all to hear: "So far as the coming election's concerned, governor, I want to wish you good luck — but not too much."

The audience, reassured the evening would be more lovefest than lambaste, visibly relaxed. I sat down to warm applause.

Expecting Bill had come with every intention of thumping me for citing his veto of university funds, I counted on him adhering closely to the prepared text he carried in quivering hand to the podium. He did not disappoint me. Starting somewhat uncertainly, he quickly warmed to his subject. Whatever I'd said to dampen his anger dried quickly in the heat of his passion. Before he had completed the first page of his script, the governor was spluttering in outrage over my alleged apostasy. The audience was clearly aghast.

Smiles turned to gasps as Bill plowed angrily through a text pockmarked with slurs and slaps. Dismayed by such ungracious response to my friendly overtures, a wave of critical muttering washed over the small ripple of embarrassed applause upon his conclusion.

While looking properly saddened, perplexed and slightly shell-shocked by the governor's flogging with my proffered olive branch, I must confess I was delighted with his display of what our audience clearly saw as most unsportsmanlike conduct.

As IN THE PRIMARY, in the general, no one tried harder to pitch me back into my Lake Clark briar patch than powerful Teamster boss Jesse Carr. So potent a force had Carr's Teamsters become, most businessmen and politicians believed, with good reason, it was the kiss of death to earn their disfavor. For survival, many chose to engage openly in osculation of quite a different sort. Despite suspicions of my environmentalist leanings, too many business people had already been clubbed by Carr's heavy hand. That I wasn't in his hind pocket, but a burr in his britches, had perverse appeal to many.

These people wrote such things as, "I don't know much about you, but anybody who's got the Teamsters against them must be okay!" Often these were unsigned, just in case.

During the course of the '74 campaign, and long after, Jesse Carr and his Teamsters exhibited far more devotion to my defeat than did I to victory. My every public appearance was attended by Teamsters, busily handing out anti-Hammond flyers or putting them on car windshields.

"If Hammond's elected there'll be a Right-to-Work Law!" "Hammond is Anti-Growth!" Or, "Protect Your Jobs/Re-Elect Bill Egan!" And later: "Can Salmon — And Hammond!"

These ploys were effective. Combined with my own diligence, hard work and indecent public exposures, we managed to whittle my discomforting lead down a few points each day. Though somewhat nervous, I remained confident I would lose handily, as in the campaign's final weeks, polls showed the rise of Egan/Boucher and the fall of Hammond/Thomas to be mutually accelerating.

As salvation seemed imminent, I began to relax. My chief regret was the one TV spot I wanted to run, never did. After months of assaulting long-suffering viewers with high-decibel political ads, in atonement I'd hoped to air one showing a tranquil mountain lake, with my voice-over saying simply: "The following 30 seconds of merciful silence are brought to you courtesy of . . ." Instead, my staff insisted on ads showing me engaged in pursuits with which most Alaskans like to identify: splitting wood, fishing, or laying up logs for a wilderness cabin.

Courage and innovation went into some of these ads. One was made by film maker Tim McGinnis, who imprudently subjected both his camera and cranium to undue hazard, placing them on my chopping block beside a chunk of wood I was splitting. If Tim's confidence in my accuracy with an ax was only barely justified, his "Woodchopper" ad is still considered an Alaskan campaign classic.

Another camera crew visiting our homestead came to understand more than most my reluctance to win the governor's chair. Arriving by floatplane one balmy late summer evening, they sighted two moose in our cove and a large brown bear just up the beach. The setting sun was turning the surrounding snow peaks into improbable hues of calendar art, reflected in the mirror-like waters below.

As we stood on the shore, a crew member shook his head and asked, "Why would you ever leave this to run for public office?"

I confessed this rude thought surfaced often, around three in the morning.

How grassroots was it? With volunteers at Anchorage Campaign Headquarters in 1978. On my left, arms akimbo, stands my communications expert Bob Clarke, obviously either dismayed by his assignment to sanitize my image or resenting the conversion of this building from an old barroom and brothel.

During the general election campaign I continued to drum my "healthy growth vs. malignant growth" theme. Unless an economic development project was environmentally sound, good for a majority if not all Alaskans, and could pay its own way, rather than become a burden to the state, I would oppose it.

"Heresy!" howled growth-for-growth's-sake advocates. To suggest any economic development should not be embraced automatically was anathema to those who would profit, even at the expense of other citizens.

Some hostility toward my "malignant growth" warnings was promulgated by Alaskans' increasing frustration with federal regulations emerging in the wake of the nation's growing environmental concerns. None of my opponents was more outraged by such "unnecessary obstructions" than crusty old Fairbanks miner, Joe Vogler. Incensed with constant federal intervention, Joe had created the Alaskan Independence Party, and was running in the general election on a secession platform.

At our first confrontation in one of those interminable "debates," I was impressed by an impassioned tirade from Vogler which, from the mouth of a less gifted orator would have been gibberish. Joe was a master at sweeping his audience spellbound into a torrent of vitriolic castigation of bureaucrats. Even I found my feet slipping in the tug of his hypnotic delivery — until the echo of jack boots and "Sieg Heils!" brought me back to reality.

But the audience, by now thoroughly saturated, responded with wave after wave of applause that seemed to crescendo when Joe referred fondly to me as "a posey sniffing swine!" I say "fondly," for as we filed from the hall after the debate, he growled to me, "If I can't win this thing I kinda hope you do, Hammond. You seem the least worst of those other guys."

Later I was asked my reaction to Joe's verbal attack. "Anyone who can come up with language like 'posey sniffing swine,' can't be all bad." I still believe this and harbor affectionate memories of Joe, who mysteriously disappeared from his cabin one spring day in 1993.

AS NOVEMBER'S FIRST TUESDAY grew closer, I was confident my ordeal was about over as we fell steadily in the polls. Though I felt some remorse in being about to disappoint those who had worked so hard for my election, it was submersed in belief the most merciful thing that could happen to me would be to just barely lose. Then, as the years passed, those disenchanted with what had happened to Alaska, might be inclined to say, "If only Hammond had been elected!" Indulgent? Perhaps. But only those who were present in Alaska at that cataclysmic time are qualified to judge.

Bill Egan, on the other hand, exuded confidence. With several thousand ballots being distributed among newly eligible trans-Alaska pipeline workers — mostly Teamsters — a huge block of votes not reflected in previous polls was predicted to elect Egan by a comfortable margin.

AND THEN IT WAS ELECTION DAY. When my campaign staff and I arrived at "Election Central" — a non-partisan Election Watch tradition at an Anchorage hotel after the polls close — I managed with difficulty to mirror their morose demeanor. Covertly, I was relieved. Convinced the nightmare was over, I could hardly wait to shuck the neckties, social obligations, and the horrendous demands imposed on those who subject themselves to campaigning for public office.

As the evening went on, however, it was evident something had gone badly awry. Egan and I remained almost neck and neck. Each time a tally was registered showing me slightly ahead, my supporters would whoop and holler, while I attempted to look as though I shared their elation. Conversely, when we dropped a few votes behind, I tried to look somber.

That election night was one of the most painful ordeals I ever experienced. I not only felt like the monstrous fraud I was; I repeatedly verified this to myself by adjusting my outward expression to contrast with what I was feeling within: Abject dismay!

When it was announced I'd won by less than a thousand votes, I couldn't believe it. My supporters went ballistically berserk. I went mentally bilious. As they thumped my back and cavorted, I wondered what in the world had gone wrong? Above the din, I could almost hear cell doors clang shut behind me.

Bill Egan not only shared my shock and disbelief, he quickly did something about it. Charging "improprieties," he demanded a recount. The first reduced my lead by half. Good. He ordered another. My lead was cut in two again. Great! Yet despite my rooting for the incumbent, it was not to be. When the smoke finally cleared, we had won — by two hundred and twenty one votes.

More accurately, I learned later, Egan lost because secessionist candidate Joe Vogler had taken five thousand votes that certainly would have gone to Bill. How bitterly divided the state had become over land and resource issues was fortunately lost on me in the moment of "victory." If I'd known the full range of problems that would boil to a head in the next four years, I might have conceded before the final recount was tallied.

As it was, weeks went by until then. Ballots from remote villages came in slowly. I was used to this; as a legislator I often didn't learn election results until after Thanksgiving. By then, I hardly cared any more. This time I cared a lot, clinging to the hope I could still have my "cake" in helping set Alaska's agenda, but, Heaven forbid, not have to eat it!

The heartburn of that alarming eventuality increased with each passing day during the recount, each day's delay allowing less and less time to select a staff and cabinet in the short transition period when one is supposed to learn at least the existence, if not the functions, of the "ropes." Then it was frighteningly official. I'd won.

Later, I was told how Red Boucher, who, as lieutenant governor supervised the Office of Elections, had performed an act of considerable courage which, if true, gave him ironic revenge on me. Boucher, according to a reporter present, had refused to surrender ballots in his care to some political operatives not under his charge. If true, my subsequent friendship with Red has enabled me to forgive him.

ON DEC. 2, 1974, I was sworn in as Alaska's third governor. No less than *Ripley's Believe It Or Not* pointed out that I had defeated every other governor in the state's history to win. Construction on the trans-Alaska pipeline was about to begin. The Greatland was about to undergo enormous change. "The Last Frontier" would soon become, according to author Peter Gruenstein, *The Lost Frontier*.

And like it or not, one who had come to seek solitude in Alaska's wilderness would find much less of either in the tumultuous years ahead.

Office photo, taken at the end of the first term, showing signs of the maturing process that serves to resculpt the features of pressured politicians as well as prunes.

24

"...a lousy Governor"

I DON'T KNOW IF I'M the only person who ever ran for governor literally praying he'd not be elected, but I suspect a multitude of Alaskans joined me in that supplication. To my prayers, however, I'd always add: "Lord, should it be your wish that I give up a good life for the burdens of public office, please help me accept it with good grace if not gusto."

While I don't for a minute believe I was elected by divine ordination, I'm no longer certain it was meant to be the divine retribution I originally thought.

In my first months as governor I was miserable, in temperament and performance. Not only had I been thrust into a job for which I was ill-prepared, I resented enormously my loss of freedom and privacy. Compounding this misery, unlike any Alaska governor before or since, instead of the normal three week transition period between Election Day and the Oath of Office, I had just three days.

Seventy-two hours allowed little time for indoctrination. I had only a thirty-minute audience with my less than effusive predecessor before he reluctantly vacated his office. Once alone, I opened the governor's desk drawers and found them stripped clean, save for a lone postcard, face down. Flipping it over I was greeted by the picture of a closed fist, mid-finger rampant, above the hand-written salutation: "Good luck — but not too much." It was unsigned.

Outgoing lieutenant governor Red Boucher, a tough, dynamic opponent who became an ardent supporter, later told me he'd felt it was "a bit tacky" for Egan to clean his desk of everything but an obscene post card and "the exploding cigar." Exploding cigar? I didn't remember an exploding cigar. Later I learned I'd given it to stogie-chewing Ed Orbeck, a former pro football player who, despite my "gift," survived the detonation to become my loyal and able labor commissioner.

Though I retained some Egan appointees in my administration, most had departed, along with their files and wealth of counsel. This was no fault of Bill Egan, who didn't know he was leaving until three days before compelled to. In any event, we assumed office in almost total ignorance.

About the only intelligence I'd gleaned from my brief summit meeting with Bill was learning to distinguish between three identical doors in the governor's office: the middle door led out to the reception area; the left was an "escape hatch" to the governor's conference room. The third door opened abruptly into the governor's toilet. To those unfamiliar with this layout, the similarity of these doors could be disorienting.

The first to verify this was Fran Ulmer, an extremely competent and lovely young woman who visited my office for a job interview. I was very impressed and somewhat intimidated by her exceptional poise and intelligence. Confident she'd made a good impression, Fran rose to make a dignified exit — only to stumble into the "john." Her embarrassed emergence and subsequent laughter thawed what reservation I might have had. Not "too good to be true" after all, she became my director of policy development and planning.

In ADDITION TO SELECTING a staff and cabinet, I had to write three major speeches on matters of which I had limited knowledge: an inaugural address to a bitterly divided Alaska, a state of the state message, and the annual budget report to the legislature. As I had never employed a speech writer, I did these on my own. That they were completed on time was remarkable. That they were pretty well received was astounding. Of my inaugural address, international journalist Lowell Thomas Sr., had this to say in his January 20, 1975, national broadcast:

> I wonder if I have attended more conventions and inaugurals than anyone? My first was Teddy Roosevelt's 'Bull Moose' convention in Chicago in 1912. Speeches at these are not always as memorable as when FDR told us 'the only thing to fear is fear itself.' Back at the 1936 Cleveland GOP convention, John Hamilton held his audience spellbound when he nominated Alf Landon. One of the most impressive; perhaps the most impressive of them all, was the Inaugural address I just heard in Alaska, delivered by an unusual political personality, Jay Hammond . . ."

Lowell Sr.'s overblown accolade can be forgiven. His only son, Lowell Jr., was sworn in as my lieutenant governor at the same ceremony. Still, I especially treasure this comment from a hard-bitten international journalist who'd seen and heard it all.

Unfortunately, Thomas's abundant praise served not only to encourage ever-widening flights of oratorical fancy, it persuaded me no one else could write speeches with which I was comfortable. As a result, I too often drowned my audiences in flurries of mixed metaphors, scrambled syntax and what the irreverent termed "Hammondese." True, some speech would occasionally soar, but not a few simply "stalled out." Still others left my audiences far behind as I swooped and swerved over the linguistic landscape, unaware no passengers had stayed aboard.

BY MY OWN MEASURE, for the first few months — some would say longer — I was a lousy governor. Too much time was spent wallowing in self-pity and resenting loss of freedom to the shackles of office.

While my sense of dread and doubts of omniscience may not have been unique — even to candidates who'd never admit to them — unlike any others I've known, I failed to find sufficient off-setting compensation in the power, prestige and other trappings of public office. I simply viewed them as additional burdens.

Though I functioned poorly, a dedicated staff and cabinet kept my head above water, barely. After stumbling blindly through those first painful months, at a cabinet meeting I reflected that, if everyone present was serving "at the governor's pleasure," as the saying goes, "How come I'm not getting any?"

The heaviest burden of all was a back-breaking load of guilt over my negative attitude. I felt like a monstrous fraud. Throughout the campaign, after the election and during those first months as governor, I'd played the role of eager candidate, then grateful recipient of the gubernatorial mantle, who now wore it with comfort and competence. I detested myself for this deception but couldn't shake it.

I tried to do penance by working ever harder at understanding all facets of government. In the process I tinkered too much with minor nuts and bolts of administrative machinery best left to department mechanics. Floundering about for extra hours each day and night, working almost every weekend and holidays, like Jimmy Carter, I learned almost too late how the fast footwork required to stay atop shifting sands of bureaucracy can ultimately trigger an inundating avalanche. Only by turning over the tools to those who could better use them did I avoid being buried.

In those awful first months I not only felt trapped in a job for which I was unprepared, I seemed unable to neutralize the character-corroding acid of self pity in which I was saturated. About 3:30 each morning I'd wake up wallowing, thrash around for a couple of hours, mentally chewing on some indigestible problem, and at 7 a.m. unenthusiastically take the short walk from the Governor's House to my office on the third floor of the Capitol building. Naturally, such a negative attitude did little to add luster to my performance,

Legendary Fairbanks bag lady Irene Sherman interrupts a dedication ceremony to offer advice to the governor. In Alaska, EVERYBODY has an opinion.

let alone the public's perception thereof. My major success in this period was proving what I'd believed all along: I should have run for the hills instead of the state's highest office.

I did my best to obscure this from my staff and the electorate, but my best was inadequate. New evidence cropped up daily. Fortunately, there was one on my staff who could empathize. Bob Palmer, my first executive assistant, had been well aware of my reluctance to run. He also felt a bit guilty, not just for helping to talk me into filing, but for managing a successful campaign. No one did more to propel me into office than Bob, and I had occasion to credit him publicly in a speech soon after the election.

"There's no doubt about it, if there's one man to whom I owe the privilege of appearing before you today as your governor, it's Bob Palmer. And someday I hope to forgive him."

The audience chuckled indulgently, certain I was joshing. Bob knew better. He came to my office later and we apologized to each other. It was apparent to us both my downbeat attitude was beating up my staff and any chance to leave a "Hammond Years" legacy any could point to with other than ridicule.

That meeting proved the turning point. If we couldn't erase my poor attitude, we could at least better obscure it. In my case, each morning in consultation with my Maker, I asked to be shown how. Gradually, things began to improve.

Around this time I came across a quotation from some ancient philosopher: "Only he deserves to lead who just as soon would not." Hmm. Maybe it wasn't so despicable after all, not to have that fire in the belly that seems to motivate those who seek positions of power and leadership.

MY STAFF AND CABINET INCLUDED some thoroughbred talent which, when given rein and adequate fodder, took the bit and carried me over many a hazardous jump. In spite of myself, I began to find certain aspects of the job rather enjoyable. Opportunities to solve some little guy's problems by shredding red tape or bruising some bumptious bureaucrat were especially zestful. Less to my credit, I also found in myself a surprisingly large slice of "ham" which, when slathered with the condiment of public applause, piques the appetite of most politicians. That this condiment was often sparse, or laced with opprobrium, only increased the savor of those times when it came unadulterated.

Because my speeches invariably reiterated themes I'd articulated in the campaign, and Alaskans were becoming increasingly divided over such issues as lands, resource development and money, applause — if and when it came -- was very well received by me. Speechmaking, of course, like theater, provides the best chance to exhibit one's ideas and sample live, public response. Speech *writing* was a chore laced with love and hate. I hated the obligation of preparing a speech; but once I had, if it succeeded, self-satisfaction leeched into my shameless soul.

Occasionally I'd write a speech that alarmed staff members assured me would outrage or insult my audience, only to have the latter applaud in wild approval. Conversely, speeches designed to placate or pander to some special audience would elicit a backfire of boos. This challenge of the unknown made speechmaking all the more intriguing.

Of course, my speeches frequently flopped with no help whatsoever from the audience. I'd said in my campaign those people who expected special treatment should not vote for me. Many had taken this advice. When they later appealed for special treatment anyhow, I felt the least I could do was to keep my end of the bargain. Consequently, to avoid the appearance of genuflecting, I bent over too far backward to craft barbed speeches for such audiences. It did little to improve communications with most special interest groups.

MY FIRST SERIOUS CONFLICT as governor involved Jesse Carr and the Teamsters. Having been catered to in the past, most of these stalwarts had complied when I suggested those who found equal treatment a comedown should not vote for me. While searching for a way to keep my side of this bargain, I was presented a platter on which Jesse's head might be served. Of course, only a vindictive, mean-spirited soul would seek such a trophy ahead of justice. So I sought both. Justice would be served — hopefully along with Carr's cranium.

My attorney general catered the affair. One morning Av Gross came to my office with a clutch of papers, spreading them before me with a reverence accorded the Magna Carta or Dead Sea Scrolls.

"Boy, is this hot. These are lease papers drawn up between the state and the Teamsters long before you were governor. The lease terms are, to say the least, most favorable to the union, but payments to the state are far in arrears. They owe a bunch of money. What do you want to do? You can foreclose and kick them off the property or sue, demanding payment plus penalties and interest. If you do the former, of course, there'll be the perception you're seeking revenge. If you do the latter, you'll simply compound the outrage of your worst enemy. What's your choice?"

"Well, Av, as you say, it's a tough choice. I'd prefer not to make it. Can't we do *both*?"

At first Av blanched. Then, presuming I was joking, he smiled. Before he could conclude the contrary, I asked him how he would handle the situation if it was anyone but Carr and the Teamsters.

"Why, we would sue," he replied.

"Then let's do it. I promised Jesse before I took office he'd be given exactly the same consideration as anyone else, no more and no less."

Informed in Anchorage of the state's lawsuit, Carr's detonation reverberated 600 miles away in Juneau. Jessie Dodson of my staff was still blinking as she related an expurgated version of his diatribe demanding an immediate audience. Since I'd never seen, much less spoken to the man, I agreed to meet with him on my next trip to Anchorage.

A few days later I was led into my Anchorage office by an unusually large contingent of state troopers, shouldering through a crowd of glowering Teamsters carrying placards: "Don't Blame Me — I Voted For Egan!"

Once inside my office, my uneasy escort grudgingly withdrew, leaving me by myself. A few minutes later, Jesse Carr was ushered in by a secretary who beat a hasty retreat. For the first time, Jesse Carr and I confronted one another in person.

A short, powerfully built, bulldog-jawed man about my age stood splay-legged facing me; dark, gun-barrel eyes bored in on mine. For a moment we stalked each other around opposite sides of the large conference table like two pitbulls. Growling in what passed for acknowledging the other dog's presence, each tried to establish dominance by every means short of lifting a leg or scratching hind paws on the carpet.

"At least he doesn't have crystal clear glacial blue eyes," was my first ridiculous thought, remembering past experiences with blue-eyed con-artists. "Maybe he can be trusted." In that vein I recalled what people who knew Carr well had told me. "Whatever else you think of Jesse Carr, when he tells you something, you can take it as Gospel — at least the Gospel according to Carr. He wouldn't say it if he didn't believe it." Jesse was the first to bite and shake the bone of contention between us.

"Look," he growled, "I was in the Marine Corps so I respect the uniform if not the man who wears it. You may be governor, but I want you to know I'm not going to take any crap from you for something that's completely above board and legal. We've done everything 'according to Hoyle' and we have all the papers to prove it."

"That's fine, Jesse," I responded with what I hoped was exasperatingly patronizing, unflappable reason. "I was in the Marines too, so I appreciate your marching straight to the point. And if you can prove that point with documentation showing you have indeed done it according to Hoyle, you'll get no grief from us. On the other hand, if you can't prove it, we're going to take you to the mat."

For a moment I thought he was about to grapple with me on the spot. Instead, his face turned an apoplectic magenta, which — the idiotic thought leaped into my mind — clashed hideously with his expensive silk tie. Blasting me one final time with those gun-barrel eyes, he stormed from the room muttering obscenities undoubtedly gleaned from his days in the corps.

When I emerged from my office a few minutes later, wide-eyed reporters schooled in, one almost tracheotomizing me with his microphone. "What in the world did you say to Jesse Carr to make him call you an S.O.B.?"

"I'm sure he meant 'Sorry Old Bureaucrat,' " I responded. "If he meant something less charitable, I'm surprised. Jesse and I were both Marines but I didn't think he thought we had anything else in common."

Until then, I'd supposed the feud between Carr and myself was a purely Alaskan affair. But now it slopped over into the national arena. A few days after this confrontation, CBS's Dan Rather arrived from New York to interview first Carr, then me, for a "60 Minutes" segment on Teamster power-brokering Alaska pipeline construction. In my interview, Rather asked, in essence, "Some people say Jesse Carr has more to say about running Alaska than even the governor. Apparently you're the first politician up here not willing to give him a free hand. Obviously he doesn't like it. What makes you think you can 'thumb your nose' at Carr and his Teamsters and survive?"

"Well," I replied, "while I'd like to have you think righteous indignation and guts shored my spine, the truth is: one, I'm too 'stove up' to grovel gracefully; two, I'm not terribly entranced with holding this office; and three, if Jesse Carr helps send me home to the hills, it might be considered a favor."

Referring to news reports of Carr's publicly impugning my ancestry, Rather asked, "I understand this was your first encounter with Jesse Carr. Tell me, what's your impression of him as a man?"

"Actually," I admitted, "aside from what he says and does, I rather like the fellow — but I don't think my Mother would."

When that "60 Minutes" program aired in Alaska, rumblings from Carr & Company rattled windows, and the ensuing shards of excoriating editorials in union publications so alarmed my staff they insisted on beefing up security. I was no longer allowed to travel without a trooper escort, new alarm systems were installed in the office and at the Governor's House. Visitors were subjected to careful scrutiny. All this probably bothered me more than it did the troopers and visitors. Until then, I had always traveled without escort, and previously — to the surprise of many callers — Bella, daughters Heidi and Dana, and I answered the phones at the Governor's House.

Word of my conflict with Carr and the Teamsters carried all the way to the White House. It was still there when President Jimmy Carter called the nation's governors to an emergency energy conference. When I arrived, the president apologized for the short notice and asked if I, as most other governors, had come in my personal plane.

"No," I replied.

"You do have a plane, don't you?" the president asked.

"You bet," I said.

"What is it, a Learjet? Saberliner? Queen Air?"

"Nothing like that, I'm afraid. All I've got is an old, single-engine 1953 Cessna 170."

"Really!?" asked the President, surprised. "Don't Alaskans worry about you flying around by yourself in an ancient aircraft like that?"

"No," I explained. "In fact, I'm encouraged by many to do so. During my campaign, Jesse Carr's Teamsters even offered to contribute a hundred gallons of aviation gas, and throw the sugar in free."

Carter looked at me blankly for a moment but laughed when I explained the effects of sugared gasoline on the digestive tract of combustion engines.

DURING MY TIME IN OFFICE, at least once a year some state or federal agency would advise that the Teamster leadership was being investigated and indictments would soon be issued. To my knowledge, none ever were. Nevertheless, Alaska's Teamster boss found his power eroding as time and truth took their toll. Some say our successful challenge of the Teamster leases was the beginning of this decline. Perhaps. But even those previously antagonistic members of both management and labor who'd been warned Hammond's policies would bankrupt them, couldn't escape the fact they were prospering beyond precedent under, or perhaps in spite of, my administration. This conclusion eventually made it much harder to march to the discordant drumbeats of anti-Hammond propaganda thumped out by Teamsters and the *Anchorage Times*.

But before this evolved, most Alaska union leaders had conditioned their members to believe I was the Prince of Darkness. This myth was exacerbated when my refusal to cave in to demands made by the Alaska State Employees' Union precipitated two painful strikes.

While inconvenient, these strikes hardly brought the state to its knees. But they did help publicize salary schedule inequities, illustrating how well paid were the strikers compared to other employees, in and outside government. The ineffectiveness of the first strike prompted one embarrassed official to wonder; "What if *all* state employees went on strike and nobody noticed?"

Not until I'd endured the second strike did I figure out how to deal with the problem. Calling in my old cohort Clem Tillion, I gave him a resolution I'd drafted which, if approved, would have the legislature direct the governor how to deal with employee salary demands.

The resolution went something like, "We, the Alaska State Legislature, hereby inform the governor we will refuse to fund any collectively bargained salary increases for employees whose salaries have kept pace with inflation, until such time as members of other bargaining units doing comparable work have achieved parity. Therefore, the governor is directed henceforth, *not to agree to any salary demands at odds with this objective.*"

Clem introduced the measure. Delighted to be "telling the governor how to do his job," the legislature passed it with hardly a ripple. When I cited this legislative directive as my grounds for rejecting the latest union proposals, labor's angry backwash splashed on the legislature, not me. Delightful. I was beginning to like this job after all!

With Clem's enthusiastic assistance, I used this process on more than one occasion when I wished to involve the legislature in business they preferred to avoid.

Having alienated Republicans and unions alike in my first term, once again I managed to irritate Big Business. In Alaska, there was no bigger business than that involved with the trans-Alaska pipeline.

Due to legal delays, pipeline construction still hadn't begun by the time I took office in December 1974. But not even by then was it politically permissible to discuss the project with candor. Any rude questioning of propaganda pumped out by pipeline promoters only showered the questioner with abuse. Being a very slow learner, I once more stuck my face in front of the nozzle.

I was on an airplane when my seat companion, ex-House Speaker Gene Guess, told me the pipeline could be delayed at least a year and cost as much as nine *billion* dollars rather than the nine hundred million dollars promoters had claimed. Gene was privy to data I was not. But since his data paralleled my own conclusions, I reiterated them to a news reporter who asked about pipeline schedules and costs.

To my astonishment, all bedlam broke loose. Editors, pipeline officials, labor unions and oil companies a shrieked I was totally wrong. They agreed pipeline costs had risen "modestly" but assured us it wouldn't cost one penny more than three billion dollars! Declining comment on the "modesty" of an increase from nine hundred million dollars to three billion dollars, I listened politely as they vowed construction schedules were "right on track" and any pronouncement to the contrary was absurd.

Meanwhile, my imprudent airing of suspicions reverberated off the canyons of Wall Street. Oil stocks plummeted. In an effort to undo the damage, pipeline owners bundled me aboard a helicopter for a grand inspection tour. One after another, key pipeline officials assured me everything was right on schedule and costs would be contained within three billion dollars.

I, in turn, relayed their assurances to the media who converged like iron filings on a magnet when our helicopter touched down in Anchorage. Subsequent headlines trumpeted that I had admitted my error and agreed everything was right on schedule! Nothing I'd said should have conveyed that conclusion. They heard what they wanted to hear. Such imprecise reporting was, unfortunately, not uncommon. I'd merely reported reassurances given by those who should know. I did not say I agreed with them, nor did I. I was not the slightest surprised when the pipeline was, in fact, delayed a year and construction costs soared to almost *ten billion dollars*. I suppose I should have learned from my resolutions regarding pipeline routes and potential delays how intellectual integrity and political prudence are often incompatible bedfellows.

ON A LATER TOUR OF THE PIPELINE in 1976, I enjoyed the company of President Gerald Ford, Henry Kissinger and Barbara Walters. Best recalled from this trip is how the windchill exuding from Barbara — unhappily out of her element — was exceeded only by that blasting off the Arctic Ocean. Henry, by contrast, insulated from both by keen wit, down parka and "bunny boots," prompted warm laughter. No one appeared more ludicrously out of place than Kissinger clad as polar explorer. His sonorous pronouncements and professorial demeanor were as out of sync in this clime as seal oil and muktuk (whale blubber) at a white tie diplomatic reception. Only his portly figure and gait seemed not to clash with the surroundings; the U.S. Secretary of State easily could have passed for a penguin.

Returning to Anchorage with President Ford on Air Force One, we discussed other matters of warmth and cold.

"Tell me, governor, where did you live before going to Juneau?" asked the President.

"A small village called Naknek," I answered.

"What's Naknek like? Describe it."

"Well," said I, "it's a little, windswept, almost treeless Bering Sea fishing community of about three hundred shivering souls, all but devoid of redeeming virtues. It's a great place to live, but I wouldn't want to visit there."

The president did a double take and then laughed. "Why? Does it get as cold as, say, Fairbanks?" (Which can fall to seventy below).

"No, but it can get pretty chilly. A while back it got down to twenty below with a forty-knot wind. I had our furnace going full blast and couldn't get the house above fifty degrees. But when I read your energy conservation plea to keep thermostats at sixty-five because of the energy crisis, I vowed to meet your mandate, even if I had to install a second furnace to do it."

*I lost the coin toss over who got to wear that abomination
of the western world — the necktie — to my lieutenant
governor, Lowell Thomas Jr.*

25

Hits and Misses:
First Term

THE "BOX SCORE" OF EVERY EXECUTIVE is a mixed bag of "win some, lose some." My first four years as governor of Alaska were no different, except for the number of issues that fell into the "no decision" category to linger into the future.

To the extent we had any "wins" at all was due to the fine staff and cabinet support I enjoyed at a time when I was neither a very willing nor able governor. To list all those to whom I owe such a debt of gratitude would change this memoir into a catalogue of competence. But some especially bore the brunt of my lack of administrative experience. My first executive secretary, Marie Matsuno, whom I'd known since she was a small child in Ugashik — a remote fishing village of perhaps two dozen people — proved as lustrous a gem as I could have unearthed in any metropolis. With Susan Greene, my special assistant on so many issues, I could even exchange accounts of past psychic experiences without fear one of us might try to have the other committed.

Of course, no one bears more of the governor's day-to-day burden than does the executive assistant who serves as chief of staff. Bob Palmer, before the legislature made him ineligible for that post on a technicality, and Bill Gordon, an Episcopal archbishop's son, served me faithfully and well. But it was a lowly, twenty-nine-year-old budget analyst unknown to me before 1975 who probably did more for less than anyone to win my awe and admiration by consolidating, and then holding down, three key positions in my first term. Any one of his demanding chores would have overwhelmed me.

Kent Dawson was and remains one of the most knowledgeable minds on the workings of government it has been my privilege to know. Unflappable, apparently without personal ego or envy, Kent made my life much easier and his more difficult by performing as budget director, chief of staff and my liaison with the legislature *concurrently*.

When Kent finally left to enter private business, Jerry Reinwand, a superb administrator, easily took the wheel and stayed as my "first mate" for the rest of my time in office.

———————————

ONE OF MY FIRST "WINS" came soon after I took office. Though at first it incurred no little political pain, it remains something I'm proudest of today.

Without holding appropriate public hearings as promised, the previous administration had sold leases for oil exploration and production in one of the most beautifully pristine eco-systems along Alaska's great coast, Kachemak Bay. It did nothing to improve my image with those who suspected I was a "preservationist," when I instructed my attorney general to explore the possibility of repurchasing these leases to protect the bay from despoilment. My environmental "extremism" was harshly criticized in 1976, when for $17 million we bought back the leases, but it gives me enormous satisfaction that no subsequent governor has dared suggest we made a mistake.

The unmatched natural beauty of Kachemak Bay remains intact — though it was until very recently threatened with a timber clear-cut. In 1991, along with many others, I appealed to the legislature and the governor to take action. In 1993 they did so, buying the land in question. Ironically, part of the money for the purchase came from settlement of the Exxon Valdez oil spill.

Today, Alaska's economic future may be destined to profit more from tourism than resource extraction. In terms of local jobs and money, tourism already has passed Alaska's timber and mining industries combined. I take some comfort that my administration worked successfully with private industry to greatly expand tourism. I take less comfort in the realization that even this benign enterprise can have a point of diminishing returns should excessive numbers of people pollute our park lands.

Another milestone of those first Hammond years was bringing Alaska into instant contact with the modern world. Before we established the State Satellite Demonstration System, with the assistance of Dr. Werner von Braun, Alaskan communities had only airmail and radio to connect them with other Alaskans and the world outside.

Unlinked by roads or telephones, bush communities relied on a radio beam that carried a popular program called "The Mukluk Telegraph." Alaskans would while away the evening eavesdropping on an entire state:

To D.J.M. in Willow,
    I'll be home Thursday with a new generator — S.
To M. in Anchorage,
    Bring toilet paper! — C.

Of course, no one living in rural Alaska before the satellite project ever saw live national television events. Even the Super Bowl, political conventions and network news reached us days late, when videotapes arrived at a few local stations located only in the larger cities.

To those living Outside, who've enjoyed live television since its inception, it may be difficult to imagine trying to maintain interest in an event after you've read about it or heard it on radio. Before the satellite, television was not a major medium in Alaska. Since for every Great Debate, there are ten Gong Shows, I won't say daily television has not had some negative impact on Alaska society. But satellite earth stations in more than two hundred villages have not only linked Alaskans with one another, the linkage has made this remote place more a part of the nation, and established Alaska as a world leader in communications technology.

AS GRATIFYING AS IT WAS to take such actions as the Kachemak buy-back, the tourism partnership and the satellite project, by far the major satisfaction of my first term came from the creation of the Alaska Permanent Fund.

Unique to Alaska, this public trust fund has many parents, none of whom were more important than Alaska's citizens themselves. By public vote, they enshrined it in our constitution. But more on that later.

IF ALASKANS' VOTE to create the Permanent Fund was unquestionably the brightest highlight of my first term, the "low light" of those years was the conflict over land issues. It's baleful glow cast dark shadows on my decision to stand for re-election. Absolutely nothing in Alaska's history has been as difficult and divisive as the Alaska lands issue. Those not here in the course of its long bitter debate cannot comprehend the economic, political and emotional havoc it created.

What became known nationally as The Great Alaska Lands War in the 1970s actually had its beginnings long before. When William Henry Seward negotiated the purchase of Alaska from Russia in 1867, he signed a document by which the United States agreed to recognize the territorial claims of Alaska's indigenous peoples: the Aleuts, Indians and Eskimos. If this was perhaps the only good thing Russia did for the people they had enslaved, more than a century later the United States had done exactly nothing to honor this clause. Even former governor Walter J. Hickel, U.S. interior secretary when the issue came to a head, apparently believed Alaska's Natives had no claims. Of course they did, and they proved it — in court and in Congress.

When Alaska became a state in 1959, it was to receive from the federal government 104 million of the former territory's 365 million acres as its state land entitlement. The federal government retained the rest. If Governor Bill Egan seemed a bit slow in selecting which lands should be Alaska's, he was bold enough to resist special interests pressing for lands that would benefit mostly themselves, and prudent enough to select a large, barren and unpopulated wasteland on Alaska's Arctic Slope, near remote Prudhoe Bay, on the Arctic Ocean on the advice of a geologist named Tom Marshall.

Ten years later, when North America's largest oil field was discovered under the frozen tundra there, a sequence of events was put in motion that would pit Alaskan against Alaskan, and Alaska against the nation for ten more years. The increasing intensity of the lands debate would preoccupy the administrations of three presidents and the U.S. Congress to become the most aggressively lobbied issue in Washington since the 1960s Civil Rights debate. As Alaska's governor for the most bitterly divisive of those years, I was in the middle but could do virtually nothing to satisfy the demands of seething factions. This painful predicament was the basis of President Jimmy Carter's comment to a group of governors meeting in Washington, "Jay Hammond probably has more problems that any of us."

With the Prudhoe Bay discovery, alert Native leaders, aware they held a trump card in allowing the transport of oil to market, filed suit to claim lands over which a pipeline must pass. Rather than let the matter languish in court for however many years it would take to resolve Native land claims, Congress preferred to get the precious oil into a pipeline as soon as possible. In 1971, it enacted the Alaska Native Claims Settlement Act, awarding $900 million and 44 million acres of land to the Natives. When another clause was inserted in the settlement act specifying additional federal land be set aside as parks or refuges in the national interest, a federal freeze was put on all state land selections until this was honored. This clause was designated, "Section 17, d-2."

When I became governor in December 1974, little had been done to resolve "d-2," and the inability to acquire our state lands was becoming an ever more festering sore on the body of Alaska society. I believed if we took the initiative by proposing sites for the parks and refuges we could resolve this problem and get on with the business of statehood. Consequently, I proposed offering 40 million acres for this purpose and was promptly denounced as a cowardly idiot by developers, speculators and politicians who felt any amount of land being "locked up" from development was either too large or an unnecessary capitulation to the federal government. Some, like Joe Vogler, called for secession.

The d-2 lands issue remained unresolved through the 1970s. An enormous, grassroots national citizen's coalition formed around the issue as environmentalists seized the delay to call for more and more Alaska land to be set aside as parks and refuges.

Then, for one brief moment in 1978, it appeared a bargain had been struck between the president and Congress. Alaska's Senator Ted Stevens worked long and hard on this compromise and everyone, including Alaska's junior Senator, Democrat Mike Gravel, had allegedly signed off on a compromise land selection plan.

Many caught up in this divisive issue breathed great sighs of relief, but some die-hard Alaskans still believed the federal government had no right to lands "in the national interest." Facing re-election in 1980, Mike Gravel had a change of mind. Congress felt betrayed when, at the eleventh hour, Gravel reneged and the settlement fell apart.

The president, meanwhile, took immediate action. Alaskans' outrage went into orbit when Jimmy Carter, to give Alaska's recalcitrant an incentive to return to the bargaining table, withdrew by Executive Order *120 million acres* of Alaska lands as National Monuments and other tightly restrictive designations — three times the amount I'd proposed and for which I'd been roundly chastised.

I remember the day of the President's order very well. It was Friday, October 13. On that same day, an Alaska court ruled my 98-vote victory in the 1978 Gubernatorial Primary invalid and ordered a new election. I was in Los Angeles when the news came in that evening. Turning in for a night's sleep before flying home to face very dissonant music next morning, I noticed there was a full moon, but resisted the urge to howl.

Bob Palmer (wearing tie) and I get an earful on the potential of agriculture in the Matanuska Valley, known for its giant cabbages.

26
Reluctant No More

IN 1974, I'D PLANNED to announce I'd serve only one term if elected. Aspiring to no more than four years, I also felt re-election would be highly unlikely for anyone who tried to get Alaska back on a "pay as we go" basis.

When I told this to Bella and my campaign staff, they counseled against a one-term announcement. "We'd hate to see you close the door if you change your mind."

They were right. Had I pronounced I'd serve only one term, my cowardly conscience would have barred me from reneging even if my attitude changed. And change it did. Too many important issues remained unresolved.

Paramount among them was my determination to evolve the Permanent Fund into what I had first proposed: an investment account, equitably disbursing benefits to all Alaskan "stock holders" in perpetuity. More than anything, this compelled me to run for a second term. Thus, election night fear I'd be elected in 1974 was supplanted four years later by fear I would not.

The 1978 election was one of the strangest ever. It was the first statewide election in the post-oil era after the campaign spending limit was removed. In 1974, gubernatorial candidates were allowed to spend no more than forty cents per person living in Alaska, a cap that had helped keep me competitive with millionaire Wally Hickel and incumbent Governor Egan. Lifting this cap in 1978 not only introduced Big Bucks to Alaska campaigns, combined with my standing in the polls, it invited the largest slate of gubernatorial candidates in memory. No fewer than nine filed for my seat.

Again, the odds-on favorite was Wally Hickel, beneficiary of a year-long "draft" campaign operated outside the state election code to promote his candidacy. In addition to this Spirit of Alaska draft, Wally would spend $640,000 in the primary alone, to my $390,000.

By contrast, my entire 1974 campaign had cost but $117,683.

The voters had changed since 1974, too. Then, large numbers of Democrats crossed over to me in the primary to assure then-Governor Egan a "weak" opponent in the general. In 1978, with a crowd of Democrats running, I could expect little cross-over help. In addition, my support from environmentalists dwindled in the perception that Democratic challenger Chancy Croft was at least as environmentally concerned as I.

A final factor weighing against me was revealed in a poll that showed almost half the voters had been in Alaska three years or less. The national perceptions of Wally Hickel they'd brought with them differed substantially from those held by long-time Alaskans who'd helped defeat Hickel in 1974. Rather than an environmentally insensitive exploiter who would plasticize and pave wilderness, newcomers remembered the U.S. Interior Secretary who "saved the alligators" and the Santa Barbara channel. Also, despite *New York Times* columnist William Safire's assertion Nixon had fired Hickel for an act of "overt disloyalty," Wally made points in the Nixon bashing that had become a national sport by 1978.

With the heightened drumbeating for Wally and against "Zero Growth Hammond" by Atwood's *Times*, now at the peak of its power, and Carr's avenging Teamsters, Wally was way ahead of everyone before the opening gun.

By contrast, I'd delayed too long in deciding to run again and had virtually no campaign organization or war chest. Experts gave me little chance of overcoming odds against re-election, and public opinion polls confirmed this wisdom. Those who controlled big money — in and outside Alaska — saw a better return on investment among the challengers than an unpopular incumbent. Meanwhile, my lieutenant governor decided he'd had enough, and did not seek re-election.

Lowell's decision not to seek re-election meant this time I'd be running alone. And it felt lonely.

Branded a "bleeding heart" for his efforts on behalf of minorities and the disadvantaged, Lowell had perhaps been the first legislator in the nation to promote a national holiday honoring Martin Luther King, Jr. Yet now he was being bombed with charges of bigotry.

These came in the wake of his return from South Africa where he had gone to represent me at an international wildlife conference. Upon return he had imprudently pronounced that he now better understood issues dividing South Africa's blacks and whites and how apartheid had evolved: many felt that because of militant tribal factions and poor education, South African blacks were not yet able to govern themselves.

Not surprisingly, Lowell's comments prompted demand for explanation. Appearing before the NAACP and Alaska Black Caucus, his remarks won him no plaudits but at least he wasn't shelled from the podium. Then, about to depart, he felt compelled to convey a thought that disturbed him: despite his ardent support of equal rights even he had to confess he was troubled by mixed marriages.

Mumbles swelled to an uproar. "What about the governor?" someone demanded. "His wife's part Eskimo."

"Oh, no," Lowell explained, spading yet another clod from the political grave he seemed determined to excavate. "Not that. I mean between blacks and whites. I believe such marriages are against nature."

At once, all of Lowell's past efforts on behalf of the needy, unfortunate or oppressed went out the window. This exceptionally decent and compassionate man was blasted from every quarter as a bigoted redneck. As might be expected, the loudest salvos came from self-righteous political opponents who greeted with gusto opportunity to assuage their consciences and enhance their own images with minority constituents through evidencing "shock and dismay."

Bella, bless her, rather than affronted by Lowell's remarks, cut right to the heart of the hypocrisy. "What a bunch of phonies. There's probably not one of them, black or white, who'd 'just as soon' have their child marry out of their race. And to the degree they'd prefer otherwise, they too, of course, are 'troubled.' But Lowell's the only politician with guts enough to admit it."

Later, Lowell told me he just couldn't leave his audience without acknowledging a prejudice most try to hide. To do otherwise, he felt, would be fraudulent.

"Lowell," I said, "that may be commendable, but not smart. It's like appearing before adoring supporters, intent on bestowing upon you the 'Man of the Year' award and announcing you really aren't worthy since at one time you'd had contracted a loathsome social disease. *It's nobody's business!*"

Ultimately, Lowell found a less painful way to end his career in politics than disembowelment before a life audience. He simply failed to file for re-election. Instead he went on to pursue his dream of flying parties into the high glacial climbing camps of Mount McKinley. Few who know him doubt that, as a top-notch mountain pilot, he has found far greater fulfillment than ever he would had he stayed in office.

Shortly before Lowell Sr. died, he asked me, morosely, what I thought of Lowell having "squandered" his political potential.

"Look," I asked, "what more can a parent ask than our children be successful and happy — not in fields to which we'd assign them, but those of their own choosing? Lowell is doing something he loves and doing it exceedingly well. In that regard he's a total success. Had he gone on in politics, he'd have been miserable. He's now casting his own shadow. In politics, yours would eclipse him. Let's face it, the name Lowell Thomas is worth points in any potential race. Whereas, while buffeting about in gale force winds at 12,000 feet, trying to touch down on a glacial washboard, it's not worth a damn thing. Perhaps for the first time in his life, Lowell doesn't resent the tag, 'Junior.' For that you should be most grateful."

I like to think he was.

WHAT LITTLE CAMPAIGN ORGANIZATION we had in 1978 was at least colorful. A big, bright, gruff graduate from Illinois politics named Bill McConkey brought much skill if little tact to his job as campaign manager. Bill and his wife, Sandy, scrounged up some support, but with funds in short supply, we relied almost completely on volunteers.

One of these was Eric Sanders, a brilliant young Anchorage attorney who quit his job as a highly successful public defender, and, when Bill left the campaign, became co-chairman with Kent Dawson, who took a leave of absence to organize what seemed to be a hopeless cause. Eric and Kent went bravely about the onerous task of raising funds. In Southeast Alaska, the wondrously lovely Mia Spear, wife of my Deputy Commissioner of Labor Bill Spear, somehow managed an energetic campaign despite little money or candidate cooperation. From his Fairbanks headquarters, Captain Jim Binkley kept us in the race, and in Anchorage, Tay Thomas organized an effective door-to-door effort.

Though we had the editorial support of Kay Fanning's small (12,000 circulation) *Anchorage Daily News*, and some smaller papers, most of the state's media were caught up in Wally's Spirit of Alaska enthusiasm. In advertising we were heavily outgunned by the collective twenty-two candidates for governor and lieutenant governor — none of whom wanted to risk damnation by saying anything positive about the present administration.

In July, we were as much as thirty points behind Wally in some polls, with the primary set for late August. Then I heard of some full-page newspaper ads running in Anchorage by a group calling itself Independent Alaskans for Hammond. On my next trip to Anchorage, I visited the small office of Independent Alaskans and met with its two principles: Sally Jones, a former journalist and state employee who'd quit her job to start the organization over which I had no control, and Bob Clarke, a man I'd never met.

Clarke had come to Alaska for six days to do a magazine story on the 1899 Harriman Alaskan Expedition when Jones sold him a bill of goods about what appeared to be Alaska's out-going governor. I first saw him sitting in a rude attic, hunched over an old typewriter, furiously spewing out begriming questions of Wally Hickel. He then showered these into print, radio and television. As the campaign went on, Clarke saw the value of Alaska's satellite system and soon had our message flowing into Alaska living rooms, surgically bypassing the *Anchorage Times*.

Though we began to move up in the polls, it seemed impossible to overcome the saturation of four years of "Zero Growth" Hammond criticism. A more intelligent candidate would have moved on to other issues, instead of continuing to beat the drum on healthy vs. unhealthy growth, something Alaskans seemed to not want to hear. My old adversary Wally Hickel meanwhile, played concert master to more popular themes by refusing to see the downside of any development project. A classic illustration of this came up in a debate over an oil refinery proposed for the Kenai Peninsula.

The project's sponsors asserted their refinery would create four hundred new year-round jobs. There was one catch. To make the refinery economically feasible, the state would have to sell the owners our royalty oil — oil we took "in kind" as part of Alaska's share of revenue from oil produced on state land — at $1.25 per barrel less than the already deflated price this oil would bring on the non-demand market created by the ban on Alaska oil export. Still, Wally thought this was a great idea, even though the number of barrels needed, at a loss of $1.25 each, would cost the state treasury $96 million a year!

"That means those four hundred jobs would cost Alaskans $240,000 each year," I pointed out. "It doesn't make sense. We could create a few *thousand* jobs tomorrow, for the same money, just by putting, say, more troopers on the state payroll."

"No, No!" Wally protested. "That would be *government* growth. I want to see growth in the *private* sector."

I argued that the extent to which the state subsidizes the private sector is nothing more than *hidden* government growth. "We could promote all sorts of growth if we're willing to subsidize it; we could grow strawberries on Mt. McKinley if we built a highway to the top, erected solar greenhouses, paid Teamster's wages and guaranteed markets. But that's not my idea of healthy economic development.

"I'd much prefer to sell our royalty oil at market value and put that $96 million into the hands of individual Alaskans as a dividend. Rather than watch benefits from their co-owned oil wealth 'trickle down' inequitably, let's let some of it percolate *up* from the grassroots."

Asserting this ridiculous concept "went out with Robin Hood," Wally reiterated the old, reliable "Zero Growth" charge — one of three false themes Hickel, Atwood and Carr continued to dump on me in 1978. The other two aroused even greater voter animosity: According to my accusers, I refused to use our new wealth to build any roads, and — most damaging of all — I failed to convey state lands to private ownership.

These patently false allegations had been repeated so frequently, the "Zero Growth Hammond" image so firmly implanted in the public mind, a cab driver even ejected a passenger on the highway when he learned his fare was a Hammond campaign volunteer. "Zero Growth" was an albatross around my neck that would not fly away, despite the fact Alaska's white hot economy should have singed its tail feathers.

True, I believed the challenge was to manage Alaska through a period of inevitable, explosive growth, to encourage what was good for Alaska's long term and to resist "growth" that would drag the state down when the boom was over. But it both baffled and aggravated me when, in the din of these inaccurate charges, the truth was not being received by the electorate.

Consequently, at an "all-candidates" debate at the Alaska Press Club, I challenged Wally Hickel to debate "one on one" what he, Atwood and Carr had made the key issues. Citing each of his charges and the facts as I knew them, I asked the Press Club's members to act as judge and jury.

"Is it true, as Wally asserts, that I'm opposed to private land ownership? Or is it true, as I contend, my administration has conveyed more state land to Alaskans than all other administrations combined?

"Is it true, as Wally asserts, I'm opposed to road building? Or is it true the seven hundred and fifty miles of roads built under my administration exceeds the total of all previous administrations combined? "Is it true, as Wally asserts, I am anti-business? Or is it true, as a University of Wisconsin study documents, my administration has provided more small business assistance than any other state in the nation?"

I asked the Fourth Estate assembled to check the facts and publish the results.

"I'll stand by your verdict and forgo any right of appeal. If you conclude it is I, rather than Wally, who is *not* telling it as it is, I will withdraw from this race and never again run for public office, if Mr. Hickel will make the same commitment."

Briefly speechless, for a moment Wally seemed caught with his political pants at half mast. But he nimbly took cover in a thicket of flowery verbiage exuding affront that I would exclude "all these other fine candidates" and unfairly narrow the field to just the two of us.

"They have as much right to be heard as we do," said Wally, finally deciding to plead the First (instead of the Fifth) Amendment.

The press did not take up my challenge. But they did report it in their coverage and suddenly we began getting mail from people questioning what they'd been led to believe. To exploit this nascent backlash, at the next debate I repeated my offer and promised to stand or fall on the findings of a panel of journalists. This time I added, "Since Mr. Hickel has rejected my challenge to debate these facts one-on-one, I'll sweeten it. Wally, I'll agree to debate you one-on-*two*; you and Bob Atwood. If a press panel concludes I'm wrong and you and the *Times* are right, I'll resign and never again run for office — if you'll make the same commitment. Someone is 'telling it like it isn't' and the voter has a right to know who."

For some reason, the press would not take this challenge seriously. When the laughter subsided, Wally again disappeared behind a smoke screen of fair play for all. But public interest in the contradiction continued to grow and two weeks later I had a final opportunity to focus attention on these distortions.

At the next confrontation, I offered to debate Wally one-on-*three*. "Me versus Hickel, Atwood and Jesse Carr. Only this time, if a majority of the media conclude I'm in error and my three opponents are right, I'll withdraw from the race entirely, if they'll simply *apologize* for 'telling it like it isn't.'"

Along with Hickel, the press again declined. By this time I'd long since lost hope of being taken up on my offer, but I realized our campaign was the beneficiary of eroding credibility of the state's largest newspaper and Alaska's most powerful union. As it happened, this erosion went on for some years. In the frustration of the campaign, I did not at first appreciate how their refusal to accept this challenge actually paid larger dividends for me than if Wally had agreed to the first one-on-one debate offer. By finessing the facts, he could have put the issue to rest. By refusing, he gave me — and those willing to listen — the issue that defined my 1978 candidacy.

Eventually I got my public confrontation with Hickel, Atwood and Carr. But that's another story.

THERE WERE OTHER DEBATES as the 1978 primary entered its last weeks. I'd moved up slightly ahead of Wally in the polls, with Anchorage insurance man Tom Fink a not-too-distant third. Then, in the final week of the campaign, Hickel unleashed a saturation media campaign urging Alaskans to elect him so he could sue the federal government — force it to bend to his will and release Alaska from bondage. In this call to arms, he neglected to mention his role as Interior Secretary in sustaining the federal freeze on Alaska's lands.

His last-minute campaign ploy was effective. Polls showed me losing ground to Wally's surge.

In spite of this, I recall most fondly one moment at the close of our last television debate. We'd been told the format would allow each of the nine candidates to ask a question of the others, then give his own answer after they'd replied. When it was my turn, to each candidate, I posed this question: "In every administration, no matter how unpopular, there are bound to be some programs you support. Tell me, which programs now being delivered by my administration would you retain if elected?"

One by one, my opponents struggled to mention those they knew were popular with the electorate, assuring voters each would be retained. After the first three candidates had answered, the next five competed to mention programs not yet cited by previous speakers. When it came time to give my own answer, I gratefully thanked them for their rousing endorsements of ninety percent of my administration's programs. Then, graciously filling in the very few they'd forgotten — and expressing "my concern for your lack of support" of some very popular programs — I happily thanked the panel for what had degenerated into a statewide televised Hammond pep rally.

Much as I'd like to take credit for this coup, it was suggested by my brilliant attorney general, Av Gross. Good as it was, however, it wasn't enough.

Late on election night and leading by six hundred votes, Wally Hickel proclaimed victory and told everyone to go home. "We've got it in the bag!"

Asked by the press if I was prepared to concede, I said while I agreed with Wally's assertion, I'd just as soon wait until it was clear just who was holding that bag.

Flying to our homestead, which remains mercifully devoid of a telephone, I waited for the pall of gloom that was supposed to descend upon me now that I'd been spurned by the electorate. I waited in vain. Instead of gloom, it felt rather good to realize I'd been shucked out of the strait jacket of public office for the freedom of my "briar patch."

My reverie while chopping wood was rudely shattered by my friend John Branson who'd taken great care of our place while we were in Juneau. "Hey, I just heard on the radio that a recount cut Wally's lead in half. You're only three hundred votes behind!"

Still sure I had no chance of making up those votes by recount, I failed to realize these were absentee ballots being counted for the first time, and mentally returned to the good life by imagining one pesky political problem after another posed on my chopping block.

A few days later, this process was again shattered by Branson running out to tell me Hickel and I were neck and neck. An hour later he re-appeared; I was *ahead* by thirty-seven votes! When I was declared the winner by ninety-eight votes, I laid my ax aside, and with a perverse mixture of gratitude and reluctance, returned to Juneau to prepare for the general election. Since John Branson is the world's best wood cutter, I thought, my wood pile will miss me less than I'll miss it.

I no sooner arrived at the state capital when word came that an Elections Office employee in Anchorage had discovered an unopened box of ballots in the trunk of his car! Hickel and his lawyer, Edgar Paul Boyko, immediately challenged the election with screams of "fraud."

My 98-vote primary victory was ruled invalid by Superior Court Judge Ralph Moody, on Friday the thirteenth, the same day President Carter withdrew 120 million acres of Alaska land in "the national interest."

When I arrived back in Alaska from Los Angeles, I learned the court had not thrown out the entire primary, however; only the two top Republican vote-getters, Hickel and Hammond, would face off in a re-run. My former friend and supporter Chancy Croft had won the Democratic nomination.

MY ATTORNEY GENERAL never had a better day "at the bar" than the night he argued the lower court's ruling against Boyko's inflammatories in a special session of the Alaska Supreme Court. In concert, the "Supremes" drowned out Boyko's dissonance, played the "blues" for Moody's decision, and harmonized unanimously in declaring the primary election was valid. The general election would be held as scheduled, now only eighteen days hence.

THE COURT DECIDED the outcome of two Hammond-Hickel elections in 1978. In addition to protesting the statewide primary, Boyko had opposed counting the lost and found box of general election ballots, once forensic experts determined it had never been opened. When it was counted by court order, I won the "election in a box," over Wally, also. But in this, the most bizarre campaign in Alaska political history, there was yet one more Hickel vs. Hammond election to come.

A few days after the Supreme Court ruling, I received a call from Wally, asking to meet. I agreed. At this meeting he demonstrated amazing powers of clairvoyance.

"Look," he told me, " 'they' want me to run against you as a write-in in the general. I don't want to do that, so I'll make a deal. For certain considerations, I'll promise not to run a write in campaign."

Rather than the eager supplication I suspect he felt this offer might prompt, I was at a loss for words. As Nature abhors a vacuum, Wally quickly filled it.

"I'll guarantee not to run a write in if you'll do three things: First, fire your attorney general, Av Gross; second, fire your natural resources commissioner, Bob LeResche; and third, fire your commissioner of revenue, Sterling Gallagher."

I told Wally I could appreciate why some who wanted to remove constraints on uninhibited, gung-ho growth might take exception to these three cabinet members. However, "I've no desire to advance myself politically over the bleeding carcasses of those who've served me faithfully and well."

Back at Lake Clark, awaiting election returns in 1978, I imagined every chunk of wood to be a pesky problem or political adversary. Lots of land-hungry new Alaskans wanted their bit of the wilderness, one of the burning issues during my second term.

Moreover, I said I could understand why some Republicans might resent Av and Bob; they were both Democrats. "However all three commissioners have one common denominator: they're brilliant. Even Gallagher, who admittedly sometimes speaks in incomprehensible tongues, often demonstrates remarkable insight and intelligence when translated. So what if he over-complicates the simplistic? The fact he can make 'Dick and Jane' sound like E=MC² doesn't bother me as long as he's doing what I want done. Sorry Wally. No deal."

"Well," he said, "if that's your answer, I guess I'll have to let my backers kickoff their write-in."

"So be it," was my departing comment.

I was fully aware Hickel had, in his money, Atwood's *Times* and Carr's Teamsters, formidable powers. In the sixty seconds it took to descend from our meeting in Wally's aerie atop his hotel to the lobby, I also found irrefutable evidence of another: his political precognition. Passing the hotel's sundry shop I saw the headline of that evening's *Times*.

"HICKEL MOUNTS WRITE IN CAMPAIGN!"

For all of a half-second I was tempted to go back and tell Wally I accepted his offer, if for no other reason than to further erode the *Times'* credibility.

Hickel not only ran his write-in campaign with an effluent flow of advertising, mail-outs and stick-on ballot decals, he "borrowed" my running mate, lieutenant governor nominee Terry Miller, as *his* running mate. In the end, Hickel/Miller garnered enough votes to come in second to Hammond/Miller in the final balloting, substantially ahead of Democratic nominee Chancy Croft and Independent candidate Tom Kelly.

Chancy had been my strong supporter in 1974. It was ironic and sad that he had reason to be disenchanted and run against me in 1978. I'd lied to him. While devoid of malice, forethought or even awareness, I had nonetheless broken my personal word to him and he'd been justifiably and unforgivingly infuriated.

Our breech evolved around passage of a bill he'd sponsored to vastly increase Workers' Compensation benefits. When it hit my desk, I had thirty days to veto or sign the bill before it became law automatically. Knowing of my opposition to what I felt were inordinate, employer-crippling workers' compensation insurance premiums, Chancy had come to my office to find out what was in store for his pet legislation. I voiced my concerns. He acknowledged them and simply asked if I would please notify him if I planned to veto the measure.

"You'll be the first to know," I promised.

As the thirty-day countdown proceeded, I gave little thought to the bill other than to conclude, unless very persuasive evidence was forthcoming to change my opinion, I would doubtlessly veto his bill. Suddenly, in late afternoon on the thirtieth day, the Attorney General's Office sent word I only had until five o'clock to veto the measure or it would become law. With no qualms, I hastily did so — totally forgetting my assurance to Chancy.

The next morning an apoplectic Chancy Croft came to my office charging I'd broken a commitment. I tried to think of something to say to mollify him. There was nothing. I'd totally forgotten my assurance he'd "be the first to know." Instead, he'd heard it on the evening news.

Chancy had every reason to be outraged. Had he been told a few days ahead I'd veto the measure, he'd have had time to try to line up votes to override. Since my perfidy probably was a major factor compelling Chancy to mount his costly, losing race, I suspect he still finds my most sincere apology less than acceptable.

Chancy had the support not only of organized labor — except for the Teamsters, who supported Hickel in both the primary, and in his general election write-in — Democratic liberals and conservationists. It proved not enough. Hammond/Miller won the 1978 General Election by 16,000 votes — my third win against Wally in 1978.

This gave rise to a trivia riddle I'm told has won more than one glass of beer for Alaska's barstool bettors. The first time it was put to me, I was stumped.

A reporter asked, "Can you tell me which Republican candidate for governor won his primary election by the largest margin; which won by the smallest margin; which one won the general by the smallest margin, and which one won the general by the largest margin?"

Knowing I must qualify for at least one of these distinctions, I was still pondering when he said, "*You're* the answer to all four. You won your first primary by a landslide; your first general by two hundred-some votes. You squeaked in on your second primary, (one hundred and thirty after the ballot box was counted). Then won your second general by the largest plurality in state history."

So much for delusions of grandeur. Rather than being swept into office on a floodtide of public support, I arrived on a small wavelet as trivia.

*I've little doubt that in 1978 I slid in on the coattails of my running
mate, Terry Miller, a brilliant young man of great potential who was
snuffed out by cancer a few years later.*

27

The Great Alaska Lands War

PERHAPS MOST CREDIT for winning re-election in 1978 belonged to my running mate, Terry Miller, a brilliant young man whose flaming potential was snuffed out by cancer a few short years later. That I'd slid in on his longer coattails I've little doubt.

Those who at the time thought that confession overly modest were given almost immediate proof to the contrary. While my oath of office still echoed, petitions were put in circulation to recall me. My sins? Three land issues that tore Alaskans asunder:

1. Demands to convey state land to private ownership;
2. Rage over the so-called "d-2" federal land freeze; and
3. Proposals to move the state capital from Juneau.

These issues so divided Alaskans they were at each other's throats. Large blocks of voters based their support on where a candidate stood on a single issue. But these issues not only divided the state in half, each did so along different fracture lines — urban vs. rural, Native vs. white, development vs. environment, city vs. city. Confusion reigned. Emotions enflamed.

Trying to govern in this atmosphere was akin to standing astride two wild horses being gelded and turpentined. All sides sought someone on whom to vent their wrath, and some had devoted half the decade to identifying that someone as Hammond. As usual, I cooperated by managing to alienate each side of all three issues.

Take the proposal to move the state capital from Juneau to a more central location: capital move proponents argued since half Alaska's population lived in Anchorage, the capital should be located in the area of greatest population

237

density and easiest access. Juneau, they argued, unconnected by road to any other Alaskan community, was inconvenient and too expensive to reach by air for citizens who wished to berate the legislature and governor. This faction maintained that government would improve by removing the legislature from its sequester in remote, often fog-bound Juneau and hauling it north, where, "if we could just get our hands on those rascals throats, they might shape up."

Actually, the motives of many "pro-move" advocates were less noble. Land speculators, businessmen, contractors and labor unions salivated over prospects of building a "Brasilia of the North." No matter its costs, the prospect of snatching the economic plum that Juneau had snatched from Sitka years before led many to invest heavily in hopes of tapping state oil revenues to finance their aspirations. Juneauites not only opposed the move; they knew as long as there remained a threat of moving the capital, potential local development prospects were grounded in Juneau, while they soared elsewhere.

Many seemed confused about where I stood, thanks not so much to my own pronouncements, but to interpretations provided by a totally polarized press in the opposing cities. The *Juneau Empire* editorialized that, despite my protests to the contrary, I was actually a "closet Capitol Mover." To prove it, the paper excerpted a quote from the minutes of a Bristol Bay Borough meeting held a decade before. Said Hammond, according to the *Empire*, "Think of all the money Alaskans would save if they had better access to their state capital."

In full context, my facetious statement had been, "Maybe we ought to move the capital and *keep* it moving. Let's put it on a ferry and move it from city to town to village. *Think of all the money Alaskans would save if they had better access to their capital.* Rather than go to it, let it come to them."

Meanwhile, the *Anchorage Times* and Teamster publications were trumpeting, "If Hammond's elected the capital will never move!" Inevitably, large numbers of people in each city came to believe I was to blame for each not getting what they wanted. In both communities, I lost an avalanche of votes over these blasts. If only I could have had the *Juneau Empire* publish the *Anchorage Times'* editorials and vice versa, I'd have probably won by at least a few more votes.

The capital move issue festered through all my eight years as governor. It was with immense satisfaction that, at the end of my term, we were able to lance this boil. But that was four years off. Meanwhile, another boil was about to burst.

Many voters on both sides of the capital move issue joined with still other Alaskans who wanted the state to convey free or cheap lands to them. Though my administration had conveyed more state acreage into private ownership in my first term than all previous administrations combined, my opponents convinced many Alaskans I was philosophically opposed to private land ownership.

"Ridiculous!" I countered, adding more fuel to the fire. "I believe very much in private land ownership. Why else would I secure all the land I could by homesteading?"

To which they re-countered, "Yeah, you got yours. Now you don't want anyone else to get any. You want to lock it all up in parks and refuges.

Of course, most state lands had yet to be conveyed from the federal government, nor would they be until "d-2" was resolved. But this did little to slake irrational demands we give away or sell at cut rate what little land we had. This sore festered hotter each passing day.

I did little to cool it by observing, "Many Alaskans worry about the federal government locking up our lands in the public domain as parks and refuges. Yet, private land ownership can be the ultimate lock-up, as is only proper, since you ought to be able to keep folks off your property if you choose. Because of this inherent right, we should be careful about conveying to private ownership lands that have a great public value, such as, for example, lands that offer access to prime fishing streams."

This evolved into an inflammatory bumper sticker: HAMMOND SAYS PRIVATE OWNERSHIP THE ULTIMATE LOCK-UP.

And among those most outraged by my presumed opposition to private land ownership was Anchorage pathologist and legislator Dr. Mike Beirne. Appointing him to a vacancy in the House was not my most astute political move. The good doctor's solution of conveying *all* state lands for *free* had the surgical finesse of disembowelment. In 1978, he introduced a bill to place on the ballot for voter approval a law that all state lands be conveyed to private parties, first come, first served! Worse yet, in an election year, the legislature passed it!

The Beirne Initiative had the same appeal to land-hungry Alaskans as would inviting the public to "help themselves" at Fort Knox. Who among our burgeoning population would not aspire to cabins at prime fishing and hunting sites, their own valley or lake, at no charge? For that matter, many non-Alaskans, including well-heeled Arabs, expressed interest in Beirne's free acreage. That prime locations would go to the most affluent and speculators seemed to escape the man on the street who would be least likely to find anything left once the land rush was on.

Though a little dense, I am not unable to profit from my past stupidity. Certain the Beirne Initiative was illegal, (Alaska's Constitution prohibits citizens from raiding State coffers for either money or land), I felt the court should share in the privilege of communicating this message. Thus, when the initiative passed, instead of committing political suicide by vetoing it, I allowed it to go on the ballot, confident it would be struck down if it passed. When the court did so, those who had thirsted with anticipation only screamed louder. But now some of those screams blew past me to blast the court.

The capital move and the Beirne Initiative, for all they divided Alaskans, were less divisive than the unresolved root of Alaska's land madness: Section 17 d-2 of the Alaska Native Claims Settlement Act.

Long before they were granted statehood, much of the land in other states already was settled and owned by private parties. Not so in Alaska. At statehood, the federal government owned 97 percent of the land, having purchased it from Russia — "Seward's Folly," remember? The remaining three percent pittance had either been conveyed to the territory or acquired by private parties through programs like homesteading. Who was going to use all that federal land — and how — was the nub of d-2.

It not only divided Alaskans, d-2 split Alaska from the rest of the Union. We could at least fumble with local issues, but our hands were tied by federal law. Alaskans never wanted to believe this, but we had almost nothing to say in how federal lands were to be used in Alaska.

To pronounce this publicly, however, would have invited impeachment. Because it was so easy to pander to the public's hysteria on this issue, most politicians did so with success, usually at my expense. As governor, I was the one held responsible for "doing something" about d-2. Of course, Alaskans were so bitterly divided, to appease one side, even if possible, would have launched the other in orbit.

In 1979, as the d-2 war intensified, most Alaska conservationists enlisted in a national Coalition for Alaska Lands, mounting one of the greatest grassroots campaigns since the Civil Rights movement. These people advocated maximum acreage be placed in parks and refuges, much of it to be designated "wilderness" where no development would be allowed.

Developers, on the other hand, banded together and objected vigorously to any proposal that would "lock up" land against potential exploitation. Of course, they too depicted themselves as conservationists and to prove it, pronounced they'd no reluctance in setting aside large enclaves of Alaska as wilderness. That most of their proposals consisted largely of inaccessible mountain tops, sterile glaciers and ice fields, did little to win over Congress.

Occupying center stage between these warring factions, and managing to offend both equally, suggests we accommodated about as well as possible concerns of both factions. In the end, perhaps, I was the most disappointed. My position on the issue differed markedly from both that of most conservationists and developers.

I felt Alaska's unique land values deserved a unique resolution; a new land use concept to assure rational resource development and yet provide adequate environmental protection over most of Alaska. To achieve these not incompatible ends required something different from the practice of creating federal enclaves such as parks and refuges within which habitat protection is complete, adjacent to lands in the same ecosystem for which little or no habitat protection was provided.

To a biologist, this not only ignored the nature of man, animals and habitat, it created unnecessary conflicts between them. What good does it do to create a federal park and provide 100 percent protection to some fish and game habitat onto which caribou and salmon migrate, if the desecration allowed to occur outside its borders in the same ecosystem is left to the discretion of state or private owners? Much better, I thought, to provide adequate protection on *most* of our land, regardless of ownership.

To accomplish this, I proposed that prime ecosystems throughout Alaska be identified and designated as Cooperative Management Areas (COMANs). All land owners within each COMAN would be consulted to draw up a land-use plan that assured basic habitat protection, yet allowed human activity that could be accommodated without damage to the ecosystem's prime values. If respective owners could not agree to such a plan, those federal lands that had been designated "prospective" parks and refuges, could then be made fully operative, with all the traditional constraints applied.

On the other hand, if landowners could reach agreement, a COMAN would be established. But no one would be locked in. Should a landowner later wish to withdraw, he could do so but only if willing to "pay the price" of having restrictive "fences" around prospective parks and refuges, (lowered under the COMAN), go back up to create full-blown parks and refuges preventing even some of the most compatible human activity.

COMANs could have provided far greater habitat protection as well as a wider range of compatible human activity over much more of Alaska's lands than is now the case.

Hoping to further this concept, immediately after taking office in my second term, I requested a special, emergency appropriation from the legislature to fund an initiative I felt would resolve the d-2 lands battle in Congress before it could tear the state further apart. (One angry Alaskan already had chained himself to the Fairbanks post office in sub-zero weather. Others threatened more violent demonstrations of discontent).

With my resources commissioner, Bob LeResche, I fashioned six basic d-2 objectives with which every faction could agree. These six consensus points touched on every contention, yet did so in a way all could endorse. When it came to "fine tuning" these six points, of course, each warring faction had its interpretation. But the differences were secondary to forging enough unity among Alaskans to allow the governor to petition Congress with a so-called "unified" state position.

The key question was who was best capable of presenting it to Congress? After exhaustive search I selected extraordinarily competent Alaska land-use attorney John Katz, and put him in full charge both in Alaska and Washington.

I'd been enormously impressed with the credibility and respect John had earned among even the most extreme developers and conservationists. If I could have run John Katz through a duplicating machine, I'd have put him in a dozen key government slots — including my own.

At the same time, I assigned to my communications director Bob Clarke the task of keeping Alaskans informed.

That Katz succeeded brilliantly in holding most factions together in a "no win" situation is perhaps best attested by the fact he has been retained by every succeeding governor to represent the state's varied interests in Washington, D.C. Since John was one, like myself, who came to Alaska for its lifestyle, I don't know how kindly John recalls me as he fights summer humidity on the streets of

Washington, or the vapors of "foggy bottom." But I have yet to hear anyone, on any side of any issue, speak without respect for his ability.

Clarke, in concert with Katz's efforts, initiated the first daily television coverage of Alaska issues in the Congress. In doing so, he provided reality therapy for all Alaskans. Courtesy of unedited daily satellite feeds to news-starved Alaska television stations, Alaskans began to comprehend d-2 problems for the first time; every evening in their living rooms, through the night and into the morning by radio, and in Alaska's only morning newspaper, the *Anchorage Daily News*, the issues unfolded. By the time Bob Atwood's post mortem *Times* got its hands on d-2 news in the afternoon, it was old news. An unexpected spin off from our d-2 initiative was, within a few months, the "Recall Hammond" campaign died aborning.

Combined with *News* publisher Kay Fanning's successful settlement of a lawsuit against the *Times* for unfair practices and the infusion of new capital, the *News* more than doubled its circulation during these same months.

Spring 1979 marked the peak of the *Anchorage Times'* influence, and the high water mark of Alaska extremism.

In Washington, Congress was going to pass a National Interest Lands bill, one way or the other, and President Carter was determined to sign it. Alaska's Senator Ted Stevens did his best to get a compromise from a Congress lobbied heavily by the powerful Alaska lands coalition. The state was obliged to reconcile Alaska's conflicting points of view, but Katz was equal to this seemingly impossible task. Only extremists on either side of this painful issue were not satisfied. When some environmentalists demanded still more set-asides, Alaska's developmental extremists decided to take matters into their own hands.

Descending on the nation's capital by the plane load, delegation after delegation of uncompromising Alaskans who thought they were playing "Mr. Smith Goes to Washington" came off as something else. Some were so rude and extreme, many congressmen told me they did more than conservationists to persuade Congress to protect Alaska from Alaskans. Their mode of travel and corrosive style prompted lobbyist Langhorne "Tony" Motley, my former commissioner of commerce and economic development, (and later President Reagan's ambassador to Brazil) to dub them "the propeller heads." Even gracious Oregon Senator Mark Hatfield told me that if he'd met "these people before, I don't know that I'd have voted for statehood."

Many Alaskans deeply resented the lack of confidence shown by Congress and the Carter Administration in Alaskans' ability to manage their own destiny. They struck back with such slogans as "We don't give a damn how they do it Outside," or "Let the Bastards Freeze in the Dark." In the end, those who whipped Alaskan emotions into a white heat did, I believe, perhaps more than environmentalists to pass what was seen by most Alaskans as an overly restrictive bill.

On one of my last excursions to Washington, I left our hotel about six one morning. Standing at the curb to hail a cab, my aide suddenly shrieked and staggered blindly into a tree. Startled, I saw his glasses askew as he frantically dabbed a handkerchief at the steaming remains of an offering conveyed by what could only have been a passing giant condor. If it was just a pigeon, as locals insisted, it gave new meaning to the word "carrier."

Since it was my aide's fiftieth birthday, he speculated morosely on his bad fortune. Of all the people in the nation's capital that morning, *he* was bombarded. "Don't worry," I reassured him as he slunk back to the hotel to shower, "it was probably just the morning flight of propeller heads."

WHEN, ON DECEMBER 2, 1980, President Jimmy Carter signed the Alaska National Interest Lands Conservation Act, with a stroke of his pen he carved a niche for himself both in history and the hearts of conservationists. By placing almost a third of Alaska's 365 million acres into protective custody, ANILCA almost doubled our nation's parks and refuges. But many developers felt Carter instead had carved the heart from Alaska.

My major disappointment was Congress' failure to implant the COMANs concept. Reluctant to accept the federal government's alternative concept of "cooperative management" — whereby "they" did all the managing and "we" all the cooperating — I'd lobbied almost all members of the House and Senate on the COMANs approach. Many were intrigued, including ardent conservationists Representatives Morris Udall and John Seiberling.

"We like the idea, but can you get conservationists to support it?" they asked. With rare exceptions, I could not. So determined were they to establish traditional parks and refuges, they refused to consider a new approach. By not doing so, we've created higher than necessary "fences" around some lands in Alaska while allowing state and private landowners to go their own way. Instead of achieving by cooperative management habitat protection for perhaps seventy percent of Alaska's prime ecosystems, we have a tattered patchwork of one hundred percent protection here, stitched to virtually no protection there, with varying protection between.

Today the most divisive issue in Alaska's state history is behind us. And most Alaskans seem persuaded ANILCA has brought neither all the horrors envisioned by opponents, nor all the blessings intended by advocates. Most are learning to live with what has been termed "the most significant piece of environmental legislation ever passed."

I suspect this measure, more than any other, will in years ahead, cast a softer glow than the harsh light history has so far reflected on Jimmy Carter. I hope so. While some may not approve the structure of the "showcases" nor the degree of diligence with which these lands are supposed to be guarded, few will dispute the need to assure that the "crown jewels" of North America, strewn about so abundantly here in Alaska, warrant something more than "business as usual."

ANILCA strove to protect these crown jewels by placing them not in impregnable vaults, but showcases — not to be locked away out of sight or touch but rather, displayed, under guard, for the admiration and enrichment of generations to come. Rather than being "locked up" as some contend, these jewels are locked open, for the enjoyment of all.

Perhaps the most ironic aspect of this incredibly divisive battle between conservationists and developers is the possibility, once oil and the minerals are depleted, ANILCA may prevent Alaska from returning to the traditional "boom — bust" cycle that has plagued its economy since the days of Russian exploitation.

Tourism, I'm told, has surpassed oil as an international monetary medium. In Alaska today, visitors spend more than a billion dollars, maintaining almost 14,000 Alaska jobs and generating millions in revenue to state and local governments. More than 52,000 Alaska jobs are now directly affected by non-resident spending — thousands more indirectly. Eighty-four percent of Alaska's visitor industry jobs are held by Alaska residents, and more local entrepreneurs are emerging to accommodate this growing activity.

Tourism has become Alaska's second largest private sector industry in terms of employment and its third largest among basic industries — including government — following only the military and the seafood industries.

Unquestionably, the crown jewels reserved and showcased by ANILCA will continue to attract those who seek experiences rapidly vanishing from other parts of the world. Barring re-emergence of international hostility such as that which seems to have faded between our nation and the old Soviet Union, Alaska as a visitor destination may indeed prevent the "busts" which followed the fur, gold and oil booms. If so, in some substantial part, ANILCA will have made this possible.

Certainly, Alaska has vast resources that will be tapped. Yet can it be both oil barrel to a nation and national park to the world? Can Alaska play both roles to the extent her charms stay unjaded? Alaska's future remains to be determined. Whatever it is, I will forever be grateful I was privileged to know her while we were both young, either oblivious to or more tolerant of each other's shortcomings.

LONG AGO, WHEN I WAS GUIDING for another outfitter, I had thrust upon me a hunting client to whom I will charitably refer simply as a "suffering sight-seer." He complained about everything under the sun and increased his complaints if the sun didn't shine, which happened to be most of the time. He complained of bad weather, lack of booze, the abundance of bugs, the cost of the hunt, the food and the state of his bowels.

After having hauled him to a mountain top where he'd emptied his rifle at a fine Dall ram (which escaped unscathed, to my secret satisfaction), he demonstrated once more how often the hunted out-nobles the hunter, and launched a profane litany of all things Alaskan, ending with the assertion, "Alaska's the last place on earth I'd ever want to live!"

I reflected on that for a moment and mused, "You know, I agree. Alaska's the last place on earth I'd ever want to live too. And with any luck at all, it will be!"

When Alaskans started applying for the first batch of Permanent Fund Dividend checks, officials were stumped by one form indicating Belle Herbert of Chalkytsik had lived in Alaska for 134 years.

In 1980, during a visit to the village, there was some disagreement over her age, but not one to quibble, I quickly recognized her as "the oldest woman in Alaska."

28

Money, Money, Money!

WHEN I BECAME GOVERNOR in 1974, the scent of anticipated oil revenues wafted like musk in the halls of the legislature. It did not require clairvoyance to sense our prudent good intentions were going to sluice away with the first turn of the money tap.

The first massive injection of oil wealth had been $900 million from the 1969 sale of oil leases at Prudhoe Bay.

Then-Governor Keith Miller agreed with a few of us legislators that prudence dictated investing the money and spending only the interest. But that idea won little support in the legislature; $900 million represented a chance to provide basic services taken for granted in the Lower 48 states.

When we opened the valve to let oil money fill those vacuums, the spigot was almost sucked dry. The state's operating budget doubled to more than $300 million a year, and our "nest egg" was scrambled.

Many swore if we received another windfall, we would not make the same mistake again.

Consequently, as governor, I believed the best approach was to divert money into a dividend-dispersing investment account, in which all Alaskans were "stockholders." To promote this idea I initiated the Alaska Public Forum, a traveling town meeting, to whip up support for a program similar to the "Bristol Bay, Inc." proposal I'd advocated unsuccessfully years before.

Public response was underwhelming. Despite lack of encouragement, I introduced a bill to create "Alaska, Inc." by amending the state constitution.

Under this proposal, Alaska, Inc. would receive 50 percent of all natural resource lease, bonus, royalty and severance tax dollars, and put them virtually

247

out of easy reach by requiring a statewide vote before the principle could be invaded. Annual earnings from this account would be divided in half: fifty percent would be dispersed in cash dividends to all Alaskans, in the form of one share of dividend-paying "stock" for each year of residency since statehood.

I'd considered providing health or unemployment insurance instead of cash dividends. Others suggested subsidized loans. Since absolute equity was a necessary objective, however, I preferred to let each Alaskan — not the politicians — decide how he or she should spend some of the resource wealth each owned.

Children's dividends would be held in an interest-bearing account until age eighteen. Persons moving out of Alaska would relinquish their "stockholder" shares.

Legislative reception for Alaska, Inc. was not cordial. The proposal was referred to a multitude of committees for interment.

Fortunately, a few lawmakers shared my concern that, unless something was done to sweep some of our coming oil wealth off the legislative smorgasbord, *all* would be consumed by programs the state couldn't possibly sustain when our one-time wealth declined.

Had it not been for the substantial efforts of a few legislators like Clem Tillion, Oral Freeman, Hugh Malone, Clark Gruening (Ernest Gruening's grandson), Terry Gardiner and a few others, Alaska would surely have followed suit. After much debate, these visionaries persuaded their colleagues to pass legislation creating an investment account. Unfortunately, it bore little resemblance to Alaska, Inc.

Rather than creating an invasion-proof account by an amendment to the Alaska Constitution, the legislature's investment account was statutory and could be tapped any time at legislative whim. Instead of depositing half of all resource lease, bonuses and royalties, deposits were halved again, to twenty-five percent. Also lopped off was any reference to severance taxes — a tax paid for 'severing' a resource from its owner — which accounts for almost half of Alaska's oil income. Legislative pruning reduced the contributions I had proposed by almost 75 percent!

In light of these mutilations I was not surprised to find also scissored out any reference to dividends or to "Alaska, Inc." In place was the misnomer, "The Alaska Permanent Fund."

"Permanent?" Only until a subsequent legislature decided otherwise. Nothing but a constitutional amendment could keep politicians from breaching the public's investment account. Anything less was an invitation to raid. Consequently, I reluctantly vetoed Alaska's first Permanent Fund. In my veto message I reiterated my concerns and insisted the issue be put to the electorate as a constitutional amendment.

The legislature grumbled but complied, and the 1976 general election saw Alaskans vote overwhelmingly to create a far more nearly PERMANENT Fund. While fund earnings can be spent as the legislature chooses, the fund itself is protected against political onslaught unless a statewide vote decides otherwise.

Again, in language the legislature approved for the amendment ballot, no dividend program was mentioned. Accordingly, the people's investment trust still lacked protection. Despite its constitutional status, I feared the Permanent Fund would die without a militant ring of voter "stockholders" to find off politicians inclined to invade the trust on behalf of special interests. This compelled my run for a second term.

I arrived in Juneau to begin my second term as governor concurrent with the torrent of wealth about to cascade down the trans-Alaska pipeline. Suddenly Alaska was about to be hip deep in one-time petro-dollars. Politicians anticipated political Nirvana: never having to say "no."

But with the combination of depressed market prices, federal price controls, the ban on Alaska oil export and resultant transportation costs far beyond what we'd expected, revenues to the state from our one-time resource were proving to be far less than anticipated.

Many Alaskans still angry with President Jimmy Carter over land issues overlook the fact the president and his energy secretary, James Schlesinger, responded positively to my administration's plea to re-classify North Slope crude as "upper tier" oil, a change that added up to millions of dollars to state coffers. Only then did the state begin to get fair return on the extraction of this finite, one-time resource.

The only credit I can assume for this windfall, aside from maintaining sincere good relations with the president — for which I was soundly criticized at the time — is in having had the good sense to appoint Sterling Gallagher and Tom Williams as my respective revenue commissioners. While I accompanied both men on forays to Washington to press for this reclassification, Alaskans can thank them and, difficult as it may be to accept, Jimmy Carter for action that increased our oil revenues dramatically beginning in 1979.

Of course, the state budget ballooned. Pressure to spend every last one of those finite, non-recurrent oil dollars proved irresistible. Every special interest demanded a piece of the action. Politicians were only too pleased to comply.

In the wake of one of my tiresome, Cassandra-like, finger-wagging lectures urging caution against the day we'd run out of oil, two of my three predecessors, Bill Egan and Wally Hickel, appeared in Juneau to present their counterpoint.

"Hammond's preaching gloom and doom," the press quoted. "He shouldn't be concerned about running out of oil. We'll never run out of oil. He should be concerned with how we should spend the next bonanza!"

Their message had much more appeal than mine. Alaskans were in no mood to forego long-awaited programs and services. Rather than "tighten the belt," the rallying cry was "loosen the purse strings!"

I once asked my press secretary, Chuck Kleeschulte, how many total dollars in legislative spending proposals I'd vetoed. Charles is an ambulatory lap-top computer whose hard drive is stuffed with instantly retrievable arcane data. Want to know, say, the incidence of inguinal hernia among Peruvian jockeys? Ask Chuck. The sexual aberrations of Mesopotamian fruit flies? Ask

Chuck. It took his chips and circuits but a moment to spit out the answer: $1.07 billion dollars!

In one session alone, legislative proposals would have cost $15 billion *more* than the state's total revenue that year! While most did not pass, state budgets still grew from $300 million in 1970 to almost $3 billion in 1980.

As governor, I was as much to blame as most for some of this budget growth. I permitted it only because the spending craze was relentless, and accommodating some of it was the only trade-off I had to sweep billions more off the table into the Permanent Fund.

History will judge if the price paid was too high. Personally, I'm convinced had I not paid it, the ultimate cost would have been the entire Permanent Fund — worth $15 billion in 1993 — plus the several billion that have gone out in dividends.

Incensed the legislature had eliminated the dividend from my "Alaska, Inc.," proposal I introduced legislation to create a Permanent Fund Dividend program soon after re-election. This too languished in committee. Several legislators advised me not to push the measure. "Dead on arrival," they said.

I was not surprised. Alaskans themselves were not interested in dividends. When in my first term I'd managed to take part of our oil wealth from the legislature and place it in the public pocket, most never knew it.

Alaska's first dividend program came in the form of an Energy Tax Credit. When I took office in 1974, the state severance tax on Cook Inlet natural gas was half the national average. I believed Alaskans, who owned this resource by unique constitutional decree, should receive at least the same tax other states imposed. Alaska's Cook Inlet gas had been sold to utilities at bargain basement prices years before to give Anchorage consumers a break. But this subsidy came from the pocket of all other Alaska co-owners of the gas. While I didn't mind so much subsidizing Anchorage consumers by sale of gas at a price minus a fair severance tax, I resented subsidizing the Japanese who were the largest purchasers.

A study showed doubling the severance tax to the national average would increase costs to the average Anchorage household by but $19 per year. However, even this was enough for the Anchorage-dominated legislature to set up roadblocks. Obviously, a detour was needed; I charted this with two pieces of legislation in an offer they couldn't refuse.

The first proposed all Alaskan taxpayers would be granted a $150 "Energy Tax Credit" against their state income tax. The second provided, however, this "credit" would not come into play unless the legislature increased the gas severance tax. Since the $150 tax credit more than compensated Anchorage gas users for the average $19 annual increase caused by the higher tax, they had no complaint. At the same time, because other Alaskans would now receive some additional benefit from Cook Inlet gas, equity was far better served.

The bill passed almost unanimously and the state took in almost $7 million more per year. Two million new dollars went out in tax credits while the remaining five million went into state coffers. Everyone, save the Japanese, seemed happy — or so I thought.

To my great surprise, in public forums discussions around the state, I later found almost no one aware of this dividend. Had Alaskans received a *check* for $150, rather than a tax credit, public awareness would have been far greater. It was a lesson I remembered in 1978.

―――――――――

WHEN ADVISED THERE WAS no legislative interest in my Permanent Fund Dividend proposal, I enlisted the services of my old cohort, Clem Tillion, to get their attention. Clem, an ardent supporter of the idea, was also the newly-elected Senate President; he could more clearly and, if necessary, painfully convey my "requests" to his colleagues. Knowing Clem took inordinate pleasure in putting thumb-screws to opponents, I handed him a new set.

"Tell them I don't care so much if they support my dividend proposal, but unless they at least take it to the floor for a vote, I'll call them back into special session the day they adjourn. What's more, anyone who votes to keep it locked in committee can expect all his 'goodies' vetoed."

Clem delivered this message with such gusto the bill shot out of committee and onto the Senate floor like a buttered watermelon. It passed overwhelmingly.

It became obvious dividend opponents hadn't believed my promise to punish them only for failing to bring the bill out of committee, not for voting against it on the floor. Virtually all voted "Aye!" on final passage.

Any affront I might have felt from their lack of faith in my promise cooled in the breeze kicked up by legislators rushing aboard to claim co-authorship of the concept they'd judged "dead on arrival" a short time before.

―――――――――

THE DIVIDEND CONCEPT is based on Alaska's Constitution, which holds Alaska's natural resources are owned, not by the state, but by the Alaskan people themselves. My proposal was to grant each Alaskan, in essence, one "share" of dividend-paying stock for each year of residency since statehood in 1959, when they had acquired ownership.

Part of my rationale for paying dividends was to help offset the nation's highest cost-of-living. It seemed grossly unfair to *not* compensate "old timers" for the twenty-one years they'd lived in Alaska bearing those costs before their oil was developed, while compensating newcomers for *every* year they would bear them. The legislature agreed, and the Alaska Permanent Fund Dividend became law. Or so I believed.

The first dividend was set arbitrarily at $50 per "share," i.e., $50 per year of state residency. Those living in Alaska since statehood would get twenty-one shares in 1980, or $1,050. On this retroactive feature the program was to founder.

A pair of newly-arrived attorneys, Ron and Penny Zobel, filed suit, contending "discrimination." They said since some Alaskans would initially receive more in dividends than they, the act violated the U.S. Constitution. Alaska Superior Court Judge Ralph Moody agreed, but the Alaska Supreme Court overturned his decision on our appeal. The Zobels then appealed to the U.S. Supreme Court and obtained a restraining order on dividend distribution.

The state's attorney general, Avrum Gross, with his brilliant co-counsel, Susan Burke, compiled a persuasive argument for the High Court. If any discrimination occurred, they contended, it was against "old timers," not "newcomers" like the Zobels. Old timers, for their first twenty-one years of residency and resource ownership, would receive a total of only twenty-one dividends, (one per year). By contrast newcomers like the Zobels, in their twenty-first year as resident/resource owners, would have received a total of *two hundred thirty-one dividends* — one for their first year, two for their second, three for the third — and so on.

If each dividend share remained at just $50, Zobel in his twenty-first year of residency would have received a total of $11,550 vs. only $1,050 for the old timer in his twenty-first year!

Compounding the irony of the Zobels' position was that the state could have legally dispersed *all* the fund's money to *only those Alaskans who were living in the state before the Zobels ever immigrated here,* denying any dividends whatsoever to those who came later.

Enormously frustrated by delay in implementing what I thought was a noteworthy departure from practices that had gotten every other oil-rich state or nation in trouble, I anxiously awaited a final decision. Av and Susan felt fairly confident these arguments would persuade the high court. Well they might have — had the court listened.

Av had argued in front of the U.S. Supreme Court before and he urged Bella and me to come and see for ourselves. "You'll find it awe-inspiring; almost like an appearance before the Almighty!"

Instead of awesome, we found it awful. The experience totally undermined my confidence in the court's ability to dispense justice or logic. From questions asked it was evident few Justices had personally reviewed the state's case. Not only did they interrupt with seemingly irrelevant questions, they never let Av present our basic arguments.

While Av assured me most justices knew our arguments from staff briefings, I heard little to support this. Justice Thurgood Marshall, rest his soul, seemed only concerned that a Black newcomer to Alaska would receive less in dividends in his first year than would a long-term white resident. Over-looked was the fact Alaska's indigenous minority, Natives — struggling to make the transition from subsistence to a cash economy in villages with unemployment as high as seventy-percent — would collectively benefit most. They had been Alaska residents and resource owners since birth.

Justice Sandra Day O'Connor, on the other hand, seemed concerned the dividend program might inhibit interstate travel. "Would Alaskans be inclined not to move freely elsewhere because to do so would deprive them of dividends?" she asked.

Av explained how the magnetic attractions of dividends could more than offset this concern by inducing non-Alaskans to move *to* the state as other states had done for years by providing land, tax breaks, etc., to attract population.

Justice William Rehnquist seemed to best grasp the issue. But the court ruled against the program and we returned to Alaska disgusted. In my twenty-two years in public office, it was by far my greatest disappointment.

In light of the high court's decision, we worked with the legislature to modify the dividend program to what it is today: roughly one half the annual earnings of the Permanent Fund are distributed equally to all Alaska residents, including children. A portion of earnings are used to "inflation proof" the Fund, and a method of five-year averaging avoids wide annual dividend fluctuations.

The first dividend check was arbitrarily set at $1,000, an amount approximating three year's dividend accumulation during litigation. While not happy to abandon the original "stockholder" concept, I reluctantly signed the program into law. Half a loaf of unleavened crumbs strewn to the public was preferable to granting politicians exclusive access to the bakery.

When it came time to make the first distribution, recalling the Zobels, I suggested dividend checks might be mailed out very slowly, in alphabetical order.

Though at the time I was outraged by their actions, by assuring every Alaskan receives precisely the same annual dividend, the Zobels strengthened the constituency that now protects the Permanent Fund from invasion by politicians who would love to get hands on those dollars.

By 1978, oil had exploded Alaska's population; a majority had been here an average of only seven years. Under my "one share per year of residency," the public's desire to protect the Permanent Fund from invasion would have been proportional to time one had lived here. Newcomers, with far less at stake, might be swayed to squander the fund on more immediate gratifications.

So it was by the time I first met Ron Zobel, my nostrils no longer quivered. A non-profit organization had asked if I would agree to a dinner with the high bidder at its annual fundraising auction. When Ron Zobel won this "privilege," I found across the table a pleasant, intelligent and articulate young man. Ron won first my attention, then my forgiveness, by confessing had he to do things over again, he might not have mounted his suit.

"Why is that?" I asked.

"For two reasons: first, everything you said the dividend would do has come true. My second reason's more personal. The only thing most people will remember me for is having delayed their first dividend checks!"

The Zobels were by no means the only critics. My old foes Hickel and Atwood were but the vanguard of many who ridiculed dividends as "a socialistic give-away" of moneys they felt should be spent instead for capital construction projects and other programs.

Alaska's dividend program is, of course, anything but socialistic. Socialism is government taking *from* a wealthy few to provide what government thinks is best for all. Permanent Fund Dividends do just the opposite. They take from money which, by constitutional mandate, belongs to *all* and allows each individual to determine how to spend some of his or her share. What could be more capitalistic?

Similarly, after the Native Land Claims Settlement Act was passed in 1971 granting Alaska's indigenous peoples almost a billion dollars in cash, I suggested they consider creating a similar account, with equal shares of dividend-paying stock going to all Alaska Natives. Some, whom I believe did not want the Native community to secure the enormous fiscal and political "clout" they would gain by keeping these monies intact, persuaded Natives to accept a different concept. Instead of a single investment account, thirteen regional corporations and more than two hundred village corporations were created, each with accompanying duplicative legal and administrative costs but with different agendae.

I feared pressures would be put on these corporations to exploit and expend their resources unwisely, and I'm not gratified to see some of my fears have been realized. Some Native corporations are in dire financial straits and have sold lands and resources over the protests of corporation members; a few Native shareholders have received thousands in dividends annually while others have received almost nothing.

Had they gone the route of the consolidated investment account, each individual Native beneficiary would now be receiving a minimum of several thousand dollars a year.

Moreover, the dividend is capitalism that works for Alaska. In a state where locals traditionally watch in frustration as most resource wealth goes Outside, the dividend's grassroots 'trickle up' distribution now accounts for the largest new capital infusion into Alaska's local economies each year.

The dividend also has increased the tax base of every community against the day when they must pick up more of the tab to fund local programs previously paid by the state — a day already dawning as Alaska's billion-dollar bubbles deflate.

Some piously refuse their dividends, asserting them to be a character corroding "something for nothing." Yet they happily use a vast array of far more costly state services for which they've paid nothing at all.

By dispersing dividends, it was my original intent to reduce state subsidies for programs based neither on need nor constitutional obligation. Though more slowly than hoped, this, too, is occurring.

When wealth began flooding state coffers, Alaskans responded no differently than have individuals, businesses and governments elsewhere when facing similar circumstances; special interests appeal for special things and politicians provide many services not normally performed by government. In Alaska, this included massively-subsidized low-interest housing and business loans, subsidies that provided hundreds of millions of dollars in "hidden dividends," benefiting a few at the expense of all.

When the state lent money at, say eight percent, when the Permanent Fund was earning fourteen percent, every million loaned cost Alaskans collectively $60,000 in lost interest the first year alone. In one year, more than the total amount dispensed in Permanent Fund dividends to all Alaskans went in such hidden dividends to less than five percent of the public. Yet I recall no special interest demanding *these* inequitably dispersed "dividends" be used for roads and schools.

Today, most Alaskans recognize that without the dividend program, the billions now invested in the Permanent Fund would have long since been squandered. To put it crudely, the dividend program pits "collective greed" against "selective greed." In the process, it serves to curb government spending, enhance the economy and achieve absolute equity in the distribution of what is actually but 1/200th of our oil wealth.

DURING THE THREE YEARS we fought to establish the dividend program, it became an on-going national news story. When the program was finally established and checks for $1,000 were distributed, these stories announced the State of Alaska was giving away "free money." Of course that's not true.

Ironically, we could have dispensed that wealth far less fairly, and few who oppose the dividend program would have objected. We could have underwritten coverage for all Alaskans who had no health insurance; wiped out local taxes; funded scholarships or granted folks no interest loans, and we would have been lauded. While the above might be worthy programs, they would have been far more socialistic, inequitable and reeking with "Big Brotherism," all of which the dividend program is not.

Some, like conservative economist Milton Friedman, suggested we divide *all* the money in the Permanent Fund among Alaskans now here. Instead, I preferred to distribute only a part of the fund's earnings, believing the bulk of that wealth should be held to benefit future generations of Alaskans as well, not only those who are here now.

I SUPPOSE, IN A STATE SO FAR AWAY from others, and with circumstances so unique, it's only natural when Alaska, not to mention its dividend program, is not well understood elsewhere. So a question asked by a National Public Radio inquisitor came as no surprise.

"What's this oddball program you have in Alaska where the state mails out checks to all the people? Aren't Alaskans a little embarrassed to get money for nothing, especially when it comes from people paying for your dividends at our gas pumps?"

"First," I responded, "you should know under Alaska's Constitution, that money and the resources it comes from, belong to *all* Alaskans; not to government nor to a few 'J. R. Ewings' who, in states like Texas, own almost all the oil. Alaska's founding fathers wanted every citizen to have a piece of the action.

"Second, even if Alaska were to *give away* its oil, you'd still pay exactly the same price at the gas pump. The retail price of oil is based on the world price of oil, as set by OPEC. Alaska's oil sells for far less than the OPEC price because Alaska oil is not sold on the world market. The money we get from our oil has nothing to do with the price you pay at the pump. We could *give* it away and it wouldn't change the retail price one penny.

"Third, Alaskans should be no more ashamed to accept a direct payment from their one-time oil wealth in the form of a check, than folks elsewhere should be ashamed of accepting lower tax rates or greater services than other states can provide."

I went on to explain how dividend dollars are not "lost" for funding *crucial* government programs. Rather, they increase the tax base of every community and have created a very healthy condition.

"If I had my way," I continued, "I'd use the dividend program to cut existing government spending, as well."

"How would you do that?" he asked.

I said I'd compile a laundry list of government programs not based on need or constitutional mandate.

"I'd put that list on the ballot and let the electorate choose which to keep. For each one wiped out, I'd propose we use half the savings incurred to further increase everyone's dividend check. Since politicians can't seem to cut spending, let's leave it up to the people."

"What a great idea!" said my host. Then a horrible thought struck him. "But wait a minute. You wouldn't put public radio on your list, would you?"

"Of course. But not to worry; I'm sure you could persuade listeners to dig into their larger dividends to come up with ample contributions," I explained.

At that he blanched, shook his head and pronounced, "Oh, No! *There are some programs the government knows are best for the people, even if the people themselves don't realize it.*"

And that, of course, is why, once a program is in place, politicians don't dare cut it. As long as re-election remains the major objective of most in public office, expect no change. It's the best argument yet for the Alaska Permanent Fund Dividend.

Bella faced her diagnosis with far more courage than I.

29

Four More Years

B_Y AND LARGE, I was far more comfortable in my second term. But it didn't begin that way; very few people know how close I came to resigning soon after re-election.

Any hope that the bitterness engendered by the virulent campaign might abate after the election was soon put to rest when Bob Atwood hired Mead Treadwell, Wally Hickel's campaign manager, to "cover" state government for the *Times*.

The state's divisiveness was at its bitter peak over such matters as the capital move and Alaska land issues. Now another arose: Who should have priority in "subsisting" on fish and game resources when and where they might be in short supply?

Believing rural villagers were those most dependent on hunting and fishing, Congress passed legislation requiring Alaska law grant priority to "rural" subsistence users if we were to be allowed to manage fish and game on federal lands. The state complied until the court struck down Alaska's "rural priority," deeming it at odds with Alaska's Constitution. Some demanded federal law be changed; others that we amend our constitution.

While the subsistence issue merely simmered during my remaining time in office, somehow I still managed to be blistered by both sides.

Before a congressional committee, I had argued, "Don't try to legislate who are subsistence *users*. Instead, require by law only that subsistence *uses* must be granted top priority, then make the state comply through regulations. To try to legislate ignores the fact that the word 'subsistence,' like the word 'pornography,' cannot be defined by law — yet we all know it when we see it."

259

My testimony affronted a few who charged I thought "subsistence" was a dirty word. But most heat came from urban sportsmen who were told I'd said rural users should get preference.

Meanwhile, far hotter fires were being fueled. With long-awaited oil dollars flowing to state coffers by the billions, virtually every aspiring entrepreneur in Alaska was demanding low-interest, no-interest, or even non-refundable loans from the state to finance get-rich-quick schemes.

A coalition of these frustrated and disgruntled detractors announced a "Recall Hammond" drive even as I was taking my second oath of office. An even darker shadow was cast on this event when a private plane returning dignitaries from my swearing-in crashed at Anchorage International Airport, killing the wife of Alaska's senior U.S. senator, Ted Stevens, and critically injuring the senator and Tony Motley, my former Commerce commissioner.

Then my life hit absolute bottom.

During a routine examination, Juneau physician Henry Akiyama discovered breast cancer in Bella. It was the beginning of my darkest hours.

We flew immediately to Seattle for surgery. For days after the mastectomy, with Bella facing long and difficult chemotherapy treatment, I seriously questioned whether to continue in office. I was more than willing to resign and remain with her in Seattle until we could return together to Lake Clark, away from the cares and seemingly thankless responsibilities of office. Who knows, I thought, with Terry Miller entirely able to assume my duties, it might prove to be my most popular decision. But Bella, though having small tolerance for politics, had always encouraged my efforts to advance my ideas. She would not hear of me quitting.

"You have goals you want to achieve, and despite those who'd love it if you quit, there are too many people who believe in you. Even those who don't will be better off if you stay," she told me. Always a source of strength, Bella's courage and determination were never more evident than during our crisis. By contrast, my political problems seemed insignificant.

Bella also saw her condition, now becoming the subject of much public speculation, as something we should not conceal, but discuss openly. Perhaps this would educate and encourage others to seek regular examinations for early cancer detection, and diminish fears of its treatment. Consequently, she gave frequent interviews, even during those most difficult early days of treatment. Her courage and concern for others over the following months were inspiring. We both were thankful to the men and women on our staff for their empathy and support, not to mention the good taste with which our predicament was handled by Alaskan reporters. Without exception, the media managed to reconcile the public's legitimate right to know the realities of our situation with concern for our sensibilities. The Hammonds will be forever grateful for this, and for the remarkable outpouring of public support so important in reinforcing our resolve and helping us through a most critical time.

Ironically, it was my strong lieutenant governor, Terry Miller — so helpful during Bella's illness — who was claimed by cancer a few short years later.

As it turned out, I'm very glad I didn't resign. The next four years saw the most critical issues dividing the state resolved — if not laid to rest. The opportunity to have played a role in their resolution provides sustaining reward for what at the time seemed to offer little but pain and anguish. Chief among these, of course, was securing the Permanent Fund Dividend program. But there were others.

The bitter "d-2" lands debate was resolved with President Carter's signing the Alaska National Interest Lands Act in December 1980. That ANILCA was not completely satisfactory to anyone appears to confirm its balance, though I regret to this day my Cooperative Land Management System concept (COMANS) was largely ignored in the settlement. Proof of this concept's validity, however, exists just outside of Haines, in Southeast Alaska, where government, industry and public organizations together created a "Critical Habitat Area" sanctuary to preserve and protect the largest population of bald eagles in North America. Bald eagles from this now-unthreatened area were transplanted to other states in the effort to restore the bird's population nationally. This living symbol of our nation was removed from the endangered species list in 1993.

Likewise, two other divisive issues, the capital move and subsistence, were put to rest by "up or down" votes in the 1982 election. At least for a few years, that is. Those who would resurrect the former might consider what Alaska's financial situation would be today, minus the billion dollars or more it would have cost to replicate a state capital and all its attendant infrastructure on barren, undeveloped land seventy-five miles north of Anchorage.

As for subsistence, it seems resolution of this complex multi-dimensional issue will forever pose dilemmas and contradictions; each time a resolution is found for one — as Alaskans achieved by ballot in 1982 — another seems to present itself. Resolution promises to remain elusive until either federal law or the Alaska Constitution is amended.

My second term also realized great revitalization in Alaska's fisheries. In 1974, when I assumed office, Alaska's salmon stocks were only beginning to recover from all-time lows. Fisheries enhancement legislation and programs that my Special Projects Assistant, Bob Palmer, was instrumental in pushing through the legislature would — along with the cooperation of Mother Nature, further constraint on foreign fleet interceptions of Alaska-bound salmon, and other measures — combine to raise annual harvests to new records.

In 1974, Alaska's vast bottom fishery (halibut, cod, pollock, which swim on the ocean floor) was a renewable resource all but ignored. By making the development of this resource a priority of my administration, by the end of my second term, bottom fishing was established as a major new renewable resource industry that continues to burgeon today.

DURING MY TWO TERMS as governor, almost $15 billion dollars flooded into the state's coffers, mostly from oil. This flood began with a trickle: just $255 million the year I took office in 1974. By 1979, the first year of my second term, the tide had risen to $1.1 billion, an amount that more than doubled the following year. In my last year, 1982, $4.1 billion flushed into the state's General Fund, a high tide that continued until the collapse of world oil prices.

With low prices and depleting oil reservoirs now deflating Alaska's billion dollar bubble, I am almost as pleased with the $1.07 billion worth of legislative proposals I vetoed as the almost $3 billion deposited into the Permanent Fund by special appropriations during my tenure — billions that would have been spent on facilities Alaskans would be forced to operate and maintain at prohibitive costs.

THERE WERE MAJOR disappointments in my second term. One, deemed by many the biggest blunder of my administration, was an attempt to promote Alaska agriculture.

Having been thumped on repeatedly by those who felt me opposed to all development, I hoped to fend off further blows by heavily investing in development of Alaska's renewable resources.

Tourism and fishing were both successful examples of efforts that paid off handsomely. But with agriculture, I concurrently violated and proved the wisdom of a basic rule I had previously tried to follow: You can't make the desert flower simply by dousing it with dollars. Money my administration sowed in agriculture reaped little but bitterness and frustration.

In my first term we had identified almost twenty-two million acres of arable land in Alaska, more than many so-called "farm belt" states combined. Skeptical at first with a proposal to put millions into a demonstration project southeast of Fairbanks, near the town of Delta, I was finally persuaded by the almost unanimous support of Alaskans who knew anything at all about farming. An Agricultural Action Council comprised of university experts and already successful farmers convinced me and later demonstrated that because of our long daylight summers, unique soil and climatic conditions, it was possible to grow crops such as barley and rape seed of extraordinarily high protein content and yield per acre.

The problem, all agreed, was that it would be necessary to forge an entire chain of conditions and infrastructure for the experiment to succeed. Absent a single link, the chain would fall apart.

One link, of course, was to prepare a massive amount of arable land to produce crops of commercial quantity. Link two: people able and willing to farm; link three: grain storage facilities for crop collection; link four: rail transportation to a seaport; link five: a grain terminal at the rail/shipping port of Seward; and, the sixth and most important link: an interested Pacific Rim market.

Bob Palmer, himself a former Kansas farm boy, played blacksmith for this project, slowly forging then hammering together, link after link of this chain. In the process, he sometimes showered sparks on nay-saying critics peering over his shoulder.

When we went out of office in 1982, each link was in place save one: the Seward grain terminal. Both site and materials for this facility had been purchased by the state, but before construction could start, the oil-flush port of Valdez offered to build a grain terminal there. The new administration and legislature, persuaded they would save money with the Valdez site, arbitrarily canceled the Seward terminal, to the dismay of almost everyone involved in the Delta Project.

Ultimately, Valdez — unconnected by railroad — built its terminal, and the state sold, at enormous loss, both the Seward terminal materials and the grain hopper railroad cars. I'm told the loss greatly exceeded the $3 million required to finish the Seward terminal. To date, not one bushel of grain has gone to the Valdez facility and moose browse has reclaimed most of the acreage cleared at Delta.

A monumental miss? Maybe. But perhaps merely a "hang fire," like the bullet delayed by a faulty firing cap. Not long ago I attended a Canadian seminar on global warming, where scientists asserted temperatures would jump several degrees over the next fifty years, especially in northern latitudes. They predicted whole eco-systems would shift northward along with the hemisphere's grain belt. And guess where that belt's buckle was centered? Right over the "bread basket" of Delta, Alaska.

A few years ago, Alaska's then-Governor Steve Cowper went to Pacific Rim countries to hawk Alaska's coal, fish and timber; he found they had far greater interest in the Delta project, from which they hoped to purchase huge amounts of rape seed and barley — not one bushel of which is Alaska now providing. Later still, the Koreans made an offer to take over the Delta Project and run it themselves. It was rejected.

Who knows? What today many believe to have been my greatest bumble may, some fifty years hence, be deemed my most visionary. Meanwhile, I regret the Delta experiment was not allowed to fail of its own weight, rather than toppling under a load of broken commitments and politics. More than the dollars wasted on this attempt, I feel regret for the families who cleared and sowed the land, built homes and made major investments in a great Alaska dream that, for many, became a nightmare.

Curiously, many Alaskans who berated me for plowing millions into Delta left completely unscathed those who lost us BILLIONS when they sold out our right to export oil in exchange for a pipeline to Valdez instead of through Canada. Could it be they don't wish to look in the mirror? Talk about pennywise and pound-STUPID!

A quite clear "miss" of my second term was a project Alaskans know as "Alpetco," acronym for Alaska Petrochemical Company, a joint venture devised by Dow Chemical Company and Shell Oil. Today, I confess I flinched on purpose.

For years, various parties interested in establishing refineries and petrochemical plants in Alaska requested we take some of our royalty oil "in kind" to fuel such enterprise, rather than sell the oil for cash. I was not entranced, but the potential for creating jobs made it politically incorrect to express that attitude outright. Rather than continue to harp on my belief that most such projects could not meet my criteria for "healthy" economic development, I decided to allow Alpetco to prove it.

"Sure, we'll sell you our royalty oil, but not at a cut rate. Anyone who will pay full market price for state-owned oil may buy it. Just don't expect us to be a bargain basement."

Of all proposals, only Alpetco contended they could build and operate their plant without a subsidy. Past protests from other bidders convinced me this was not economically feasible, but with some malice aforethought, I signed the Alpetco contract, fully expecting them to return to the table for a rate reduction once public expectations had been aroused.

That's precisely what happened. Alpetco announced its plans, public expectations soared in anticipation of the major new facility, and Alpetco came back to plead for a discount to make its venture "economically feasible." Their plea was denied and the petrochemical plant died aborning.

This project communicated far more clearly than I could in words, how many development projects can not possibly pay their own way in Alaska. By so doing, at long last Alaskans began asking rude questions of other proposals that, only a few years before they would have blindly embraced simply because "they create jobs." That those jobs might cost every other Alaskan far more than they were worth, had, until Alpetco, been almost ignored.

A "miss?" In targeting public enlightenment, rather than blindly shooting for a new, subsidized mega-project, I think we scored a bull's eye.

———————

At THE SAME TIME I was pushing the Permanent Fund Dividend program forward in the legislature, a far more popular proposal to repeal Alaska's personal income tax was steamrolling ahead. If the dividend was the most gratifying accomplishment of my second term, my inability to stop income tax repeal is my biggest disappointment, and may prove one of our most serious mistakes.

As oil dollars began to inflate our treasury, public demand to repeal the income tax grew apace.

As usual, I was on the wrong political side of a popular issue. I thought repeal was stupid. Worse, I imprudently said so. "Reduce it if you will; suspend it if you must. But for heaven's sake, don't repeal it or you'll cut the one string connecting the citizen's pocketbook to the government purse, and see state spending soar. If people no longer feel it's their tax dollars 'those idiots in Juneau are spending,' a major restraint on government growth and spending will be lost. Once repealed, we'll never get it back until we've raided all other revenue sources, and/or traumatically cut even crucial state programs."

Not only was repeal legislation introduced, enough signatures had been gathered to place the issue on the ballot at the next election. In spite of clearly overwhelming support for repeal, I continued to speak out against it.

Paradoxically, the same core group promoting tax repeal — the business community as represented by the Chamber of Commerce and its house organ, the *Anchorage Times* — was the primary opponent of the dividend program. In the ensuing debate, I tried to convince these opponents how money paid out in dividends would glean far more collective benefits for Alaska businesses than would the same amount of money they'd save through tax repeal.

To make my case, I pointed out that, in the late 1970s, the income tax brought in about $200 million annually. With repeal that $200 million benefit would not only go mostly to those who least needed it, but to nearly one quarter of Alaska's work force who were non-residents. By contrast, $200 million in dividend payments would enrich each of our 500,000 residents — and only Alaskans — by $400 each.

One would think that Alaska business, as the prime beneficiaries of dividend spending would be the first to register preference for the dividend program over tax repeal. Instead, they scoffed at the former while salivating over the latter. Of course, the degree of enthusiasm for tax repeal was directly proportionate to one's income level.

Many if not most who favored repeal but opposed the dividend were ardent champions of more state spending in the form of additional subsidies such as 'low interest loans' to 'spur economic development.' An equally ardent opponent of such hidden subsidies, I lobbed out mangled metaphors that only seemed to increase the conviction I truly was "Zero Growth" Hammond.

Speaking to a group badgering me to support tax repeal, I pronounced: "You folks complain our state is 'living beyond its means.' You're right. The remedy, of course, requires two things: either cut down on high living or increase our means. Eliminating the income tax will do precisely the opposite. Not only will we reduce our means, we'll cut the one prime restraint on government spending.

"What's more, though you seem perfectly willing to cut down on the little guy's 'living' by slicing social programs like welfare, you seem unconcerned about boosting 'living' for select interests through subsidies such as lower than market rate loans and other 'hidden dividends' not based on need. Some might call that 'corporate welfare.' And believe me, legislators won't be selective. They'll fund welfare for everyone, if they can in the process inflict pain on none but the oil companies. The result will be huge increases in state spending that will leave this state high and dry when the oil runs out.

"To compound the irony of your position, repeal of the income tax plays into the hands of those whom you believe advocate zero growth. With neither an income tax nor significant severance taxes on any resources other than oil, the quickest way for the state to go broke is to spur economic development that cannot pay its own way."

I felt prudence dictated we at least keep the income tax on the books against the day declining oil wealth compelled its revival. Otherwise, when that day arrived, before the tax would be reimposed, politicians would divine some way to invade the Permanent Fund and devastate even vital state programs.

As an alternative to outright repeal, some like-minded legislators and I introduced a bill exempting people who had paid state income taxes in three previous years. Others would pay three-thirds the first year; two-thirds the second and one-third in the last year. This bill passed easily but was immediately challenged. A reporter asked, "If the court strikes down the bill, would you permit an income tax repealer to become law?"

Naively assuming common sense would prevail, I expressed confidence the court would sustain the new income tax law. Should it be struck down, I admitted I probably did not have enough nerve to veto a tax repealer.

"After all, the legislature would delight in shoving a veto override down my gullet. Besides, even if sustained, there's no question the public would then pass that proposition putting income tax repeal on the ballot for voters come next election. Repeal would pass overwhelmingly."

As it turned out, common sense did not prevail. To my amazement, the court struck down our modified tax proposal. The legislature then quickly repealed the tax. I lament I did not veto it. I should have. I like to think I would have, had the press not reported, inaccurately, that I'd vowed to not veto a repealer. Once again, I felt trapped by a statement I never made, but for which the public would think I'd broken a commitment were I to take an action they'd been led to believe I'd "promised" not to.

The most regrettable aspect of income tax repeal is that it exerts pressure to invade the Permanent Fund to replace the money lost by income tax repeal. This, of course, will shift the burden for state spending entirely from those who can best afford to pay taxes — including the non-residents who make up about a quarter of our workforce — to the shoulders of each and every Alaskan, regardless of income. None would feel the burden more than the low and middle income groups.

OF COURSE, I HAD MY OWN weaknesses for gratification and I succumbed to these when the rare occasion permitted.

It took me a long time to learn that a wise man does not do public battle with those who buy ink by the barrel. But Bob Atwood seemed my daily nemesis, opposing my proposals and politics in his news columns and editorial page without let-up. One had to seek revenge where one could find it.

Like the evening at Atwood's palatial home for a dinner in honor of Norway's visiting King Olaf. I confess I disported in a crude and shameful manner. Ushered into a living room seemingly transported intact from the Palace of Versailles, I stood amid the statuary and small groups of formally attired dignitaries speaking in tones muted for the pomp and circumstance of the occasion.

Wending my way uncomfortably across the vast floor of polished oak, strangling in black tie and penguin suit, I felt totally out of my element — until suddenly I was made to feel entirely at home by the loud, squalling of a pinched floorboard underfoot. Since each of the four houses I have built came complete with squeaking floor boards, I felt a certain form of home companionship that even a multi-million dollar mansion could harbor such defect.

Growing more comfortable by the moment, I rocked back and forth on the complaining floorboard, pretending to ignore the frowns being flung my way by Bob's daughter, Elaine. After several sublime moments, during which my serenade threatened to drown out the chamber music, Elaine, descended with a frosty smile.

"I see you've found it."

"Huh?"

"The floor board. You're standing on the squeaky floor board," she explained through teeth tightly clenched.

"Oh! You mean they're not supposed to do that? I wonder what I did wrong in all the houses I built?"

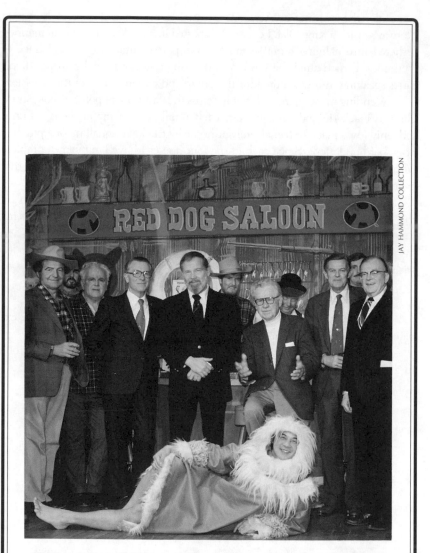

Flanked by Lowell Thomas Junior and Senior, I attended an uplifting musical focusing on Alaska performed by the all-male Bohemian Club in San Francisco. Anchorage banker Elmer Rasmuson, far right, was master of ceremonies. Feminists were critical of my attendance.

30

Media Mania

CONCLUDING A 1980 SPEECH to the National Press Club in Washington, I was asked: "As a public official, what's your assessment of the press' reporting news fairly and accurately?"

With appropriate caution, I responded: "If you think I'm stupid enough to address the shortcomings of the press to a legion of press people with nothing between us but a flimsy podium, you're absolutely right; I am. Unfortunately, however, the time remaining simply doesn't permit."

Apparently they thought I was kidding; I sat down to warm applause.

The truth is, I sometimes marvel how reporters capture what they do of a story's complexities. As one who's tried his hand at both news making and news raking, I have empathy for both rakers and rakees. Other times, I share with all who serve in office a dismay for the media's frequent failure to report accurately, completely and with balance. Certainly, I felt this was a major problem when the *Anchorage Times* seemed to deliberately distort not just what I said or did, but misinformed the public on issues critical to the state.

Unfortunately, as the state's dominant news medium in my first term, the distortions did not stop with the *Times*' afternoon editions; picked up and circulated by wire services, they became common fare in smaller newspapers as well as radio and television news. Consequently, how the *Times* chose to see things was, by and large, how things appeared to most Alaskans.

Not that I didn't contribute to my own bad press. Even for the most conscientious reporters, my inability to staunch verbiage too often had me awash in it. Sometimes, in an effort to make me comprehensible to readers, the press would haul me feet first from the quagmire and sluice off the murk. Sluiced off as well,

all too often, was any semblance of common sense. There seemed far more interest in catching me with verbal trousers half-masted, indecently exposing either
much more — or much less — of the naked truth. In this effort I often unwittingly cooperated. In the process, much got lost in translation and any semblance
of the statesman-like image to which I aspired became coincidental.

MANY WONDER TODAY: "Where are the Washingtons, Lincolns and
Jeffersons of yesteryear? Has that breed of giant been supplanted by a hybrid
group of conniving little men and women? Or does the luster of leadership dim
in an excess of media illumination?"

Certainly it's hard for public figures to pose nobly on pedestals while the
media expose one's blemishes to public view. Heroic images blur in the glare of
publicity relating, say, to the state of one's gastrointestinal tract or penchant for
the grape or for extramarital frolicking.

In these days of competitive mass communication, it's unlikely we'll find
the public again accepting the omniscience of a leader. The result is a dimin-
ishment of followership. Of course, this may be a healthier situation. For while
it may prevent an Honest Abe from election to the city council, it could prevent ascendance of an Adolf Hitler.

Some reporters compound the difficulties of those in leadership by zeroing
in on whatever ulterior motive *might* have prompted a decision. A biased journalist who seeks sensation rather than substance can easily project what he wants;
if we were capable of walking on water, headlines would explain it as our inability to swim.

In addition to convoluting my messages in "Hammondese" I contributed
to confusion by often thinking out loud about alternative methods for resolving
problems. Invariably, some reporter would select the most outrageous option as
my preferred proposal. At other times, I read assertions of what I was about to
do — and found them news, indeed, to me. Then, when I failed to fulfill the
prediction, I'd either vacillated or backed down.

Most in public office ask only to be held accountable for what they *really*
do or say, not what some suggest we may have done or said. While I believe
most times the media wants to tell it like it is, too often they tell it as they'd
like it. Consequently, many in public life are contemptuous of media coverage.
For the few who dare show it, the media make it worse. Though often impressed
that reporters glean as much as they do from interviews, more often I'm appalled or amused by omissions and distortions. Though most of us take as gospel
what the media tells us, their subjects will tell us otherwise.

Newspersons are no more infallible than are doctors, lawyers, plumbers or
even politicians. But one simple practice would go far to avoid misinformation,
ensure greater access to public figures and vastly increase public knowledge and
confidence in our institutions — the press included. In many cases, competitive

news deadlines will not permit, but when they do, a reporter who would grant those interviewed the chance to check copy for accuracy before publication, would vastly enhance credibility and future access to news sources. Of the hundreds of reporters who have interviewed me, a rare few were self-confident enough and sufficiently concerned for comprehension and accuracy, to submit their stories for review. Each earned my deep respect, immediate future access and candid disclosure.

I particularly recall *U.S. News and World Report*. After an exhaustive interview on highly complex issues, the editor sent me their pre-publication copy for review. Retaining the right to print the story as it had been written unless persuaded otherwise, "for the sake of accuracy and clarity," he asked if their report truly captured my views. I suspect this practice contributed in no small degree to the magazine's reputation for objective reporting.

Public figures would fall all over themselves to accommodate reporters who employed this practice. But most reporters are aghast at the suggestion. They deem it the ultimate desecration to allow their virginal copy to be seen by its subject before publication. Too bad. If the practice were commonplace, public figures would evidence less reluctance to confide fully in the media. A more informed citizenry would be far better qualified to vote.

In my first four years as governor, my press secretary had been a thoroughly decent, competent and totally honest young fellow who, as a reporter, earned respect among both peers and politicians. Scott Foster caused me to re-evaluate my perception that press people were primarily intent on pillorying politicians.

Adherence to substance rather than style, coupled with reluctance to add "spin" to stories to enhance our political advantage, earned Scott my admiration. Unfortunately, engaged as we were in a one-sided war with the forces of distortion led by the *Times* and the Teamsters, it also earned Scott less than accolades from some of my cabinet and staff who demanded his help in the formidable job of sanitizing the Hammond image. The ensuing tension prompted Scott's resignation shortly after my 1978 re-election.

Seeking a replacement I asked the counsel of an astute if controversial political consultant. Bill McConkey urged me to replace Scott with someone more inclined to propagandize for us to counter those propagandizing against us.

"I know just the guy for the job," Bill said. "I knew him in Washington. I'll bring him up for an interview if you want."

"Fine," I said. "Let's do it."

A week or so later, Bill ushered his candidate into my office. A somewhat rotund fellow with a puckish sense of humor, I liked him immediately and came close to hiring him. Two things gave me pause. First, he knew almost nothing of Alaskan issues. Second, I was already strongly considering someone else for the job. Thanking him for his interest I said we'd be in touch. With that he walked out of my office and into history. Back in Washington he became Ronald Reagan's press secretary. His name, James Brady, became household words when his brain stopped a would-be assassin's bullet aimed at his president.

MY ULTIMATE CHOICE for press secretary was Bob Clarke, who I'd discovered when tracking a noise in the attic of an Anchorage campaign office in 1978. Rather than a rummaging rodent, Clarke had been sifting through discarded files for old issues to recycle. Bob proved a remarkable fellow whose impressive intellect was obscured by a self-deprecating sense of humor and occasional flashes of irascibility. That he could paw through pages of Hammondese and sift the occasional nugget from the clinkers, impressed me. That he readily saw merit in my proposals demonstrated clearly, of course, his exceptional wisdom. That he could then translate my thoughts from convolution to clarity incurred my great appreciation.

Bob completely revamped our approach to media relations in my second term. In my first, we'd solicited audiences with even such unfriendly media as the *Times'* editorial board. I frequently submitted myself to such inquisitions in the naive belief editors would better understand and more clearly report what I was up to and why, if they heard it directly from me. To my inevitable dismay, ensuing editorials seemed even more vitriolic and unfocused. Points I attempted to make were ignored and quotes out of context were used to convince readers I was an even more dangerous lunatic than previously reported.

"Governor," counseled Bob, "it should be clear by now the *Times* has no interest in reporting your position on any issue that shows you as reasonable. Still, it's the state's largest newspaper and dominates all others in Alaska. You've got to go around the *Times* and get into Alaska's homes through another portal."

Having worked in every mass communications medium, Clarke saw in the state's satellite telecommunications apparatus and Alaska's undeveloped commercial television industry the means to do so.

"Instead of editorial board conferences, we'll put you on the satellite and give local TV stations something more than still photographs and wire stories to 'rip and read' for news programming," he proposed.

Two months into my second term, Alaskans started receiving daily television coverage of the Alaska land debates in Congress. From Juneau, stations received periodic feeds of the governor or his cabinet on critical state issues As audio portions of these television feeds also were picked up for radio news, the majority of Alaskans for the first time were getting first hand news and information undistorted by the state's largest newspaper. Since our communications office took care to maintain accuracy and balance, often presenting opposing views, the system rapidly gained credibility. By the time the afternoon *Times* got its hands on the facts, it was working with day-old news already received statewide on radio and television the previous evening, and by the morning *Anchorage Daily News*.

As Alaska's commercial television news came of age, almost simultaneously, publisher Kay Fanning's refinanced and rejuvenated *Anchorage Daily*

News began its climb to fill the credibility vacuum in the state's largest city. The days of the *Times* as the dominant moulder of public opinion were over. Clarke also conceived satellite television specials, by which citizens in their living rooms, thousands of miles from their capital, could conduct direct question/answer sessions with me and my cabinet. These gave Alaskans unique access to state government on issues of local concern.

Meanwhile, public perception shifted remarkably. By summer 1979, upon my return from several weeks in Washington D.C. on the Alaska Lands debate, (for which the Times and other opponents had previously been excoriating me), we found my public approval rating had risen well over 50 percent. It was to continue upward for the remainder of my term.

In my 1978 campaign, national political consultant David Sawyer had taken numerous opinion polls. About the only thing most voters agreed on was that I "could be trusted." The hitch was, many thought this meant I could be trusted to do the wrong thing. At its best, according to Sawyer, my favorable rating through 1978 was forty-two percent. Of the remaining fifty-eight percent, most had no opinion at all. Only seventeen percent were "unfavorable," a small saving grace, according to Sawyer.

In 1982, then counseling Terry Miller's run for governor, Sawyer conducted statewide polls for similar information. He brought his findings to my office, expressing amazement at the dramatic change from four years before. My approval rate had doubled to more than eighty percent!

"I've never seen such a remarkable turn around," enthused David. "In 1978 most Alaskans couldn't care less whether you sank or swam. Now they seem to think you walk on water. How did you do it?"

The truth is, I didn't. Most credit for this reversal goes to our communications office. While other staff and cabinet members discretely confined their efforts at cleaning up the Hammond image with occasional verbal beard or toenail trimmings, Clarke blasted away with water cannon and extra-terrestrial devices.

But I believe Bob Atwood may have contributed almost as much. By continuing to charge I intended to change Alaska into a howling wilderness by stifling growth at a time when we seemed about to swamp in growth of all kinds, he squandered his credibility while enhancing mine. For this generosity, I almost came to suspect he was actually a "closet" Hammond supporter. Audiences that previously had glowered through yet another Hammond "malignant growth" speech, now were applauding the same ideas they had scorned only months before.

My chief lament when it came time to vacate the governor's chair was the loss of contact with co-workers. After eight years of weathering crises together we had become a family. And like family, they often made me look good in spite of myself. These days, Bella and I enjoy the Hammond Reunions organized periodically by Peggy "Can Do" Hackett, formerly an outstanding aide in my Washington office.

As THE LAST WEEKS of my eight year tenure passed, I did not lament Alaska's constitutional limit of two consecutive terms for governors. When asked if I'd consider running for a third term, I was happy to say I was constrained from doing so by our constitution and common sense. Instead, I was eager to shed the trappings of office for our Lake Clark homestead. After eight years of tumult I had achieved the most important items on my agenda and there was much to be thankful for — not the least of which that it was almost over.

My last regret came, however, with Terry Miller's surprising last minute loss in the Republican primary to another old adversary, Tom Fink — a disappointment mollified somewhat when Fink, in turn, was soundly trounced by the election of Democrat Bill Sheffield.

Remembering all too well the abbreviated transition period allotted me in 1974, not to mention the exploding cigar and mid-finger salute that welcomed me to the office, I instructed my cabinet and staff each to prepare detailed status reports on any and all pending problems within their purview, and to be fully available to Sheffield's transition team. I never meant anything more sincerely than my pronouncement at a joint news conference with the governor-elect:

"I hope Bill Sheffield is the best governor Alaska has ever had, and we'll do everything we can to help."

WHILE THE JOINT TRANSITION teams were hard at work, I received an odd invitation to give my final speech as governor to an audience of old friends and non-supporters at the Anchorage Chamber of Commerce. Momentarily suspecting a sick joke and contemplating the bullet-proof vest facetiously offered by Public Safety Commissioner Bill Nix, I accepted nevertheless.

After a gracious introduction by newly-elected Anchorage Mayor Tony Knowles, I delivered what I termed my "Out-augural" address. I told my smiling audience that of all the numerous forums in Alaska, theirs was the most appropriate for the event. "Certainly no group would more appreciate hearing from my very own lips that I am departing public office forever."

Though I went on to say the same offensive things I'd said before that had elicited their apoplectic scorn, on this occasion, the chamber responded to each point with applause and, at the end, a standing ovation!

Momentarily stunned, I preferred to conclude the chamber's salute was prompted more by improved perception of my intents and performance than elation over my imminent departure. This conclusion was confirmed, I thought, when I saw my old nemesis, Bob Atwood, approached the podium, hand extended. As we shook hands and the applause grew louder, he spoke.

"You know, governor, I think at long last I'm beginning to understand just where you're coming from and I'm kind of sorry for the eight years of grief my paper gave you. If you'd talked this way before, maybe we could have worked together."

If I'd have talked this way before? It seemed the way I'd always talked! I found this confession, though belated, both touching and confusing. After so many years of tilting with Bob on his editorial page — where he always got the final blow — that he should even momentarily lay down his lance and sword to give a hand to one he'd unhorsed so often, suggested there might, after all, beat a heart 'neath his baldric.

On the other hand, considering all who'd indicated they'd supported me *because* Atwood, Carr and Hickel were against me, I wondered if my "Out-augural" could have let *those* folks down.

My disquiet was short lived.

Three days later, an *Anchorage Times* editorial crowed how splendid everything was going to be, now that we'd replaced old "Zero Growth" Hammond with pro-development Bill Sheffield. With that, I slept much better.

Above: *Daughter Heidi and Bruce Stanford at their 1982 wedding at the Governor's House in Juneau.*
Below: *Jay and Lauren Stanford, Hammond grandchildren.*

31
Life in the Governor's House

BUILT FOR $32,000 IN 1912, the four-story Governor's House in Juneau would seem more at home amid magnolia trees and strumming minstrels than perched beneath snow-covered peaks overlooking a small coastal town. Nor did its white-columned colonial plantation facade carry over into the building's interior. In December 1974, when Bella, Heidi, Dana and I moved into the "mansion," it was more igloo than antebellum until a new heating system and insulation were installed.

In my first term, Alaska was still strapped for cash, and renovating the Governor's House had very low priority on my agenda. In my second term, as billions bubbled into state coffers, we were able to make several overdue improvements. Curiously, we were criticized for not making more. When my successor remedied this deficiency by spending $2 million for a complete renovation, he, of course, was loudly criticized for spending too much.

Most of the old building's modern conveniences were installed during Wally Hickel's two-year reign. By far the most elaborate of Governor Hickel's renovations was the plush, silk and gilt-plated "Grace Kelly Suite." Like an Iowa farmer who converted his cornfield to a baseball diamond hoping "Build It and They Will Come," one-time Kansas carpenter Wally royally re-did the mansion's top floor in hopes the Princess of Monaco would accept his invitation. The Princess never graced the facilities, however, and they remained pristine even after our arrival. More accustomed to bush outhouses, it seemed somehow sacrilegious to perform bodily functions amidst such gold-plated splendor; we preferred the less intimidating atmospheres of the building's ten other bathrooms.

Slightly overwhelmed by the mansion's size, during our eight year occupancy, we confined ourselves mostly to a five-room apartment-like complex on the second floor, entertaining when we had to on the spacious, main floor.

Bella and the girls did their best to adapt to this home away from home, at least from fall through late spring. Come the thaw however, they chaffed anxiously to escape the Governor's House for Bristol Bay. Juneau's government and politics were poor alternatives to planting gardens and harvesting salmon. By June, they were gone and I confess to a deep, almost daily resentment I'd not gone with them.

All of us were accustomed to doing things for ourselves, and it took some time to realize we were expected to retain a house-keeper and cook. Fortunately, Bella's extremely competent personal secretary and "house manager," Connie Stewart, made sure things ran smoothly — including house tours she conducted.

Of all the mansion's modern "conveniences," the one I prayed most might fall apart was its telephone system. When we moved in, I was aghast to find our quarters infested with phones. One of my first official directives was to exterminate most of them. Unfortunately, those few that escaped detection by the pest control people all worked to perfection.

There's a lot to be said for telephones. There's gotta be. Otherwise most folks wouldn't have one in the house. While much of what I feel about telephones can't be printed here, take it from me: they're fractious, time-robbing, ganglia-jangling devices ranking somewhere between the "rack" and the "iron maiden" in rendering torture. Because for some time our phone number was listed in the directory and we answered calls ourselves — a fact that surprised many callers — we experienced much pain unnecessarily.

As these phones were equipped with both visual and audible means of disturbance, they constituted a constantly irritating electronic mutation akin to crossing lightening bugs with mosquitoes. Many's the night I might have slept through the buzz, had the blinking light not wakened me. Is it any wonder I'm pleased not to have one of these contraptions at Lake Clark?

Compounding the agony, as the hours grew later, telephone conversations grew longer and more eccentric. If you've been awakened at three a.m. by some drunk willing to selflessly grant you an hour or two of his time to deliver profane counsel on how to govern the state, you know what I mean.

Of course, the problem could have been avoided simply by removing our number from the directory. I'd like you to think dedication to open government caused me to resist. A listed phone number seemed but one other price to pay for the "rewards" of public service, a price I was prepared to pay — up to a point. That point arrived with a call I received a few months after I took office — at two in the morning! Because it came from a long-time acquaintance and fellow fisherman, I suffered almost an hour of alcoholic pleas, demands, threats, cursing and counsel. Verbatim, (I swear on a stack of telephone directories) it went like this:

"Governor, I have received a revelation from the Lord. He has instructed me to demand you send National Guard cargo planes to Bristol Bay and fly salmon to canneries in Cook Inlet. Unless you heed this counsel, prepare to spend eternity in the fires of Hell!"

That did it. Next day I had them grant me a new, unlisted number.

DESPITE CRANK CALLS and letters, during my first years as governor security was quite relaxed. After a spate of threats, however, my staff insisted security be tightened. New locks and other devices were installed at the mansion, and I was no longer permitted to travel from Juneau unescorted; an armed, plain-clothed trooper came along.

The first threat I recall came when a disgruntled citizen imprudently told a Coast Guard officer he intended to shoot the governor. One suspects he was not too bright or only half serious. Since one likes to believe one's detractors must be of limited intellect, vanity suggests the former.

Alerted by the Coast Guard of my would-be assailant's intent, state troopers apprehended him on his arrival at my empty office. During a brief incarceration he underwent psychological testing. Despite flunking, he was out on the street in a few days. Dismissing the assumption he'd been found sane in his desire to shoot me, a short time later I had scheduled a flight to Seattle when my security people were not as bemused to learn my "stalker" was booked on the same plane. From then on, I was accompanied by a security guard on all trips.

At first I was resentful of this additional lack of privacy. However, I came to admire the outstanding men assigned this onerous duty, not only for their high professional competence; most became personal friends. Not that they caused me no problems. At times they insisted I wear a bullet-proof vest, a bulky, uncomfortable contraption that did little for my limited wardrobe, not to mention the gubernatorial figure. The first such occasion was a Fourth of July parade in Palmer, near the state fair grounds. It seems someone had gotten word the governor was to be "blown away" while seated in the reviewing stand.

Arriving by car to the point where I was to mount the steps to my seat, I struggled to button my jacket over the vest and stepped out into the milling throng. Feeling a bit portly, I sucked in my gut, stood especially erect and, aware of every eye fixed on me, attempted to stride casually to my seat. Midway up the stands, I became aware that the smiling vibrancy of the crowd seemed excessive. Only then did I glance down to see I'd buttoned my jacket two buttons off the norm; one side was elevated to scarf level, the other pulled down past my pocket. With the vest underneath, I looked ridiculous. Feeling as big a fool as I looked, I slunk to my place in the bleachers.

That the threat on my life might be only a hoax was not something security people could assume. They took no chances. Among other measures, they clustered a half dozen plain-clothed troopers above, alongside and below me on the bleachers. While I felt these precautions somewhat over done, I admit becoming acutely aware of my "companions" swiveling this way and that to check buildings and vehicles to my rear, and fought the inclination to sit in one of their laps.

ON MOST JOURNEYS outside Alaska, I was accompanied by a tall, handsome, professional trooper captain named Harkey Tew. Harkey's full head of steel-gray hair and patrician profile provided unexpected security. Outside Alaska, most people mistook *him* for the governor. This occasionally caused me some embarrassment.

To illustrate this, at Harkey's retirement party, I told his fellow officers, "I view Harkey's departure with mixed feelings. He looks so much more distinguished than I, most people thought *he* was the governor. But the crowning indignity occurred on a recent flight to Washington, D.C., when a little old lady had learned from a stewardess that 'Alaska's governor is on board up front.' When the seat belt sign was turned off, the kindly soul scurried forward to our usual bulkhead seat behind the first class compartment in order to offer the governor a bonbon. Noting the distinguished looking silver-haired gentleman seated on the aisle, she tapped him on the arm.

"'Are you the governor of Alaska?'

"'No Ma'am' replied Harkey. 'I'm Captain Tew of the Alaska State Troopers.'

"'Oh my!' she stuttered, stepping back and clapping her hand to her mouth in embarrassed confusion. Then nervously flicking her eyes at the suspicious-looking bearded hulk in the next seat staring out the window with a blanket over his lap — presumably covering handcuffs — she whispered conspiratorially above the hum of the engines:

"'Where are you taking your prisoner?'

"That did it!" I told his fellow officers; "Harkey's got to go!"

So much more gubernatorial did Harkey appear, even at national governors' conferences, some who'd seen us together would ask me which state Harkey governed. Harkey's quiet and unassuming manner could be deceiving, however. He took his work seriously and not even the governor was exempt from admonishment when it came to security, as I learned one balmy night in San Francisco.

An aide and I decided to walk around the block from our hotel to find an ice cream parlor before turning in for the night. Not bothering to tell Harkey, we set out only to pass a number of provocatively dressed, somewhat earthy women who stared suspiciously when we asked where we might get an ice cream cone. Long before circling the block back to the hotel, where Harkey stood, fuming, I realized we had traversed a local red light district. Duly chastised, cones melting, we slunk back to our rooms, Captain Tew marching sternly a few feet behind.

LIFE IN THE MANSION was more bearable when Bella was there. She accepted the role of First Lady more gracefully than I'd anticipated. Though we entertained minimally, she was always a most gracious hostess, equally at home dining on Beef Wellington at the White House or on agutuk in a Kobuk Eskimo fish camp, winning respect and admiration from all who came to know her.

Totally devoid of pretensions and guile, she is the most honest person I know. Among her attributes is an uncanny knack for flushing out phonies, with which, of course, the political world is overpopulated. Bella often detected character blemishes long before her husband saw past the cosmetic charisma and social flair with which some politicians powder their public persona.

Bella often stood in at functions I couldn't attend. In the process she won far more hearts than I would have. After such a visit to Nome, Albro Gregory, the irascible old curmudgeon who wrote, edited, published, hawked and fish-wrapped with his beloved *Nome Nugget*, gushed editorially: "We don't know about this guy Hammond, but as far as we're concerned, his wife Bella can do no wrong." Shortly after, both Bella and I flew to Nome. Taxiing to the parking ramp, the first thing to catch my eye was a huge sign on the wall of a hangar. Letters six feet high pronounced, "WELCOME BACK BELLA!" Beneath, in letters less than six inches high, was inked in: "Oh yes, and you too, Jay."

In her capacity as my roving representative, Bella sometimes encountered the unexpected, as when she stood in for me at the annual Alaska Day Parade at Sitka. In company with our good friend Dee Longenbaugh, Bella watched the procession of floats, musicians and costumed dignitaries celebrate the 1867 purchase of Alaska from Russia. Dee, a charming, loquacious lady who greatly appreciates the fact Bella is a world-class listener, bubbled on effervescently, when suddenly, to Bella's astonishment, rolling by on the main street came an antique pick-up bearing spectacular cargo. At the wheel was local bon vivant and prankster, Porky Bicar, renowned for his wild imagination. Porky recently had embellished his reputation and created near panic among Sitkans who feared the nearby dormant volcano, Mt. Edgecumb was about to erupt. Ever the innovator, Porky had helicoptered a number of old tires into the crater and set them afire.

Now, as the parade rolled past, Bella saw Porky again at the wheel of his antique truck, happily waving and smiling as onlookers gaped at his cavorting cargo, a local go-go dancer he'd hired who — unbeknownst to Porky — had been paid by some of his previous victims a few dollars more to do her routine topless.

Though the noble beat of the "Alaska Flag Song" does not lend itself well to go-go gyrations, the young lady was doing her unlevel best to keep everything metronoming in tempo, while an oblivious Porky nodded and grinned to greater audience appreciation than he had expected.

Meanwhile, an astonished First Lady glanced at her friend Dee, who continued her soliloquy uninterrupted.

"Golly," thought a perplexed Bella, "I guess they do things differently here in Sitka."

After the parade, she asked Dee about her casual attitude toward what would cause consternation elsewhere.

"What?" shrieked Dee incredulously. "I can't believe it!" So engrossed had Dee been in her one-sided conversation, she had been as oblivious as Porky to the spectacle.

"No!" declared Dee. "Sitkans do not condone topless dancing al fresco on *any* occasion!"

Condoned or not, Porky's X-rated float in the First Lady's presence was widely reported. When the press later asked my reaction, I expressed outrage that my wife would be exposed to such a shameful performance.

"It's the last time I'll subject my wife to that sort of behavior. Next year, I'll go to Sitka myself !"

LONG BEFORE Barbara Bush's Millie invaded the White House, Alaska had a First Dog in charge of its Governor's House; a small, hairy beast of neurotic temper, dubious pedigree, indeterminate age and debatable intellect. To confess my wife has a soft spot for such creatures will not surprise those given pause by her selection of mate. Truth to tell, for all her practical approach to life, Bella is a sucker for strays, birds with wings down, the abused and unwanted. This accounts for her taking, first Sparky, and later, Orphan Annie, Usook (Eskimo for "hey you") and finally, Goofy Charlie into our home — and often our bed. To this day, I dare not turn Bella loose in a dog pound unless prepared to re-linquish the small remnant of household left me. No sir! From now on I put my foot down — with less trepidation, I might add, since the dogs are now all house-broken.

All in the above named menagerie are small beasts, devoted to Bella. Me, I always liked big dogs. I considered small feisty yappers the indulgence of blue-rinsed matrons, apartment dwellers or ladies of the evening. Sparky, Annie, Usook and Charlie? Good grief! My preference was for brutes with brawny, venturesome names. Names with hair on the chest: Buck, Spike, Thunder, Duke. Of late, however, the disturbing thought surfaces that such preference might reflect the pathetic subconscious need of the insecure, unfulfilled male to en-hance his macho self-image.

In the brave new plastic world of the 90s, an itch for swashbuckling derring-do seems increasingly scratched by names we append to our toys:

"Mustang . . . Barracuda . . . Thunderbird." There's something vaguely depressing about all this but I can't quite put my finger on it. Suffice it to say, only a man with his act together — or a nerd — would drive, for example, a Chrysler "Cottontail" or a Ford "Fink." So it is with the heroic handles we hang on our dogs.

Though I confess I've had my share of Kobuks and Spikes, in my defense, my last team of sled dogs were "the Jones Boys." There was Daniel, Henry, Suzie, Shadrach, Meshach and Abednego Jones and Sally.

Sparky came to us already named by the little old Naknek Eskimo neighbor lady whom he'd adopted. Each morning we'd see this tiny terror leading a pack of large mongrels up the road is search of a handout or randily racing them back down the road in pursuit of some female. Since any of his consorts could consume Sparky with one nip, his position as dominant male seemed curious — until we got to know him. Like a small hairy Houdini, Sparky was a master of illusion. Not until we learned he was actually a 180-pound bull mastiff masquerading for humans as a 9-pound poodle did we fully appreciate how he came to be packmaster.

Rarely did Sparky let us mortals see his true dimensions, though we should have guessed as much from his bark. So explosive was his delivery, when he sounded off, all four legs would be propelled into the air. This not only intimidated other dogs, it infuriated people he serenaded at night.

At first, this unappreciative audience included my wife. Many's the time I heard Bella's midnight mumble, "I wish they'd do something about that terrible little dog." Since they didn't, she did. After several months of mooching at our house, Sparky had wormed his way into Bella's affections. In 1974, when we left Naknek for the Governor's House, our neighbor told Bella she could have Sparky. Thus Sparky commenced a new life as "First Dog," so identified by the miniature T-shirt presented by an admirer.

Sparky was equal to his new title. In Juneau, he quickly took over the governor's grounds — until the geese arrived. One spring morning we awoke to find four large white geese, strutting about the fenced yard. Put there by some practical joker, the joke was on him, if he expected them back. Bella would not hear of the geese leaving, either via stew pot or the humane society. Again, our household enlarged.

When Sparky discovered the new arrivals, he at once proceeded to show the geese who was boss. As he barked in pursuit, the birds frantically scurried about, squawking to his immense satisfaction. Having clearly established his rank, Sparky smugly resumed his rounds, re-staking the territory.

As First Dog, Sparky especially enjoyed the copious bloom of flowers surrounding his grounds. Once, however, blissfully intent on sniffing a primrose, he failed to detect an old gander sneak up slowly behind him. When in range, the bird's bill snaked forward with deadly accuracy, impaling the two most immediately available appendages. Sparky emitted a falsetto shriek and shot several feet skyward, never again to enter the garden until the geese departed, much later.

Sunday mornings I walked Sparky while Bella readied for church. I did this with some trepidation, trying to disassociate myself from the ridiculous creature who, with a grin, invariably disgraced us both by doing his business the instant townsfolk and sightseers chose to pass by. One observer stopped long enough to note I appeared to be walking a dry fly at the end of a hawser.

Little good it would have done to try to explain that the heavy tether was to protect other dogs ten times Sparky's apparent size. Unlike us humans, these animals recognized Sparky's true dimensions and cowered before him.

On those Sunday morning treks, he would try to mark an ever-enlarging expanse of territory. He was astonishingly accomplished at this. So great were Sparky's territorial ambitions, however, at the end of our walks I fear he did little more than "puff dust."

On one such occasion we passed a yard party celebrating Mother's Day, where squealing grandchildren made such a fuss over the strange little "Is it really a dog?!" the rest of the family came over to laugh or marvel. Among these was the gray-haired guest of honor. Recognizing the governor at one end of the leash, her conversation turned to politics, on which the dear old soul held some quite outspoken opinions.

Suddenly, in the midst of a chiding discourse on bureaucratic deficiencies, the poor woman shrieked and erupted in what appeared to be a St. Vitus Dance. Apoplexy? Coronary?

No, none of these. Resenting either her inattention or political philosophy, Sparky had determined to reclaim center stage, at the expense of one pair of open-toed, sensible shoes. This time, lamentably, "dust puffing" Sparky was not.

My staff was like family and treated me much like a father —
arrogant, disrespectful, disobedient, mouthy, but extraordinarily
competent and greatly loved. From left, the staff included
Chuck Kleeschulte, Vanetta Hildebrand, Lynda Gignere,
Sue Green, Ron Lehr, Louise Mundell, Jesse Dodson,
Jerry Reinwand and Robert Clarke.

32

Name Droppings

As WE PREPARED TO VACATE the Governor's House for Lake Clark, of all the Hammonds hoped to regain, nothing was more precious than a private life we'd not had for eight years. Of discomforts that come with public office, second only to being throttled daily by neckties was loss of privacy. Bad as it was for me as governor, at least when I left the state I could settle into comfortable anonymity. A bearded sleeper flying economy class is seldom suspected of status. But what must it be like for those instantly identifiable the world over?

To most of my generation, the two-edged sword of celebrity vs. privacy was thrust home at an early age by the example of the one man who, when I finally met him, completely over-awed me. Accepting an invitation from Lowell Thomas Jr., I arrived to find myself virtually speechless when introduced to our dinner companion, Charles Lindbergh. Here was history in the flesh. I doubt I would have been more impressed had Abe Lincoln or Tom Jefferson resurrected across the table.

General Lindbergh quickly put me at ease, however. Like many truly great men I've met, he had the ability to make *you* feel important, downplaying his own unique accomplishments. When he learned I had flown Corsairs in the South Pacific, he asked penetrating questions. A casual listener would have thought I was the expert rather than he. But the first man to fly the Atlantic Ocean alone, non-stop — gaining unprecedented international celebrity for the feat — had, very quietly during World War II, tested the Corsair, shooting down enemy aircraft while so engaged.

I found "Lucky Lindy" — whose fame made him one of the most unfortunate of men — a fascinating, fatherly figure for whom I quickly felt both admiration and affection. His delight with having lived enough years out of the spotlight that he could travel without recognition was both obvious and touching.

LATER, I HAD A CHANCE to discuss celebrity and privacy with Robert Redford, when he came up for the Alaska premiere of his movie, *All The President's Men*. Our mutual friend, Kay Fanning, had asked if I might like to accompany Redford, his young son and daughter, who were seeking a sample of Alaska wilderness. Opportunity to both shuck the shackles of office and meet one of my favorite screen actors was irresistible, and one fine day we flew up the Susitna River, spotting moose and brown bear below, toward my friend Gray Mower's fishing lodge on Chulatna Lake, nestled in the long shadows of Mt. McKinley.

During the flight Redford showed surprising awareness of Alaskan issues. I found him not at all the slick, cynical, self-indulgent Hollywood type I'd encountered before. A dedicated environmentalist in the best sense of the word, he proved remarkably sensitive, intelligent and endowed with a warm sense of humor. After thirty minutes, I felt I'd known him thirty years.

When I asked if he mourned the loss of privacy, he answered wistfully. "Oh, it gets tedious at times. It's nice to escape for a while. Any chance we could get lost for three or four days?"

"As much as I'd like, probably not," I replied. "But we'll get out from under the hammer at least for a while. Only the Mowers know we're coming."

To my dismay, as our plane landed and taxied to the Mower's dock, about a dozen people burst out of the woods and surged down to greet us.

"Gee," I groaned, "I'm sorry, Bob. Apparently word got out you were coming. I thought only Gray and his wife would be here, not a horde of fans." I also wondered if he thought the reception something cooked up by a publicity-seeking politician.

"Oh well," he said graciously, "it goes with the territory. Let's get it over with."

Disembarking first, I walked up the dock when, to my surprise, the small crowd rushed forward and engulfed *me*!

Hiding regret that the Redford family's wilderness experience had been so tamed, I dutifully began shaking the hands extended to me by men I learned were National Guard officers from various states on Alaska maneuvers. Their helicopters having picked up state trooper radio transmissions that "the governor is landing," they'd flown to Mower's to meet me.

In the midst of these exchanges, I glanced back to see Redford leaning casually against the Widgeon, wearing dark glasses, battered jeans and a broad grin, wriggling his fingers at me. Camouflaged, he remained just where he was: happily incognito.

IF THE NATIONAL GUARD officers were unaware of the celebrity in their presence that day, circumstances were dramatically different when I accompanied President Jimmy Carter and his Secretary of State Ed Muskie on a fishing trip in 1979.

An ardent and expert fly fisherman, Carter concealed disappointment when told flood conditions in coastal streams prevented us going for rainbow trout. Instead, I explained, we'd be heading into the Talkeetna mountains to a remote fishing cabin owned by a friend.

Unlike the small fishing parties I'd guided before, almost thirty people boarded two giant Huey helicopters at Elmendorf Air Force Base — enough for a small invasion. In the lead chopper, I accompanied Carter and Muskie (for whom we had great difficulty finding size 14 rubber waders), and numerous Secret Service agents.

When the great, whirring Hueys put down at a small creek mouth near the remote cabin, amid the buffeted brush and dust kicked up by the choppers we spotted two figures hunkered down at the inlet of the supposedly deserted lake. A phalanx of armed Secret Service men hurtled out to identify the interlopers — who proved to be newlyweds, hoping to honeymoon in dreamy privacy, deep in the solitude of Alaska's mountains. Astonished enough by the invasion of what appeared to be combat gunships, they gaped in disbelief when a score of plainclothes agents armed with automatic weapons jumped out and moved quickly to "take the high ground."

The couple went goggle-eyed when next they saw descending on them a pair of rubber waders containing the president of the United States!

Once on the creek, the president seemed completely transported from cares of office. Handling his fly rod with finesse, he worked the stream with flies he tied himself. Moreover, he out-fished us all.

The interlude was all too brief, however. The helicopter radio informed the president of the as yet unannounced release of the very first hostage held at the American embassy in Iran. Arriving back at Elmendorf to an impromptu news conference, Jimmy Carter was again immersed in the heavy responsibilities of the presidency. It was a privilege to have helped him escape those obligations, if only for a few hours.

If the honeymooners took home a story I suspect they had difficulty persuading some to believe, at least two dozen witnesses can verify it. One, the expert fly-fishing president, took home an iced-down catch of Arctic Grayling for dinner at the White House.

CELEBRITY COMES IN ALL SHAPES and sizes. In February 1979, as a member of the National Governors Conference committee on International Trade,

I attended a dinner party in Georgia hosted by Governor George Busby to honor Deng Xiaoping, premier of the People's Republic of China.

My table companion was Ohio Senator John Glenn, with whom I'd gone through Naval Flight Training in the early 1940s. Glenn, a Marine pilot who also served in China during the last days of Chiang Kai Shek's Nationalist government, learned I was about to leave on a trade mission to Japan, Taiwan and Korea.

"You also ought to visit China," Glenn suggested. To my surprise, in response to our interest, Deng issued an invitation. But when I became the first U.S. governor to visit the People's Republic after diplomatic relations were restored, I came perilously close to re-shattering them.

In Beijing ("Peiping" when I was hospitalized there in 1945), I met with Premier Deng for what was asserted to be the first full-length television program produced in the PRC and beamed by satellite into the United States. In a forty-five minute audience with Deng, I was surprised to learn he was fully aware I'd been in China under the auspices of his old antagonist Chiang Kai Shek. Seated in chairs so overstuffed the diminutive premier was virtually engulfed, we spoke through an interpreter. Aware of grinding cameras that might expose and record anything I might say to offend my host, or indicate to those back home that I was a "pinko comsymp," I weighed my words very carefully. Deng's first question was, "Governor, you have seen the old China and the new. What do you think of our progress?"

Visualizing my rabidly anti-communist brother, Bill, and conservative friends in Alaska leaning forward to catch any hint of apostasy, my mind coughed up but one thought:

"Well, Mr. Premier, any regime that has done away with the necktie can't be all bad."

The interpreter conveyed my profundity to Deng in Mandarin, whereupon the premier slapped his thighs, laughed and sing-songed off a response the interpreter relayed to me without the slightest smile:

"The premier says you 'crack him up.'"

Crack him up? Like many Orientals, Deng seemed not to speak English. Preferring to speak through interpreters offers advantages during negotiations to those who speak both languages: twice the time for reflection. That Deng understood English, I have little doubt. After all, an idiom such as "cracks me up" is not likely found either in Mandarin or Mao's little red book.

Deng followed this exchange with some symbolic talk about the "threat of 'bears'" to Alaska, just across the strait from Russia. In spite of my earlier vow not to venture into the field of geopolitics from areas less strewn with land mines, I almost self-destructed when I pronounced, "Actually, we in Alaska are physically closer to Beijing than to Washington, D.C." Then, unthinkingly, I mused, "As a matter of fact, sometimes because of indifference or misunderstanding in our nation's capital, we may even be politically closer."

These words no sooner stumbled from my lips than I tried to grab their ankles to haul them back. To no avail. Their utterance was accompanied by a collective gasp from my wall-eyed staff members. "What I mean is . . ." I began in feeble explanation. In the grind of the video camera, the rest, I'm sure, was entirely lost on the grinning Deng.

Desperate to change the subject, I acknowledged the good health and popularity of the Panda bears Deng had given the United States, and asked the premier about the Alaskan musk oxen President Nixon presented in exchange to the People's Republic. "Whatever happened to those musk oxen?"

To my horror, in a stage whisper just loud enough for me to hear, Bob LeResche, my commissioner of natural resources, cupped his hands to the ear of my Attorney General Av Gross and intoned, *"They were delicious!"*

I thought: Let's hope the cameras jam or the satellite falls from orbit. Otherwise, this program will set U.S.-China relations back by as many light years distant as I'm now seen by the right wing of the Republican party.

Mercifully, I needn't have worried. When the special finally aired in the United States, Chinese censors had excised all dialogue and replaced it with a "politically correct" voice-over travelogue of the Forbidden City and other points of interest.

However imprudent my gratefully censored gaffe to Deng Xiaoping, it was nonetheless accurate. Geographically, Alaska *is* closer to China and Japan than to Washington, D.C. Closer still to Russia. But as a consequence of the Alaska National Interest Land Claims Act and the Ronald Reagan presidency, Alaska's political proximity to Washington changed dramatically in the last two years of my term. None of the ensuing encounters are more memorable than those with the man charged with authority over twice as much Alaska acreage than is the governor.

U.S. Secretary of the Interior James Watt had a firm agenda for Alaska's federal lands and waters. Unlike his predecessor Cecil Andrus — who in the Carter Administration worked to conserve Alaska's "crown jewels" for future generations — Jim Watt's development agenda required a 180-degree shift in state/federal relations. Atop Watt's agenda were plans to develop oil deposits believed to lie beneath the Arctic National Wildlife Range and the pristine waters of Bristol Bay.

The degree of federal protection to be accorded ANWR had been hotly debated in Congress in the late 1970s. Conservationists saw the area uniquely representative of Arctic coastal habitat on which the Porcupine caribou herd annually calve. They demanded it be declared wilderness. Conversely, oil interests wanted federal permission to drill for the enormous pool of oil they felt lay beneath the tundra. Faced with these conflicting demands, Congress compromised by doing neither. A provision for "future study" was structured in the Alaska National Interest Lands Act.

As for Bristol Bay, "known" oil deposits amounting to something less than sixty days' energy supply for the nation seemed hardly worth risking the world's most productive fishery.

I was not unacquainted with either area. Forty years before, as a wildlife biologist, I'd helped conduct the first comprehensive study of the ANWR area's Porcupine caribou herd. I'd been a Bristol Bay fisherman for thirty years, and as a legislator, I had created the Bristol Bay Fish Sanctuary to protect its sensitive environment and prime fishery values against oil drilling. Shortly after I bought back oil leases in Kachemak Bay, I became the first governor to protest oil drilling in Bristol Bay's federal waters, as well.

Of the two areas, the thought of drilling Bristol Bay gave me much more concern than ANWR. And when the Reagan administration announced its intention to auction federal oil leases in Bristol Bay, I almost succeeded in talking Interior Secretary James Watt out of it.

Soon after his Senate confirmation, I traveled to Washington and won a temporary "stay" on the Bristol Bay oil lease auction. Subsequently, however, these leases were put back on the schedule, and when James Watt made his first visit to Alaska in 1981, he was welcomed with open arms by pro-development interests, and with clenched fists by conservationists.

*Unlike politicians proud of having come up from a log cabin
to a fine mansion, I went from a mansion to a fine log
cabin in 1982 — and felt blessed. We retired to our Lake
Clark homestead. Best of all,* it has no phone!

33

Back to the Briar Patch

MORE THAN TEN YEARS have passed since we left the Governor's House in December 1982. When I returned to our homestead 180 miles from Anchorage and the nearest road system, relief was so overwhelming I was compelled to question my dedication to public service. It felt so good not to be rendering any, or to be rendered by it. When asked if there was life after politics, I cited Don Harris' comment: "I'm not sure. It feels as though I may have died and gone to heaven."

As I set about catching up on eight years of accumulated chores, my time soon became fully occupied. In addition to the always depleting woodpile, I served on some boards, gave a few speeches, and did some writing.

Today, my guiding is confined to a few old clients. Most, as I, long ago lost whatever "blood lust" we may have had and far prefer to see game on the hoof than on the wall. Even our fishing is more for food or fun than to mount a trophy. So averse have I grown to increasing encroachment by "slob" hunters who have neither reverence for game nor appreciation for the country, I've lost my zest for hunting.

Not that I have anything against hunting when "fair chase" is employed and game is abundant. After all, without hunters, Alaska's wildlife would be in far worse shape. Ethical hunters' concerns and license fees provide prime deterrent to loss of habitat and game populations.

Actually, most game species in Alaska are in better shape than they were when I came here almost fifty years ago, and that includes the wolf. In today's scenario, it is the hunter who is increasingly threatened. Militant, anti-hunting organizations have burgeoned, "Animal Rights!" their rally cry.

In an increasingly urbanized America incapable of dealing with crime and violence, many focus frustrations on those who would "prey" on what they perceive as more innocent and noble than much of humankind.

Content to have others slaughter their food for them, they see hunting as cruel, archaic, unjustified blood sport. Most believe themselves enlightened liberals, possessed of a superior appreciation of life's sanctity than the lowly hunter. Yet, clean dispatch by bullet is far less "cruel" than slow, natural death by starvation or disease that are a wild animal's alternative fates.

And so far as sanctity of life is concerned, anti-hunters seem curiously inconsistent. Most would apply this ethic only to the more "noble" species. True believers, of course, must sanctify life wherever it is found; not only in wolves, moose, bear or deer, but in the stockyard or chicken coop, the Norway rat, mosquito and the cockroach — not to mention the human womb. To those who deem themselves enlightened "pro-choice," I suggest they extend the same considerations to those who'd hunt. After all, anthropology tells us it is the origin of the cooperation and community from which our civilization has evolved.

BELLA AND I try to spend as much time as possible at the lake, except when we fly to our "city house" in the little coastal village of Naknek for the annual sockeye salmon run. Salmon harvests had been declining until the early 1970s, when several factors — including, I like to think, fishery enhancement programs employed by my administration — turned things around. Runs have been generally bountiful since.

Despite our plans to do so, travel has lost much allure for Bella and me. We have so much to do at home, in surroundings hard to surpass, we find ourselves wishing we were back home after a day or two's absence. Though we normally go into town only under considerable provocation, and then with protest, this has changed somewhat since the birth of our grandchildren, Lauren and Jay Hammond Stanford in Anchorage. Now, the trip through blustery Lake Clark Pass is more frequent. As a grandmother, Bella can be lured from the homestead almost as easily as she was from the Governor's House each spring to go fishing.

In the deep, white cold winter of 1989, I wished I'd gone with her. For the first week our Lake Clark thermometer hit thirty below zero, but as usual with such low temperatures, there was no wind. This seems simply "brisk" to a hard-bitten old sourdough, I mused smugly. When the mercury sank to forty below, to my surprise the wind began to blow. At sixty below, to my dismay, the wind began to scream! Our sewer and water pipes locked up along with my generator. Trekking long yards to and from the outhouse rivaled Perry's dash to the Pole, but Perry didn't have to sit half-naked on it! An inch or two of rime did little to prolong meditation.

In the house, I had three stoves going at capacity, yet twenty feet away from one, our indoor thermometer read two degrees below zero! In trying to fire-thaw a pipe beneath the cabin floor, I burned my hands in barely avoiding setting the place ablaze.

SOMETIME AFTER LEAVING office, I began a book about my Alaskan experiences. But as the 1980s slipped by, I never found time to complete it. When asked how I was enjoying all my spare time in retirement, I was forced to admit I was still looking for it; I'd never been busier. Overly obliged and extended, I resolved to take on no new ventures, including one proposed by my old friend, Larry Holmstrom.

A very talented broadcaster, Larry had been a key person in the Fairbanks governor's office in my first term and gone on to become one of the state's most accomplished radio and television producers.

Larry had gotten to know and work with CBS newsman Charles Kuralt on one of his popular "On The Road" programs done in Alaska. Kuralt suggested that a wealth of untapped raw material justified a kindred series featuring Alaskans. When Larry called to ask me to narrate such a program, I explained I had no desire to be plucked from the anonymity of my briar patch and again exposed to public scrutiny.

"Well," said Larry, "don't say 'no' too quickly. I'll draft a proposal. Mull it over, then give me an answer."

According to Larry's concept, "Jay Hammond's Alaska" would focus on Alaskans doing unique things, often under adverse circumstances. In Larry's words, ". . . an upbeat celebration of those colorful folk who've found their lives and longings better fulfilled in Alaska than anywhere else."

Intrigued, I agreed to narrate a pilot program; but the name of the show still caused me concern. One was prompted by a voice crowing from the peanut gallery of my subconscious: "Jay Hammond's Alaska? Instead of trying to copy Kuralt's 'On The Road,' maybe you should call it 'Jay Hammond's Off The Wall.' Who are you trying to kid? The only thing you have in common with Charles Kuralt is your hairline!"

Another concern was that the Alaska I found when I got here years ago no longer exists, except in my mind. Perhaps it never did. Moreover, all Alaskans have their own version of and vision for "their" Alaska, and both yield grudgingly, if at all, to another's interpretation.

On the other hand, I reflected, the threads that stitched together the fabric of my years in Alaska have been spun largely by people — some good, some bad and some ugly, but often beautiful. Perhaps by plucking those threads we could share scraps of what makes Alaska and Alaskans unique.

Executives at the communications corporation, Alascom, saw the pilot and sponsored five programs. In making these shows, we found a lot of stories out there, blowing like warm, fresh, dry winds amid the wet blankets too many folks flap these days: people doing unusual, uplifting and often courageous things

JOAN RAY

Larry Holmstrom directs a segment of "Jay Hammond's Alaska" near one of the old double-ended sailboats fishermen used when I first went to Bristol Bay in the mid-1940s.

against heavy odds, and doing them remarkably well in an exceptional land they'd trade for no other. Still, even with the pilot completed, I was bothered. Seeing that raddled old gray beard on screen completely shattered my self-image of the thirty-year younger stalwart I presumed yet capering about inside.

Nevertheless, when we completed the first five programs, Alascom asked for another series of eight. It was while filming this second series that tragedy struck.

As producer, Larry made arrangements to visit Ultima Thule, the guiding operation of the Claus family, deep in Alaska's spectacular Wrangell Mountains. Larry, his daughter Marcie, cameraman Ron Eagle and I flew into Chitina, where the Clauses met and flew us to their remote, river-bar airstrip, a hundred miles up the Chitina River.

That evening, we flew to the mountain sheep pastures on McCall Ridge, directly behind the Claus lodge. Ron Eagle and Paul Claus lugged Ron's heavy camera gear up to the summit, spry and seemingly unconcerned as mountain goats, the rest of us panting behind. Breathtaking in yet another way, the climb was worth the effort. Under the midnight sun, a spectacular panorama unfolded beneath us, spreading clear to the Canadian border.

Ron was entranced by the scene in that special late-day light which, when properly caught, bathes landscapes in the far North with a wash of such surreal color artists who paint it accurately are accused of creating unrealistic "calendar art." Ron shot several minutes of dall sheep, grazing hundreds of feet down the almost sheer wall falling to the valley floor far below.

Once again, I was impressed with Ron's iron nerve. Focusing the heavy Betacam on his shoulder, he stood, toes bridging the edge, bending over for a clear shot of the sheep while I stayed timorously back four feet, trying to ignore the tugging, acrophobic pangs that taunt the less intrepid when standing, unfettered, on the brink of a precipice.

Reviewing Ron's footage later, we found he'd captured several shots of Alaska's state flower, the Forget-Me-Not.

The next morning, we flew several miles up the Tana River to film some sport fishing before floating this lusty side-stream. With Class Four rapids on a par with those of the great Colorado River, our Tana River float promised to be an exciting segment of the next program.

I'd done considerable white water canoeing but had little experience with rafts. Paul and Donna Claus, by contrast, had rafted the Tana many times, the last just two days before. We all put on rain gear and life jackets. Marcie tried to don a dry suit; finding it uncomfortable, she decided against it.

After an extensive safety briefing by Paul, Larry, Marcie and Donna climbed into the bow; Ron and I in the stern. Paul and Dan, his assistant, manned the oars and we were off, into the swift current. The first several minutes, while exhilarating, seemed hardly hazardous. Ron shot a lot of good footage and all aboard seemed to find the experience enjoyable.

Paul and Dan guided the raft with great finesse through the first rapids. I was impressed both with their ability and that of the large raft to traverse waters into which I'd never take a canoe. Certainly at no time did I feel endangered. Then, the rocky canyon walls narrowed, squeezing the rushing water into less space and increasing the river's hydraulic actions. With deepening holes and standing waves ahead, Paul urged Ron to stow his camera in its waterproof bag. A consummate professional in a profession where risk frequently results in the best pictures, Ron declined, eager to capture the action.

"We've got some big water ahead," Paul shouted well before we entered the blue-gray chute. "Hang on tight!"

I took this advice and clung with both hands. We shot through the first stretch of boiling rapids, the looks of excitement on the passengers' faces showing they were having the time of their lives. That for some, it was to be the very last time, never entered my mind.

Again, Paul yelled his instructions: "Hang on! The heaviest rapids are coming up!"

Again we shot down into a deep hole, then climbed a towering wave. At the crest of this giant spume, the raft twisted and seemed about to flip and come down on top of us. My inclination was to turn loose my grip and throw up my hands to ward off a falling raft. Instead, I consciously ordered my hands to stay locked, concluding if the raft flipped, I would be better off firmly attached. Apparently, one or more of our passengers gave in to that instinctive reaction and let loose.

As the swamped raft easily righted itself and shot onto calmer water, I spotted four people in the water, none more than forty feet behind. All had their heads up and eyes on us. In none did I detect sign of panic; rather their expressions reflected a mix of tentative confidence and but a touch of supplication. At that point, none of us still aboard felt the situation perilous. The water had flattened with our friends only a few yards behind, moving downstream with the current. Paul and Dan maneuvered to position the raft for recovery as I bailed rapidly with a five-gallon bucket.

Almost immediately the closest person, Paul's wife Donna, was hauled aboard. Within another two minutes, Paul went into the water, and together we pulled in Ron Eagle. Even before he was out of the water, Paul was rendering CPR. But Ron's color was bad, and as Donna and I worked on him in the raft we detected no vital signs. His 35mm camera had twisted five or six times around his neck and, according to one doctor, this may have contributed to larynx spasm.

Within another five minutes, Paul and Dan had picked up Marcie. When hauled aboard, her color was good. She was unconscious, but her survival seemed probable. Meanwhile, however, Larry, had disappeared. Depositing Donna and me with the two victims on shore, Paul and Dan headed downstream to search. Donna and I continued CPR on Ron for more than two stressful hours before we accepted the inevitable.

The ensuing hours were grim. A roaring fire soon allowed us to dry out and make camp. After collecting a few days worth of firewood, we constructed a shelter of interwoven alders that proved surprisingly water-tight in the light rain that fell through the long night.

About dusk, Paul, who'd been picked up downstream by his father John in the Beaver, flew over and dropped sleeping bags. Unfortunately, these landed in water. Paul, however, had also arranged for mountain guide Bob Jacobs to trek the six miles up river from his camp. Bearing sleeping bags and ample food, Bob was a welcome sight. But he brought no word of Larry.

Next morning, a Park Service helicopter skillfully rested one skid on a huge boulder and hovered a few feet off the rushing water while Donna and I were lifted aboard. Inside, we were informed the crew had found Larry's body downstream, where it had washed up on a sand bar.

Hoping to assure accurate news accounts, we carefully outlined precisely what had occurred at Park Service headquarters in Chitina. Nonetheless, initial press coverage contained several errors. It was reported that the river had been exceptionally high, the raft had flipped over, and all three victims had died of head injuries. Actually, the river was down from what it had been two days before when Paul and Dan had last run it. The raft had not flipped, and examinations showed none had died of head injuries. All drowned.

Since the Tana is glacier-fed, water temperature was less than forty degrees. While such extreme cold can render a person virtually helpless in very short order, people have been resuscitated from cold water "drownings" of more than half an hour's duration with no vital damage.

Naturally, the incident prompted a spate of armchair suggestions of what should have been done to avoid the accident: dry suits and crash helmets should have been worn; seatbelts and tether lines attached, etc., etc.

Both Paul and Donna Claus, as well as oarsman Dan, impressed me greatly. Should I engage in such a trip in the future, there are no three people I would more prefer to have accompany me. I saw no dearth of competence to suggest there was much they might have done that would likely have changed the outcome.

When tragic accidents occur, survivors ask rude questions — "Why them, Lord, and not me?" for one. A certain sense of guilt descends on one's shoulders and it's mighty hard to shake, especially when someone in their twilight years survives, while those for whom the sun stood directly overhead have it eclipsed by a much too early death.

My last glimpse of the three victims detected only exaltation. Even after being hauled out, their faces bore no signs of that fearful, frozen look I've seen far too often fixed on the faces of the dead. Instead, each face held a peaceful serenity which we, who must each in turn meet that eventuality, perhaps could envy. Like President John Kennedy who also died too young, Larry, Ron and Marcie did so under circumstances which, when considered objectively, should ease the burden of their loss. There are worse ways to go than almost instantly and painlessly doing what you love to do, oblivious to the prospect of death and while yet held in high esteem. Most are not so fortunate.

Larry Holmstrom, Ron Eagle, and Marcie Holmstrom were exceptionally achieving, talented professionals who excelled not only in their chosen line of work, but at the business of living. Much more than that, they all were friends — friends who generously gave far more of themselves than ever they extracted in return.

I'M COMPELLED TO RELATE a prologue, despite the possibility it may discomfort those who cling tenaciously to their dogma of disbelief in divine providence, to say nothing of serendipity.

Until about six months before this fateful accident, both my hands had become so crippled from arthritis I had difficulty even holding an ax or hammer. This was especially troubling during fishing seasons, when picking salmon from a gillnet requires both hand strength and dexterity. By spring of 1988, my hands were so bad I asked Heidi to make a doctor's appointment for the next time I came to town. Anchorage real estate agent Ray Dahl was showing us a house and overheard my request, but made no comment.

I returned to Lake Clark where, in resuming household chores, it was all I could do to grip wood without substantial pain, let alone chop it.

Then, approaching the woodshed one morning, I found virtually all pain and stiffness gone. I could close my fists completely and cling even to the handle

of a heavy splitting maul with no difficulty. I was at a loss to explain the overnight change. I had not yet seen the doctor. I was on no medication. My diet
regimen was the same and so was the weather. Yet, for the first time in two long
years, my hands were fully functional and free of pain.

On my next trip to Anchorage, Ray was once again driving Heidi and me
about. The conversation had not once touched on the subject of my hands when
suddenly Ray asked, "By the way, Jay, how are your hands?"

I told Ray what had happened. "I can't explain it, but they're about as
good as new. I can do anything I could before."

Ray smiled indulgently. "The last time you were here, I heard you mention your hands. Our Abbott Loop prayer group has been praying for their
healing."

Coincidence? Psychosomatics? Alpha-waves? Believe so if you must, but
pardon me if I can't make that leap of faith in temporal powers. Had I experienced any previous temporary relief, or known Ray's group was trying to
intercede, you might make the a case for one or the other. But my relief was so
dramatic, only the most gullible can ascribe it to coincidence. To remain a skeptic
in spite of many such experiences would require me to accept a far less substan-
tiated credo than belief in the good Lord's intercession.

I most certainly credit this intercession with surviving the Tana River rafting accident. Had my hands and grip been as feeble as they were only weeks
before that trip, there's no question in my mind: I'd have been flung into the
water also.

I lost three close friends in that tragedy, but not before they privileged me
to meet some others. Paul and Donna Claus were as deeply hurt as I by the
Tana River accident. But they are a family that combines a fearless zest for high
adventure with a conviviality so exceptional that adversity, I know, will never
dampen their spirit or spirituality. Sustained by inspirational reliance on the
Lord's guiding hand, they've shrugged off body blows that would've decked
anyone lacking their moral and spiritual underpinnings.

I trust these underpinnings will sustain their next generation, the latest
addition to which is a strapping boy: Jay Claus.

AFTER THE DEATHS of Larry, Ron and Marcie, the thought of continuing
"Jay Hammond's Alaska" seemed unthinkable. It was Larry Holmstrom's show
and the thought of doing it without him brought back both guilt and sorrow.
We were obliged by contract to deliver the second series of programs, but I felt
our sponsor would understand my reluctance to continue.

In the studio, watching Ron Eagle's footage of sheep pastures beneath
McCall Ridge with its unintended message of "Forget-Me-Nots" only reinforced
these emotions, until someone suggested dedicating this last show to the memory
of our three friends. This thought, in turn, prompted Larry's partner, Richard

Taylor, to observe that continuing the series would provide an on-going memorial. "If Larry were here, I believe he'd want his creation to live on."

Since I'd not before met Richard, I had some reservations. Yet the sensitivity, intelligence and professionalism with which he put together our "last" program, replaced these reservations with great respect and regard for another new-found friend.

In 1993, "Jay Hammond's Alaska" had been capturing stories about unusual Alaskans for almost seven years. Larry's creation will provide a film record of extraordinary men and women of Alaska, active during a particularly significant period in its history.

For myself, all the people these programs have enabled me to meet have enriched the Mother Lode of my Alaska experience, none more so than did Larry Holmstrom.

Time for reflection has moved me to be far less judgmental of others than before. No human being can withstand nor deserves unstinting scrutiny. All have flaws.

34

Foes, Friends, Family and Faith

THE LATTER PART of Ken Burns' outstanding Civil War television series depicts a post war reunion at Gettysburg. There, crickety, cotton-bearded old men in Blue tearfully embrace Gray-clad contemporaries. Though they had fought with fury years before, the sharing of events that shaped history had created a bond which, in time, evolved as affection.

So it is that I reflect on my erstwhile foes, Jesse Carr, Bob Atwood and Wally Hickel. While in times past there were moments I'd cheerfully have burned all three at the stake, there smolders now not one small angry ember. Rather, their memories evoke a warm glow of fondness; yes, even appreciation. For truth to tell, I owe all three more than they or I had once believed. It was their individual and collective opposition that, I've come to realize, did more than I to define and inadvertently enhance whatever public service I may have performed.

Satisfaction from triumph is directly proportionate to the formidableness of one's adversaries. And these guys were about as formidable as foes could be. But whatever else one may say about them — and I've said entirely too much — all three have been outstanding Alaskans. Though each made a fortune in Alaska, rather than departing the state to invest it elsewhere as do so many fair-weather snowbirds, they plowed both their fortunes and great energies into trying to fashion their vision of a better Alaska. That their visions and mine were not always in focus, makes their commitments no less commendable.

Jesse is gone now. Bob's beloved *Anchorage Times* has folded, and Wally's regained the governor's chair, which must seem far hotter than when he first sat in it.

Frankly, a few years ago these events would have flushed few tears from me. Today, each brings a tinge of sadness and regret for any unkindness I may have shown. To all of them, and those who hold them in affection, I'd like to offer apologies and this salute:

"Bob, Wally, and you too, Jesse, if you can read me, in making my life so much more interesting than it would have been otherwise, you bestowed on me a treasure trove of memories I'll forever cherish. For these, thanks, and God bless!"

Of course, I'm not alone in mellowing. Since leaving office eleven years ago I've found most Alaskans appear to be wondrously forgiving or forgetful. Even in Anchorage, where anti-Hammond sentiment ran rampant, today I seldom encounter anyone who wasn't, they contend, a firm supporter back then. So, let my all my successors take heart; one's blemishes seem far less detectable when viewed through the veil of time.

Of course, occasionally someone rips aside that veil to hand me humble pie: like the old curmudgeon who once stopped me on the street to grump, "Hey! I thought *you* were a lousy governor, but this new guy is making you look *good!*"

To illustrate the persistence of this trend, more recently I emerged from an Anchorage hardware store, and shouldered past a glowering behemoth clad in a jacket embroidered "LOCAL 959" — a Teamster's emblem I once perceived as an Alaska version of the Sign of the Beast.

"Hey!" I heard a gruff voice shout from behind. Turning, I looked upward a head and a half into a pair of boiling eyes.

"Are you who I think you are?" the goliath demanded.

"I'm afraid so," I replied meekly.

Whereupon the largest Teamster I've ever seen jabbed a salami-sized finger into my chest, growling, "Hammond, I was a shop steward when you and Jesse Carr were blasting each other, and I gotta tell you, I thought you were the worst governor this state could ever have."

"Oh, oh," I thought; "Here it comes. Why hadn't I shaved my beard and gone incognito?"

Then extracting his finger from my paralyzed pectoral, he extended a ham-sized hand, adding: "But I want to shake your hand; you did ten times as much for me and my family than Jesse ever did."

NOT ALL ALASKANS are forgetful or forgiving, however. An Anchorage columnist took indignant exception when a poll indicated I had achieved far greater public support out of office than I'd enjoyed while in. Ignoring the obvious possibility most Alaskans are simply happier to have me out than in, Mike Doogan denounced those polled as deluded, amnesiac and inconsistent. His theme: What has Hammond done to be held in such high esteem in a town where people at one time would have been pleased to impale him on the City Hall flag pole? That the writer had been campaign manager for Chancy Croft, my Democrat opponent in the 1978 governor's race, may have sharpened his memory along with his sense of affront and confusion. Still, he posed a perplexing question.

After all, there were times I feared stoning in the streets after reading some *Anchorage Times* editorial charging I meant to bankrupt the city and deny its people employment. As one writer had put it: "Hammond won't be content until moose are rubbing velvet off their antlers on darkened downtown lamp posts and bear roam the deserted lobby of Hickel's Hotel Captain Cook."

The phenomenon of late-blooming popularity continues, at least in the imaginations of some. In 1993, the Alaska Journal of Commerce listed me among its "Twenty-five Most Powerful Alaskans" for my "continued influence" on the electorate:

"Alaskans love Jay Hammond. Bush pilot, former fighter pilot, guide, fisherman, trapper, lodge owner, poet, politician . . . Alaskans would have elected him forever. Hammond hasn't been governor for years but when he speaks . . . he is listened to."

Influential? Powerful? Listened to? Tell that to the unsuccessful political candidates I've endorsed over the years. My batting average was so low, before I vowed to make no more I considered offering my endorsements only to those who refused to pay me *not* to.

My view of opinion polls suggesting I could be returned to office merely by declaration is this: the day I indicated any such aspiration would be the day I'd be inundated with regurgitated recollections of all my past transgressions — both real and suspect. When folks ask if I'm inclined to run again, I tell them in all the honesty, I've tasted freedom and love it. I miss the attractions of public office about as much as I might those of a bleeding ulcer.

People seem increasingly to hold their leaders in wildly fluctuating extremes of high esteem and rank disfavor. The higher the profile, the more vulnerable to being clouted by that swinging pendulum.

Take the case of another old friend, a naval aviator who went through training at Corpus Christi, shortly after I did in 1942. I hadn't seen him for years when some former sport fishing clients who lived in Houston offered to hold a fundraiser for my impoverished 1978 re-election bid. George Bush and his gracious wife, Barbara, generously opened their home to put me up for my three-day visit.

Perhaps no candidate has had a greater breadth of preparation for the job of president. In business, in Congress, as ambassador to China and the United Nations and as head of the CIA and vice president, George Bush had already spent a lifetime in the service of his country.

George's main problem was he is a gentleman of the old school at a time when honor, decency, loyalty, devotion to family, God and country don't mesh all that well with Joe Sixpack's cynical conception of politicians. If we can't brand our leaders venal, corrupt or immoral, we must diminish them with other labels, like "sanctimonious" (Carter), "bumbling" (Ford), or in George's case, "wimp."

Wimp? Let me tell you folks: Wimps don't fly torpedo bombers, especially back when George Bush did. Shortly before he enlisted, famed Torpedo Squadron 8 was wiped out in an attack on Japanese warships. Everyone knew the lumbering TBMs and TBFs were flying coffins. They could not engage in evasive maneuvers; once committed to a torpedo run, it was 'home-in' straight to the target through unrelenting fire. That any survived such combat seems remarkable. That any willfully volunteered to strap themselves on top of a ton of TNT, to ride it down to lethally objecting targets, might call into question sanity, but never guts. To those of us, in contrast, "safely" tucked in Corsair cockpits, torpedo bomber pilots and crew were considered Kamikazes, before we ever knew the word. Egocentric fighter pilots may tend to think of themselves as the elite. But those I knew held in higher awe the men who flew torpedo bombers. That George Herbert Walker Bush would never qualify as a wimp was known all along to Barbara and friends. Too bad no one told Saddam.

I believe I may have been the first U.S. governor to endorse George Bush's presidential candidacy in 1978, and I have not regretted it. Even though his patrician character seemed rather out of place in politics, I for one was mighty grateful to have George at the controls during the Cold War's thaw and the Berlin Wall's crumble. He is that rare combination of "old pilot" and "bold pilot," and even those who do not share my high regard must credit the man for having wooed and won a most remarkable First Lady.

My point is: George Bush held a public approval rating of more than eighty percent as president. Hardly a year later, polls showed him at less than twenty-five. Harry Truman was approved by only twenty-one percent in 1951; today we view him as one of the 20th Century's greatest presidents. Just as I believe the fates conspired to dump on Jimmy Carter, I fear circumstances over which he had too little control, helped retire my old friend George Bush. And, like Gerald Ford, whom Chevy Chase showed as a pratfaller, and Jimmy Carter, whom some labeled too pious, I believe Gentleman George's persona which seemed to unduly discomfit Joe Sixpack, will in time be obscured by recognition of his monumental contributions to our peace and security.

Now that Barbara and George have returned home to Texas, I suspect both will grow in stature as criticism abates — and critics realign their sights on their newest target.

During the last two National Governors Conferences I attended, I made the pleasant acquaintance of an extraordinarily charismatic and impressively intelligent young fellow whom I predicted could go far in politics if he weren't careful. Thus, it is with no great surprise that I view former Arkansas Governor Bill Clinton as president.

With the continuing bombardment of seemingly insolvable national and international problems raining on Bill Clinton's parade into history, should he emerge no more folded, spindled and mutilated than George Bush at this writing, he'll be fortunate.

Passage of time not only dulls memories and allows us to forgive our public servants, it also matures those who were too young to know or care about earlier political wars. In Alaska, time also brings new arrivals to the state, which helps a has-been like myself sink more comfortably into anonymity. The descent is not entirely "free fall," however. Not long ago I entered a store where a nubile young cashier kept glancing suspiciously my way. Unable to suppress her curiosity, she walked over to where I was examining some hardware.

"Didn't you used to be somebody?" she asked.

"Not really," I replied.

Unsatisfied, she continued to study me as I made my rounds, apparently sifting through mental flashbacks of pictures she'd seen on post office walls or "Missing Fugitive" television shows. When I came to pay my bill, her face suddenly lit up in recognition.

"I got it! McGovernor, right?"

"Close," I smiled, bemused by how her memory tapes had cross-filed a former bush rat governor with a 1972 presidential nominee.

Vividly remembering the days when recognition usually meant dealing with some irate citizen's diatribe, it's not at all affronting when folks fail to penetrate my disguise of age and attire. Recently, when my daughter Heidi and I were ushered to a table at a restaurant, Heidi overheard our hostess enlighten a young waitress.

"See that man over there? He used to be governor!"

I turned just in time to catch the young lady's eye and observe a classic double-take. Measuring the bearded hulk seated at our table, she turned, grinning widely at her informer.

"Him? Naaaaw!"

Some things never change.

As I've "matured," however, there have been changes; some I find perplexing. Though I hear as well as ever, increasingly, people mumble. This can be interesting.

Not long ago a woman asked me: "Who was pregnant the year you were born?"

Taken aback, I replied, "Why, my mother, of course."

Noting her bewilderment, I asked her to repeat her question.

"Who was *president* when you were born?" she answered, louder.

PASSING SEVENTY, I seem to have the best of all worlds. People are wondrously forgiving or forgetful. Old foes have become friendly and most folks who do remember, seem not to hold the past against me. More and more, people recognize me either from television or as the father of my children, rather than for offenses in public office.

Though father of daughters only, I've never felt short-changed for failing to sire sons. I'd not trade any of my three girls for half a dozen boys. Besides, I've found a surrogate son in my nephew, David McRae, who far better fills that void than could almost any father's son I've known. Tall, strong, brilliant and handsome, David seems almost too capable and caring to be true. Had I been able to design a model son, compared to David I fear I'd have fashioned an Edsel to his Porsche.

Fortunately, in the case of my daughters, their mothers' genes over-rode most of mine; all three girls are exceptional.

Wendy, my oldest, I once believed a treasure lost irretrievably. After our divorce, her mother took Wendy south and, for years, we lost close contact. In the interim, I received extraordinarily literate and incisive travelogues of her peregrinations to exotic places: Easter Island, Manchu Picchu, Bogota, Tanzania, Thailand and Cambodia. First a Peace Corps volunteer, she later joined *Redd Barna*, a Norwegian affiliate of Save the Children. In this service to the world's most helplessly underprivileged and oppressed, she met and married a like-minded soulmate, Norwegian Per Wam.

Even so, it was with no little apprehension I anticipated seeing Wendy for the first time in many years when she wrote she was bringing my new grandson, Nick, to visit us at Lake Clark in 1987. Anxieties were never more unjustified. Wendy proved so warm, compassionate and understanding, my family immediately fell in love with her and her handsome, happy little boy.

Heidi, Bella's and my oldest daughter, is another jewel I'd not refacet even were it were possible — which it is not. Strong-willed, confident, extremely able and accomplished, Heidi can do almost anything better than most. Had she so desired, I've little doubt she could have been a champion athlete, outstanding musician, business executive and, certainly, a far better governor than the one she has observed most closely. Known as "the Boss" by her parents for her take-charge inclinations, Heidi has blessed us with little Lauren — who, at age five is a clone of her mother at that age — and my two-year old namesake, Jay Hammond Stanford — an obvious first round draft pick for the Pittsburgh Steelers, despite his father's perverse hope he'll sign with the Forty-Niners.

My youngest, Dana, is an enigma within a conundrum. For years she tried to withhold her good looks, fine mind and potential from too close inspection. One walked on unshelled eggs around Dana, one moment coddled, the next, briskly scrambled. In recent years, she has mellowed and her talents, which include a remarkable artistic ability and a wondrously off-beat sense of humor, are being ever more appreciated by those who've come to know them, including herself.

Among my most cherished treasures are splendid wood carvings she has made. Perhaps mercifully, I can no longer find caricature sketches she'd made of friends and family before age six. Done in a huff, these were so remarkably funny and brutally accurate we dared not show them to the subjects for fear of insult.

Somebody, no doubt an apprehensive father-in-law, once observed how turning your daughter over to a young swain has about as much appeal as permitting a gorilla to fondle your Stradivarius. I have yet to meet Wendy's husband, Per, an experience I anticipate. But when Heidi announced her engagement to Bruce Stanford, a burly, California law student, at first it drew as discordant a note from my heart strings as one sawed by an unresined bow.

An attorney?! Oh no! How often had I stated publicly: "I have nothing against attorneys. Some of my best friends are attorneys. I just don't want my daughter to marry one!"?

Oh well, I consoled myself in 1982 as theirs became one of the rare Governor's House weddings; he's a pretty fair fly fisherman so he can't be *all* bad. While my lawyer-son-in-law struggles to confirm this hopeful presumption, his role as a devoted, much loved father to our grandkids, Lauren and Jay, has earned him considerable redemption.

TIME FOR REFLECTION has also moved me to be far less judgmental of others than before. No human being can withstand nor deserves unstinting scrutiny. All have flaws.

There's only one role model who warrants emulation, and He died 2,000 years ago. My father came as close as anyone I know to meet that standard.

While both my parents were fine examples of joyous, abundant living through deep, spiritual conviction, in my youth I found such beatitudes quaint, but not compelling. Only much later did I find there are three dimensions to every being: mental, physical and spiritual. For years I exercised the first two only; focusing on physical or mental accomplishments, I remained spiritually flabby. Unless I could see, understand, touch or experience something directly, I had little time for it. Only when I came to recognize there were other dimensions that cannot be explained, did I conclude my folks were right after all. That condition was a long and painful time in coming.

In college I had wrestled with calculus unsuccessfully until I found that, whether or not I understood just how it worked, it really did. So it was with religious conviction. But unlike, say, Eldridge Cleaver, who saw Christ's face in the moon, or Chuck Colson, who was traumatically born again and baptized in tears shed in the backwash of Watergate, my own spiritual enlightenment was far less dramatic.

Rather than a cataclysmic sunburst of revelation, mine was more like reverse Chinese water torture. Drop by drop, the hard crust of disbelief and rejection was eroded through a multitude of experiences; among them, witnessing innumerable cases of what acceptance of the Lord had done for others. I envied these experiences until I finally realized that, at least in the spiritual realm, all mankind could achieve equity. While rewards for our mental and physical efforts and circumstances will vary, each of us can achieve absolute equality through that salvation doled out by the Good Lord for all in precisely equal measure.

Do I today have any doubts? Of course. But they are doubts of the intellect, not the spirit. While I envy those who "know" without question all tenants of their religious beliefs to be absolute, I have not reached that state of grace, nor am I certain I would want to. I wonder if the Good Lord looks with any less favor upon those who believe despite doubts, than He does upon those who believe because they have no doubts whatsoever? I'm not sure whose belief is more firmly founded: one who believes because he "knows" or one who believes despite the fact he does not know absolutely?

Perhaps it's the degree to which we let those beliefs influence our performance here on earth which matters most. Certainly, there are a lot more "sayers of the word" than "doers." The former too often assert spiritual conviction verbally, yet express doubt daily through their actions or inactions.

My own stumbling odyssey of the spirit is perhaps best summed up in a bit of verse I once wrote.

THANKSGIVING

Lord, when I was young I hadn't time
To give to the likes of you.

The world was hung here just for me.
Roads ran clean out of view.

You were some stranger in the night
Whose face I seldom saw.

Except at times when I was scared
Or when my soul rubbed raw

Upon the shards of broken dreams
Or promises unkept.

And, Yes, Lord, I guess at times I slipped
On tears that others wept.

But I was much too smart for you
To hang onto very long.

Besides I just could not believe
That "meek" could outlast "strong."

And yet at times when I was scared
Or old man death came near me,

I'd take a chance and call your name,
Not sure that you could hear me.

Like the time you joined me in a cockpit
When at 600 feet
Some bandit knocked my tail off
And pinned me in the seat.
You placed your hand on mine, Lord,
And you brought us down okay.

Yet somehow when I hit the deck,
Again, you'd slipped away.

Or take that time out on the trapline
When the dogs went through the ice.
We very nearly bought the farm
But again you paid the price

By taking time to haul us out.
Did I thank you Lord or not?
Got so busy warming up my hide,
Perhaps my heart forgot.

Then of course there was the time
I'd broken both my pins
And laid for days out in the bush
Reflecting on my sins.

Sure was a hard-learned lesson, Lord,
I guess some guys can't hear "please"
And so you've got to knock them off their feet
To bring them to their knees.

Yes, I've been shot at, Lord; been kicked and cussed
And sliced once with a knife. But it wasn't till
I turned to you,
learned anything of life.

I guess I'm not too smart, Lord,
Or I'd have learned long in the past
That trails I'd been traveling
Led to nowhere mighty fast.

How come a guy can live so long
And all that time can't tell
He's been standing in the valley
Looking up to Hell?

Perhaps one's brain gets cluttered up
With junk that blocks the light
And makes it hard for him to tell
What's really wrong from right.

So forgive my brain, if it still has doubts;
My heart has none at all.
Yet like a baby trying to walk
The soul first must learn to crawl.

So it's a wonder, Lord, you found me
For my soul was so darned small
I'm surprised that you could find it
Among others twice as tall.

Yes, sometimes I marvel that you bothered
To take time to search the ranks
Of sinners till you spotted me.
For that, most of all Lord, Thanks.

At Lake Clark, our nearest neighbor is almost on the horizon.
Anchorage is beyond the mountains — a million miles away.

35

Whither Alaska?

ALASKANS HAVE OFTEN been spared economic catastrophe by the timely occurrence of disaster. The advent of world wars — the first of which boosted settlement of Anchorage, the second much of our infrastructure — the Good Friday earthquake in 1964, the Fairbanks flood of 1967 and the Exxon Valdez oil spill of 1989, all rescued Alaska from potential bankruptcy with massive infusions of dollars for disaster relief. Small wonder Alaskans have diverse views on issues that pit environment against economic development.

So many imponderables, conflicts, misconceptions, factions and dichotomies are harnessed together — often head-to-head instead of in tandem — that rather than proceeding down a well-defined trail, what some term Alaska's "sled of state" seems ever about to plunge into the brush, fall through the ice or crash into a windfall.

Some contend this stems from lack of strong leadership. They are wrong. Alaska has too many leaders. The problem is a dearth of fearless followers among timorous politicians concerned chiefly with re-election. Consequently, our sled of state often has lead dogs hitched not only up front, but aft as well, with another dozen snarling and plunging about in the basket, tails tucked tightly between their legs.

Further confusing destiny's course are multitudes living elsewhere determined to save Alaska from Alaskans. Much of this absentee interest is understandable. After all, the bulk of Alaska belongs not to those who live here, but to the federal government. Failure of many Alaskans to appreciate the patronizing and often ignorant concerns of outsiders serves but to increase our protective, parochial zeal.

Among Alaskans themselves, vision of the future is kaleidoscopic. To the ardent developer aspiring to create "Manhattan on the Muskeg," environmental constraints tarnish their golden image of a booming land over run by consumers. To environmentalists who'd close the door behind themselves upon arrival, development that lures others to follow, like a stone thrown in Walden Pond, distorts their mind's-eye reflection of unspoiled wilderness.

In trying to focus on a future to which most Alaskans could aspire, I preached, ad nauseam, my belief development should be encouraged only when its economic benefits to all Alaskans outweighed environmental costs. Most of my sermons fell on deaf ears. Deeming my words heretical, developers continued to believe all growth was good, while environmentalists decried my preaching as overly burdened with economics at the expense of concerns for "quality of life and vision for the future." To developers, I said Alaska's long-term economic health depends on a healthy environment. To environmentalists, I said, "You can more likely derail projects that threaten quality of life by holding growth proponents' feet to the fire on the economic self-interest of Alaskans than you can by fanning flames of environmentalism. Folk who couldn't care less about dicky birds will sit up and take notice of some economic turkey that pecks at their pocket books."

If we limit arguments to purely a battle between "the buck and the biota," the quick buck will win every time. I am convinced that only through an amalgam of economics and environmentalism can Alaska hope to sustain values which make this the place most of us wish to live.

Development that actually costs the state, remains at once Alaska's least understood and most pressing economic problem. Few politicians seem concerned we do not extract enough wealth from new resource development to offset its costs. Instead, they talk of spurring even more growth by "diversified" economic development, blithely ignoring the fact that without drastic changes, we'll simply "diversify" the means by which we go broke.

What good would it do, for example, to boost economic development of Alaska's immense mineral resources and create 10,000 new jobs when, as has been the case with all our past resource development, most would go to folks flooding up with their families from elsewhere?

Without an income tax, each of these 10,000 new jobholders will cost the state thousands of dollars in service costs, above what they contribute to state coffers — not to mention the additional costs for family members. These costs, of course, will be paid from our finite pool of oil wealth — which is exactly the same whether our population is 500,000 or 5,000,000 — so long as industries other than oil don't pay their way.

Failure to recognize this has fostered Alaska's past boom and bust cycles and if not changed could lead to economic disaster.

IT'S NOT SURPRISING that most Alaskans fail to distinguish between healthy and unhealthy economic development. Most come from other states where development pays its own way simply because it has to. Unlike Alaska, these states have no great pool of oil wealth from which they can ladle subsidies. Drain our pool and almost all other Alaskan development could go belly up.

Elsewhere, corporate and personal income taxes must generate enough new revenue to offset costs incurred by providing basic public services. Not conditioned to the contrary, small wonder Alaska newcomers bring with them presumption any development which creates jobs must be good for the economy.

Perhaps the best way to bring enlightenment would be to send all Alaskan Permanent Fund shareholders an annual statement reflecting how each of their resources performed over the previous year. I suspect recipients would sit up and take notice if their statement read: "Your dividend from oil: $1,000. From Fishing, Tourism, Timber and Mining: Minus $1,500. Please remand a check for $500 within 30 days to cover your negative dividend balance."

Wally Hickel likes to refer to Alaska as an "Owner State." I prefer to term Alaskans as an "Owner People" to reflect our constitutionally mandated public, rather than state, resource ownership.

Despite this collective ownership, however, Alaskans receive but a tiny portion of their resource wealth through annual Permanent Fund Dividends. Since this dividend is but one half the earnings derived from investments of roughly only *one-tenth* of their oil wealth, it's clear that most of every Alaskan's share is retained by the state in a "hidden dividend tax" used to fund government. Currently, that "hidden tax" extracts from Alaskans — and only from Alaskans — about 85 percent of our government costs; whereas in other states, those costs are paid by "above board" corporate, sales, income or property taxes.

Because of this hidden tax policy, many people, including Alaskans, are deluded into thinking Alaskans are not taxed at all. Instead Alaskans collectively may be the most taxed of any. Currently, each and every Alaskan — children included — are taxed almost nine-tenths of their annual oil wealth — in 1993 about $6,000 *per year per person!*

To bring this point home, perhaps each should be paid his full share, and the state required to take it back through user fees or increased taxes needed to fund government. This would not only re-attach citizens' fingers to the public purse strings; the one-quarter of our work force comprised of non-residents would at least have to pay something for the price of admission, instead of enjoying the almost free ride they get currently, at the expense of every Alaska resident.

Such an approach is, of course, abhorrent to most politicians. Rather than continue to permit them to spend our oil wealth as *they* deem fit, they'd be compelled to come to the electorate, hat in hand, and make the case that each of their pet programs warrants the increase in taxes or user fees. My, how "needs," demands and priorities realign when voters perceive themselves as having to pay for them. I suspect were every Alaskan annually granted his full per capita share of the wealth we could eliminate or vastly curtail all welfare programs, unemployment insurance and subsidies along with much of the government workforce. At the same time, we could painlessly reduce salaries of remaining employees by an amount equal to their increase in dividends. Even prisoners' increased dividends could be used for restitution to victims — or at least offset costs of their room and board.

Heady thought, but of course it will never happen. Politics preclude it.

Lamentably, politicians talk increasingly of reducing or "capping" dividends to postpone the inevitable day when re-imposing a state income tax is necessary. Once more, political expediency fosters stupidity.

Capping dividends not only equates with imposing a head tax on *every* Alaskan and *only* Alaskans — regardless of income — it staunches the flow of what every study has shown to be the one dispersal of money that produces the biggest bang for the buck in bolstering Alaska's economy.

Cap dividends, and you'll infect the Permanent Fund with a virus which could lead to its demise. Once assured of only an inflation-eroding, fixed return on their investment account, Alaskan shareholders would no longer protest each time politicians tried to raid the fund or attempt to invest it in less prudent schemes.

Rather than "cap" dividends, far better to *uncap* them so Alaskans will know precisely how much of their true share of wealth has been retained by government through its "hidden dividend tax." Were the state to send every shareholder an Internal Revenue Service 1099 Form, showing we'd each been credited, say, $10,000 of which $9,000 has been withheld in state taxes, Alaskans would pay far more attention to just how their resource ownership income was used. As would the IRS, no doubt, when suddenly smothered under a blizzard of "early tax filings" by Alaskans claiming a $9,000 deduction from their federal income tax obligations.

Ironically, some non-Alaskans seem to grasp far more readily how the Permanent Fund and its dividends will determine our destiny.

A 1992 article by *Anchorage Daily News* reporter Wesley Loy bolsters my conviction that the Permanent Fund and its dividend program must remain intact, if we are to protect Alaska's future.

In his story, "Piggy Bank Politics," subtitled "Many governments try to save their windfalls, but Alaska's effort is different. It works," Loy interviewed Johns Hopkins University economist and energy expert Thomas Stauffer, who he reported to be "in constant awe" of Alaska's Permanent Fund.

By all rights, Stauffer says, the fund shouldn't exist, because "People are reluctant to save and politicians are compelled to spend." He says Alaska's Permanent Fund fascinates political scientists as well as economists because almost every other attempt at large scale public savings around the world — in Saudi Arabia, Oman, Abu Dhabi, Venezuela and British Columbia — have "flopped badly." Alaska's Permanent Fund "shouldn't have happened [and] it shouldn't have been successful. Human nature being what it is, people will not save and will try to raid the savings if they can, particularly politicians."

The reasons Alaska's fund has worked, Stauffer believes, are the following: The fund was designed to save by investment, not used to fund capital

Governors Jay Hammond, Bill Sheffield, Walter J. Hickel, Keith Miller and Steve Cowper in 1993 at the filming of a statewide TV special discussing Alaska's future.

projects; the fund's investments are made outside the state and bring money from outside into Alaska's economy; and the Permanent Fund Dividend — a "brilliant" stroke to protect the fund from political raids and infuse new capital into Alaska's local economies — "gave everybody a stake [in the Fund] every year. Absolutely brilliant."

Stauffer credits "the unique success of such a fund" thusly: "You were damn lucky that you had some statesman-like leaders . . . at the critical time."

Well, lest we forget, it was the people of Alaska, not its politicians, who provided the leadership and created their Permanent Fund. Politicians wanted a fund they could get their fingers into when they had spent the rest of our one-time windfall. The people voted a resounding "No!" to this by amending their state constitution to protect it.

Likewise, it is the people of Alaska, today and tomorrow, who collectively retain a stake in their fund's future. I can only hope they will spurn the political pressures to cap the dividend; to do so would diminish that stake, becloud its brilliance and embark Alaska on the same slippery path that has led almost every other oil-dependent state, province or emirate toward the brink of financial confusion, if not collapse.

Unfortunately, many Alaskans believe once government spending has been cut, and income taxes imposed we should next consider dividend caps. Yet *economically, it never makes more sense to cap dividends* than to simply ratchet up taxes to raise the same amount. In effect, capping dividends taxes only — and all — Alaskans. Increasing most taxes spreads the burden to those best able to pay — and also includes transient workers who currently remove so much wealth from our state. In fishing, for example, nonresidents cart off about two-thirds of the annual payday, yet contribute virtually nothing for the privilege.

THOSE WHO BELIEVE new, non-petroleum resource development and the creation of new jobs will necessarily bail out Alaska's fiscally floundering Ship of State are deluded.

Unless resource-related jobs create sufficient new state tax or royalty income offsetting attendant increased government service costs required to sustain inevitable population increases, we'll find we've not only simply pumped our ballast tanks into the bilges, but opened the sea-cocks as well.

Those who ignore this — and that includes most politicians — are like a ship owner who sells cargo at the same price he paid for it, then finding to his distress he's losing money, believes the answer is to buy a larger vessel so he can haul and sell even more.

Make no mistake: without a state income tax, adequate severance taxes or royalties on resources other than only oil, unlike any other state, Alaska has made it almost impossible for additional growth to pay its own way.

Curiously, those most unconcerned with this anomaly seem also to be those most alarmed by state budget increases. Apparently, they fail to recognize every new job that does not go to a person already residing in Alaska is the same as putting that new job-taking immigrant and all accompanying family members on the state payroll at roughly $6,000 a year — the current annual cost of state services paid out per capita.

It is understandable, of course, why members of the business community love population increases: the more houses, insurance, goods and services sold, the more the private sector economy booms.

The trouble is, there are *two economies* with which we must be concerned in Alaska: the private sector and the public, i.e. government. When one parasites off the other, the resultant waste product causes what might be called "economic pollution." Unless those two economies can be balanced by siphoning revenues from one to the other, we will face fiscal chaos.

In failing to achieve that balance, we're in the ridiculous position where what's good for one economy is bad for the other. For example: our private sector economy would certainly boom if our population doubled; conversely, our public sector economy would be far better off if Alaska's population were cut in half.

There are two ways to remedy this: Either increase revenue flow from the private sector to the public sector through royalties, taxes, and user fees, or reduce the size of government. So far, politicians have been remarkably successful in avoiding the pain of doing either.

So long as re-election remains their Holy Grail, don't expect politicians to trade it for a tin cup filled with the dregs of defeat.

Decreasing likelihood of legislative remedies further, is that it takes but a single truculent committee chairman, to bottle up a bill in committee. This must change before there can be any hope of avoiding a financial crisis in Alaska.

Since the legislature has been unable to balance the books, and breach barriers that prevent solving Alaska's most pressing problems, perhaps it's time to *give the public a crack*!

Why not put the following on the ballot and allow voters to accept or reject them?

1. Shall Alaska impose severance tax or royalty on all citizen-owned natural resources, and deposit part in the Permanent Fund?

2. Should we allow the public to vote for or against all non-mandated government programs not based on need, and for each eliminated, deposit the savings in the Permanent Fund?

3. Should we permit the electorate to be the binding arbiter in public employee collective bargaining disputes?

4. Should we impose term limits on elected officials?

5. Should we require public approval before any earnings reserve of the Permanent Fund be expended by the legislature?

If our constitution decrees we can only cast advisory votes, *let's amend our constitution to require the legislature at least to vote on each publicly approved proposal within a time certain*, instead of simply burying these matters in committee.

I MADE THESE PROPOSALS at an economic summit held by Governor Hickel in 1993, and I concluded my presentation by pointing out how these propositions had two things in common:

"Let the public vote on each, and I suspect all would pass. Leave them up to the legislature and none will. By placing all on the ballot, the broad *public interest* might control politicians, prevail over special interests, and restrain government spending."

After years of futilely expressing these views, I was taken aback recently by the enthusiastic response of a once hostile audience. When approached by a broadly smiling Bob Atwood, I was almost speechless.

"By Golly, Jay," he gushed, "I agreed with everything you had to say! Why weren't you talking that way when you were governor?"

Looking into my old friend's eyes, I suddenly felt disoriented.

"I was, Bob. You just weren't listening."

Moments later, a political figure several light years to the left of Atwood, but who also had opposed my policies for many years, said much the same thing. Could it be all I'd done is once again confuse everyone?

Whatever, the parade continues. Several members of the Hickel administration, legislators, business persons and community leaders have subsequently expressed enthusiastic support for almost all those proposals.

Yet, not to worry; even as I conclude this memoir, not one has been introduced, let alone enacted.

Could it be, politicians remember too well what Alaska voters did in 1976, when allowed to deal with an issue fumbled by their elected representatives? Back then, by voting to create the Permanent Fund, Alaska's citizens slapped the lid on billions of dollars politicians would have happily spent and still would today, if they could.

It's almost enough to persuade one to run for governor. Almost, but not quite. When asked if I've any inclination to do so, my standard reply is: "No thanks. I've tasted freedom and I love it."

One reporter pressed further. "Aren't there any circumstances under which you'd run again?"

"Sure, if the legislature granted me total dictatorial powers. Permit them to provide counsel, but for heaven's sakes not muck around with or deny me my programs!"

HAVING PASSED THREE-SCORE and ten, I've grown far too cantankerous to suffer again the frustrations of dealing with politicians. Rather than engage in the cushion plumping required to elicit support from recalcitrant legislators, I'd be more inclined to induce compliance by forcibly jamming those cushions and letting solons choose to consume them or choke. Of course, I'd never abuse such dictatorial powers. But I'd never trust anyone else not to. When one begins to think in that vein, it's time to leave public office forever.

And back in the real world — Bella and I take a break before returning to the end of our set-net site at Naknek.

Epilogue

FOR YEARS, I WAS PLAGUED with a recurrent nightmare: once more, I'd be back in college, confined to campus and a torturous study schedule. No longer. That nightmare's been supplanted. Now I occasionally dream I've been re-elected. Relief upon awakening is exquisite. Not that I don't deem public service a privilege if not always a pleasure; just that, like childbirth, it's not the pangs one remembers with warm feeling.

So it is with other facets of life in Alaska. Here one can yet carve out a life to one's own design, and though in the process the fingers may be nicked and bloodied, somehow the grandeur of the land and the warmth of its people help focus one's view on the horizon instead of the hurt.

Here, lifestyles that would brand one "eccentric" elsewhere may be indulged without raising an eyebrow.

Our nearest and only year-round neighbors, Tish and Howard Bowman — who happen to be the best of all possible neighbors — live some ten roadless miles up the lake. That Bella and I chose to live one hundred and fifty miles off the road system in a log house we built prompts but mild interest. Of course, that we elect to feed several voracious wood stoves a dozen cords of spruce and birch annually, have no telephone and must produce our own power prompts some to question our sanity.

That we occasionally have wolves, wolverine, otter, beaver, bear, caribou and moose in our front yard, which is backdropped by some of the most spectacular real estate this side of Shangri La prompts envy in others.

Alaskans, perhaps more than most, romantically aspire to "live off the land." Many who try find it a little too gritty for a steady diet on learning, as one oldtimer put it, "After a while, that land don't taste so good!"

So it was with Bella and me. Though we have an immense garden, put up fish and have ample access to wild game, we are far from self-sufficient. It costs a great deal even to live frugally in the bush. At about four dollars per gallon for fuel, we pay more than double its city price.

Freight and groceries run an additional half dollar a pound to be flown just to Port Alsworth. And the expense of maintaining an aircraft, at times the only means of access to our homestead several miles across the lake, runs into five figures annually.

Even the blessing of having no phone is not without cost. If they could be used at our place, which they cannot, we could purchase a whole bank of cellular phones and even an 800 number for the price of the mobile and fixed marine and aircraft radios used to keep in contact.

While, of course, we have no car at Lake Clark, we have a tractor for hauling wood, a bucket loader (purchased for flood control when a beaver dam broke in heavy rain and washed one of our cabins out into the lake), an all-terrain Honda and our most recent acquisition, a twenty-seven foot industrial-strength cabin cruiser.

I bought the boat when it became evident sometimes we couldn't cross to Port Alsworth where there were telephones, a post office and access to Anchorage via instrument-equipped, twin engine aircraft able to fly when my old Cessna can't.

That we seldom got newspapers until several days stale didn't disturb me, but the six days spent at Port Alsworth vainly trying to fly to our homestead where Bella was storm-bound prompted me to have a craft built that can cross under almost any condition.

Though forty-five-mile-long Lake Clark sometimes does not freeze, usually by mid-October the lake level drops enough to permit me to replace my floats with ski/wheels and land on a slowly emerging narrow rock beach. Similarly when the ice goes out I can change back as the small bay where I tie up begins to fill. Both seasons can present problems. Before the lake level falls, beach landings can be almost as exhilarating as night carrier landings. And mooring a floatplane in spring on the open lake can grab your attention when the wind clocks over fifty.

Like many homesteaders, we once thought we'd raise some livestock and ducks. Coyotes, lynx and an eagle snatched most of the latter, and we gave our goats away before they could become bear or wolf bait. Just as well. Bella could never abide consuming her newfound friends. Besides, we can stock our larder with spruce grouse that foolishly bumble into our yard each fall. Since these fend for themselves, rather than bond through costly hand feeding, Bella appears to find their utilization tasty instead of traumatic.

While the presence of wolves, bear and moose may pose some small hazard by contrast to beasts roaming the urbs these days, they, for the most part, are good neighbors. Knowing they were here first modifies intellectually, if not emotionally, our response to the occasional rampage. When bear or moose break down the pole fence surrounding the garden or bust into the smokehouse we fume a bit and then fix it.

Less repairable, however, was trauma incurred the day the wolves came and took Annie.

Of all Bella's dogs, Annie squirmed furthermost into our hearts. Seemingly a cross between an Ewok and the Cookie Monster, Annie was embued with unbounded affection and enough endearing traits to win over most everyone.

One spring morning Bella was in the front yard, I at my outdoor work bench and Dana was gathering kindling across our log bridge. Suddenly I heard Dana shriek. Startled, I looked up to see her racing downhill, flailing away with a stick at a wolf attempting to snatch one of the dogs. Suddenly, eight wolves appeared silently as if conjured up. As Bella and I ran toward Dana shouting, several dashed down the beach, one with Annie in its jaws. The eighth wolf held its ground belligerently and fled only after I'd flung a rock.

Obviously, we'd permitted the wolves to become too used to us. Instead of scaring them off in prior weeks when this pack and another of ten often visited, Bella and I enjoyed watching them gambol about in our yard and would howl them back when they'd ghosted off into the woods. More than once, we'd commented we couldn't imagine ever again killing one of these beautiful creatures. Yet, I'd have gladly rolled the one who'd grabbed Annie. Animal rights, just like human rights, are countenanced only so long as the fist stops short of one's nose.

While I empathize with those who envy our life and find foreclosed most chances to emulate it, with too many invaders the prime attraction of "wilderness" living is gone. Accordingly, we tread as lightly as we can on the land, recognizing we can never "own" it. Instead, we are but brief stewards. As such, we felt obligated to blend our structures to the landscape and bend our spirits to the natural rhythms around us. Though we often fail by, say, imposing the flatulence of a gas engine on the cry of a loon, or by snatching a salmon en route to spawn, we've tried to do penance. To assure our homestead will in large part forever be wild, we've turned half over to the Nature Conservancy, thereby foreclosing any chance that portion may be developed.

Magnanimous? Not at all. By contrast to monetary value lost along with development "rights," the privilege of current occupancy and knowledge that values we hold dear will remain in our wake is substantial reward. (Besides, there are some very significant immediate tax write-offs and estate considerations attending such "unselfish" actions!)

At a time when most Alaskans were yet pretty well confined to their home villages or to a few small cities, my work as a fish and wildlife biologist, government hunter, guide and bush pilot, took me almost everywhere throughout the Greatland.

From Alaska's mountains, woods and waters, I've gleaned an abundant fortune in coin of the spirit, if not the realm. From Alaskans themselves, I've

JAY HAMMOND COLLECTION

*My grandfather, William Jefferson Hammond, a sergeant in
the 77th New York State Volunteers, who served in the Civil
War. Lamentably, I know almost nothing about him, save that
he carried his wounded brother, Delos, from the flaming hell
of the Battle of the Wilderness. Thus, I am prompted to write
this book for my antecedents. I'd hate for them to draw their
conclusions only from newspaper stories!*

garnered far more. Most prized is the life and family I'd never have known had
serendipity not lured me North.

Surely my cup runneth over. So what if that cup be a mite chipped, cracked
and dented! I'd not trade its content for any other libation the fates have de-
canted since time began.

— *the end* —

Appendix

As Alaska's governor from 1974 until 1982, I remain ultimately responsible for any oversights or shortcomings of my administration. Those who were, and are, responsible for whatever success we achieved for the people of our state are represented in the incomplete list of names that follows:

OFFICE OF THE GOVERNOR
Bob Palmer, Bill Gordon, Kent Dawson, Jerry Reinwand, executive assistants.

Charlene Abbey, Charles Adams, Allan Adasiak, Danith Anderson, Jane Anvik, Donald Argetsinger, Lynn Bartlett, Jim Beltran, Diane Bergstrom, Darwin Biwer, Zela Boseman, Janet Bradley, Elsa Bronson, Carole Burger, Penelope Burke, Randall Burns, Pete Carran, Cathi Carr-Lundfeldt, Mary Capobianco, Charles Champion, Earl Costello, Larry Chaplin, Robert Clarke, Vicki Clayman, Steve Cramer, Karen W. Cory, Terry Dale, Phil Deisher, Howard DeVore, Jesse Dodson, Richard Dowling, Jim Edenso, Kim Elton, Rebecca Engen, Ronald Evans, John C. Flanigan, Scott Foster, Robert A. Frederick, John Garner, Lynda Giguere, Janet Green, Susan Green, Peggy Hackett, John Halterman, Michael Harper, Roy Helms, Jeffrey Hiatt, Betty Hickling, Mary Jo Hobbs, Larry Holmstrom, Wilda Hudson, Katie Hurley, Derrill Johnson, Myrtle Johnson, Yoshio Katsuyama, John Katz, Peter Keating, Robert Kemp, Kurt Kerns, Chuck Kleeschulte, Don Kubley, Reva LaFavour, Beatrice Langness, Donna Lehr, Ron Lehr, Diane LeResche, Robert LeResche, Ron Lind, Susie Lowell, Bill Luria, Ron Maerjeweski, Ann Mawn, James Mayer, Charles Meacham, Larry Mix, Sandra McConkey, Bill McConkey, Betsy McGuire, Betty Michael, Jay Moor, Rod Mourant, June Nelson, Chris Noah, Penny Pearson, Frank Peratrovich, Marie Pignalberi, Marco Pignalberi, Bob Pollock, Gladys Reckley, Roy A. Rickey, Douglas A. Riggs, Pete Rouse, Sally Rue, Carole Sather, John Schaeffer, Daveed Schwartz, Barbara Shaffer, Brian Shortell, Robert Simon, Mia Spear, Keith Specking, Anne Speilberg, Barbara Stelly, Charles Stovall, Janos Sturm, James N. Souby, Larry Talbert, Neil Thomas, Robert Thwing, Frances Ulmer, Robert Waldrop, Robert Walp, Murray Walsh, Karen Ward, Bob Weeden, Janice White, Mike Whitehead, Clarke Young.

DEPARTMENT OF ADMINISTRATION
Andrew Warwick, B. B. Allen, William R. Hudson, Carol Burger, commissioners.

Paul Arnoldt, Javan Beitinger, Bryan Biesanz, Craig Bracken, Richard C. Bradley, Edna Caldwell, L. Jay Campbell, Bruce Carlson, Kenneth Cates, Judith Crondahl, George F. Crowder, Bruce Cummings, Ed Dahl, Jan Daniels, Daryel Donaldson, Kent Dawson, Mike DeBerry, Diana DeSimone, Steve Dozier, Tom Dunne, Gene Durkee, George Elgee, Tom Farnan, Richard W. Freer, Robert S. Gates, David George, John George, Arlene Goodman, Mary A. Gray, Gordon Griffin, Dale Griggs, Tom Haas, Chuck Harrigan, John Haywood, Robert Head, Duane Herrick, Carolyn Hinke, Pete Hoepfner, Patrick Hunt, Ken Humphreys, Aaron Isaacs, Richard Jablonoski, Barry Jackson, Kenneth L. Kareen, Carl Krefting, Darrell Keith, Dick Kent, John M. Kinney, Dan Knauss, Darlene Levy, Penny Lefevre, Ronald Lind, Robert Link, John Logan, Tom Main, Robert Marcisak, Henry Masters, George Michael, John Mitchell, Gary Motley, Larry Morris, Daniel Morrissey, William Mullen, Collen Roguska Murphy, Frederick Muller, Rod Mourant, Bruce Moore, Michael P. McMullen, Michael Parisi, John Paul, Vernon Perry, Earl Prince, Russell Phillips, Don Reyes, Kenneth Ryals, Arthur Sanford, A.M. Saylors, Richard A. Smith, Kellus Sewell, Frank Sisson, Charlene Stewart, Robert Stewart, Larry Stevens, Jerry Shoenborn, Marian Schafer, Marie Swanson, Wayne Thompson, George Trzesniowksi, Caroline Venusti, Jon Walcott, Ron Walt, Michael Wheeler, Gerald White, Richard Winchell, Earl Wischmeier.

DEPARTMENT OF COMMERCE & ECONOMIC DEVELOPMENT
Langhorne A. Motley, Phillip Hubbard, Charles R. Webber, commissioners.

Frank Adams, Frank Adkins, Sharon Andrew, Janet Barnes, Donald W. Baxter, Victor Bernasoni, Karen Bernstein, John Bitner, Richard Block, Nancy Blunck, Everett O. Bracken, Julius J. Brecht, Bob Breeze, George Briggs, Robert Cacy, Domonic Carney, Jan Clemetson, Lois Cook, Earle Costello, John Curtis, James Deagen, Quentin de Boer, Robert Dindinger, Harry Donahue, Richard H. Eakins, Jim Edenso, B. Richard Edwards, Torbert Elliott, Dewey Emerick, John Farleigh, Mary Fiorucci, Michael Ford, Roger Frawley, John George, N. Win Germain, Charles Gibson, Harry Goldbar, Shari Gross, Carolyn Guess, Stuart C. Hall, Hoyle Hamilton, James Hendeshot, Hank D. Hodge, Don Hoover, Don Hostak, H.A. Hoffman, Ken Humphreys, Cheri Jacobus, Pete Jeans, James Johnson, Everett Kent, Rick Kiefer, Willis Kirkpatrick, Susan Knowles, Wally Kubley, Harry Kugler, James Lawson, Jean Lancaster, Ronald Linder, Craig Lindh, Marty Lentz, Jack Linton, Jim Lyon, Richard Long, Royce Lowe, William Ludwig, James Magowan, Gloria Manni, David Massey, Red Mayo,Thomas Meyer, Alan McGregory, Gail McGuill, Terry J. McGuire, Bill McConkey, Ruth McMahan, Bill Miles, Terry Miller, Keith Miller, Robert A. Mohn, Ken Moore, Richard Montague, Russell Mulder, Fred Muller, Diana Murphy, Archie W. Neill Jr., James Nuttall, John O'Shea, Fred Overstreet, Clarissa Quinlan, Grant Peterson, James E. Pfiefer, Kay Poland, Tom Powers, Kenneth O. Price, David Reaume, June Reiger, Richard Reynolds, Douglas Riggs, Robert Rocker, Dale Rusnell, Miles Schlosberg, Donald F. Searcy, Del Simpson, John Sims, George W. Skladal, Donna Smathers, Lonnie Smith, Joseph Swanson, Jim Sullivan, Donald Tandy, Jane Templeton, Jack L. Tinsely, Harry D. Traeger, Sharon Traylor, Bert Wagnon, Catherine Wallen, Ron Walt, Marvin R. Weatherly, John Werner, Larry Werner, Rich Whitbeck, James Wiedeman, James Williams, John Williams, Karen Wilory, Donald G. Wold, Eric Yould, Gordon Zerbetz.

DEPARTMENT OF COMMUNITY AND REGIONAL AFFAIRS
Lee McAnerney, commissioner.

Fred Ali, Donald Argetsinger, Richard Austerman, Clark Boston, Charles Bridgewater, Lauren Bruce, Jim Caldarola, Susan Charles, Veronica Clark, Kathleen Dalton, Patricia Dieterich, S. Robert Dozier, Debra English, Terry Earley, Michael Harper, Herv Hensely, Barbara Hipsman, Terry Hoefferle, David Jensen, Tom Judson, Dan Kanouse, Dottie Kauffman, Paula Kelley, Larry Kimball, Lawrence H. Kimball Jr., Ms Lare', Lois Lind, Eric Lee, Sue Lowell, Linda Low, Linda Luther, Marie Matsuno, Palmer McCarter, Beverly McCartney, Mary McClinton, Pat McConnell, Mark Mickelson, Rebecca Miller, Barbara Morse, F. Harvey Pitts, Patrick Poland, Frank Ramous, Willie Ransome, Patrick Poland, Jim Sanders, Bruce Silverthorne, Nancy Slagle, Sally Smith, Don Smith, Mark Stephens, Reed Stoops, Jack Smodey, John Tetpon, Charles Troyon, Pauline T. Valha, Kevin Waring, Lynn A. Wegener, Don Wilson, Robert Wolden, Art Zillig.

DEPARTMENT OF EDUCATION
Dr. Marshall L. Lind, commisioner.

August Anderson, Sue Arnold, Carolyn Barry, James Beima, Ruth Benigno, John Blain, John Borbridge Jr., Glenn Byington, Thomas Brown, Sylvia Carlsson, Jac Caruthers, Vince Casey, Bob Clark, Janet Clarke, Nathaniel H. Cole, Wanda Cooksey, Charles Craig, Pat Darby, Marge Dawes, Robert Davis, Bill Diebels, Richard B. Engen, Glen Erickson, Harry Gamble, Bill Gillespie, Ken Grieser, Gayle Groff, Paul Gulyas, Mary Halloran, Bill Hanable, Tom Healey, Darwin Heine, Jan Hohman, Beverly Horn, Gerald Hilley, Katherine T. Hurley, Bob Isaac,Verdell Jackson, Jefferson C. Jeffers, Barnard Jones, Margaret Justice, Romayne Kareen, Donn Kruse, E. Meg Lamey, Thelma Langdon, Margaret Leibowitz, Robert Lintott, Marilou Madden, Mark Maddox, Jane Byers Maynard, Donald McKinnon, Ruth McLean, Hans Mercer, Beth Mitchell, Michael Morgan, Bill Mulnix, Alan Munro, D.M. Murphy, Frank Nelson, June Nelson, Richard Penrod, Ernest Polley, Mike Porcaro, Malcom Roberts, Kerry Romesburg, Chris Roust, Eula Ruby, Kay Schilz, David Scott, Richard Spaziani, John Stamm, Alair Stanton, Greg Thies, William D. Thomson, Yvonne Tremblay, Stanley Truelson, Vern Williams, Wendell Wolfe, Phyllis Woodman, F. Pat Young.

DEPARTMENT OF ENVIRONMENTAL CONSERVATION
Ernst Mueller, commissioner.

Glenn Aikens, Kay Allred, Ames J. Alter, Mike Angelo, Woodruff Angst, Randy Bayliss, Tim Bergin, Alan Boggs, Harold Brighton, William Burgoyne, Charlette Chastain, Kyle J. Cherry, C.

Deming Cowles, Larry Dietrick, Al Eagle, Marti Early, Kurt Fredriksson, Bill Gillespie, Dennis Grimmer, Tom Hanna, Ronald G. Hansen, George Hart, Jim Hayden, Gary Hayden, Lee Hays, Deena Henkins, Gerald Hiley, F. S. Honsinger, Stan Hungerford, Keith Kelton, Evelyn LaPoint, Les Leatherberry, Doug Lockwood, Douglas Lowery, Robert Lundell, Dick Luther, Dick Marcum, Robert Martin, Tom McCarty, Sue McKechnie, Rob McMahon, Roger Moulton, Chris Noah, Dave Parker, Clark Pearson, William Publicover, Doug Redburn, Gene Rehfield, Jerry Reinwand, Eula Ruby, Jim Sanders, Jerry Sargent, Jonathan Scribner, Richard Spaziani, Andrew Spear, Kathleen Stewart, Richard Stokes, Dave Sturdevant, Tom Trible, Alex Vitari, Dale Wallington, June Ward, Margo Waring, Daniel Wilkerson, Richard Williams, Betty Young, Shiela Zagars.

DEPARTMENT OF FISH & GAME
James Brooks, Ronald Skoog, commissioners.

Judith Akrep, Fred Anderson, Rupert Andrews, Bruce Barrett, Roger F. Blackett, Richard Bishop, Bob Burnett, Dave Cantillion, Russell H. Clark, Don W. Collinsworth, Gregory Cook, David A. Daisy, William Demmert, Gene Doss, Douglas Dvorak, Sterling Eide, J. Scott Grundy, Gary K. Gunstrom, Ed Huizer, Mary K. Jablonski, Derrill Johnson, Dennis Kelso, Richard C. Lee, Burdette Lechner, Carl Lehman, Jack W. Lentfer, Robert LeResche, E. Richard Logan, Thomas D. Lonner, Alex McRea, Ronald W. Miller, Stanley A. Moberly, Jeffrey J. Morrison, Delores A. Moulton, Dean Paddock, Roger E. Pegau, Steven Pennoyer, Robert A. Rausch, Richard D. Reed, R. Russell Redick, Ronald Regnart, Burke Riley, Carl Rosier, Robert Roys, Kurt Schelle, Robert Simon, Roger Smith, Ronald T. Stanek, Don Stewart, Don H. Strode, Ronald J. Somerville, Patricia Szabo, John Underwood, Frank VanHulle, George Van Wyhe, Roger Wadman, John W. Wayman, John Williams, Marian Williams, Alice Wolcott.

DEPARTMENT OF HEALTH & SOCIAL SERVICES
Francis S. L. Williamson, Helen D. Beirne, commissioners.

Charles G. Adams, Jr., Rod Betit, Deborah Behr, Jack Bodine, Joan Brooks, Larry Burton, Charles Campbell, Robert L. Cole, James Fox, Robert Frasere, David W. Freer, Paul Frith, Janice K. Gates, Sam J. Granato, Martha Graumann, Robert P. Gregovich, Dana Grendell, Faye Gutherie, Paula Gruwell, Richard C. Hacker, Gloria Hawkins, Lee Hendrickson, Mary Beth Hilburn, Marsha Hubbard, William H. Huston, V. L. Iverson, Lois M. Jund, Vivian Kirkevold, Allen Korhonen, Roger Lange, Phoebe Lindsey, Catherine M. Lloyd, Bradford Matsen, Jack McCombs, Frederick McGinnis, Patrick McGinnis, Elizabeth Muktarian, Phil Nash, D. Sharon Osborne, Maurice Plotnick, Lloyd Pukis, John Pugh, Richard Renninger, Judy Shuler, Jerry L. Schrader, Kay Smith, Vernon Stillner, Lawrence Sullivan, Kay Tibbles, Dean F. Tirador M.D., Elizabeth Tower, Samuel Trivette, Carol M. White.

DEPARTMENT OF LABOR
Edmund H. Orbeck, commissioner.

Rebecca Branchflower, Nico Bus, Charles R. Caldwell, Don Cather, James R. Carr, John Cook, Judy Knight DuBois, Larry Chaplin, Dale Cheek, Lee Dalby, Calvin C. Dauel, B. W. Finley, Lottie C. Fleeks, Joseph S. Godsoe, Roger A. Harman, Ray Joregensen, Benjamin Joy, Naomi Kipp, J. E. Kirkpatrick, Judy G. Knight, Helen Lee, E.T. Leland, R. M. Levy, Glenn H. Lundell, Lew McFerren, Jacquelyn L. McClintock, Lynda McCurry, J. Allan McKinnon, Darrell Miller, Russ Molt, Lucille Odom, James O'Rourke, Larry Plessinger, John Post, B.D. Richardson, Doris Simon, Naomi Smith, Dennis L. Smythe, James Souby III, William Spear, Harry Sturrock, Ken Swift, Paul Troeh, Earl Turner, Elaine VanderSande, Tim Vogl, Darwin R. Walter Jr., Donald R. Wilson, Grace Wilson, R. Scott Withers, A. G. Zillig.

DEPARTMENT OF LAW
Avrum Gross, Will Condon, attorneys general.

Charles Adams, Lauri J. Adams, Glenn C. Anderson, Yako Andrew, Elizabeth Arnold, Michael Arruda, Mark E. Ashburn, Mary Ellen Ashton, E. John Athens, James L. Baldwin, Joseph D. Balfe, Ernest Beauchamp, Martha Beckwith, James A. Bergland, Josh Berger, Frederick Boness, Bruce M. Botelho, Richard A. Bradley, Stephen E. Branchflower, Julius J. Brecht, Michelle D. Brown, Robert Bundy, Wyanne S. Bunyan, Susan Burke, Richard D. Burnham, Jeanne A. Bussey, Rhonda F. Butterfield, Steven J. Call, Anne Carpeneti, Robert Coats, Chris Cobb, Charles W. Cohen,

Jeffrey W. Cole, Stephanie J. Cole, William Cook, Patrick W. Conheady, Susan Connolly, William T. Council, William Cummings, Geoffrey Currall, Eugene P. Cyrus, John Davies, Harry L. Davis, Laura L. Davis, Jacquelyn DeHaven, Susan Delbert, Donna Dell'Olio, Abigale Dodge-Ogawa, Loren Domke, Joseph K. Donohue, James P. Doogan Jr., James E. Douglas, Anthony D.M. Doyle, Stephen G. Dunning, George Edwards, Sharon Emley, Mark A. Ertischek, Robert A. Evans, Natalie K. Finn, Stanley T. Fischer, Peter B. Froelich, Sareh E. Fussner, John. B. Gaguine, Hal P. Gazaway, John G. Gissberg, Edith A. Glennon, Betty Glover,J ames V. Gould, Meg Greene, Peter Gruenstein, Dean J. Guaneli, Patrick Gullufsen, Dorothy Awes Haaland, James L. Hanley, William H. Hawley, Jr.,James C. Hayes, Geoffrey Haynes, Douglas A. Hebbel, Mary Anne Henry, Daniel W. Hickey, Shelly J. Higgins, Joseph Hill, Gayle Horestski, Stanley Howitt, Stephen H. Hutchings, Dennis P. James, Tom Jahnke, Thomas F. Janidlo, Monica Jenicek, Linda Jesser, Carol Barclay Jones, Carolyn E. Jones, Donald M. Johnson, Robert M. Johnson, Jane F. Kauver, Sarah T. Kavasharov, Michael Keenan, Elizabeth Kennedy, Richard P. Kerns, Moira Kirkpatrick, Thomas G. Koester, Kathryn M. Kolkhorst, Ross Kopperud, Victor Krum, Robert W. Landau, Sandra Landis, Eugene G. Lawn, Ivan Lawner, David LeBlond, Leonard N. Linton Jr, Jeffrey Lowenfels, Ron Lorensen, Leslie Ludtke, Louise F. Ma, William L. Mackey, David Mannheimer, Gerald Markham, Genelle Massey, Robert Maynard, Malcom McCain, Dwayne McConnell, H. Russ McKeever, Jack B. McGee, Thomas E. Meachem, William G. Mellow, Louis J. Menendez, Douglas R. Mertz, Charles Merriner, John. R. Messenger, Peter Michalski, Martha Mills, Thomas Miller, Barbara Miracle, Bill D. Murphree, Eugene P. Murphy, Paul E. Olsen, Randy Olsen, Eric Olson,Lauri Otto, Peter Partnow, Rodger Pegues, Richard L. Peter, Arthur H. Peterson, Edward Peterson, Timothy J. Petumenos, Cynthia Pickering, Nancy L. Potter, Ray Preston, Ann Prezyna,Michael D. Randall, Richard J. Ray, Dickerson Regan, James N. Reeves, Joyce Rivers, Thomas H. Robertson, Elizabeth Ross, Gayle Savage, William R. Satterberg, Michael W. Seawright, Sanford Segalkin, Michael W. Sewright, George Schmidt, Linda Scoccia, John Scukanec, Elizabeth Shaw, George Sheldon, David Shimek, Connie Sipe, Larry I. Spengler, Teo Spengler, Michael Stark, Niesje J. Steinkruger, Amy Stephson, Barry Stern, David C. Stewart, Robert Stoller, Cynthia Stoltenberg, Richard A. Svobodny, Richard B. Tennant, Michael A. Thompson, Jonathon K. Tillinghast, Thomas B.. Turnbull, Shannon Turner, Susan Urig, Melissa F. Verginia, Deborah Vogt, Gail Voightlander, Timothy D. Waisanen, David J. Walsh, Linda L. Walton, Thomas Wardell, Larry Weeks, Michael N. White, Thomas R. Wickwire, Janice C. Williams, L. Eugene Williams, Larry Wood, Mark Wood, Gary Vancil, Clarke Logan Young, Larry Zervos.

DEPARTMENT OF MILITARY AFFAIRS
Major General C. F. Necrason, adjutant general.

Brigadier General William J. Sharrow, Assistant Adjutant General, Col. Eward Belyea, Judy Coleman, Col. R.A. Goodman, Col. John Hoyt, Col. Edward M. Johnson, Fran Kinney, Edward Newberry, Terry Nidiffer, Jill O'Neil, Lois Richardson, Richard Rountree, Col. Clarence H. Ryherd, Col. Roger T. Schnell, Lloyd Turner, Lois Wingo.

DEPARTMENT OF NATURAL RESOURCES
Guy Martin, Robert LeResche, John Katz, commissioners.

Harry S. Aase, Robert O. Baker, Charles Behlke, Javan Beitinger, Tom Bergstrom, Kay Brown, Marilyn Brustad, Joe Burch, Russell W. Cahill, Domonic L. Carney, Al Carson, Tom Cook, William Copeland, William Dennerline, Lawrence A. Dutton, William C. Fackler, Charles Gamble, O.K. Gilbreth Jr., George A. Hall, Henry L. Hall, Hoyle Hamilton, David G. Hanson, Glenn Harrison, Geoffrey Haynes, Marta Hensel, Claud Hoffman, George K. Hollett, F. S. Honsinger, Doug Jacobson, Robert R. Jensen, Richard Lefebver, Allan Linn, Terry McWilliams, Ron Mitchell, Stan Muchewicz, Beverly Muller, Daniel Nelson, Al Ott, Bob Parkerson, Gar Pessel, Jerry Reinwand, Daniel A. Robinson, Jack Roderick, Ross Schaff, Robert D. Shaw, Lonnie C. Smith, Michael C.T. Smith, Theodore G. Smith, Henrietta Sofoulis, Reed Stoops, Ed Thompson, Dale Tubbs, Amos Mathews,Thomas Marshall, Mar Winegar, Donald Wold, Hilton Wolfe.

DEPARTMENT OF PUBLIC SAFETY
Richard L. Burton, William R. Nix, commissioners.

Col. T.R. Anderson, Red Bradley, Nola Capp, Capt. Walt Gelmore,Trygve Herman, Ronald A. Hendrie, Walter V. Lawson, Diana Long, James F. Mayer, Donald L. McQueen, Vern Roberts,

Robert Rowan, Carol Scott, Charles Smith, Cpl. Leon Steel, Col. Robert J. Stickles, H.J. Sydnam, Larry W. Talbert, Col. Fred W. Woldstad, J. "Pat" Wellington.

DEPARTMENT OF REVENUE
Sterling Gallagher, Thomas K. Williams, commissioners.

Donald W. Barnes, Frederick P. Boetsch, Richard D. Brewer, Linda Brown, Nancy Brown, Don Bullock, Peter Bushre, Betty Calhoun, Daniel Copeland, Joseph K. Donahue, Donald F. Durkin, Jim Edenso, Janette Edwards, Lawrence C. Eppenbach, Gerald D. Heier, Lois Hicks, Noreen Hirsh,G il Hjellen, Rose Hohl, Allen Jahner, Gary Jenkins, Robert Johnson, Deena Kaye, Ralph Kimlinger, Elsie King, Fred Kings, Darrell Knox, Albert Kuntz, Linda Lockridge, Mavis Magnuson, John Messenger, Michael McCormick, Faith Mitchell, Maureen O'Brien, Dean Olson, Agnes Osborne, Robert Pilcher, Eddy Prince, David Rose, Patrick Sharrock, Anselm Staack, Vernon Voss, Philip Wall, Lawrence Williams.

DEPARTMENT OF TRANSPORTATION & PUBLIC FACILITIES
Walter B. Parker, Don Harris, Hesden D. Scougal, Robert Ward, commissioners.

Richard Armstrong, Kenneth Arnold, John Bates, Frank Baxter, John C. Becker, Jack T. Bodine, James Brayton, Donald Candey, William Chambers, Dick Chitty, Ronald Davena, Dennis M. Dooley, Kit Duke, James Eide, Charles Freymueller, Thomas Gallagher, Ken Gehring, Carl Gonder, Lindsa Hartenberger, Paul Haggland, Richard Holden, John Horn, Mel Hoversten, Clayton Hueners, William Hudson, Harold Hume Jr., Howard Isberg, Richard Jensen, H. Woodrow Johansen, Ginger Johnson, Tom Johnson, Tracy D. Kaldor, Chris Karp, Harry Keller, Rick Keifer, Robert LaRue, Herbert Lehfeldt, Ron Lind, Thomas Lunsford, Charles Matlock, Audrey Mayer, Charles A. Meggitt, Larry Michou, Gerald Miller, Claude Milsap, James F. Moody, Jack Morrow, Virgil Nordgulen, Martin Nussbaum, Jo Ann O'Connor, Eleanor Ouzts, Donna Page, Roy Peratrovich, William Race, Loren Rasmussen, R.D. Redick, W.L. Riddle, Doyle Ross, Patrick P. Ryan, A.M. Saylors, H.D. Scougal, Harry Shawback, R.D. Shumway, Jack M. Spake, Warren Sparks, Henry Springer, Don Statter, Chuck Taylor, Roger Thayer, Jeanne Tramp, John Umlauf, Bert Wagnon, Billy Walker, Wayne Weeks, Warren Wild, W.K. Williams, Andy Zahare.

Source: Alaska Blue Book editions for 1975, 1977, 1979 and 1981, or provided by other sources. In no event should these lists be considered more than a majority of those managerial personnel serving the Hammond Administration. We regret those names inadvertently omitted.

Index

A

Adams, Al 178
Aircraft
  A-20 twin-engine bomber (also A-20-A)
    36
  Aeronca 91
  B-25 Bombers 45
  Bellanca 116
  Cessna 170 114, 214, 328
  Cessna 185 115
  Corsair 37, 42, 49, 287, 308
  F-4U 46
  Fokker 116
  Huey helicopter 289
  Japanese Zero 46
  Loening amphibian biplane 52, 54–58,
    61, 69–70
  N3N biplane 35
  OS2U Kingfisher floatplane 36, 38, 63
  PA11 81
  PBY Flying Boat 63
  Piper J5C 117–118
  Sikorski 116
  Spartan Jeeps 35
  Stearman 35, 63
  Stinson 63, 91, 116
  Travelaire 116
  Waco 91, 116
Akiyama, Dr. Henry 260
Alaska Aviation Heritage Museum 52, 58
Alaska, cities of
  Alexander Creek 63
  Anchorage 52, 53, 54, 57, 58, 61, 63, 73,
    82, 89, 92, 93, 94, 97, 117, 118, 127,
    133, 159, 186, 187, 193, 196, 197, 203,
    212, 216, 228, 232, 237, 239, 250, 260,
    295, 296, 302, 306, 316, 317
  Chitina 298, 300
  Clear 157
  Cold Bay 93, 94, 95
  Cordova 135, 149
  Delta (also Delta Junction) 224, 262, 263
  Dillingham 73, 75-76, 80, 128, 151
  Elmendorf Air Force Base (also
    Elmendorf) 289
  Fairbanks 57, 67–71, 93, 113, 132, 139,
    161, 176, 178, 187, 200, 202, 210, 216,
    228, 241, 262, 297

  Fort Richardson 97
  Gakona 93
  Haines 261
  Homer 132
  Juneau 127, 128, 137, 141, 144, 156,
    159, 188, 212, 216, 232, 237, 249,
    260, 265, 272, 276
  King Cove 93–94, 95, 121
  King Salmon 77, 85, 96–97, 99, 151
  Kotzebue 90–91, 117
  Manakutuk 159
  Mary's Igloo 89
  Naknek 82, 83, 97, 123–124, 127, 128,
    139, 144, 146, 148, 151, 156, 185,
    187, 190, 194, 216, 283, 296
  Nikolai 158
  Nondalton 159
  Nulato 159
  Pilot Point 84, 86
  Port Alsworth 328
  Port Moller 97
  Skwentna 63
  South Naknek 151, 159
  Talkeetna 61
  Tyonek 63
  Ugashik 84–86, 219
  Valdez 173, 177, 178, 263
  Wiseman 157
Alaska Constitution 138, 149, 221, 239,
    248, 251, 256, 259, 261
  Borough governments 149–151, 152–153
Alaska Elections
  General, 1974 199–205
  Primary, 1974 187–188, 191–197
  General, 1978 236, 237
  Primary, 1978 223, 225–235
Alaska, Inc. 247–248, 250
Alaska Journal of Commerce 307
Alaska Legislature 131
  Committee system 129–130
  Legislative pay 129
  Length of session 129
  Lobbyists 147–148
  Natural Resources Committee 130–132,
    136, 138–140, 148, 162
  School financing 150–151, 153
  Senate Finance Committee 183

Alaska National Interest Land Conservation
    Act, 1980 (also ANILCA) 243–244,
    261, 291
Alaska Native Claims Settlement Act, 1971
    222, 239, 254
Alaska Native Health Service Hospital 97
Alaska Peninsula 73, 84, 95, 102, 104, 105,
    115
Alaska Permanent Fund Dividend Program
    153, 221, 225, 246, 248, 250–256, 261,
    262, 264, 266, 319–321, 323, 324
    Permanent Fund dividends 250–256,
    265–266, 319–321
Alaska Petrochemical Co. (also Alpetco)
    264
Alaska Press Club 194–196, 229
Alaska Public Forum 247
Alaska, State of
    Alaska National Guard (also National
        Guard) 278
    Alaska State Employees' Union 192, 215
    Alaska State Troopers 279, 280
    Delta Barley Project (also Delta project)
        224, 262–263
    Fish and Game Department 103, 186
    General Fund 262
    Satellite Demonstration Program 220,
        221, 228
    Seward Grain Terminal 263
Alaska Statehood movement 124
Alaska, Territory of
    Game Commission 107
Alaskan Independence Party 203
Aleutian Chain 74, 93, 94, 95, 99, 158, 169
Amchitka Island nuclear test (see also
        Cannikin Project) 169–170
Ames, Phil 92–93
Anchorage Chamber of Commerce 168–
    169, 265, 274–275
Anchorage Daily News (see also Kay Fanning)
    170, 178, 228, 242, 272, 320
Anchorage Times (see also Robert Atwood)
    170, 175–176, 179–180, 192, 214, 226,
    228, 234, 238, 242, 259, 265, 269,
    271, 272–273, 275, 305, 307
Andre, Dora 108, 109
Andre, John 108
Andrus, Cecil 291
Animal rights issue 103, 295, 329
Arab Oil Embargo, 1973 174, 178
Arctic National Wildlife Refuge (ANWR)
    291–292
Arctic Slope 157, 222
Army Air Corps 46–47
Atwood, Elaine 267
Atwood, Robert (see also *Anchorage Times*)
    175, 179–180, 192, 197, 226, 229, 230,
    234, 242, 253, 259, 266–267, 273,
    274–275, 305–306, 323

B

Baggen, Ed 139
Baker, Bob 90–91
Baker, Forbes 139
Banfield, Dr. Frank 103
Baranof Hotel, Juneau 155–156
Bartlett, Bob 137, 160, 161
Bears 89–90, 108–109, 110, 111–113, 115–
    116, 296, 327, 328
Becharof Lake 80, 83, 111, 113
Beijing, China 290
Beirne, Dr. Mike 239
Beirne Initiative 239
Bering Sea 123, 216
Bicar, Porky 281
Binkley, Jim 139
Blodgett, Bob 133–134
Boone and Crockett Club 108
Borneo 42
Boucher, Red 187, 199, 201, 204, 207
Bowman, Howard 327
Bowman, Tish 327
Boyko, Edgar Paul 184–185, 232
Brady, James 271
Branham, Bud 53–54, 60, 61, 64, 66, 67,
    107
Branson, John 232
Bristol Bay 73, 82, 123, 127, 128, 132, 139,
    150, 151, 152, 238, 278, 291, 292, 298
Bunnell, Charles 70
Burkholder, Bob 90–91, 92–93
Busby, Gov. George 290
Bush, Barbara 282, 307, 308
Bush, George 307–308

C

Canada, cities of
    Hooverville, Ontario 18–19
    Smith River, B.C. 55–57
Cannikin Project (see also Amchitka Island
    nuclear test) 170
Caribou 66, 73, 102, 103, 105, 108, 109,
    116, 118, 291, 292, 327
Carr, Jesse (see also Teamsters Union) 175,
    192, 197, 200–201, 211–214, 226, 229,
    230, 234, 275, 305–306
Carter, Jimmy 209, 214, 222, 223, 232, 242,
    243, 249, 261, 289, 291, 308
Chatelaine, Ed 92, 93
Chiang Kai-shek 49, 290
Chignik Lake 108
China, Nationalist 45, 49–51, 69, 290
China, People's Republic of 50, 290–291
Clark, Lake 74, 97, 99, 114, 120, 166, 168,
    185, 200, 233, 260, 274, 278, 287,
    294, 296, 301, 310, 316, 328
Clark River 108
Clarke, Bob 202, 228, 241, 242, 272, 273
Claus, Donna 298, 299–300, 302
Claus, John 300

Claus, Paul 298, 299–300, 302
Clinton, Bill 308
Coalition for Alaska Lands 240
Cook Inlet 170, 250–251, 279
Cooperative Land Management Areas
    (COMANs) 241, 243, 261
Cowper, Steve 263
Croft, Chancy 226, 232, 234–235, 307
Crowley, Jim 32

D

d-2 lands 222–223, 237, 239–243, 261
Dahl, Ray 301, 302
Davidson, Harry 127–128
Davidson, Mark 127–128
Dawson, Kent 219–220, 228
Deacon, Henry 158
Democratic Party 127, 128, 132, 137–138,
    159, 180, 188, 194, 197, 199, 226,
    232, 234, 235, 274
Deng Xiaoping 50, 290–291
Dodson, Jessie 212
Dogs 65, 66
    Annie, killed by wolves 329
    First Dog in Governor's House 282–284
    MacKenzie River husky 66
Drew, Jimmy 123
Dykema, Dick 84

E

Eagle, Ron 298–301, 302
Earthquake, 1964 Alaska 142–143, 161, 317
Egan, Bill 137, 143, 151, 159, 180, 183,
    184, 187, 188, 193–194, 197, 199–201,
    203, 204, 207–208, 212, 222, 225–226,
    249
Environmental Protection Agency, U.S. (also
    EPA) 178
Exxon Valdez oil spill 171, 178, 220, 317

F

Faiks, Jan 178
Fairbanks Daily News-Miner 139, 161, 176
Fanning, Kay (see also Anchorage Daily
    News) 178, 228, 242, 272, 288
Ferguson, Archibald "Archie" 91, 118
Fink, Tom 274
Fish & Wildlife Service, U.S. 71, 78, 89–
    98, 100, 101, 108, 124, 141, 142
Ford, Gerald 216, 308
Foster, Scott 271
Franz, Charlie 144
Freeman, Oral 248
Friedman, Milton 255

G

Gallagher, Sterling 233–234, 249
Gardiner, Bella (see also Hammond, Bella)
    75–77
Gardiner, Terry 248

Gardiner, Tom 75, 76, 77
Gilbert, Dr. Richard A.C. 108–109
Glaser, Frank 101–102
Glenn Highway 92
Glenn, John 290
Governor's House, Juneau 77, 214, 276,
    277–284, 287, 295, 296, 311
Gravel, Mike 223
Greene, Susan 219
Gross, Avrum 192, 212, 231, 233–234, 252–
    253, 291
Gruening, Clark 248
Gruening, Ernest 137, 138–139, 140, 141–
    142, 248
Guess, Gene 215

H

Haggland, Dr. Paul 68–69
Hamilton, Adm. Tom 33–34
Hammond, Bella (see also Gardiner, Bella)
    97, 104–105, 107, 120, 128, 144, 156,
    157, 187, 190, 214, 227, 252, 258,
    260, 273, 277–278, 281–282, 283, 296,
    310, 326, 327, 328, 329
Hammond, Dana 120, 146, 154, 156, 190,
    214, 277–278, 310, 329
Hammond, Edna Sterner 2, 4, 5, 22, 23–26,
    77
Hammond, Heidi 120, 146, 154, 156, 190,
    214, 276, 277–278, 301, 302, 309, 310,
    311
Hammond, Rev. Morris A. 2, 4, 5, 6, 20,
    21, 22, 23–26, 72, 74, 99, 311
Hammond, Wendy 70, 72, 73–74, 190, 310,
    311
Hammond, William "Bill" 3, 6, 23, 48, 290
Hansen, Harold "Horrible" 149
Harris, Don 158, 295
Hatfield, Mark 242
Headaches 31, 33
Hickel, Walter J. "Wally" 159–163, 175,
    184, 187, 191–192, 193–194, 196, 197,
    199, 221, 225–226, 228–232, 235, 249,
    253, 259, 275, 277, 305, 307, 319, 323
Hohman, George 183
Holmstrom, Larry 297–301, 302–303
Holmstrom, Marcie 298, 299, 300, 301, 302
Hood, Lake 58
Hope, Andrew "Andy" 132
Hunting, ethics of 64–65, 101–105, 106,
    108, 110, 295–296

I

Iditarod Trail Sled Dog Race 65
Independent Alaskans for Hammond 228
International North Pacific Fisheries
    Management Council 160, 161
Izembek Bay 74

J

Jacobs, Bob 300
Japan 46, 47, 110, 174, 177, 180, 250, 251, 290, 291
"Jay Hammond's Alaska" TV show 297–301, 298, 302–303
Jensen, Dick and Iris 83, 144, 157
Jensen, Marc 156–157
Joiner, Gene 90–91
Jones, Bob "Sea Otter" 93–96, 99
Jones, Sally 228
Juneau Empire 238
Juve, Henrietta "Hank" 39, 54, 55, 56, 61, 62, 67, 70, 73–74

K

Kachemak Bay 187, 220, 221, 292
Katz, John 241–242
Kay, Wendell 133
Keitahn, Beverly 183–184
Kejulik River 80, 81
Kelly, Maury 101–102
Kelly, Tom 234
Kenai Peninsula 170, 229
Kendall, Bruce 138
Kent, Rockwell 24, 53
Kerttula, Jay 185
Kessler, Whitey 42
Kissinger, Henry 216
Kleeschulte, Chuck 249
Kuskokwim River 74

L

Ladd Field, Fairbanks 67
Lee, Bobby 93
LeResche, Bob 233–234, 241, 291
Leu, Reiny 41–42
Lindbergh, Charles 287
Longenbaugh, Dee 281–282
Lopez, Barry 89, 104

M

MacArthur, Gen. Douglas 46–47, 50
Mahaffey, Bob 75, 80–81
Malone, Hugh 248
Marshall, Thurgood 252
Matsuno, Marie 219
McConkey, Bill 228
McConnaughy, Lucy 109–110
McConnaughy, Mack 109–110
McGill, Joe 151–152
McGinnis, Tim 201
McKinley, Mount 227, 229, 288
McNabb, George 144
McNease, Maggie 95–96
McNeil River 74
McRae, David 310
Methodist Church 2, 24
Meyers, Bob 99

Miller, Henry 82–83
Miller, Keith 159, 187, 191, 193–194, 247
Miller, Terry 234, 235, 236, 237, 260, 273, 274
Miner, Joe 117
Missisagui River 15
Moody, Ralph 232, 252
Moore, Harry 38
Motley, Langhorne "Tony" 242, 260
Mowatt, Farley 103
Mukluk Telegraph, The 90, 91, 220
Munsey, Park 83–84
Musk oxen 162–163, 291

N

National Environmental Policy Act, U.S. 174
National Press Club 269
National Public Radio 255–256
Nature Conservancy, The 329
Nekeferoff, Billy 82–84
Nemeti, Irene 55
Nemeti, Lee 54, 55
News media, coverage by 85, 86, 89–91, 97, 161, 175–176, 178, 179–180, 184, 188, 191, 192, 213, 215–216, 228, 230–231, 238, 242, 259, 260, 266, 269–275, 300, 306–307
Nichols, Robert "Nip" 15–20, 28–29
Nix, Bill 274
Nixon, Richard 159, 192, 197, 226, 291
Nome Nugget 281
North Slope 173, 177, 249
Nunivak Island 162

O

O'Connor, Sandra Day 253
Orbeck, Ed 207
Order of the Purple Chrysanthemum 49

P

Pacific Rim 263
Palmer, Bob 161, 175–176, 193, 197, 210, 219, 224, 261, 263
Paxson's Lodge 92, 93
Pennsylvania State College 31, 69
Peterson, Ray 118
Philippines 42, 43, 46, 51
Phillips, Brad 157
Prince William Sound 174, 177, 178
Prudhoe Bay 170, 173, 222, 247
Puntilla Lake 61, 62, 63, 67

Q

Quinton, Griff 54, 61, 66, 108

R

Rader, John 140–141
Rainy Pass 54, 58, 62, 65, 66

Rainy Pass Lodge 62–66
Rampart Dam proposal 138–142
Ray, Bill 179, 184
Recall Hammond movement 237, 242, 260
Redford, Robert 288
Reeve, Bob 61, 118
Rehnquist, William 253
Reitz, Augie 160
Religious beliefs 4, 25, 301–302, 311–314
Republican Party 127, 132, 137–138, 157,
     159, 160, 173, 180, 188, 192, 194,
     196, 197, 215, 232, 234, 235, 274
Rick, Sam 84–86

S

Sackett, John 157, 159, 178
Safire, William 226
Sandy River 104
Sapsuk, James 85
Sapsuk, Valentine 84–86
Sawyer, David 273
Schlesinger, James 249
Seiberling, John 243
Sheffield, Bill 274, 275
Sheldon, Todd 111–113
Siegel, "Murderous Manny" 44–45, 46
Smith, Maury 176
Smith, "Mudhole" 118
Somerville, Ron 186–187
South Africa 226
Spear, Bill 228
Spear, Mia 228
Stanford, Jay Hammond 296, 310, 311
Stanford, Lauren 296, 310, 311
Sterner, Suzie 2, 23, 24
Stevens, Ted 222, 242, 260
Stewart, Connie 278
Susitna River 288
Susitna-Devil Canyon Hydro Project 141,
     142

T

Taiwan 290
Tana River 299–300, 302
Taylor, Richard 302–303
Taylor, Warren 138, 141, 142
Teamsters Union, Alaska Local 959 175,
     192, 200–201, 203, 211–214, 226, 234,
     235, 238, 271, 306
Tew, Harkey 280
Thomas Jr., Lowell 179, 185, 191, 196, 197,
     199, 201, 218, 226–227, 268, 287
Thomas Sr., Lowell 208, 227, 268
Thomas, Tay 228
Tillion, Clem 126, 132–133, 134–135, 136,
     140, 141, 159, 160–161, 175, 215, 248,
     251
Trans-Alaska Pipeline 172, 173–178, 203,
     205, 213, 215–216, 249

Alternative Canadian route 173–177,
     263
Trapping 65–67, 70, 103, 104
Treadwell, Mead 259

U

U.S. Marine Corps 30, 36, 41–51
     Black Sheep Squadron 41
U.S. Navy 32–39, 46, 50, 54
U.S. News and World Report 271
Udall, Morris 243
Ugashik River 85
Ulmer, Fran 208
Ungaluthluk River 74
United States, cities of
     Chapel Hill, N.C. 32, 36
     Corpus Christi, Texas 36, 38, 39, 53,
          307
     Dallas, Texas 34, 35, 36
     Jacksonville, Fla. 36, 39
     Los Angeles 223, 232
     Middletown, N.Y. 23, 24
     Schuylerville, N.Y. 121
     Scotia, N.Y. 2, 4, 7, 13, 20, 21, 24, 27
     Troy, N.Y. 2
     Washington, D.C. 141, 159, 160, 188,
          222, 241, 242, 249, 269, 271, 273,
          280, 290, 291
University of Alaska 69, 70–71, 77, 199
Utech, Mike 94, 95

V

Vogler, Joe 203, 204, 222

W

Wallace, Mike 213
Walrus Islands 74
Walters, Barbara 216
Walton, Chuck 110–111
Watson, Gordon 141
Watt, James 291–292
White House, The 214, 281, 289
White, Sam 118
Wien, Noel 118
Wien, Sig 118
Williams, Tom 249
Wolf-hunting issues 101–105
Wolford, Ray 93
Wolves 77, 101–105, 116, 295, 296, 328–
     329
World War II 38, 40, 41–49, 287
     Kamikaze missions 46, 308

Z

Zobel, Penny 252–253
Zobel, Ron 252–253